The American Community College

· ·

Third Edition

Arthur M. Cohen
Florence B. Brawer

The American Community College

Third Edition

Jossey-Bass Publishers
San Francisco

• •

Jossey-Bass Web address: http://www.josseybass.com

Tables 1.2 and 1.3 reprinted from Torsten Husen and T. Neville Postlethwaite (eds.), *The International Encyclopedia of Education, Second Edition*, Vol. 2. Copyright 1994, Pages 894 and 896, with kind permission from Elsevier Science Ltd, The Boulevard, Langford Lane, Kidlington 0X5 1GB, UK

Manufactured in the United States of America

Library of Congress Cataloging-in-Publication Data

Cohen, Arthur M.
  The American community college / Arthur M. Cohen,
Florence B. Brawer. — 3rd ed.
    p.   cm. —(The Jossey-Bass higher and adult education series)
  Includes bibliographical references and index.
  ISBN 0-7879-0189-X
  1. Community colleges—United States. I. Brawer, Florence B.,
date. II. Title. III. Series.
LB2328.C55   1996
378'.052—dc20   95-33293
                                                              CIP

THIRD EDITION
HB Printing   10 9 8 7 6 5 4 3

The Jossey-Bass
Higher and Adult Education Series

· ·

Clearinghouse for Community Colleges

The material in this publication is based on work sponsored wholly or in part by the office of Educational Research and Improvement, U.S. Department of Education, under contract number RI-93–00–2003. Its contents do not necessarily reflect the views of the Department or any other agency of the U.S. Government.

Contents

. . . .

Foreword to the First Edition

. . . .

This book appears at a time of great significance to the community college. The decade of the 1980s will mark a turning point in its history. It is already evident that the community college is experiencing the effects of lean years, following an unusually long succession of fat years when a new college appeared each week and double-digit enrollment increases were announced annually. Especially threatening are the public's efforts to curtail spending by propositions such as 13 (California) and 2½ (Massachusetts) and by caps on enrollment. Significant for the future may be the end of the campaign to transmute the community college into a new kind of institution, neither college nor high school—an idea espoused by Edmund J. Gleazer, who recently retired as president of the American Association of Community and Junior Colleges. These developments and many others mentioned by Cohen and Brawer may denote for the community college maturity, as well as the end of the Golden Age.

Cohen and Brawer's book will take its place alongside books by such community college giants as Koos, Eells, Bogue, and Medsker. Their comprehensive, incisive, interpretive analysis of the community colleges covers nearly all facets of the college. They start with a historical analysis of the origins and development of the college and end with a critique of the college's critics. In between, chapters are devoted to administrators, students, and faculty. Four chapters, almost one-third of the book, are devoted to the curriculum functions. Chapter One offers the rationale used throughout most of the book. The authors state that their function is to present information and examine the many viewpoints that have been advanced. From this approach, they do not expect to find ultimate answers but hope that better questions will result.

Those acquainted with the authors will not be surprised that they undertook this formidable task. They know that Cohen and Brawer have been immersed in community college research for more than two decades. During that time they have visited hundreds of community colleges, associated with nearly all those who have written on the college, reviewed thousands of documents sent for inclusion in the collection of the ERIC Clearinghouse for Junior Colleges since it was organized in 1966, edited the quarterly *New Directions for Community Colleges* series from its origin in 1973, and conducted major research in the humanities and sciences through the Center for the Study of Community Colleges. There is hardly a subject or topic on community college education that does not appear in one or more publications that have been written by them or produced under their guidance. Their book is a distillation of this vast experience and knowledge and is a capstone to the many articles and books they have written individually and as coauthors.

The [original] thirteen chapters describe, probe, and dissect every facet of the institution, sometimes sympathetically, at other times critically, although seldom superficially. Despite the kaleidoscopic nature of the community college, the authors' comprehensive, incisive treatment brings into focus the changes it has undergone since its modest beginnings as a liberal arts junior college to the multifaceted giant community college of the 1960s and 1970s. Now, the incipient reform movement calls into question the sacrosanct principles of the open door and equal opportunity. Instead of the new institution, neither high school nor college, the authors see a return to an expanded version of the college of the postwar era of the 1940s and 1950s.

In chapter after chapter the authors make clear that research as often as not raises more questions than answers. In the areas of teaching and especially learning, the profession has made very little progress in evaluating its efforts. A historical survey of the research in these two areas would, if presented graphically, look much like graphs depicting the course of the economy, with cyclical changes representing the rise and fall of particular theories. One would like to see the trend line in community college learning slope upward, but as Cohen and Brawer intimate, the trend line here, as in nearly all segments of education, would have a downward slope. Despite all the labors, the results, except as reported by those in charge of the experiments, are of minor significance unless one gains some comfort that the educators have learned which ideas and theories do not produce results.

Although the authors modestly assert that answers to current problems will not be found, one wonders whether it is possible for two of the most prominent students of the community college, with strong convictions expressed in many publications, to submerge those convictions in questions in such a comprehensive, wide-ranging book. Their strategy of wondering, offering information, and examining many viewpoints has enabled them to range further afield speculatively, seemingly without committing themselves. Yet questions, no matter how carefully worded, often suggest the answers the authors would have given if they had been taking the test instead of administering it. It is noteworthy that in the four curriculum chapters the authors dispense with questions; they substitute their convictions. How could it be otherwise with authors who have been immersed in the study of the community college for two decades?

The reader will be confronted with the many paradoxes surrounding the community college. The most nettlesome is, as the authors point out, that it is called a college, but elementary-grade subjects—arithmetic, reading, writing—rank high in terms of courses offered and students enrolled. Another: although it has been the fastest-growing segment of education, it seems to be the least known. After seventy-five years it has yet to adopt a name that describes its functions. "Identity" or "image" remains one of the most serious concerns of community college educators—a concern that has been with them almost from the beginning. It will, the authors imply, remain with them as long as the community college remains for students a second or lower choice rather than an equal choice with other higher education institutions and as long as educators and leaders of their professional organizations continue to emulate chameleons in adopting and dropping one educational fad after another, all in the name of innovation.

One of the most intriguing chapters is "The Social Role." The reader will find here the arguments of the leading critics that the community college has failed to provide upward mobility or access to higher education. Briefly, the authors describe the criticisms and, at times, raise questions about their validity. They resist the temptation to be apologists, pointing out that the persistence of doubts concerning the community college's role in furthering upward mobility derives "from a gap in perception" of the educators.

In their chapters "Collegiate Function" and "General Education," the authors make a strong plea for "liberal education for the informed citizen." The community colleges, they maintain, must "provide some portions of the education for the masses that tends toward encouraging exercise of the intellect." They offer a "model for effecting general education for a free people in a free society."

Because this book records the many changes that affect the community college and, more important, the way educational leaders react to them, it will appeal to those who seek only the "facts." How many? What courses and curricula? Where from? At the other extreme it will help those seeking to understand the philosophy— philosophies perhaps—that has propelled this institution to its present status. The critics—the community college personnel and the authors' colleagues who are involved in research on the institution— will find much to applaud and probably more to contend with. Although the authors will welcome the plaudits, they will not be disappointed if they elicit disagreement. They have strong beliefs and they are critics. So they will welcome the opportunity to be on the receiving end for the sake of starting a dialogue that they believe is urgently needed as educational leaders struggle to find solutions in the new, unfamiliar environment of zero growth and fiscal retrenchment.

September 1981   John Lombardi
                                                    Former President
                                                    Los Angeles City College

Preface

This is the third edition of a book published originally in 1982 and updated in 1989. It is about the American community colleges, institutions that offer associate degrees and occupational certificates to their students, and a variety of other services to the communities in which they are located. These 1,250 colleges range in size from fewer than one hundred to more than thirty thousand students. Around one-sixth of them, mostly the smaller institutions, are privately supported. The others, the larger, comprehensive structures, are found in every state.

Audience

In this edition, as with the previous books, our purpose is to present a comprehensive, one-volume text useful for everyone concerned with higher education: college staff members, graduate students, trustees, and state-level officials. The descriptions and analyses of each of the institution's functions can be used by administrators who want to learn about practices that have proved effective in other colleges, by curriculum planners involved in program revision, by faculty members seeking ideas for modifying their courses, and by trustees and officials concerned with college policies regarding curriculum and student flow.

The book focuses mainly on the period since 1960, when the community colleges underwent several major changes. During that time the number of public two-year institutions doubled, and their enrollments increased tenfold. The relations between administrators and faculty changed as multicampus districts were formed and as contracts negotiated through collective bargaining became common. Institutional financing was affected both by tax limitations and by a continuing trend toward state-level funding. The proportion of students transferring to universities fell, and those transferring from universities rose. The collegiate function was shaken as career and community education made tremendous strides and as the colleges grappled with problems of teaching the functionally illiterate.

The book is written as an interpretive analysis. It includes data summaries on students, faculty, curriculum, and many other quantifiable dimensions of the institutions. It explores the inversion of institutional purpose that resulted in the career programs serving as the basis for transfer and the transfer programs becoming areas of terminal study. It explains how students' patterns of college attendance forced a conversion from a linear to a lateral curriculum pattern, from students taking courses in sequence to students dropping into and out of classes almost at will. It shows how general education can be reconciled with the career, developmental, community, and collegiate education functions, and how counseling and other auxiliary services can be integrated into the instructional program. And it examines some of the criticism that has been leveled at the community college by those who feel it is doing a disservice to most of its matriculants, especially the ethnic minorities.

A revised edition of our work is warranted now because several changes have occurred since the second edition appeared. In the colleges faculty power has consolidated, only to be met by countervailing power concentrated at the state level. Mandatory testing and placing of students has spread along with enrollment limitations. Developmental education has become more prominent, taking its place as a curriculum function second only to career and collegiate education. Administrators have had to become more attentive to state-level directives regarding institutional functioning and funding.

Yet many things have remained the same. Few new public colleges have been formed, and the ratio of full-time students to part-time students and of full-time faculty to part-time faculty has not changed. College organization, instruction, and institutional purpose are not different. The colleges are still concerned with providing relevant educational services to their clients, who attend for various reasons. Most of the issues that we noted at the end of each chapter in the second edition are repeated herein; the most intractable problems are never solved. As I. F. Stone said in *The Trial of Socrates*, "Change is a constant but so is identity. The whole truth can only be achieved by taking both into consideration" (1987, p. 69).

We have made several changes in the book. The chapter organization remains the same, but we have added a chapter on research in and about the community college (Chapter Thirteen). Within each chapter we have updated the tables and graphs to depict the most recent data, and we have incorporated new examples of the services that the colleges provide. We have expanded our discussions of student flow, institutional finance, instruction, student services, and curricular functions by providing recent information in these areas. We have simplified definitions and reanalyzed the relationships among the various college purposes and functions. We have tried to keep pace with the terminology most commonly employed to describe aspects of the institution. For example, although *remedial education, developmental education, basic studies,* and *compensatory education* are used interchangeably to describe those areas of the curriculum that suggest less-than-college-level studies, we have retitled the second edition's chapter on compensatory education because that term is not as commonly used as the term *developmental education* (Chapter Nine).

Overview of the Contents

Chapter One recounts the social forces that contributed to the expansion and contemporary development of the community colleges. It examines the ever-changing institutional purposes, showing how their changes come in conflict with funding patterns and structures. It traces the reasons that local funding and control have given way to state-level management, and it questions what the shape of American higher education would be if there were no community colleges.

Chapter Two displays the changing patterns of students from the point of view of their age, ethnicity, and goals. The reasons for part-time attendance patterns are explored. There is a particular emphasis on minority students. The chapter also examines attrition, showing that the concept is an institutional artifact masking students' true achievements, and it reviews the most recent data on student transfer rates.

Chapter Three draws on national data to show how the full-time and part-time faculty differ. It examines tenure, salary, work load, modes of faculty evaluation, professional associations, and faculty preparation. It discusses the relations between moonlighting and burnout, and the conflict between instructors' desires for better students and the realities of the institutions in which they work.

Chapter Four reviews the modifications in college management that have resulted from changes in institutional size, the advent of collective bargaining, reductions in available funds, and changes in the locus of control. Examples of varying modes of college organization and the role of each administrator within them are presented.

Chapter Five describes the various funding patterns, showing how they have followed shifts in mode of organization. Relations between the level of tuition and equity and efficiency in institutional operations are explored. The chapter details the effects of fiscal limitation measures and shows how various cost-saving practices have been installed. It also considers the effects of state-level funding changes.

Chapter Six reviews the stability in instructional forms that have been maintained in the colleges. It discusses instructional technology, and such instructional techniques as the use of television and computers, writing across the curriculum, and supplemental instruction. Notes on mastery learning, learning resource centers, and competency-based instruction precede a discussion of the assessment of instructional effects.

Chapter Seven traces the student personnel functions, including counseling and guidance, recruitment and retention, orientation, and extracurricular activities. It also considers financial aid and the shifting patterns of articulation, detailing efforts to enhance student flow from community colleges to senior institutions.

Chapter Eight considers the rise of occupational education as it has moved from a peripheral to a central position in the institutions. No longer a terminal function for a few students, career education now serves people seeking new jobs and upgrading in jobs they already have, students gaining the first two years of a career-oriented bachelor's degree program, and candidates for relicensing. The chapter also discusses career education's contributions to the community.

Chapter Nine traces the decline in student literacy at all levels of education and shows how community colleges are bearing the brunt of students' ill-preparedness. It reviews specific college programs to enhance students' basic skills, examines the controversies surrounding student mainstreaming and restrictive programming, and explores the options of screening students at entry on a course-by-course basis or, instead, allowing students to enter any course of their choice but requiring simultaneous remedial assistance. The chapter details the rise of developmental education to a level of importance second only to that of collegiate and career studies.

Chapter Ten considers adult and continuing education, lifelong learning, and community services. It recounts numerous examples of cooperative arrangements between colleges and community agencies, asks how funding can be maintained for this function, and explores how the major institutional associations continue to promote community education. The chapter also considers the assessment of effects and the validation of services that fall outside traditional collegiate offerings.

Chapter Eleven considers the rise, fall, and subsequent stabilization of the liberal arts. How collegiate studies affect student transfer to senior institutions is included, as are discussions of the academic disciplines, the faculty as a liberal arts support group, transfer rates, and assessment of student learning in the liberal arts.

Chapter Twelve traces the ebb and flow of general education through interdisciplinary courses and shows how the concept has suffered from failure of consistent definition. The chapter offers a model for reviving general education in each of the colleges' dominant curricula.

Chapter Thirteen discusses research in and about the community colleges, an area that until recently has received little acknowledgment from sources outside the colleges. It reviews the groups that conduct research, the types of research they report, the external mandates that affect their studies, and some of their findings.

Chapter Fourteen examines the philosophical and practical questions that have been raised about the community college's role in leveling the social-class structure in America in general and in enhancing student progress toward higher degrees in particular. It shows how the same data can be used to reach different conclusions when the critics do not properly consider the differences between social equalization and equal access for individuals. The chapter poses alternative organizational forms within existing community colleges so that the colleges can provide equity, access, and an avenue for individuals to attain higher degrees.

Chapter Fifteen projects the trends in student and faculty demographics and indicates the areas where change will occur in college organization, curriculum, instruction, and student services. It also comments on the ascendant role of developmental education and projects the future of moves toward assessing college outcomes.

Sources

The information included in this book derives from many sources but predominantly from published observations and findings. Major books and journals and the Educational Resources Information Center (ERIC) files have been searched for documents pertaining to each topic. We have also relied on our own surveys, conducted since 1974 through the Center for the Study of Community Colleges.

This attention to the extant literature has both positive and negative features. On the plus side, it enables us to plot trends in curriculum, faculty functioning, patterns of student attendance, and college organization. On the other side, it limits our sources of information to surveys and written material. Surveys necessarily condense unique activities into percentages, thereby muting some of the vibrancy that colleges and their offerings manifest. Researching just the available literature limits our awareness of college practices to a view of institutions where staff have written descriptions for general distribution.

Although we have relied primarily on printed sources and on our own research studies, we have also sought counsel from the many community college staff members around the country whom we meet during their visits to the ERIC Clearinghouse for Community Colleges at UCLA, at conferences, and during our visits to their own institutions. However, even though we have drawn on all these sources and tried to present an evenhanded treatment, we must admit that we have our prejudices. We are advocates for the community colleges, believing that they have an essential role to play in the fabric of American education. We are advocates for their educative dimension, the aspect of their efforts that affects human learning. And we favor especially the collegiate and general education functions, feeling that they must be maintained if community colleges are to continue as comprehensive institutions, and if students are to be prepared for life in an ever-changing world.

Above all, we are critical analysts, concerned more with examining the ideas undergirding the community colleges' functions than with describing the operations themselves. We wonder about the interrelations of funding, management, curriculum, and teaching. And we are concerned about the shape that the institutions have taken as increasing percentages of their students attend part-time and as their curricula have taken more of a lateral than a linear form.

The latter point deserves elaboration. Which college serves best? One with 10,000 students, each taking one class? One with 5,000 students, each taking two classes? Or one with 2,500 students, each taking four classes? In all cases the cost is about the same, but the institutions are quite different. In the first example, the college has a broad base of clients, and its curriculum has a lateral form composed of disparate courses, such as those offered through university extension or adult education centers. In the second, the curriculum has taken a more linear shape, and the implication is that students are expected to progress toward a certificate or degree. The third type of college has apparently restricted admission to those who can attend full-time, and its courses are arrayed in sequential fashion, each of them demanding prerequisites.

The shape that an institution takes is not derived accidentally. Deliberate measures can be effected to bring about an emphasis in one or another direction. The policy makers who would serve the broadest base of clients would offer courses at night and in off-campus locations, allow students to enter and withdraw from classes without penalty at any time, and engage in vigorous marketing campaigns to attract people who might not otherwise consider attending college. Those who see their college as serving best if it enrolls full-time students would offer courses on campus only, install strict academic probation and suspension standards, demand advance registration, and enforce course prerequisites. The point is that either extreme, or any position between, could be taken by officials operating colleges within the same state, under the same sets of regulations. We believe that the function of the analyst is to bring these types of options to the attention of people within the colleges so that they might realize that their institutions can be changed and that these changes need not be undertaken haphazardly. At the same time, we recognize that in an institution whose budget depends on student enrollments and whose mission is to serve as many people as possible, most college managers see no need to standardize disparate attendance patterns.

Numerous changes in American society and in public outlook have occurred in recent years, but the colleges have been affected hardly at all. The national debt has skyrocketed, along with interest payments that must be borne for decades to come. The number of homeless people and immigrants, documented and undocumented, has grown substantially. Drug abuse, white-collar crime, gangs armed with automatic weapons, and antigovernmental sects have become national threats. Yet the colleges continue as always, adjusting somewhat to students' tendencies to take fewer courses per term but not at all to the cosmic issues noted above. What can they do? They are schools, able only to minister to their clients. They cannot directly resolve any of the major issues confronting society. Broad-scale social forces swirl about them, but the colleges are propelled mainly by their internal dynamics—a point that can be readily recognized by viewing the differences between institutions in the same types of communities.

Acknowledgments

No long-sustained project of this kind ever operates in isolation, nor is it the work of its authors alone. For this book and the research on which it is based, many agencies provided assistance: National Endowment for the Humanities; National Science Foundation; the Andrew W. Mellon Foundation; the Ford Foundation; the Carnegie Foundation for the Advancement of Teaching; and the E. M. Kauffman Foundation's Center for Entrepreneurial Leadership. We are indebted also to the National Center for Education

Statistics, whose numerous studies provide baseline data regarding all sectors of education.

We have included the foreword to the first edition, by the late John Lombardi, in this volume because we continue to value his insights. He dedicated his professional life to the community colleges. His writings, several of which we cite in this book, reveal his analytical approach to every issue concerning the institutions.

Several staff members of the U. S. Department of Education-sponsored ERIC Clearinghouse for Community Colleges at UCLA helped put the edition together. Elizabeth Foote used her expert knowledge of the ERIC data base to find documents regarding all aspects of institutional functioning. Amy Pape did much of the typing; Janel Henriksen was diligent in helping to update tables and obtain bibliographic citations. UCLA and the Center for the Study of Community Colleges supported all our work. Jim Palmer, Bill Armstrong, and Trudy Bers provided comments on the research chapter (Chapter Thirteen). Anita Colby created the index.

We have referred to the second edition as the Son of the American Community College, and to the current edition as the Granddaughter. Accordingly, we dedicate this volume to our grandchildren, with the hope that their educational experiences, whatever and wherever they may be, will be personally fulfilling and socially rewarding.

Los Angeles, California   Arthur M. Cohen
November 1995   Florence B. Brawer

The Authors

Arthur M. Cohen has been professor of higher education at the University of California, Los Angeles (UCLA) since 1964. He received his B.A. (1949) and M.A. (1955) degrees in history from the University of Miami. He received his Ph.D. degree (1964) in higher education from The Florida State University. He has been director of the ERIC Clearinghouse for Community Colleges since 1966 and president of the Center for the Study of Community Colleges since 1974. Cohen has served on the editorial boards of numerous journals and has written extensively about community colleges. His first book was *Dateline '79: Heretical Concepts for the Community College* (1969); his latest is *Managing Community Colleges: A Handbook for Effective Practice* (with Brawer and Associates, 1994).

Florence B. Brawer is research director of the Center for the Study of Community Colleges. A former research educationist at UCLA, psychometrist, and counselor, she received her B.A. degree (1944) in psychology from the University of Michigan and her M.A. (1962) and Ed.D. (1967) degrees in educational psychology from UCLA. She is the author of *New Perspectives on Personality Development in College Students* (1973) and the coeditor of *Developments in the Rorschach Technique*, vol. 3 (1970).

Cohen and Brawer together wrote *Confronting Identity: The Community College Instructor* (1972), *The Two-Year College Instructor Today* (1977), and *The Collegiate Function of Community Colleges*

(1987). Together with other ERIC staff members, they also wrote *A Constant Variable: New Perspectives on the Community College* (1971) and *College Responses to Community Demands* (1975). Cohen and Brawer have edited several series of monographs published by the Center for the Study of Community Colleges and the ERIC Clearinghouse for Community Colleges. Since 1973, they have been editor-in-chief and associate editor, respectively, of the Jossey-Bass quarterly series *New Directions for Community Colleges*.

The American Community College

Third Edition

1

Background

Evolving Priorities and Expectations
of the Community College

The American community college dates from the early years of the twentieth century. Several social forces contributed to its rise. Most prominent were the need for workers trained to operate the nation's expanding industries; the lengthened period of adolescence, which mandated custodial care of the young for a longer time; and the drive for social equality, which supposedly would be enhanced if more people had access to higher education. Community colleges seemed also to reflect the growing power of external authority over everyone's life, the peculiarly American belief that people cannot be legitimately educated, employed, religiously observant, ill, or healthy unless some institution sanctions that aspect of their being.

[handwritten margin note: Social forces]

The ideas permeating higher education early in the century fostered the development of these new colleges across the country. Science was seen as enhancing progress; the more people who would learn its principles, the more rapid the development of the society. New technologies demanded skilled operators, and training them could be done by the schools. Individual mobility was held in the highest esteem, and the notion was widespread that those people who applied themselves most diligently would advance most rapidly. Social institutions of practical value to society were being formed. This was the era of the Chautauqua, the settlement house, the Populists. And in the colleges the question "What knowledge is of most worth?" was rarely asked; the more likely question was "What knowledge yields the greatest tangible benefit to individuals or to society?" The public perceived schooling as an avenue of upward mobility and as a contributor to the community's wealth. Veblen's (1918) and Sinclair's ([1923] 1976) diatribes against domination of the universities by industrialists were ineffectual outcries against what had become a reality.

Publicly supported universities, given impetus by the Morrill Acts of 1862 and 1890, had been established in every state. Although many were agricultural institutes or teacher-training colleges little resembling modern universities, they did provide a lower-cost alternative to private colleges. The universities were also pioneering the idea of service to the broader community through their agricultural and general extension divisions. Access for a wider range of the population was increasing as programs to teach an ever-increasing number of subjects and occupations were introduced. Schools of business, forestry, journalism, and social work became widespread. People with more diverse goals demanded more diverse programs; the newer programs attracted greater varieties of people.

Probably the simplest overarching reason for the growth of community colleges was that an increasing number of demands were being placed on schools at every level. Whatever the social or personal problem, schools were supposed to solve it. As a society we have looked to the schools for racial integration. The courts and legislatures have insisted that schools mitigate discrimination by merging students across ethnic lines in their various programs. The schools are expected to solve problems of unemployment by preparing students for jobs. Subsidies awarded to businesses that train their own workers might be a more direct approach, but we have preferred paying public funds to support career education in the schools. The list could be extended to show that the responsibility for doing something about drug abuse, alcoholism, teenage pregnancy, inequitable incomes, and other individual and societal ills has been assigned to schools soon after the problems have been identified. Schools were even supposed to ameliorate the long-standing problem of highway deaths. Instead of reducing speed limits and requiring seat belts in the 1960s, many states enacted laws requiring schools to provide driver education courses.

Despite periodic disillusionment with the schools, the pervasive belief has been that education—defined as more years of schooling—is beneficial. It was not always that way. In earlier centuries, and in other societies, people did not ascribe such power to or make such demands on their schools. Instead the family, the workplace, and various social institutions acculturated and trained the young. Illich has said, "We often forget that the word 'education' is of recent coinage. . . . Education of children is first mentioned in French in a document of 1498. . . . In the English language the word 'education' first appeared in 1530 . . . in Spanish lands another century passed before the word and idea of education acquired some currency" (1971, p. 8). But the easily accessible, publicly supported school became an article of American faith, first in the nineteenth century, when responsibility for educating the individual began shifting to the school, then in the twentieth, when the schools were unwarrantedly expected to relieve society's ills. The community colleges thrived on the new responsibilities because they had no traditions to defend, no alumni to question their role, no autonomous professional staff to be moved aside, no statements of philosophy that would militate against their taking on responsibility for everything.

Institutional Definitions

Two generic names have been applied to two-year colleges. From their beginnings until the 1940s, they were known most commonly as junior colleges. Eells's definition (1931) of the junior college included the university branch campuses offering lower-division work either on the parent campus or in separate facilities; state junior colleges supported by state funds and controlled by state boards; district junior colleges, usually organized by a secondary school district; and local colleges formed by a group acting without legal authority. At the second annual meeting of the American Association of Junior Colleges, in 1922, a junior college was defined as "an institution offering two years of instruction of strictly collegiate grade" (Bogue, 1950, p. xvii). In 1925 this definition was modified slightly to include the statement: "The junior college may, and is likely to, develop a different type of curriculum suited to the larger and ever-changing civic, social, religious, and vocational needs of the entire community in which the college is located. It is understood that in this case, also, the work offered shall be on a level appropriate for high-school graduates" (p. xvii). But the instruction was still expected to be "of strictly collegiate grade"; that is, if such a college had courses usually offered in the first two years by a senior institution, "these courses must be identical, in scope and thoroughness, with corresponding courses of the standard four-year college" (p. xvii). Skill training alone was not considered sufficient to qualify an institution for the appellation *community college*. A general education component must be included in the occupational programs: "General-education and vocation training make the soundest and most stable progress toward personal competence when they are thoroughly integrated" (p. 22).

During the 1950s and 1960s, the term *junior college* was applied more often to the lower-division branches of private universities and to two-year colleges supported by churches or organized independently, while *community college* came gradually to be used for the comprehensive, publicly supported institutions. By the 1970s the term *community college* was usually applied to both types.

Several names in addition to *community college* and *junior college* have been used. Sometimes these names refer to the college's sponsor: "City College," "County College," and "Branch Campus" are still in use. Other appellations signify the institutions' emphases: "Technical Institute" and "Vocational, Technical, and Adult Education Center" have had some currency. The colleges have also been nicknamed "People's College," "Democracy's College," and "Anti-University College"—the last by Jencks and Riesman (1968), who saw them as negating the principles of scholarship on which the universities had been founded.

Sometimes, deliberate attempts have been made to blur the definition. For example, during the 1970s the American Association of Community and Junior Colleges (AACJC) sought to identify the institutions as community education centers standing entirely outside the mainstream of graded education. In 1980 the AACJC began listing "regionally accredited proprietary institutions" in addition to the nonprofit colleges in its annual *Community, Junior, and Technical College Directory.*

We define the community college as *any institution accredited to award the Associate in Arts or the Associate in Science as its highest degree.* That definition includes the comprehensive two-year colleges as well as many of the technical institutes, both public and private. It eliminates many of the publicly supported area vocational schools and adult education centers and most of the proprietary business and trade colleges that are accredited by the National Association of Trade and Technical Schools, but not by the regional accrediting associations. However, numerous institutions in the latter group, the fastest-growing sector of postsecondary education in the 1980s, are being accredited to award associate degrees; hence, some lists include them in the two-year college category. By 1985, "half of the private two-year institutions were organized as profit-making entities," according to the U.S. Department of Education's National Center for Education Statistics, which had begun counting them as part of the group (Adelman, 1987, p. 5).

Development of Community Colleges

The development of community colleges should be placed in the context of the growth of all higher education in the twentieth century. As secondary school enrollments expanded rapidly in the early

1900s, the demand for access to college grew apace. The percentage of those graduating from high school grew from 30 percent in 1924 to 75 percent by 1960; and 60 percent of the high school graduates entered college in the latter year. Put another way, 45 percent of eighteen-year-olds entered college in 1960, up from 5 percent in 1910. Rubinson has contended that the growth of schooling in the United States can be predicted by a "model in which the proportional change in enrollments at any given level of schooling is a simple function of the numbers of people in the relevant age group and in the previous level of schooling" (1986, p. 521). Green (1980) put it more simply, saying that one of the major benefits of a year of schooling is a ticket to advance to the next level. (Notably, as high school graduation rates stabilized at 72–75 percent in the 1970s, the rate of college going leveled off as well.)

However, the states could have accommodated most of the people seeking college attendance simply by expanding their universities' capacity, as indeed was the practice in a few states. Why community colleges? A major reason is that several prominent nineteenth- and early-twentieth-century educators wanted the universities to abandon their freshman and sophomore classes and relegate the function of teaching adolescents to a new set of institutions, to be called junior colleges. Proposals that the junior college should relieve the university of the burden of providing general education for young people were made in 1851 by Henry Tappan, president of the University of Michigan; in 1859 by William Mitchell, a University of Georgia trustee; and in 1869 by William Folwell, president of the University of Minnesota. All insisted that the universities would not become true research and professional development centers until they relinquished their lower-division preparatory work. Other educators—such as William Rainey Harper, of the University of Chicago; Edmund J. James, of the University of Illinois; and Stanford's president, David Starr Jordan—suggested emulating the system followed in European universities and secondary schools. That is, the universities would be responsible for the higher-order scholarship, while the lower schools would provide general and vocational education to students through age nineteen or twenty. Harper also contended that the weaker four-year colleges, instead of wasting money by doing superficial work, might better become junior colleges. In fact, by 1940, of 203 colleges with enrollments in 1900 of 150 or fewer students, 40 percent had perished, but 15 percent had become junior colleges (Eells, 1941a).

In California it probably would have been feasible to limit Stanford and the University of California to upper-division and graduate and professional studies because of the early, widespread development of junior colleges in that state. Such proposals were made several times, especially by Stanford's President Jordan, but were never successfully implemented. Grades 13 and 14 were not given over exclusively to community colleges in any state. Instead, the colleges developed outside the channel of graded education that reaches from kindergarten to graduate school. The organization of formal education in America had been undertaken originally from both ends of the continuum. Dating from the eighteenth century, four-year colleges and elementary schools were established; then, during the nineteenth century, the middle years were accommodated as colleges organized their own preparatory schools and as public secondary schools were built. By the beginning of the twentieth century, the gap had been filled. If the universities had shut down their lower divisions and surrendered their freshmen and sophomores to the two-year colleges, these newly formed institutions would have been part of the mainstream. But they did not, and the community colleges remained adjunctive well into the middle of the century.

Their standing outside the tradition of higher education—first with its exclusivity of students, then with its scholarship and academic freedom for professors—was both good and bad for the community colleges. Initially, it gained support for them from influential university leaders who welcomed a buffer institution that would cull the poorly prepared students and send only the best on to the upper division. Later, it enabled them to capitalize on the sizable amounts of money available for programs in career education, to accept the less well-prepared students who nonetheless sought further education, and to organize continuing education activities for people of all ages. But it also doomed community colleges to the status of alternative institutions. In some states—notably Florida, Texas, and Illinois—upper division universities were built so that the community colleges could feed students through at the junior level, but few of those innovative structures survived.

Organizationally, most of the early public community colleges developed as upward extensions of secondary schools. Diener (1986) has compiled several nineteenth- and early-twentieth-century papers promoting that idea. Included are statements by Henry Barnard, the first United States commissioner of education; John W. Burgess, a professor at Columbia College; William Rainey Harper; and Alexis Lange, of the University of California. In 1871, Barnard proposed that the schools in the District of Columbia be divided into five sectors, one of which would be "*Superior and Special Schools*, embracing a continuation of the studies of the Secondary School, and while giving the facilities of general literacy and scientific culture as far as is now reached in the second year of our best colleges" (Diener, 1986, p. 37). In 1884, Burgess recommended that high schools add two or three years to their curriculum to prepare students for the work of the university. Harper also proposed that high schools extend their programs into the collegiate level: "Today only 10 percent of those who finish high school continue the work in college. If the high schools were to provide work for two additional years, at least 40 percent of those finishing the first four years would continue until the end of the sophomore year" (Diener, 1986, pp. 57–58). (His figures on the ratio of college attendance were remarkably prescient.) Lange regarded the junior college as the culmination of schooling for most students, with the high school and junior college together forming the domain of secondary education. But in his view the junior college would do more than prepare

young people for college; it would also train for "the vocations occupying the middle ground between those of the artisan type and the
professions" (Diener, 1986, p. 71).

Rationalizing the New Form

Reasons for the growth of community colleges in their early years
have been stated by numerous commentators, each with an argument that has some appeal. The idea that rapid growth in the high
school population in the early years of this century led to student
demand for additional years of schooling could be rationalized, but
so can many others. The claim that business people supported the
institutions so that they would have a ready supply of workers
trained at public expense has some adherents; this seems more valid
in light of contemporary events as states put forth low-cost funding
and education projects in attempts to attract industry, with the community colleges as central elements in their presentations. And the
literature certainly supports the idea that community leaders saw
the formation of a college as an avenue to community prestige.
Even the notion of a grand scheme to keep poor people in their
place by diverting them to programs leading to low-pay occupational positions has found some acceptance, particularly among
those who perceive a capitalist conspiracy behind all societal events.
    Which belief has the most credibility? Each has its adherents.
But why can't they *all* be true? There certainly does not need to be
one reason above others for any major shift in institutional forms.
Each year of schooling does give rise to a desire for an additional
year. School superintendents may want to be college presidents,
and teachers to be college professors. Communities erect signs
pointing to their local college and announce its availability in all
their displays. Industries and professions need skilled practitioners.
All the reasons mentioned can be justified as contributing to the
opening of one thousand public community colleges in not much
more than fifty years. Why must one argument be more valid than
the others?

Harder to reconcile is the fact that the other developed nations, especially those of Western Europe from which most of the American ideas of education were imported, did not develop community colleges of their own. They all faced the same phenomena of rising populations, changing technologies, different expectations for child rearing, a shifting pattern of preparation for the work force. However, they built adult education centers and vocational schools separate from each other and rarely founded institutions that would enable people to transfer credit to baccalaureate programs. Were their school superintendents less eager to become college presidents? Were their high school populations more docile in accepting the decision that they would never have a chance for a baccalaureate? Were their communities less eager to enjoy the prestige that goes with a local college? Were they more subject to conspiracies to keep the lower classes in their place, hence to keep poor people out of school entirely?

The best answer might be that since its founding, the United States has been more dedicated to the belief that all individuals should have the opportunity to rise to their greatest potential. Accordingly, all barriers to individual development should be broken down. Institutions that enhance human growth should be created and supported. Talent is potentially to be found in every social stratum and at any age. People who fail to achieve in their youth should be given successive chances. And perhaps most crucially— absent a national ministry of education or even, until recently, much state control or oversight—the local school districts could act on their own.

Much recent scholarship (Pedersen, 1987, 1988; Frye, 1992; Gallagher, 1994; Dougherty, 1994) has documented the influence of local officials in forming the colleges. Frequently operating in high school facilities, the colleges were local institutions with much civic pride surrounding their development. As they were formed, schoolteachers became college professors and school superintendents became college presidents, a significant force for building an institution that would accord prestige to its staff and its township. Prior to mid-century, the notion of statewide systems or a national agenda hardly existed.

Historical Development of the New Form

The thesis attributing the rise of the two-year colleges to the efforts of local, civic, and professional leaders has merit. For one, it provides an explanation for the two-year colleges as a twentieth-century phenomenon even though calls for their development had been made by university leaders decades earlier. The need for trained manpower had been apparent, too, but apprenticeships were the dominant way into the work force. Until the 1900s, two essential components were not yet in place: sizable numbers of students graduating from high school, and public school districts managing secondary schools to which they could readily append two more years of curriculum, with or without special legal sanction.

In 1919, McDowell submitted the first doctoral dissertation describing the junior college movement. He found the roots of the junior college in the works previously cited and acknowledged that the universities had supported the junior college because of their need to divert the many freshmen and sophomores whom they could not accommodate. He also traced the expansion of secondary schools into grades 13 and 14 and the conversion of many church colleges and normal schools into junior colleges.

Much of the discussion about junior colleges in the 1920s and 1930s had to do with whether they were expanded secondary schools or truncated colleges. The school district with three types of institutions (elementary schools with grades 1–6, junior highs with grades 7–10, and combined high schools and junior colleges with grades 11–14) was set forth as one model. This 6–4–4 plan had much appeal: curriculum articulation between grades 12 and 13 would be smoothed; the need for a separate physical plant would be mitigated; instructors could teach in both high school and junior college under the same contract; superior students could go through the program rapidly; occupational education could be extended from secondary school into the higher grades; and small communities that could not support self-standing junior colleges would be helped by appending the college to their secondary schools. The 6–4–4 plan also allowed students to change schools or leave the system just when they reached the age limit of compulsory school attendance. Most students did (and do) complete the tenth grade at age sixteen. A high school that continues through grade 12 suggests that students would stay beyond the compulsory age, whereas a system that stops at grade 10 coincides with the age when students can legally leave.

Would a four-year junior college beginning at grade 11 enhance schooling for most students? Those who completed the tenth grade and chose to go beyond the compulsory age would enter a school in their home area that could take them through the sophomore year or through an occupational program. But hardly any public school districts organized themselves into a 6–4–4 system—possibly because, as Eells (1931) suggested, this system did not seem to lead to a true undergraduate college, complete with school spirit. He mentioned also the ambition of junior college organizers to have their institutions elevated to the status of senior institutions. However, the idea did not die; the notion of a Middle College High School, a secondary school built within a community college (described by Cullen and Moed, 1988), has gained some interest recently.

Arguments in favor of a new institution to accommodate students through their freshman and sophomore years were fueled by the belief that the transition from adolescence to adulthood typically occurred at the end of a person's teens. William Folwell contended that youths should be permitted to reside in their homes until they had "reached a point, say, somewhere near the end of the sophomore year" (quoted in Koos, 1924, p. 343). Eells posited that the junior colleges allowed students who were not fit to take the higher work to stop "naturally and honorably at the end of the sophomore year" (1931, p. 91). "As a matter of record, the end of

the second year of college marks the completion of formal education for the majority of students who continue post–high school
studies" (p. 84). They would be better off remaining in their home
communities until greater maturity enabled a few of them to go to
the university in a distant region; the pretense of higher learning
for all could be set aside. Harvard president James Bryant Conant
viewed the community college as a terminal education institution:
"By and large, the educational road should fork at the end of the
high school, though an occasional transfer of a student from a two-
year college to a university should not be barred" (quoted in Bogue,
1950, p. 32).

The 1947 President's Commission on Higher Education articulated the value of a populace with free access to two years of study
more than the secondary schools could provide. As the commission
put it, because around half of the young people can benefit from formal studies through grade 14, the community colleges have an
important role to play. The commission also suggested changing the
institutional name from *junior college* to *community college* because
of the expanded functions.

Expansion of Two-Year Colleges

Junior colleges were widespread in their early years. Koos (1924)
reported only 20 in 1909 but 170 ten years later. By 1922, thirty-
seven of the forty-eight states contained junior colleges, this within
two decades of their founding. Of the 207 institutions operating in
that year, 137 were privately supported. Private colleges were most
likely to be in the southern states, publicly supported institutions
in the West and Midwest. Most of the colleges were quite small,
although even in that era public colleges tended to be larger than
private colleges. In 1922 the total enrollment for all institutions was
around 20,000; the average was around 150 students in the public
colleges and 60 in the private. California had 20 private junior colleges in 1936. But those institutions together enrolled fewer than

2,000 students, and by 1964, all but three of them had disappeared (Winter, 1964).

By 1930 there were 450 junior colleges, found in all but five states. Total enrollment was around 70,000, an average of about 160 students per institution. California had 20 percent of the public institutions and one-third of the students, and although the percentages have dropped, California has never relinquished this early lead. Other states with a large number of public junior colleges were Illinois, Texas, and Missouri; Texas and Missouri also had sizable numbers of private junior colleges. By 1940 there were 610 colleges, still small, averaging about 400 students each.

The high point for the private junior colleges came in 1949, when there were 322 privately controlled two-year colleges, 180 of them affiliated with churches, 108 independent nonprofit, and 34 proprietary. As Table 1.1 shows, they began a steady decline, merging with senior institutions or closing their doors. No new ones have been organized since the mid 1970s (Woodroof, 1990). Never large, by the latter 1980s the median-sized private, nonprofit college had fewer than 500 students. By contrast, the median public college enrolled nearly 3,000 students. These sources of information on the number of colleges vary because they may or may not include some of the two-year branch campuses of public universities, schools accredited by the National Association of Trade and Technical Schools but not by the regional accrediting associations, and various categories of technical institutes. Not only do the data vary among the directories, but because of revised survey procedures or definitions they are not consistent from year to year within the same directories.

Although the number of colleges has changed little recently, enrollments have grown. Even so, this has not changed the median college size, because most of the growth has taken place in the larger institutions. In Fall 1991, one-third of the public community colleges had enrollments of 2,200 or less, one-third enrolled between 2,200 and 6,000, and one-third were from 6,000 on up to 30,000

Table 1.1. Numbers of Public and Private Two-Year Colleges, 1900–1994.

		Public		Private	
Year	Total	Number	Percentage	Number	Percentage
1900–01	8	0	0	9	100
1915–16	74	19	26	55	74
1921–22	207	70	34	137	66
1925–26	325	136	42	189	58
1929–30	436	178	41	258	59
1933–34	521	219	42	302	58
1938–39	575	258	45	317	55
1947–48	650	328	50	322	50
1952–53	594	327	55	267	45
1954–55	596	336	56	260	44
1956–57	652	377	58	275	42
1958–59	677	400	59	277	41
1960–61	678	405	60	273	40
1962–63	704	426	61	278	39
1964–65	719	452	63	267	37
1966–67	837	565	68	272	32
1968–69	993	739	74	254	26
1970–71	1,091	847	78	244	22
1972–73	1,141	910	80	231	20
1974–75	1,203	981	82	222	18
1976–77	1,233	1,030	84	203	16
1978–79	1,234	1,047	85	187	15
1980–81	1,231	1,049	85	182	15
1982–83	1,219	1,064	87	155	13
1984–85	1,222	1,067	87	155	13
1986–87	1,224	1,062	87	162	13
1988–89	1,231	1,056	86	175	14
1990–91	1,238	1,078	87	160	13
1992–94	1,236	1,082	88	154	12

Source: American Association of Community and Junior Colleges, *Community, Junior, and Technical College Directory*, 1960, 1976, 1979, 1980; Palmer, 1987b; National Center for Education Statistics, 1990, 1993.

and more. This is essentially the same breakout of small, medium, and large-size colleges as was apparent in the early 1980s. In the early 1990s, more than one million students were enrolled in colleges that had over twenty thousand students each.

More than any other single factor, access depends on proximity. Even the highly selective University of California's urban campuses draw three-quarters of their entering freshmen from within a fifty-mile radius. Hence, the advent of the community college as a neighborhood institution did more to open higher education to more people than did its policy of accepting even those students who had not done well in high school. Throughout the nation, in city after city, as community colleges opened their doors, the percentage of students beginning college expanded dramatically. During the 1950s and 1960s, whenever a community college was established in a locale where there had been no publicly supported college, the proportion of high school graduates in that area who began college immediately increased, sometimes by as much as 50 percent. The pattern has not changed. According to a survey by the College Entrance Examination Board (1986), 94 percent of the two-year-college matriculants nationwide are residents of the state in which the college is located; 96 percent commute to the campus. (The figures for four-year colleges are 76 and 41 percent, respectively.)

Fueled by the high birthrates of the 1940s, this rapid expansion of community colleges led their advocates to take an obsessive view of growth. Growth in budgets, staff, and students was considered good; stasis or decline was bad. It is a peculiar, but readily understandable, view. When budgets, enrollments, and staff are on an upswing, anything is possible; new programs can be launched, and new staff members can be found to operate them. It is much easier to hire a new composition teacher than to assign remedial English classes to a history instructor whose course enrollments have declined. Small wonder that college leaders made growth their touchstone. The philosophy is that new programs serve new clients;

the conclusion is that the institution that grows fastest serves its district best.

Obviously, though, the number of new institutions could not continue expanding forever. In 1972, M. J. Cohen studied the relationship between the number of community colleges in a state, the state's population density, and its area. He found that community colleges tended to be built so that 90 to 95 percent of the state's population lived within reasonable commuting distance, about 25 miles. When the colleges reached this ratio, the state had a mature community college system, and few additional colleges were built. As that state's population grew larger, the colleges expanded in enrollments, but it was no longer necessary to add new campuses. In the early 1970s seven states had mature systems: California, Florida, Illinois, New York, Ohio, Michigan, and Washington. In these states the denser the population, the smaller the area served by each college, and the higher the per-campus enrollment. Applying his formula of the relationship between number of colleges, state population, and population density, Cohen (1972) showed that 1,074 public community colleges would effectively serve the nation. In 1994, 1,082 such colleges were in operation; thus, the formula seems valid.

Diversity marked the organization, control, and financing of colleges in the various states. Like the original four-year colleges and universities, junior colleges grew without being coordinated at the state level: "Without doubt, the weakest link in the chain of cooperation for junior colleges is in the lack of authority for leadership and supervision at the state level. . . . By and large, the junior college in the United States has been growing without plan, general support, or supervision, and in some states almost as an extralegal institution" (Bogue, 1950, pp. 137–138). According to Blocker, Plummer, and Richardson, the colleges were "a direct outgrowth of customs, tradition, and legislation," and their "confused image . . . [was] related to state and regional differences and legislation and to the historical development of the institution" (1965, p. 76).

Various organizing principles dictated construction of the junior colleges. Decapitation was one. Four-year private colleges struggling to maintain their accreditation, student body, and fiscal support might abandon their upper-division specialized classes to concentrate on freshman and sophomore work and thus become junior colleges. The University of Missouri helped several struggling four-year colleges in that state to become private junior colleges. In other southern states where weak four-year colleges were prevalent, this dropping of the upper division also took place, accounting for the sizable number of private junior colleges in that region. Originally, over half of the private colleges were single-sex institutions, with colleges for women found most widely in New England, the Middle West, and the South.

Junior colleges were also organized by public universities wanting to expand their feeder institutions. The first two-year colleges in Pennsylvania were established as branch campuses of the Pennsylvania State College. The state universities of Kentucky, Alaska, and Hawaii also organized community colleges under their aegis. Some public universities established two-year colleges on their own campuses. A University Center System gave rise to several two-year institutions in Wisconsin, and the University of South Carolina founded several regional campuses.

Although community colleges now operate in every state and enroll half of the students who begin college in America, they found their most compatible climate early on in the West, most notably in California. One reason may have been that many of the ideals of democracy first took form in the western states, where women's suffrage and other major reforms in the electoral process were first seen. But the expansion of the community college in the West must also be attributed to the fact that during the eighteenth century and the first half of the nineteenth, while colleges sponsored by religious institutions and private philanthropists grew strong elsewhere, the West had not yet been settled. In the twentieth century it was much easier for publicly supported institutions to advance where there was little competition from the private sector. California became the leader in community college development because of support from the University of California and Stanford University, a paucity of small denominational colleges, and strong support for public education at all levels. Even now, more than half of the college students in Arizona, Washington, and Wyoming, as well as California, are in community colleges.

A 1907 California law authorizing secondary school boards to offer postgraduate courses "which shall approximate the studies prescribed in the first two years of university courses," together with several subsequent amendments, served as a model for enabling legislation in numerous states. Anthony Caminetti, the senator who introduced the legislation, had been responsible twenty years earlier for an act authorizing the establishment of high schools as upward extensions of grammar schools. Actually, the law only sanctioned a practice in which many of the high schools in California were already engaged. Those located at some distance from the state university had been offering lower-division studies to assist students who could not readily leave their home towns at the completion of high school. When Fresno took advantage of the law to establish a junior college in 1910, one of its presenting arguments was that there was no institution of higher education within nearly 200 miles of the city. (Such justifications for two-year colleges have been used throughout the history of the development of these institutions.) Subsequent laws in California authorized junior colleges to open as districts entirely independent of the secondary schools, and this form of parallel development continued for decades. Indicative of the inchoate nature of the institution in its early years, in 1927 California had sixteen colleges organized as departments of the local secondary schools, six as junior college departments of state colleges, and nine organized as separate junior college districts. In 1936 the number operated by the high schools had increased to twenty-three and those by separate junior college districts to eighteen, but the junior college departments of state universities had declined to just one. By 1980, nearly all the junior college districts had been separated from the lower-school districts.

The beginnings of the two-year college in other states that now have well-developed systems followed similar patterns, but with some variations. Arizona in 1927 authorized local school districts to organize junior colleges. In Mississippi they were spawned by county agricultural high schools. In 1917, a Kansas law allowed local elections to establish junior colleges and to create special taxing districts to support them. Michigan's authorizing legislation was passed the same year. Public junior colleges had already begun in Minnesota before a law was passed in 1925 providing for local elections to organize districts. Missouri's legislation permitting secondary schools to offer junior college courses dates from 1927, although junior colleges were established there earlier. Most of the community colleges in New York followed a 1949 state appropriation to establish a system of colleges to "provide two-year programs of post-high-school nature combining general education with technical education, special courses in extension work, and general education that would enable students to transfer" (Bogue, 1950, p. 34). Each state's laws were amended numerous times, usually to accommodate changed funding formulas and patterns of governance.

But these patterns are not uniform. Many aspects of college operations continue as they were when the institutions were under the local control of school boards; faculty evaluation procedures and funds awarded on the basis of student attendance are prime examples. And sometimes, just as one characteristic of the college changes in the direction of higher education, another moves toward the lower schools. In 1988, the California legislature passed a comprehensive reform bill that made many community college management practices correspond with those in the state's universities; but in the same year a proposition that was passed by public initiative placed college funding under guarantees similar to those enjoyed by the K–12 system.

Curricular Functions

The various curricular functions noted in each state's legislation usually include academic transfer preparation, vocational-technical education, continuing education, remedial education, and community service. All have been present in public colleges from the start. In 1936, Hollinshead wrote that "the junior college should be a community college meeting community needs" (p. 111), providing adult education and educational, recreational, and vocational activities and placing its cultural facilities at the disposal of the community. Every book written about the institution since then has also articulated these elements.

Academic Transfer

Academic transfer, or collegiate, studies were meant to fulfill several institutional purposes: a popularizing function, a democratizing pursuit, and a function of conducting the lower division for the universities. The popularizing activity was to have the effect of advertising higher education, showing what it could do for the individual, encouraging people to attend. The democratizing function was realized as the community colleges became the point of first access for people entering higher education; by the late 1970s, 40 percent of all first-time-in-college, full-time freshmen and around two-thirds of all ethnic minority students were in the two-year institutions. The function of relieving the universities from having to deal with freshmen and sophomores was less pronounced, because the universities would not relinquish their lower divisions. Instead, community colleges made it possible for them to maintain selective admissions requirements and thus to take only those freshmen and sophomores they wanted.

In 1930, Eells surveyed 279 junior colleges to determine, among other things, the types of curricula offered (Eells, 1931). He found that 69 percent of the semester hours were presented in academic subjects, with modern foreign languages, social sciences, and natural

sciences predominating. The 31 percent left for nonacademic subjects included sizable offerings in music, education, and home economics, and courses similar to those offered in extension divisions.
At that time there was little difference between the curricula presented in public colleges, whether state controlled or locally controlled, and in private denominational or independent institutions;
but the older the institution, the more likely it was to be engaged in
building a set of nonacademic studies. The universities accepted the
collegiate function and readily admitted transferring students to
advanced standing, most universities granting credit on an hour-for-
hour basis for freshman and sophomore courses. Bogue reported that
"60 percent of the students in the upper division of the University
of California at Berkeley, according to the registrar, are graduates of
other institutions, largely junior colleges" (1950, p. 73).

Vocational-Technical

Vocational-technical education was written into the plans in most
states from the earliest days. In the 1970s the U.S. Office of Education popularized *career education*, which phrase is used throughout
this book as a collective term for all occupational, vocational, and
technical studies. Originally conceived as an essential component
of "terminal study"—education for students who would not go on
to further studies—career education in the two-year colleges was
designed to teach skills more complicated than those taught in high
schools. Whereas secondary schools in the 1930s were teaching
agriculture, bookkeeping, automobile repair, and printing, for example, junior colleges taught radio repair, secretarial services, and laboratory technical work. Teacher preparation, a function of the
junior college in the 1920s, had died out as the baccalaureate
became the requirement for teaching, but a sizable proportion of the
occupational curriculum in the 1930s was still preprofessional training: prelaw, premedicine, pre-engineering. According to Eells
(1931), in 1929 the proportional enrollment in California public
junior colleges was 80 to 20 in favor of the collegiate; in Texas

municipal junior colleges, it was 77 to 23. By the 1970s the percentage of students in career education had reached parity with that in the collegiate programs.

Continuing Education

The continuing education function arose early, and the percentage of adults enrolled increased dramatically in the 1940s. The 1947 President's Commission on Higher Education emphasized the importance of this function, and Bogue noted with approval a Texas college's slogan, "We will teach anyone, anywhere, anything, at any time whenever there are enough people interested in the program to justify its offering" (1950, p. 215). He reported also that "out of the 500,536 students reported in the 1949 [AAJC] *Directory*, nearly 185,000 are specials or adults" (p. 35).

Remedial Education

Remedial education—also known as developmental, preparatory, or basic skills studies—grew as the percentage of students poorly prepared in secondary schools swelled community college rolls. Although some compensatory work had been offered early on, the disparity in ability between students entering community colleges and those in the senior institutions was not nearly as great in the 1920s as in the 1980s. Koos (1924) reported only slightly higher entering test scores by the senior college matriculants. The apparent breakdown of basic academic education in secondary schools in the 1960s, coupled with the expanded percentage of people entering college, brought remedial education to the fore.

Community Service

The community-service function was pioneered by private junior colleges and by rural colleges, which often served as the cultural centers for their communities. Early books on two-year colleges display a wide range of cultural and recreational events that institutions of the time were presenting for the enlightenment of their communities. Public two-year colleges adopted the idea as a useful aspect of their relations with the public, and in some states special funds were set aside for this function. By 1980 the AACJC *Directory* listed nearly four million community education participants, predominantly people enrolled in short courses, workshops, and noncredit courses. The community-service function also included spectator events sponsored by the colleges but open to the public as well as to students.

This book presents separate chapters on each of the curricular functions: collegiate (academic transfer), career (vocational-technical), and remedial (developmental) education. Community service and continuing education are merged, and general education is accorded treatment on its own. Student guidance, often mentioned as a major function, is covered in the chapter on student services. Yet all the functions overlap, because education is rarely discrete. Community college programs do not stay in neat categories when the concepts underlying them and the purposes for which students enroll in them are scrutinized. Although courses in the humanities are almost always listed as part of the collegiate program, they are career education for students who will work in museums. A course in auto mechanics is for the general education of students who learn to repair their own cars, even though it is part of the offerings in a career program. Collegiate, career, continuing education—all are intertwined. Who can say when one or another is being provided?

Such definitions are pertinent primarily for funding agents and accreditation associations and for those who need categories and classification systems as a way of understanding events. "Career" education is that which is supported by Vocational Education Act monies and/or is supposed to lead to direct employment. When a course or program is approved for transfer credit to a senior institution, it becomes part of the "collegiate" function. When it cannot be used for associate-degree credit, it is "developmental" or "community" education. That is why community college presidents may honestly say that their institutions perform all tasks with great facility. When confronted with the charge that their school is not doing enough in one or another curriculum area, they can counter that it is, if only the courses and students were examined more closely. All education is general education. All education is potentially career enhancing. All education is for the sake of the broader community.

Colleges in Other Countries

All nations face similar issues of work-force development, societal cohesion, and providing avenues of individual mobility. As Tables 1.2 and 1.3 indicate, most of the countries in Europe and Asia support institutions that provide functions similar to those in American community colleges. (Still other institutions, not listed, have been formed in Africa and South America.) However, no countries but the United States (and to some extent Canada) have formed comprehensive community colleges. The primary reason is that compulsory schooling continues for a greater number of years for America's young people than it does in any other nation, a phenomenon seeding the desire for more schooling. The second reason is that Americans seem more determined to allow individual options to remain open for as long as each person's motivations and the community's budget allow. Placing pre-baccalaureate, occupational, and remedial education within the same institution enables students to move from one to the other more readily than if they had to change schools.

Changing Emphases

Community colleges have effected notable changes in American education, especially by expanding access. Well into the middle of the twentieth century, higher education had elements of mystery within it. Only one young person in seven went to college, and most students were from the middle and upper classes. To the public at

Table 1.2. Institutions Providing Community College Functions in Europe, Asia, and Other Countries.

Institution	Country
College of Advanced Education	Australia
College of Applied Arts and Technology	Canada
Collège d'Enseignement Général et Professional (CEGEP)	Canada
College of Further Education	Australia, Britain
Community College	Canada, New Zealand, United States
Fachhochschule	Germany
Folkhighschool	Denmark
Higher Technicians' Section	France
Institut Teknologi	Malaysia
Junior College	Japan, Republic of China, United States
Regional (or District) College	Norway, Israel
Regional Technical College	Ireland
Special Training School	Japan
Technical College (or Institute)	United States, Malaysia, New Zealand
Technological Education Institution	Greece
Two-Year Vocational University	People's Republic of China
University Institute of Technology (IUT)	France
Upper Secondary School	Sweden
Volkshochschule	Germany
Workers' College	People's Republic of China

Source: Cohen, 1994a.

large, which really had little idea of what went on behind the walls, higher education was a clandestine process, steeped in ritual. The demystification of higher education, occasioned by the democratization of access, has taken place steadily. After World War II, as a result of the GI Bill, which made available the first large-scale financial-aid packages and made it possible for people to be reimbursed not only for their tuition but also for their living expenses while

Table 1.3. Major Emphases.

	General	Pre-University	Technical	Vocational	Cultural/Social
Australia					X
Britain					X
Canada	X	X	X	X	
Denmark					X
France			X	X	
Germany					X
Greece			X		
Ireland				X	
Israel	X		X		
Japan	X	X	X	X	
Malaysia				X	
New Zealand			X	X	
Norway		X			
People's Republic of China				X	X
Republic of China				X	X
Sweden	X			X	
United States		X	X	X	X

Source: Cohen, 1994a.

attending college, the number of people going to college increased rapidly. By the 1990s, 24 percent of all American adults had completed four years of college, an achievement matched by no other country except Japan.

The increase in enrollments was accompanied by a major change in the composition of the student body. No longer were colleges sequestered enclaves operated apparently for the sons of the wealthy and educated, who were on their way to positions in the professions, and for the daughters of the same groups, who would be marked with the manners of a cultured class; now colleges were opened to ethnic minorities, to lower-income groups, and to those whose prior academic performance had been marginal. Of all the higher education institutions, the community colleges contributed most to opening the system. Established in every metropolitan area, they were available to all comers, attracting the "new students": minorities, women, people who had done poorly in high school, those who would otherwise never have considered further education.

During this same era community colleges contributed also to certain shifts in institutional emphasis. They had always been an avenue of individual mobility; that purpose became highlighted as greater percentages of the populace began using colleges as a step up in class. The emphasis in higher education on providing trained personnel for the professions, business, and industry also became more distinct. Admittedly, it is difficult to identify the students who sought learning for its own sake, or who went to college to acquire the manners that would mark them as ladies or gentlemen; perhaps students whose purposes were purely nonvocational were rare even before 1900. But by the last third of the twentieth century, few commentators on higher education were even articulating those purposes. Vocationalism had gained the day. College going was for job getting, job certifying, job training. The old value of a liberal education became supplemental: as an adjunct to be picked up incidentally, if at all, along the way to higher-paying employment.

Other shifts in institutional emphasis have been dictated not by the pronouncements of educational philosophers but by the exigencies of financing, state-level coordinating bodies, the availability of new media, and new groups of students. There has been a steady increase in the public funds available to all types of educational institutions, but the community colleges have been most profoundly affected by sizable increases in federal appropriations for occupational education. Beginning with the Smith-Hughes Act in 1917 and continuing through the Vocational Education Acts of the 1960s and later, federal dollars have poured into the education sector. Community colleges have not been remiss in obtaining their share. Their national lobbyists have worked diligently to have the community college named in set-asides, and the colleges have obtained funds for special occupational programs. The career-education cast of contemporary colleges is due in no small measure to the availability of these funds.

State-level coordinating agencies have affected institutional roles. Coordinating councils and postsecondary education commissions, along with boards of regents for all higher education in some states, have attempted to assign programs to the different types of institutions. These bodies may restrict lower-division offerings in community colleges. In some states continuing education has been assigned; in others it has been taken away from the colleges.

The new media have had their own effect. Electronic gadgetry has been adopted, and elaborate learning resource centers have been opened on campus. Because learning laboratories can be made available at any time, it becomes less necessary for students to attend courses in sequence or at fixed times of day. The new media, particularly television, have made it possible for institutions to present sizable proportions of their offerings over open circuits. The colleges have burst their campus bounds.

But the new students have had the most pronounced effect. The community colleges reached out to attract those who were not being served by traditional higher education: those who could not afford the tuition; who could not take the time to attend a college on a full-time basis; whose ethnic background had constrained them from participating; who had inadequate preparation in the lower schools; whose educational progress had been interrupted by some temporary condition; who had become obsolete in their jobs or had never been trained to work at any job; who needed a connection to obtain a job; who were confined in prisons, had physical disabilities, or otherwise unable to attend classes on a campus; or who were faced with a need to fill increased leisure time meaningfully. The colleges' success in enrolling these new students has affected what they can offer. Students who are unable to read, write, and compute at a level that would enable them to pursue a collegiate program satisfactorily must be provided with different curricula. As these students become a sizable minority—or, indeed, a majority—the college's philosophy is affected. Gradually, the institution's spokespersons stop talking about its collegiate character and speak more of the developmental work in which it engages. Gradually, faculty stop demanding the same standards of student achievement. Part-time students similarly affect the colleges as new rules of attendance are adopted to accommodate students who drop in and out. And new types of support systems and learning laboratories are installed for those who do not respond to traditional classroom-centered instruction.

Overall, the community colleges have suffered less from goal displacement than have most other higher education institutions. They had less to displace; their goals were to serve the people with whatever the people wanted. Standing outside the tradition, they offered access. They had to instruct; they could not offer the excuse that they were advancing the frontiers of scholarship. Because they had expanded rapidly, their permanent staffs had not been in place so long that they had become fixed. As an example, they could quite easily convert their libraries to learning resource centers because the libraries did not have a heritage of the elaborate routines accompanying maintenance and preservation of large collections. They could be adapted to the instructional programs.

In 1924, Koos was sanguine about the role of the junior college in clarifying and differentiating the aims of both the universities and the secondary schools. He anticipated an allocation of function "that would be certain to bring order out of the current educational chaos. . . . By extending the acknowledged period of secondary education to include two more years . . . allocation of purpose to each unit and differentiation among them should take care of themselves" (p. 374). Koos believed that most of the aims and functions of the secondary school would rise to the new level, so that the first two years of college work would take on a new significance. These aims included occupational efficiency, civic and social responsibility, and the recreational and esthetic aspects of life. The universities would be freed for research and professional training. Further, the college-entrance controversy would be reduced, and preprofessional training could be better defined. Duplication of offerings between secondary schools and universities would also be reduced by the expansion of a system of junior colleges.

Clearly, not many of Koos's expectations were borne out. He could not have anticipated the massive increase in enrollments; the growth of universities and colleges and the competition among them; or the breakdown in curriculum fostered, on the one hand, by part-time students who dropped in and out of college and, on the other, by the institutions' eagerness to offer short courses, workshops, and spectator events. His scheme did not allow for students who demanded higher degrees as a right, crying that the colleges had discriminated against them when degrees were not awarded as a matter of form. And he was unaware of the importance that students and educators alike would place on programs related to job attainment.

Issues

The revolution in American education, in which the two-year college played a leading role, is almost over. Two years of postsecondary education are within the reach—financially, geographically, practically—of virtually every American. Two generations have passed since President Truman's Commission on Higher Education recommended that the door to higher education be swung open. Now community colleges are everywhere. There are systems with branches in inner cities and rural districts, and with programs in prisons and on military bases. Classes are offered on open-circuit television, on Saturdays, and at all hours of the night. Open-admissions policies and programs for everyone ensure that no member of the community need miss the chance to attend.

Riding the demographics of the World War II baby boom, the fiscal largesse resulting from an expanding economy, and a wave of public support for education, community colleges had been organized in every state by the 1960s. Less than ten years later, in the 1970s, the institution matured. The overall number of two-year colleges was 1,230 in 1976. In 1977, part-time student enrollment exceeded 60 percent and occupational degrees awarded were at 60 percent of the total. Part-time faculty members in 1976 represented 55 percent of the total faculty. All these figures have changed little in intervening years. The community colleges enrolled 34 percent of all students in U.S. higher education in the mid 1970s; in the early 1990s, it was 37 percent.

In summation, the number of colleges, student-attendance patterns, faculty-employment patterns, and types of degrees awarded were level from the mid 1970s to the mid 1990s. Although this stasis refers to the basic characteristics of the institution as a whole and not to notable changes that might have occurred in one or another college, it does reveal a mature system that has taken its place as a central element in the fabric of American postcompulsory education.

This maturity has not changed the colleges' perennial problems of funding, public perception, relative emphasis, purposes, and value. To Bogue in 1950, the critical problems of the community colleges were: devising a consistent type of organization, maintaining local or state control, developing an adequate general education program integrated with the occupational, finding the right kinds of teachers, maintaining adequate student guidance services, and getting the states to appropriate sufficient funds. These problems have never been satisfactorily resolved.

Recent changes in both intra- and extramural perceptions of community colleges have led to further issues. Some of these shifts are due to educational leadership at the state and the institutional level, but more are due to changing demographic patterns and public perceptions of institutional purposes.

First, there has been an inversion in the uses of career and collegiate education. Career education was formerly considered terminal. Students were expected to complete their formal schooling by learning a trade and going to work. Students who entered career programs and failed to complete them and then failed to work in the field for which they were trained were considered to have been misguided. Collegiate programs were designed to serve as a bridge between secondary school and baccalaureate studies. Students who entered the programs and failed to progress to the level of the baccalaureate were considered dropouts.

Since the 1970s, however, high proportions of students who complete career programs have been transferring to universities. Career programs typically maintain curricula in which the courses are sequential. Many of these programs, especially those in the technologies and the health fields, articulate well with baccalaureate programs. Most have selective admissions policies. Students are forced to make an early commitment, satisfy admissions requirements, maintain continual attendance, and make satisfactory progress. This pattern of schooling reinforces the serious students, leading them to enroll in further studies at a university. The collegiate courses, in contrast, are more likely to be taken by students who have not made a commitment to a definite line of study, who already have degrees and are taking courses for personal interest, or who are trying to build up their prerequisites or grade point averages so that they can enter a selective admissions program at the community college or another institution. Thus, for many students enrolled in them, the collegiate courses have become the catchall, the "terminal education" program.

A second issue is that by the 1970s the linear aspect of community colleges—the idea that the institution assists students in bridging the freshman and sophomore years—had been severely reduced as a proportion of the community colleges' total effort. The number of students transferring was reasonably constant, but most of the expansion in community college enrollments was in the areas of career and continuing education. The collegiate programs remained in the catalogues, but students used them for completely different purposes. They dropped in and out, taking the courses at will.

Among California community college students, Hunter and Sheldon (1980) found that the mean number of credit hours completed per term was between seven and eight, but the mode was three—in other words, one course. The course array in the collegiate programs was more accurately viewed as lateral rather than linear. Not more than one in ten course sections enforced course prerequisites; not more than one course in ten was a sophomore-level course. What had happened was that the students were using the institution in one way whereas the institution's patterns of functioning suggested another. Catalogues displayed recommended courses, semester by semester, for students planning to major in one or another of a hundred fields. But the students took those courses that were offered at a preferred time of day, or those that seemed potentially useful. In the 1980s many colleges took deliberate steps to quell that pattern of course attendance, but nationwide it was still the norm.

Third, a trend toward less-than-college-level instruction has accelerated. In addition to the increased number of remedial courses as a proportion of the curriculum, expectations in collegiate courses have changed. To take one example, students in community college English literature courses in 1977 were expected to read 560 pages per term, on average, whereas, according to Koos (1924), the average was three times that in *high school* literature courses of 1922. These figures are offered not to derogate community colleges but only to point out that the institutions cannot be understood in traditional terms. They are struggling to find ways of educating students whose prior learning has been dominated by nonprint images. The belief that a person unschooled in the classics was not sufficiently educated died hard in the nineteenth century; the ability to read *anything* as a criterion of adequate education has been questioned in an era when most messages are carried by wires and waves.

But all questions of curriculum, students, and institutional mission pale in the light of funding issues. Are the community colleges—or any schools—worth what they cost? Have the colleges overextended themselves? Do their outcomes justify the public resources they consume? Can they, should they, be called to account for their outcomes? These questions have appeared with increasing frequency as public disaffection with the schools has grown. Whether the community colleges stand alone or whether they are cast with the higher or lower schools, their advocates will be forced to respond.

Several other current issues may also be phrased as questions. How much more than access and illusory benefits of credits and degrees without concomitant learning do the colleges provide? Are they in or out of higher education? How much of their effort is dedicated to higher learning, to developing rationality and advancing knowledge through the disciplines? How much leads students to form habits of reflection? How much tends toward public and private virtue?

Is it moral to sort and grade students, sending the more capable to the university while encouraging the rest to follow other pursuits? Commenting on the terminal programs—the commercial and general education courses that did not transfer to the universities—Eells noted: "Students cannot be forced to take them, it is true, but perhaps they can be led, enticed, attracted" (1931, p. 310). And in his chapter on the guidance function, he stressed: "It is essential that many students be guided into terminal curricula" (p. 330). The "cooling-out" function (so named by Clark in 1960), convincing students that they should not aspire to higher learning, yielded an unending stream of commentary—for example, an issue of New Directions for Community Colleges entitled *Questioning the Community College Role* (Vaughan, 1980). But the question is still unanswered.

What would the shape of American education be if the community colleges had never been established? Where would people be learning the trades and occupations? Apprenticeships were the mode in earlier times. Would they still dominate, as they do in Europe? Would the less-than-college-level regional occupational centers and area vocational schools be larger and more handsomely funded? Would different configurations have developed?

What would have happened to the collegiate function? How many fewer students would be attending college? Would the universities have expanded to accommodate all who sought entry? Community colleges certainly performed an essential service in the 1960s, when a mass of people demanded access. By offering an inexpensive, accessible alternative, these colleges allowed the universities to maintain at least a semblance of their own integrity. How many universities would have been shattered if community colleges to which the petitioners could be shunted had not been available?

If there were no community colleges, what agencies would be performing their community service? How many of the services they provide would be missed? Would secondary schools better maintain their own curricular and instructional integrity if community colleges were not there to grant students absolution for all past educational sins? Would other institutions assume the remedial function?

Although such questions have been asked from time to time, they have rarely been examined, mainly because during most of its history the community college has been unnoticed, ignored by writers about higher education. Books on higher education published from the turn of the century, when the first community colleges appeared, through the 1980s rarely gave even a nod to the community college; one searches in vain for a reference to them in the index. In 1950, Bogue deplored the lack of attention paid to the junior colleges, saying that he had examined twenty-seven authoritative histories of American education and found only superficial treatment of junior colleges or none at all. Rudolph's major history of the higher education curriculum, published in 1977, gave them a scant two pages. Pascarella and Terenzini's massive review, *How College Affects Students* (1991), offered little more. Recently, however, a small body of literature, noted in the chapter on research, has been filling in some of the gaps.

Perhaps community colleges should merely be characterized as untraditional. They do not follow the tradition of higher education as it developed from the colonial colleges through the universities.

They do not typically provide the students with new value structures, as residential liberal arts colleges aspire to do. Nor do they further the frontiers of knowledge through scholarship and research training, as in the finest traditions of the universities. Community colleges do not even follow their own traditions. They change frequently, seeking new programs and new clients. Community colleges are indeed untraditional, but they are truly American because, at their best, they represent the United States at its best. Never satisfied with resting on what has been done before, they try new approaches to old problems. They maintain open channels for individuals, enhancing the social mobility that has characterized America; and they accept the idea that society can be better, just as individuals can better their lot within it.

2

. . . .

Students

Diverse Backgrounds, Purposes, and Outcomes

Two words sum up the students: *number* and *variety*. To college leaders the spectacular growth in student population, sometimes as much as 15 percent a year, has been the most impressive feature of community colleges. The numbers are notable: enrollment increased from just over five hundred thousand in 1960 to more than 2 million by 1970, 4 million by 1980, and nearly 6 million by the early 1990s. During the 1960s, much of the increase was due to the expanded proportion of eighteen- to twenty-four-year-olds in the population—the result of the World War II baby boom. More people were in the college-age cohort, and more of them were going to college.

Table 2.1 shows the number of undergraduates in all types of colleges relative to the number of eighteen- to twenty-four-year-olds in the American population for each decade from 1900 to 1970. The table accurately depicts the proportion of the age group attending college for those years, but because many undergraduates—half the community college population currently—are older than twenty-four, it is not reasonable to extend the table. A more accurate depiction of the rate of college going now is to divide the number of eighteen- to twenty-four-year-olds enrolled in college by the number of that age group in the population; the figure equaled 28 percent in 1991. Whereas in the early 1960s one-half of the high school graduates went to college, by the 1980s two-thirds of them

Table 2.1. Undergraduate Enrollment in U.S. Colleges and
Universities as Compared to Eighteen- to Twenty-Four-Year-Old
Population, 1900 to 1970.

Year	College-Age Population Eighteen to Twenty-Four Years (in Thousands)	Undergraduate Enrollment (in Thousands)	Percentage
1900	10,357	232	2.2
1910	12,300	346	2.8
1920	12,830	582	4.5
1930	15,280	1,054	6.9
1940	16,458	1,389	8.4
1950	16,120	2,421	15.0
1960	15,677	2,874	18.3
1970	24,712	6,274	25.4

Source: National Center for Education Statistics, 1970, p. 67.

were entering some postsecondary school—an increase occasioned
in large measure by the community colleges' availability. By 1987,
45 percent of the American population aged twenty-five to thirty-
four had attended college for at least one year.

This chapter reports data on the numbers and types of students
attending community colleges, including reasons for the different
enrollment patterns, college effects on various student groups, and
student goal attainment and dropout. Student transfer rates are
examined, but information on jobs attained appears in Chapter
Eight, on career education.

Reasons for the Increase in Numbers

The increase in community college enrollments may be attributed
to several conditions in addition to general population expansion:
older students' participation; financial aid; part-time attendance;
the reclassification of institutions; the redefinition of students and
courses; and high attendance by low-ability, women, and minority

students. Community colleges also recruited students aggressively; to an institution that tries to offer something for everyone in the community, everyone is potentially a student.

Demography has a profound effect on college enrollments. The number of eighteen-year-olds in the American population peaked in 1979, declined steadily throughout the 1980s, and was 23 percent lower in 1992. In the twenty years following 1969, overall enrollments in public two-year colleges increased by 149 percent, with the bulk of that increase occurring during the 1970s. Enrollments in the 1980s increased by only 19 percent; with the exception of Florida, enrollments in all states that had mature community college systems showed considerably less increase—and New York, California, and Washington actually registered decreases for the decade (National Center for Education Statistics, 1992a).

In order to make up for the shortfall in potential younger students, the colleges expanded programs attractive to older students. Numbers of working adults seeking skills that would enable them to change or upgrade their jobs or activities to satisfy their personal interests were attracted because they could attend part-time. Older students swelled enrollments. According to the AACJC *Directory*, the mean age of students enrolled for credit in 1980 was twenty-seven, the median age was twenty-three, and the modal age was nineteen. A 1986 national survey conducted by the Center for the Study of Community Colleges found that by then the mean had gone up to twenty-nine, the median had increased to twenty-five, and the mode had remained at nineteen. By 1991, the mean had surpassed age thirty-one (National Center for Education Statistics, 1993).

Note the discrepancy among these three measures. The mean is the most sensitive to extremes; hence, a program for even a few senior citizens affects that measure dramatically. The median suggests that the students just out of high school and those in their early twenties who either delayed beginning college or entered community colleges after dropping out of other institutions accounted for half the student population. This 50 percent of the student body that was composed of students aged eighteen to twenty-five was matched on the other side of the median by students ranging in age all the way out to their sixties and seventies. The mode reflects the greatest number; nineteen-year-olds were still the dominant single age group in the institutions. Thus, a graph depicting the age of community college students would show a bulge at the low end of the scale, a peak at age nineteen, and a long tail reaching out toward the high end.

The availability of financial aid brought additional students as state and federal payments, loans, and work-study grants rose markedly. From the 1940s through the early 1970s, nearly all the types of aid were categorical, designed to assist particular groups of students. The largest group of beneficiaries was war veterans; in California in 1973, veterans made up more than 13 percent of the total enrollment. Students from economically disadvantaged and minority groups were also large beneficiaries of financial aid; more than thirty thousand such students in Illinois received state and local funds in 1974. Since the middle 1970s more of the funds have been unrestricted. Overall, one-third of the students entering community colleges in 1989–90 received some form of financial aid during their first year of attendance, with total aid averaging $2,000 per aid-receiving student (National Center for Education Statistics, 1994i, p. 64). When spread across the entire student population, these scholarships and grants averaged $671 per credit full-time-student equivalent (FTSE) in 1993 (Dickmeyer, 1994).

As the age of the students went up, the number of credit hours each student attempted went down. In the early 1970s one-half of the students were full-timers; by the mid 1980s only one-third were (see Table 2.2). In 1986 just over one-fourth of the one million students in California were enrolled for more than twelve units, while nearly half were taking fewer than six units (California Community Colleges, 1987a). Nationwide more than one-third of the stu-

Table 2.2. Part-Time Enrollments as a Percentage of Total Enrollments, 1970–1992.

Year	Total Fall Enrollments	Part-Time Enrollments	Percentage
1970	2,195,412	1,066,247	49
1975	3,836,366	2,173,745	57
1980	4,328,782	2,733,289	63
1985	4,269,733	2,772,828	65
1988	4,615,487	3,047,514	66
1990	4,996,475	3,279,632	66
1992	5,485,512	3,567,796	65

Source: National Center for Education Statistics, 1994j, p. 182.

dents were enrolled for fewer than six units in 1993 (Dickmeyer, 1994). And these figures do not include non-credit students enrolled in community or continuing education, high school completion courses, and short-cycle occupational studies. The pattern was consistent throughout the country; in nearly all states with community college enrollments greater than fifty thousand, part-time students outnumbered full-timers. In Illinois part-timers outnumbered full-timers seven to three in 1991 (Illinois Community College Board, 1992).

The rise in the number of part-time students can be attributed to many factors: a decline in eighteen-year-olds as a percentage of the total population, an increase in students combining work and study, and an increase in women attending college, to name but a few. The colleges have made deliberate efforts to attract part-timers by making it easy for them to attend. Senior citizens' institutes; weekend colleges; courses offered at off-campus centers, in workplaces, and in rented and donated housing around the district; and countless other stratagems have been employed. Few noncampus colleges count *any* full-timers among their enrollees. The Community College of the Air Force, headquartered in Alabama but with classes offered around the world, claimed 330,000 students in 1994, with about 10 percent of them attending full-time (American Association of Community Colleges, 1995).

The rise in part-time attendance has lowered the percentage of students attending community colleges past their first year. AACJC data for 1963–1973 showed a relatively constant ratio of about 2.4 freshmen to one sophomore; by the end of the decade, however, the proportion of students *completing* two years had dropped to less than one in five. Part of this decrease may be attributed to certificate programs that could be completed in one year, part to the massive increase in students without degree aspirations taking only a course or two for their own interest. The AACJC's dropping of "freshman" and "sophomore" categories from its *Directory* after 1975 reflected the tendency of most colleges to avoid referring to their students' year of attendance. The preferred mode of classification was to designate those who wanted credits for transfer to a baccalaureate institution, those who sought occupational training, and "other." Not necessarily more accurate, at least this type of information differentiated students according to the ways that many states allocate funds: degree credit, occupational studies, and adult or continuing education.

The growth in total enrollments did not result alone from the colleges' attracting students who might not otherwise have participated in education beyond high school. Two other factors played a part: the different ways of classifying institutions and a redefinition of the term *student*.

Changes in the classification of colleges are common. Private colleges become public; two-year colleges become four-year (and vice versa); adult education centers and proprietary trade schools enter the category, especially as they begin awarding degrees. The universe of community and junior colleges is especially fluid. From time to time, entire sets of institutions, such as trade and vocational schools and adult education centers, have been added to the list. As examples, in the mid 1960s four vocational-technical schools became the first colleges in the University of Hawaii community college system, and in the mid 1970s the community colleges in Iowa became area schools responsible for the adult education in their districts. Sometimes, institutional reclassification is made by an agency that gathers statistics; in the 1990s, the National Center for Education Statistics and the Carnegie Foundation for the Advancement of Teaching began adding accredited proprietary schools to their community college data bases. All these changes add to the number of students tabulated each year.

Reclassification of students within colleges has had an even greater effect on enrollment figures. As an example, when the category "defined adult" was removed from the California system, students of all ages could be counted as equivalents for funding purposes. In most states the trend has been toward including college-sponsored events (whether or not such activities demand evidence of learning attained) as "courses" and hence the people attending them as "students." The boundaries between the categories "degree-credit," "non-degree credit," "non-credit," and "community service" are permeable; student tallies shift about as courses are reclassified. Further, the community colleges have taken under their aegis numerous instructional programs formerly offered by public and private agencies, including police academies, hospitals, banks, and religious centers. These practices swell the enrollment figures and blur the definition of *student*, making it possible for community college leaders to point with pride to enhanced enrollments and to gain augmented funding when enrollments are used as the basis for accounting. They also heighten imprecision in counting students and make it difficult to compare enrollments from one year to another.

Nonetheless, the proportion of Americans attending college has increased steadily through the twentieth century, and the availability of community colleges has contributed notably to this growth. By 1989–90, one-half of all students beginning postsecondary education enrolled first in a two-year college (National Center for Education Statistics, 1994i). Of the students who delayed entry until they were thirty or older, 68 percent began in a community college. As the following sections detail, the colleges have been essential especially to the educational progress of people of lower academic ability, lower income, and other characteristics that had limited their opportunity for postsecondary enrollment.

Student Ability

Classification of students by academic ability revealed increasing numbers of lower-ability students among community college entrants. As Cross (1971) pointed out, three major philosophies about who should go to college have dominated the history of higher education in this country: the *aristocratic*, suggesting that white males from the upper socioeconomic classes would attend; the *meritocratic*, holding that college admission should be based on ability; and the *egalitarian*, which "means that everyone should have equality of access to educational opportunities, regardless of socioeconomic background, race, sex, *or ability*" (p. 6). By the time the community colleges were developed, most young people from the higher socioeconomic groups and most of the high-aptitude aspirants were going to college. Cross concluded: "the majority of students entering open-door community colleges come from the lower half of the high school classes, academically and socioeconomically" (p. 7).

Various data sets reveal the lower academic skill level of the entrants. The American College Testing Program's entering-test means for community colleges have been considerably lower than the norm for all college students. Whereas in 1991 the average national ACT composite score was 20.6, for students who indicated "Two-Year College Degree" as their objective it was 17.0 (National Center for Education Statistics, 1993, p. 130; American College Testing Program, 1990, p. 7). These differences showed up on statewide tests as well. Scores on the New Jersey College Basic Skills Placement Test showed that 46.8 percent of the students entering the county colleges in 1993 "lack proficiency" in verbal skills; this compares with 19.6 percent at the state colleges. Comparable figures for computation are 54.0 versus 20.7 percent, and for elementary algebra 72.9 versus 30.9 percent (New Jersey State Department of Higher Education, 1994).

However, like most other institutions of higher education, the community colleges have also sought out high-ability students and made special benefits available to them. For example, in 1979 Miami-Dade Community College began giving full tuition waivers to all students graduating in the top 10 percent of their local high school class, and in 1991 it extended that offer to the top 20 percent. In 1994 the college was drawing around one-fourth of the eligible group, totaling around 1,300 such students, for a total college investment of $1.5 million per year (Cathy Morris, telephone conversation, September 29, 1994).

The prevalence of honors programs suggests also that the colleges have welcomed the better-prepared students. White (1975) surveyed 225 colleges in the North Central region and found that about 10 percent had formalized honors programs and that nearly half of the others made some provision for superior students. Twenty years later, *Peterson's Guide to Two-Year Colleges* listed honors programs in over 25 percent of the institutions.

Gender

Probably because it is easier to sort students by gender than by any other variable, differences between male and female college students have long been documented. Historically, among students of questionable ability, fewer women than men attended college. When funds were limited, more male than female high-ability students from low-income families entered college. Further, the women who went to college were more likely to be dependent on their families for support. Not until 1978 did the number of women attending college in the United States equal the number of men. (By 1991 women were ahead, 55 percent to 45.)

The percentage of women students in community colleges has increased even more—to 57.5 percent by 1991—with 66 percent of them attending part-time. This compares with a part-time attendance rate of 60 percent for men. Overall, in each year since 1978, more women than men have earned associate degrees; in 1990, 58 percent of the degrees went to women.

There has been some slight change in the types of programs that community college students enter, although the traditionally gender-differentiated fields persist. The associate degrees awarded reveal these differences. In 1990, women earned 92 percent of the degrees in nursing, 95 percent in dental assisting, and 98 percent in medical assisting. Of the 14,302 degrees awarded in secretarial programs, all but 190 went to women. Men dominated in transportation, with 85 percent of the degrees; engineering technology, 91 percent; and fire control, 94 percent. Interestingly, the degrees awarded in computer and information science and in public affairs were about equally divided (National Center for Education Statistics, 1993, p. 247).

Ethnic Minorities

The community colleges' diligence in recruiting students from segments of the population that had not previously attended college yielded sizable increases in the college attendance of ethnic minorities. By 1991, community colleges, with 39 percent of the total enrollment in American higher education, were enrolling 47 percent of the ethnic minority students (National Center for Education Statistics, 1993). Minority students constituted 25 percent of all community college enrollments nationwide, up from 20 percent in 1976. Naturally, the pattern differs from state to state depending on the minority population. California, Hawaii, Louisiana, Mississippi, New Mexico, and Texas had the highest percentages of minorities among their community college students. Minorities were also enrolled in significant numbers in other states that have well-developed community college systems.

When the enrollment figures are disaggregated by ethnic groups, they are even more revealing of the community colleges' contributions to access for minority students. As shown in Table 2.3, the Hispanic proportion of community college enrollment *exceeds* the Hispanic proportion of the population in forty-one states. Comparable figures for African-American enrollments are found in twenty-one states.

More so than in the universities, the community college student population tends to reflect the ethnic composition of the institution's locale. Community colleges in cities with high proportions of minorities—Chicago, Cleveland, El Paso, Los Angeles, Miami, New York, Phoenix—enroll sizable numbers of minority students. The evidence of neighborhood attendance is revealed where the community college has several campuses in the same city. At East Los Angeles College in 1994, 73 percent of the students were Hispanic; at Los Angeles Southwest College, 76 percent were black; at Los Angeles Pierce College, 56 percent were white; and at Los Angeles City College, 25 percent were Asian. This pattern was not confined to the cities; community colleges in rural areas with high minority populations, as in many areas of Mississippi, Texas, and California, similarly attracted large numbers of minorities. Several community colleges were established especially to serve Native Americans. Oglala Lakota College (North Dakota), Haskell Indian Junior College (Kansas), Navajo Community College (Arizona), and Bacone Community College (Oklahoma) are notable examples.

Because the issue of minority students' progress in college has been so charged politically, the question of whether the community colleges have enhanced or retarded progress for minority students has been debated at length (see, for example, Astin, 1982; Richardson and Bender, 1987; Richardson and de los Santos, 1988). Those who say that the community colleges have assisted minority students point to ease of access, low tuition, and minimal entrance requirements. They note the numerous programs that provide special services to minority students, and they applaud efforts made to

Table 2.3. Percentages of African-American and Hispanic Population
by State, Compared with Ethnic Enrollments in Two-Year Colleges.

| | African-American | | Hispanic | |
	State Population	Two-Year College Enrollment	State Population	Two-Year College Enrollment
Alabama	25.3%	17.8%	0.3%	2.6%
Alaska	4.1	0.9	1.6	1.5
Arizona	3.0	3.5	9.1	15.1
Arkansas	15.9	12.8	0.5	0.6
California	7.4	8.0	11.8	18.2
Colorado	4.0	4.1	7.5	11.6
Connecticut	8.3	10.8	3.2	6.2
Delaware	16.9	14.7	1.0	1.8
Florida	13.6	11.4	9.9	13.4
Georgia	27.0	24.3	0.9	1.3
Hawaii	2.5	1.1	2.0	1.9
Idaho	0.3	0.4	2.2	2.4
Illinois	14.8	13.9	3.5	9.8
Indiana	7.8	8.2	1.0	1.1
Iowa	1.7	2.6	0.7	1.1
Kansas	5.8	5.7	1.7	2.7
Kentucky	7.1	6.7	0.3	0.6
Louisiana	30.8	24.3	1.5	3.5
Maine	0.4	0.6	0.4	0.4
Maryland	24.9	21.0	1.4	2.1
Massachusetts	5.0	6.7	2.0	5.2
Michigan	13.9	10.3	1.1	1.7
Minnesota	2.2	2.3	0.7	1.2
Mississippi	35.6	24.8	0.4	0.4
Missouri	10.7	12.4	0.8	1.1
Montana	0.3	0.0	0.9	0.9
Nebraska	3.6	4.1	1.3	2.6
Nevada	6.6	6.0	5.6	8.2
New Hampshire	0.6	1.2	0.7	3.3
New Jersey	13.4	12.9	5.3	7.9
New Mexico	2.0	3.6	25.2	31.4

Table 2.3. Continued.

	African-American State Population	African-American Two-Year College Enrollment	Hispanic State Population	Hispanic Two-Year College Enrollment
New York	15.9	13.8	5.1	9.5
North Carolina	22.0	19.2	0.6	0.9
North Dakota	0.6	1.1	0.4	0.3
Ohio	10.6	10.4	0.7	1.4
Oklahoma	7.4	6.9	1.1	1.6
Oregon	1.6	1.7	2.0	2.5
Pennsylvania	9.2	11.1	0.8	1.8
Rhode Island	3.9	4.9	2.1	4.8
South Carolina	29.8	23.9	0.5	0.9
South Dakota	0.5	0.0	0.4	0.0
Tennessee	16.0	15.3	0.4	0.6
Texas	11.9	10.3	14.6	21.8
Utah	0.7	0.6	2.6	3.3
Vermont	0.3	0.1	0.5	0.1
Virginia	18.8	13.7	1.4	2.1
Washington	3.1	4.1	1.8	2.8
West Virginia	3.1	3.2	0.4	0.3
Wisconsin	5.0	5.9	0.9	2.0
Wyoming	0.8	0.7	3.2	3.7

Source: Bureau of the Census, 1992; National Center for Education Statistics, 1992b.

recruit them. Their most telling argument is that a sizable percentage of those students would not be in college at all were it not for the community colleges.

Several analysts have charged that minority students who begin their college education at a community college will do less well than those of equal ability who enroll at the senior institution, and that this differential is greater for them than it is for the majority students. These detractors have taken the position that because students who begin at a community college are less likely to obtain baccalaureate degrees, minorities are actually harmed by two-year institutions. What is the evidence? The best estimates suggest that white students, who comprise 74 percent of community college enrollment, obtain 81 percent of the associate degrees; African-American students, 10 percent of enrollment, obtain 8 percent of the associate degrees; Hispanic students, 8.5 percent of enrollment, obtain 5 percent of the degrees; Asian students, 4.5 percent of enrollment, obtain 3 percent of the degrees (National Center for Education Statistics, 1993, p. 272). (These figures suggest not only differential achievement but also the imprecision of the term *minority student*.)

It is difficult to disaggregate the effects of community colleges from the characteristics of the students who enter them. In general, students who enter community colleges instead of universities have lower academic ability and aspirations and are from a lower socio-economic class. The various studies that have attempted to control for those variables frequently also attempt to control for the fact that minority students are more likely to attend school part-time, and the community colleges encourage part-time attendance. Minority students are also more likely to be from low-income families, and community colleges have low tuition.

The question of whether community colleges are beneficial to minority students is thus unresolved. If sizable percentages of minority students would not attend any college unless there were a community college available, and if the act of attending college to take even a few classes is beneficial, then community colleges have certainly helped in the education of minority students. But if the presence of a convenient community college discourages minority students from attending senior institutions and reduces the probability of their completing the baccalaureate, then for those students who wanted degrees the college has been detrimental.

The question is not whether minority students tend to be concentrated in two-year colleges; they do. The question is not whether they tend to go through to the level of the associate degree and then transfer to the university; as a group they do not. The question is what effect the community colleges have on *all* their students. And the answer is that they have a similar effect on all their students, minority and majority. As an example, nationwide the student transfer rate is higher for white and Asian students than it is for African-American and Hispanic students. However, in colleges that have a transfer rate substantially higher than the national norm, the transfer rate for African-American and Hispanic students is higher than the national norm for all students. The colleges are not designed exclusively for the purpose of passing students through to the baccalaureate. The issue must be seen in its total context; it does not merely affect the minorities.

The program completion rate of minority groups in community colleges must also be viewed in association with their record in other levels and types of institutions. During the 1960s, around three million pupils began their first grade each year and in the 1980s, around one hundred thousand first-professional and doctoral degrees were awarded annually. Obviously, most students left the school system somewhere along the way, but where? The progress made by these three million students in graded education was different for minority and majority students. As a group, minority students began at a point of lower academic achievement, and the difference between them and the majority students increased through the grades toward graduate school. Similarly, the number of minorities dropping out of graded education was greater at each year along the way.

Those who would understand the effect of community colleges should visualize two lines representing continuance in school. If one line shows majority students' persistence and the other minorities', the two will not be parallel; the line representing the majority will show the lesser attrition. The lines will be farther apart (the difference between minority and majority students will be greater) at grade 14 than at grade 12; fewer of the minorities are in college. Figure 2.1 depicts the trends graphically. Those who argue that the

Figure 2.1. Progress in the Educational System. Percentage of Cohort Entering Fifth Grade.

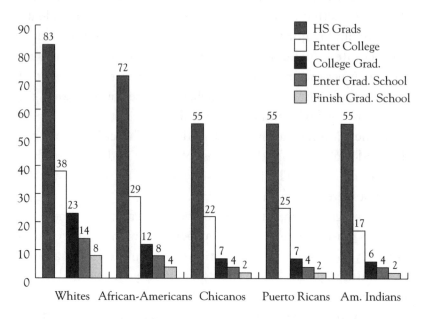

Source: Astin, 1982, p. 175.

community college does a disservice to minorities will point to the gap between minority and majority students' persistence in college. But they usually fail to note that a comparison between the groups for *any* two years of graded education, from kindergarten through the doctorate, would show a similar difference. Thus, because minority students tend to be clustered more in community colleges, the charge is made that they do less well in those institutions.

Whom do the community colleges best serve? Egalitarians would say that the institutions should maintain parity in the percentage of each ethnic group attaining each of the following goals: entering college, enrolling in transfer-credit courses, persisting in any courses, gaining the associate degree, gaining admittance to a high-level technological program, graduating from such a program, transferring to the university at any point, and transferring to the university at the junior level. In practice, however, this level of equivalence is impossible to attain, short of imposing strict quotas at every step. For the minorities as for any other identifiable student group, the question should be put more broadly: "The community college or what?" For most students in two-year institutions, *the choice is not between the community college and a senior residential institution; it is between the community college and nothing.*

Classifying the Students

The classification of students into special groups is more politically inspired than educationally pertinent. Women, ethnic minorities, and people with disabilities were able to have their concerns translated into special programs only after they became politically astute. From the college perspective, the temptation to place courses or students in separate categories was always present. The mature woman with a bachelor's degree, taking an art class for credit because it was taught by someone she admired and was scheduled at a time of day that was convenient for her, was not deserving of the special treatment accorded to "returning women," "the aged," or "students intending to transfer." She was there for her personal interest. Yet, because of politically and institutionally inspired definitions, she would be counted each time the institution reported its numbers of women, aged, and transfer students.

Classifying students takes other forms as well. Assessments of community college students have been made from perspectives that span the social sciences: psychological, sociological, economic, and political. To the psychologist, community college students are pragmatic, little concerned with learning for its own sake. They are not self-directed or self-motivated; they need to be instructed. To the sociologist, the students are struggling to escape from their lower-class backgrounds; some do, but many are inhibited by a bias against leaving family and friends that a move in class would engender. To the economist, students from low-income families pay more in the form of forgone earnings as a percentage of total family income than their counterparts from higher-income groups, a differential that more than offsets the savings gained by attending a low-tuition institution. To the political scientist, students attending community colleges are given short shrift because the institutions are funded at a lower per capita level than the universities, and hence the students do not have equivalent libraries, laboratories, or faculty-student ratios available to them.

But determining the reasons that students attend college is not an exact exercise. They come for a variety of reasons, and the same person may have a half-dozen reasons for attending. Much depends on the way the questions are asked and the interpretations that the respondents make. There can be little doubt that, although most students attend community colleges to better themselves financially, a sizable percentage are there for reasons of personal interest having nothing to do with direct fiscal benefit. The Center for the Study of Community Colleges' 1986 national survey found 36 percent seeking transfer, 34 percent job entry skills, 16 percent job upgrading, and 15 percent personal interest.

The conventional belief is that community college students—in contrast to students in four-year colleges—are less interested in academic studies and in learning for its own sake; instead, they are interested primarily in the practical, which to them means earning more money. Although some research evidence supports that belief, the perception that higher education is particularly to be used for occupational training seems to be pervasive among students in all types of institutions.

Whether or not these characterizations are correct, they mean little to institutional planners. Certainly, community college students are realistic, in the sense that they use the institutions for their own purposes. But what students do not, in schools where attendance is not mandated? Certainly, many are from lower social classes than those attending the universities, but their class base is higher than that represented by the majority of Americans who do not attend college at all. Certainly, many are from the lower-income groups, but their attendance usually leads to higher earnings. Certainly, they welcome an instantly responsive institution, but the effects of nonpunitive grading and of forgiveness for past educational sins on their proclivities for learning have not yet been traced.

Unaware of all these analyses, the students continue attending the community colleges for their own purposes. Those just out of high school may matriculate merely because they have been conditioned to go to school every time September appears on the calendar. Students of any age wanting a better job may attend because career programs are connected to employers. Those who have jobs but want additional skills may hope to find a short-term program that will teach them to use the new equipment that has been introduced in their industry. Many begin at the introductory level and learn complete sets of jobs skills enabling them to qualify for trades that they might have known nothing about before entering the programs. Some students seek out special-interest courses, ranging from "The Great Books" to "Poodle Grooming," taking a course or two whenever one that strikes their fancy appears in the class schedule. Some use the community colleges as stepping stones to other schools, finding them convenient and economical entry points to higher education and the professions.

The community college certainly serves a broader sector of the local population than does any other higher education institution. In colleges that have compared their enrollment to the population of the district they serve, enrollments usually range from a low of 1.5 or 2 percent to a high of 5 percent of the total population. Howard Community College (Maryland) enrolled 2.29 percent of its district's population (Heacock and Jenkins, 1993); the San Diego Community Colleges, 3.3 percent (Barnes, 1992). William Rainey Harper College, north of Chicago, enrolled 3.9 percent of its district's population, ranging from 34 percent of the nineteen-year-olds to 0.36 percent of people over fifty-five.

Statewide figures are similar. The percentage of a state's population that is enrolled in its community colleges varies widely. Much depends on demography—the percentage of population that is over seventeen—but more relates to the overall college-going rate in the state, the availability of other forms of colleges and universities, and the accessibility of the community colleges (Table 2.4).

The socioeconomic status of students attending two-year colleges tends to be lower than that of students attending four-year institutions. Of the students entering the senior colleges in 1989–90, 6.0 percent came from the bottom socioeconomic quartile and 56.4 percent from the top quartile. For those entering the two-year colleges, comparable ratios were 18.5 and 30.3 (National Center for Education Statistics, 1994i).

Transfer Rates

Much work has been done recently on calculating student transfer rates. In 1989, the Center for the Study of Community Colleges began collecting data on transfer, using the definition: *all students entering the community college in a given year who have no prior college experience, and who complete at least twelve college credit units within four years of entry, divided into the number of that group who take one or more classes at an in-state, public university within four years.* By collecting data from individual colleges and state agencies, the Center published national transfer rates for students entering in each year, beginning in 1984. Table 2.5 displays those findings.

Figures for the 1989 entrants were corroborated by the National Center for Education Statistics, which found that 50 percent of the students entering community college in 1989 had left by 1992 while 27 percent were enrolled at a postsecondary institution. The slightly higher transfer rate found by the NCES is probably due to the fact that their data include students who transferred out of state and/or to independent universities in state (National Center for Education Statistics, 1994i, p. ii). The transfer rates would be further inflated

Table 2.4. Estimated Percentage of State Populations Aged Eighteen and Over Attending Community College, 1992.

State	Estimated Percentage	State	Estimated Percentage
Alabama	2.78	Montana	1.13
Alaska	0.25	Nebraska	3.77
Arkansas	1.19	Nevada	3.48
Arizona	5.94	New Hampshire	1.58
California	5.66	New Jersey	2.40
Colorado	3.43	New Mexico	4.16
Connecticut	1.87	New York	2.17
Delaware	2.23	North Carolina	3.23
Florida	3.30	North Dakota	1.80
Georgia	1.83	Ohio	2.16
Hawaii	3.18	Oklahoma	2.80
Idaho	2.16	Oregon	3.79
Illinois	4.40	Pennsylvania	1.80
Indiana	1.08	Rhode Island	2.31
Iowa	3.05	South Carolina	2.37
Kansas	3.60	South Dakota	0.07
Kentucky	1.92	Tennessee	2.22
Louisiana	0.95	Texas	3.42
Maine	0.97	Utah	3.26
Maryland	3.21	Vermont	1.36
Massachusetts	2.01	Virginia	2.95
Michigan	3.23	Washington	4.38
Minnesota	2.84	West Virginia	0.61
Mississippi	2.95	Wisconsin	3.03
Missouri	2.13	Wyoming	6.12

Source: Phillippe, 1995a.

if longer than four years were allowed before tabulating the transfers. However, since community college matriculants arguably are potential transfers until they either show up at a university or die, the transfer rate calculations can never be fully reflective of student performance. Using data from the National Longitudinal Study of the High School Graduating Class of 1972, Adelman reported that "1 out of 5 individuals who attend two-year colleges eventually

Table 2.5. Transfer Rates for Students in Participating Colleges.

Students Entering in Four Years	Percentage Receiving 12+ Credits Within Four Years	Percentage Transferring Within Four Years	Number of Colleges in Sample
1984	50.5	23.7	48
1985	46.7	23.6	114
1986	46.7	23.4	155
1987	46.9	22.6	366
1988	45.5	22.1	395
1989	44.3	21.2	383

Source: Center for the Study of Community Colleges, 1995.

attends a four-year college. . . . This is the true 'de facto' transfer rate" (1988, p. 40).

The transfer rates for community college students can be modified by adding in different types of information. For example, how many entering students aspire to further education? Different data support different conclusions. When students in degree-credit classes are asked their primary reason for attending, as in studies done in Virginia (Adams and Roesler, 1977), Maryland (Maryland State Board for Community Colleges, 1983), Illinois (Illinois Community College Board, 1986), California (Field Research Corporation, 1984), Washington (Meier, 1980), and nationwide by the Center for the Study of Community Colleges (1986), the proportion of bachelor's degree aspirants approximates one-third. Other studies have calculated the community colleges' contribution to students attaining the baccalaureate by conducting retrospective studies, examining the transcripts of baccalaureate recipients to see how many transferred credits from community colleges. These types of studies usually report that from 30 to 60 percent of the people obtaining baccalaureate degrees from public universities have some community college courses on their record.

Interestingly, even though the transfer rate in most of the states with comprehensive college systems clusters around the 22 percent national mark, the range between states is from 11 to 40 percent. Some of the reasons for this wide interstate disparity are related obviously to the structure of higher education within a state. Where the two-year colleges are organized as branch campuses of the state university, the transfer rates are high; where they function as technical institutes that emphasize trade and industry programs, the transfer rates are low. Deviations from the norm appear also in states where transfer to independent universities is a prominent feature of the higher education system or where policies related to enrollment have been effected. For example, state-mandated limitations on college growth eventually elevate the transfer rate because the community colleges tend to react to enrollment caps by cutting the programs that attract adult, part-time students, that is, those least likely to transfer. Transfer rates among colleges in the same state similarly show wide variations, undoubtedly because of local conditions, community demographics, college proximity to a university campus, and employment or economic conditions in the district. Nonetheless, for the analyst seeking evidence of the role of the community college in assisting people toward the baccalaureate, the data that have been collected uniformly across the states are indispensable.

Dropout

To transfer to a senior institution, enter the job market, get a better job, or merely learn for one's own purposes: these are students' chief reasons for attending community colleges. How do they fare? The community colleges pride themselves on open access, which translates into ease of entry. In general, this means that students may register with little advance commitment and enroll in classes without completing a plan of study. Part-time attendance is encouraged, and withdrawing from classes without penalty and re-enrolling is considerably more typical student behavior than that found at the universities. The colleges have made numerous efforts in recent years to tighten requirements, by demanding advance registration, pre-enrollment counseling, filing of matriculation plans, and mandatory testing and advisement. But the attendance patterns that were encouraged during an era of laissez-faire, open-access policies still dominate.

Which students persist? Who drops out, and when? Who completes the programs, transfers, or satisfies the reasons for entry? More studies of student attendance patterns have been conducted than of any other phenomenon within the institutions. Students are tracked, transcripts are analyzed, the dropouts are surveyed, and grade point averages earned by transferring students are reviewed, all in an attempt to learn how and why students stay or leave. The presenting reason is to determine how the college can better serve its matriculants; the result is a wealth of study tracking community college students into and out of the institutions.

This group of studies has yielded much information on who persists. To name only a few, studies done at Metropolitan Community College (Falcone, 1990), Prince George's Community College (Clagett, 1988b), and William Rainey Harper College (Lucas and Meltesen, 1991b) have pointed out that the students who stay in school are those who began as full-time attendees, had higher grade point averages, were younger, attended classes during the day, and were involved in college activities that included student clubs, advisement sessions, and interacting with faculty members outside of class. In other words, the students who persist in community colleges are much like those frequently called traditional college students. They are committed to their studies and involved in their institution's activities and processes.

The other side of the equation considers the students who drop out. Most of these studies rely on surveys of nonreturning students, such as those done at Johnson County Community College (Conklin, 1992), Monroe Community College (Cotnam and Ison, 1988), Charles County Community College (Von Wald, 1992), Cumberland Community College (Stolar, 1991), and San Jose City College

(Kangas, 1991). The reasons why students drop out are quite varied, but in general, most of them are related to situations beyond the college's control.

First, many of the early leavers have already attained the objective for which they attended. They only wanted to take a course or two. Hence their leaving had nothing to do with college policies or procedures; they got what they wanted and then they withdrew. Conklin and Cotnam and Ison reported finding that three out of four respondents to their surveys indicated they had achieved the educational objective for which they enrolled. And in studies that asked students whether they intended to return, a majority of the respondents indicated that they would be back one day. The availability of the institution seemed quite popular and may even have contributed to the lack of persistence: why not leave when other demands interfere? You can always return.

Students give varied reasons for leaving. A change in work schedule is often cited, along with such personal reasons as health problems, difficulty in obtaining child care, financial burdens, inconvenient class scheduling, change in residence, or attendance at another institution. Most indicated that no college service could help. For example, in the Cotnam and Ison study, 85 percent of the former students reported that no intervening college service would have affected their decision to leave. Put another way, only 20 percent of the respondents to the survey said that the college could have influenced them to return.

Even though most of the reasons for leaving school are beyond the institution's ability to amend, some of the reasons suggest that institutional intervention might be helpful. One discovery is that decisions to drop out are usually made early on. As an example, Kangas (1991) interviewed students who withdrew and found that 71 percent of them thought about leaving in the first four weeks; 85 percent did not talk to their instructor about withdrawing. And even though he found that only around one student in six offered reasons related to the classroom, the instructor, or the college, the students who withdrew indicated that they had never really gotten involved with the college; most of them studied alone and most were working forty or more hours per week. Nationally, of the students entering community colleges in Fall 1989 and leaving by the end of their first year, 39 percent indicated they had never participated in a study group, 34 percent had never socialized with faculty or advisors, and 45 percent had never spoken with faculty outside of class (National Center for Education Statistics, 1994i). Lucas and Meltesen (1991b) found that only 8 percent of the students indicated the college was in any way responsible for their decision to withdraw; nearly half the dropouts had never consulted a counselor.

This issue of involvement or college assistance suggests that some actions could be taken to integrate the students with the college. But these actions need to be taken early, beginning even before the instructional term begins. Programs of early start and summer involvements have been tried and have been demonstrably successful. But these reach only a few students, those who in the main are already committed. The rest of the beginning students need to be alerted to the availability of advising and, more important, to the campus services that can help them in making the transition from their life in the community to life as a student. Child care facilities, now found in most colleges, are essential. But only a few colleges have created sizable numbers of on-campus jobs for aides, paraprofessionals, peer tutors, teaching assistants, clerical workers, or custodial assistants, all jobs that might bring the students into closer association with the institution and thereby allow them to work fewer hours away from the campus. And only a few colleges have installed early-alert systems, arrangements whereby if a student has missed more than two classes, a staff member seeks out the student to find out if there are any problems with which the college can help.

Goal Attainment

Numerous studies have been made of the students who transfer from community colleges to baccalaureate-granting institutions. Once the students arrive, they seem to do as well eventually as the native juniors, although they may take longer to obtain the bachelor's degree. Another consistent finding is that those students who transfer with greater numbers of community college credits do better than those with fewer. And the phenomenon of transfer shock, the first-term decline in grade-point average that has been observed for decades, is still apparent.

Transfer-student performance is detailed routinely in state-level documents, such as the annual articulation and transfer reports from the Florida State Board of Community Colleges, Illinois Board of Higher Education, Washington State Board for Community and Technical Colleges (1994), and the Colorado Commission on Higher Education (1992). Single-college studies confirm the findings. Johnson County Community College studied the students moving from community colleges to universities in Kansas and Missouri and found their academic performance in the first semester four-tenths of a grade point lower than that of the native university students (Soltz, 1993). Similar shortfalls were reported in studies of transfers from Piedmont Virginia Community College to universities in Virginia (Head, 1993), from Brazosport College to universities in Texas (Preston, 1993), and from Lehigh County Community College to universities in Pennsylvania (Moyer, 1992).

The reasons that students transferring to universities have had a difficult time there can only be surmised. Possibly the native students were tied into an informal network that advised them on which professors and courses were most likely to yield favorable results. Transfers may have satisfactorily completed their distribution requirements at the community colleges but could not do as well when they entered the specialized courses at the universities. Community colleges may have been passing students who would have failed or dropped out of the freshman and sophomore classes in the senior institutions. And, as a group, the community college students were undoubtedly less able at the beginning. All these variables probably operated to some degree and tend to confound the reasons for junior-level dropout and failure.

Astin has said that, for those who begin at a community college, "even after controlling for the student's social background [and] ability and motivation at college entrance, the chances of persisting to the baccalaureate degree are substantially reduced" (1977, p. 234). He found that the following factors lead to the attainment of a degree: residence on campus, a high degree of interaction with the peer group, the presence of good students on the campus, and full-time-student status. But these factors are rarely found in community colleges. Few two-year institutions have residence halls; in most states, especially those with a hierarchical public higher education system, the community college students are of lesser ability; most are part-timers; and most have jobs off campus. Thus, the combination of individual and institutional factors at the community college level operates distinctly to reduce the probability that any student will complete the two years and transfer to a baccalaureate-granting institution. Pascarella and Terenzini echo these contentions, pointing out that "Although where one enters college makes little difference *once the baccalaureate degree is earned*, the fact remains that students at two-year colleges are substantially less likely than their peers at four-year colleges to complete a bachelor's degree program and to reap the associated benefits" (1991, p. 641).

Determining the intrainstitutional procedures that affect dropout tells only part of the story. The colleges' efforts to recruit and enroll sizable numbers of students must also be considered. Community colleges have made tremendous efforts to bring in a variety of students. They established off-campus recruitment centers and sent vans staffed with counselors into shopping centers and parks. They advertised in newspapers and conducted telephone solicitations. Some of the advertising campaigns were planned as carefully as sophisticated marketing plans used by private business enterprises.

Johnson (1979) defined marketing as an integration of promotional activities with programs designed particularly for certain population segments and offered at times and places convenient to those groups. He considered it important for college managers to understand marketing, convince other staff members of its importance, and put all elements of the college into a marketing stance, and he advocated organizing marketing task forces to work with instructors and other staff members in devising and promoting new programs. By 1988, a sizable percentage of the nation's community colleges had organized marketing divisions (Bogart and Galbraith, 1988). These efforts shifted in the 1980s as budget reductions made it more difficult to provide noncredit activities for special groups. But attracting students to degree-credit programs remained a high priority in institutions where fiscal survival was tied directly to the number of people in classrooms. These efforts certainly contributed to maintaining enrollments, but they also tended to attract sizable numbers of students with only a casual commitment to college-level studies.

The admissions procedures alone, which allowed students to enter classes almost at will, certainly contributed to the dropout rate. Studies of the reasons that students drop out of college rarely considered the strength of their initial commitment, but it seems likely that a student who petitions for admission, takes a battery of entrance tests, and signs up for classes six months in advance of the term is more genuinely committed to attending than one who appears on the first day of classes without any preliminary planning. Data on students' ethnicity, prior academic achievement, and degree aspirations pale in comparison with the essential component, the degree of their personal commitment. Tinto has asserted that any valid study of dropout must consider the intensity of the student's "educational goal commitment . . . because it helps specify the psychological orientations the individual brings with him into the college setting" (1975, p. 93).

Studies of student dropout may be only marginally relevant to an institution that regards accessibility as its greatest virtue. The community colleges have organized themselves around the theme of ease in entrance, exit, and reentry. Having made a considerable effort to recruit students and to offer them something useful, most faculty members and administrators do want to keep them enrolled, at least until degree or program objectives have been fulfilled. But it is difficult for an institution built on the theme of easy access to limit easy exit.

Still, as confirmed in the studies of dropouts, most students seem to attain at least their short-term goals. Students usually have more than one reason for attending, and the importance of one or another may shift over time. The students who attend for only a short time and then transfer or go to work without receiving a degree or certificate of completion may be the pragmatic ones. The associate degree itself has had little value in the marketplace—a fact acknowledged by the AACJC, which organized a short-lived "Associate Degree Preferred" campaign (Parnell, 1985) to encourage students to obtain degrees and employers to give preference to those who have them. The proponents of program completion policies must continually battle not only the students' and employers' perceptions but also the universities that readily accept transfers without associate degrees and the educators whose goal is to maintain the community colleges as passive environments providing ad hoc studies for anyone at any time.

Assessment and Tracking

Curriculum tracking within the colleges has risen and fallen with the times. Throughout their early years, the community colleges typically administered achievement tests to matriculants and attempted to place students in courses presumed consonant with their abilities. Students were shunted from transfer to remedial or occupational programs, a practice that gave rise to the "cooling-out" thesis. Most institutions also maintained academic probation, F grades, one-term dismissal of students not making satisfactory progress, transcripts required for admission, entrance tests, midterm grades, penalties for dropping classes after the eighth week, mandatory exit interviews, required class attendance, and mandatory orientation courses. However, during the early 1970s these practices fell into disfavor as many students demanded the right to enter courses of their own choosing. Further, measuring students' abilities has never been an exact science; a student deficient in one area of knowledge may be well qualified in another, and stories of abuses in program tracking are common. Educators rationalized their inability to assess their students accurately by saying that anyone had the right to try anything, even if it meant failure. The 1970s saw an erosion of course prerequisites as surely as dress codes had been abandoned in an earlier day.

By the end of the decade, the pendulum had swung back, propelled more by the students than by changes in institutional philosophy. The career programs were being reserved for the favored few, while the transfer curricula were entered by those unqualified for the technologies or uncertain of their direction. This use of the collegiate courses by the less able, by those waiting for billets in the more desirable programs to open, and by those trying to make up deficiencies in prior preparation may have contributed to high dropout rates. Subtly but decisively, the collegiate programs were being transformed into catchalls for the unable and/or uncommitted students.

During the 1980s the community colleges groped for a middle ground between linear, forced-choice, sequential curricula and the lateral, laissez-faire approach of letting students drop in and take any course they wanted. Recognizing that neither of the extremes was tolerable and that neither best served the clients, the staff in most institutions attempted to maintain some semblance of counseling, orientation, and testing to determine why students had appeared and how they could best be helped. But students were using the college for purposes other than those anticipated by program planners. Except for those enrolled in the selective-admissions, high-technology and allied health fields, few students attended courses in the sequence envisaged by program planners.

Moves toward encouraging students to matriculate in and to complete programs gained momentum during the 1980s. One of the first requirements was to test the students at entry, place them in the programs commensurate with their aspirations and abilities, and demand that they make steady progress toward completing the program. For example, Miami-Dade Community College established a policy of assessing students, mandating certain courses, and placing on probation or suspending students who were not making satisfactory progress toward completing a program—in short, reinstating the policies under which most institutions had operated fifteen years earlier (Middleton, 1981). During the first two years that the policy was in effect, several thousand students were dropped from the rolls, but enrollments eventually stabilized and student attendance patterns increasingly reflected the changed policy.

The practice of requiring testing and program placement spread, often prodded by legislators who were appalled at the dropout rates. Florida, Georgia, New Jersey, Tennessee, and Texas rules mandated that all entering students or students seeking degrees or transfer take tests in the basic skills. And numerous community colleges in states where testing had not been mandated were beginning to require testing on their own. The Southern Regional Education Board (Abraham, 1987) found that twice as many two-year colleges as four-year colleges in its region had policies governing testing and placement. A national survey found that, although the majority of the two-year colleges accepted all persons over eighteen who had earned a high school diploma, almost 90 percent of them used tests to place first-time students (Woods, 1985).

The move was not without its detractors. Some felt that state-mandated testing would lead to a reduction in institutional ability to serve various types of clients. In 1988, a group of Latino rights organizations sued a California college on the grounds of discrimination in access. This led to a state mandate that entrance tests be validated in relation to student achievement. Others deplored the tests' effects on curriculum; students take the courses that teach them to pass the tests, and mandated exit tests invariably are built on generalized content.

Still, any institution needs to demonstrate its usefulness to society if it is to continue to be supported. When a school that people are not obligated to attend continues to enroll greater segments of the population, its administrators can argue that it must be offering something of value to those who are investing their own time and money. They can also argue that enrolling ever greater percentages of the population is a social good because the more people who are exposed to schooling, the more likely it is that intellectual leaders will emerge from among them. If intellectual ability in the population is distributed on a probability basis, intelligent people will come forth if more are given access to schooling. By that line of reasoning, any restricted educational system runs counter to social policy, whether the restriction is by wealth, sex, race, or scholastic test.

Questions of program completion pale in that light. The better question to ask is "*Of what value is the community college even to those people who do not graduate or transfer to a baccalaureate-degree-granting institution?*" By their nature, by deliberate intent, the community colleges sought to become open-access institutions. They vigorously recruited part-timers, commuting students, and students who were working off campus. To attract these students, they abandoned most of the punitive grading, academic probation, class attendance requirements, and other policies designed for the more traditional students. Who can estimate the extent of the social need they were fulfilling?

In summation, if the purpose of the collegiate enterprise is to pass most students through to the baccalaureate degree, then the community college is a failure by design. Its place in the total scheme of higher education ensures that a small percentage of its matriculants, minority or majority, will transfer to universities and obtain the baccalaureate. It accepts poorly prepared students and encourages part-time and commuter status. Its students perceive the institution as being readily accessible for dropping in and out without penalty. They know they need not complete a program soon after leaving secondary school; the institution will be there to accept them later.

Issues

Institutional planners will continue to face questions about the numbers and types of students properly enrolled in community colleges. For example: which groups have first claim on the institution? If enrollment limitations mean that some students must be turned away, who shall they be? Those of lesser ability? Those with indistinct goals? Those who already have baccalaureate degrees? Lists placing the categories of potential students in order from highest to lowest priority may have to be developed.

The designations "transfer," "remedial," and "occupational" are institutionally inspired. They do not accurately describe the students' intentions. What more realistic categories might be defined?

Colleges can control the types of students they attract by expanding or contracting off-campus classes and by enforcing student probation and suspension procedures more or less stringently, to name but two obvious means. Who should decide on the policies and hence the student types?

Historically, the community college student has been defined as one who is enrolled in a course. Yet some colleges have taken steps to purge their rolls of those who were not making satisfactory progress toward completing a program. Must the definition of *student* rest on sequential attendance? Can colleges find some other way of classifying people who want only to use the campus for the social interaction it provides?

How will the recent moves toward assessing students at entry and demanding that they make continual progress toward completing a program affect enrollments of various groups? How will they affect retention and program completion?

And the broadest questions of all: Which people benefit most from, and which are harmed by, an institution that allows all to attend at their pleasure? For which students should society pay full fare? The personal and social implications of these questions give way rapidly to the political and fiscal as soon as they are put to the test.

Faculty

Building a Professional Identity

As arbiters of the curriculum, the faculty transmit concepts and ideas, decide on course content and level, select textbooks, prepare and evaluate examinations, and generally structure learning conditions for the students. In common with nearly all teachers, they are not independent practitioners. They work in institutions and are subject to the rules thereof; the workplace shapes their behavior. At the same time, they communicate with their colleagues and take on the mores of the profession.

This chapter views many aspects of the faculty: their demography, preparation, and salary; their working conditions, including tenure, workload, and evaluation; and the less tangible concerns of faculty satisfaction, desires, and professionalism.

The Workplace

Community college instructors rarely write for publication, but when they do, and when they speak at conferences or respond to surveys, they often reveal persistent concerns about their workplace. In an issue of *New Directions for Community Colleges* on the theme of "Responding to New Missions," one instructor began an article, "Let's be candid about the major issue in the community college today: the low academic achievement of its students" (Slutsky, 1978, p. 9). Noting the demoralization of faculty members who had expected to be teaching college-level students but who found few able students in their classes, she reported the concern felt by instructors who believed that the decline in student ability was encouraged by institutional policies over which the instructors themselves had no control. And she deplored the colleges' attempts to retain on the rolls even those students who would not show up for class, let alone keep up with their course work. Mooney (1989) echoed this sentiment when she reported that professors are deeply troubled by the attitudes and academic credentials of their students.

Similar attitudes about the peculiarities of the community college environment were reported by the instructors interviewed by Seidman (1985). Those in the traditional academic disciplines were most likely to feel out of place because of their institutions' commitment to students and to curricula with which they had little affinity. But many found the community college a personally satisfying environment. They welcomed their role and were highly involved with their teaching.

People willingly endure incredible levels of discomfort when they believe that they are striving for a higher cause. The history of saints and soldiers, monks and missionaries reveals that when superordinate goals are dominant, participants relinquish the tangible rewards that they might otherwise think are their due. But when faith or patriotism wanes, demands for more immediate benefits increase, and the group must provide extrinsic incentives to sustain its members' allegiance. Eventually, a formal organization evolves, with ever stricter rules of conduct guiding the lives of its people, who themselves have since been transformed from participants into workers.

Many two-year colleges began as small adjuncts to public secondary schools, and their organizational forms resembled the lower schools more than they did the universities. Their work rules and curricula stemmed from state education codes. Mandated on-campus hours for faculty members, assigned teaching schedules, textbooks selected by committees, and obligatory attendance at college events were common. Institutional size fostered close contact among instructors and administrators. The administrators held the power, but at least they were accessible, and face-to-face bargains could be struck regarding teaching and committee assignments. And as long as the institution enrolled students fresh from high school, the faculty could maintain consistent expectations.

The major transformation in the community college as a work-place came when it increased in size and scope. Size led to distance between staff members; rules begat rules; layers of bureaucracy insulated people between levels. Decision making shifted from the person to the collectivity, decisions made by committees diffusing responsibility for the results. The staff became isolates—faculty members in their academic-freedom-protected classrooms, administrators behind their rulebook-adorned desks.

As the colleges broadened their scope, the transformation was furthered: first career education, then adult basic studies, compensatory programs, and—unkindest of all from the faculty viewpoint—the drive to recruit and retain apathetic students. Numerous instructors—who may have regarded themselves as members of a noble calling, contributing to society by assisting the development of its young—reacted first with dismay, then with withdrawal or antagonism, to the new missions articulated by the college spokespersons. Feeling betrayed by an organization that had shifted its priorities, they shrank from participation, choosing instead to form collectivities that would protect their right to maintain their own goals. The *Gemeinschaft* had become a *Gesellschaft*.

Whether or not collective bargaining in community colleges resulted from this transformation, it did enhance faculty well-being, although not nearly as much as its proponents had hoped or as much as its detractors had feared. The working conditions most obviously affected were class size, the number of hours instructors must spend on campus, the out-of-class responsibilities that may be assigned to them, the number of students they must teach per week, and the funds available for professional development opportunities. Because all these elements were associated with contractual requirements, informal agreements between instructors and administrators about switching classes, trading certain tasks for others, and released time in one term in return for an additional class in another were rendered more difficult to effect. Work rules often specified the time that could be spent on committee service, media development, and preparing new courses. In brief, the contracts solidified the activities associated with teaching, binding them by rules that had to be consulted each time a staff member considered any change; hence, they impinged on the instructors as though they had been mandated by an autocratic administration.

The People

Although it is possible to generalize in only the grossest way when one is describing a quarter-million people, demographically the community college faculty differ from instructors in other types of schools. The proportion of men is lower than in universities, higher than in secondary schools. Most of the faculty members hold academic master's degrees or have equivalent experience in the occupations they teach; they are less likely to hold advanced graduate degrees than university professors are. Their primary responsibility is to teach. They rarely conduct research or scholarly inquiry. They are more concerned with subject matter than are their counterparts in the secondary schools, less so than university professors. On a full-time basis they conduct four or five classes per term, thirteen to fifteen hours a week. Over half are part-time employees at their colleges, but they teach only one-fourth of the classes. Many, both full- and part-timers, sustain other jobs in addition to their teaching.

The demographics of community college faculty have changed in recent years, with increases in women and minorities. The 1988 and 1993 national surveys of postsecondary faculty show the differences. In 1987, 9 percent of the full-time faculty in two-year public colleges were classified as Native Americans, Asians, blacks, or Hispanics, but that proportion rose to 14.5 percent in 1992. The ratio of women rose from 38 to 44 percent during the same period. The comparable figures for all of higher education in 1992 show 13.2 percent of full-time instructional staff as minorities and 32.5 percent as women (National Center for Education Statistics, 1994a).

Preparation

When the size and number of community colleges were increasing rapidly, the question of proper training and experience for instructors was frequently debated. Should instructors have prior experience in the lower schools? Should they hold the doctorate? What qualities were needed? The answers varied, but the flow of instructors into the community colleges can be readily traced.

Beginning with the earliest two-year colleges and continuing well into the 1960s, instructors tended to have prior teaching experience in the secondary schools. Eells (1931) reported a study done in the 1920s showing that 80 percent of junior college instructors had previous high school experience. In the 1950s, Medsker (1960) found 64 percent with previous secondary or elementary school experience. Around 44 percent of new teachers of academic subjects entering two-year colleges in California in 1963 moved in directly from secondary schools, and others had had prior experience with them (California State Department of Education, 1963–64). In 1973, Bushnell reported that 70 percent of the two-year college faculty nationally had previously taught in public high schools. However, as the number of newly employed instructors declined in the 1970s, the proportion of instructors with prior secondary school experience declined with it. More were coming from graduate programs, from the trades and from other community colleges.

Preservice Training

The master's degree obtained in a traditional academic department has been the typical preparation. The doctorate has never been considered the most desirable degree; arguments against it may be found from Eells in 1931 (pp. 403–404) to Cohen and Brawer in 1977 (pp. 119–120). During the 1920s fewer than 4 percent of the instructors at two-year colleges held the doctorate. By the 1950s the proportion had climbed to between 6 and 10 percent, and there it remained for two decades; Blocker (1965–66) reported 7 percent, Bayer (1973) 6.5 percent, and Medsker and Tillery (1971) 9 percent. By the mid 1970s it had reached 14 percent as fewer new instructors without the degree were being employed, and many of those already on the job were concurrently receiving advanced degrees. In the early 1980s the proportion exceeded 20 percent—largely because of the relatively stable employment scene, coupled with the tendency for instructors to obtain doctoral degrees so that they would move higher on the salary schedule. As an example, between 1973 and 1984 the proportion of male faculty with no more than a master's degree dropped from 74 to 59 percent, while men with doctorates rose from 6 to 27 percent. In this same period, women with the master's as their highest degree fell from 73 to 61 percent, while women with doctorates increased from 5 to 13 percent.

Table 3.1 shows the proportions of instructors holding bachelor's, master's, and doctor's degrees from 1930 through 1989. Graduate degrees were rarely found among teachers in career programs, where experience in the occupations along with some pedagogical training was considered the best preparation; but among the liberal arts instructors in many colleges, the proportion with the doctorate surpassed 25 percent (Cohen and Brawer, 1987, p. 67).

Regardless of the degree titles and types of programs, an emphasis on breadth of preparation and on sensitivity to the goals of the community colleges and the concerns of their students has been a standard recommendation. Calls for these types of people have been made not only by community college administrators but also by major professional and disciplinary associations. But few community college instructors were prepared in programs especially designed for that level of teaching. Few had even taken a single course describing the institution before they assumed responsibilities in it. And although Eells (1931) had recommended that people entering two-year college

Table 3.1. Highest Degree Held by Instructors at Two-Year Colleges (Percentages).

Year and Source	Less Than Bachelor's	Bachelor's	Master's	Doctorate
1930 Wahlquist (cited in Eells)	7%	29%	54%	9%
1941 Koos (cited in Monroe)	3	27	64	6
1957 Medsker (cited in Monroe: includes administrators)	7	17	65	10
1969 National Center for Education Statistics	17 (includes both)		75	7
1972 National Center for Education Statistics	3	13	74	10
1979 Brawer and Friedlander	3	8	74	15
1984 Carnegie Faculty Study (cited in Ottinger)	5	10	63	22
1989 Astin, Korn, and Dey	11	10	61	18

Sources: Eells, 1941a, p. 103; Monroe, 1972, pp. 148, 248; National Center for Education Statistics, 1970, 1980; Brawer and Friedlander, 1979; Ottinger, 1987, p. 118; Astin, Korn, and Dey, 1991.

instruction after having secondary school experience take intervening work at the university, not many took that route.

Several well-integrated graduate-school-based programs for preparing community college instructors have been established, and especially tailored degrees have been introduced on numerous occasions. The Master of Arts in Teaching received some support during the late 1960s, when colleges were expanding rapidly and seeking well-qualified staff, and the Doctor of Arts was promoted by the Council of Graduate Schools and the Carnegie Commission on Higher Education. The programs usually include a base of subject matter preparation in an academic department, some pedagogical preparation, and a period of practice teaching or internship. These programs continue to be offered, some at the more prestigious universities, but they have not become widespread; well over half of the Doctor of Arts in Teaching degrees awarded in 1981 were granted at just four institutions, and even at these institutions program enrollments had declined by one-third over the prior four years (Dressel, 1982). None, including the especially sponsored programs for instructors in areas of short supply, has ever developed as a major source of community college instructors. However, the programs continue, with new ones developed occasionally, as at George Mason University (Virginia) in the late 1980s.

The drive to attract minority-group instructors has led to various special efforts. Anglin and others (1991) described a working model for a community college-university minority teachers recruitment project. Suggesting that structural changes be made to recruit students for the teaching profession, they recommended that the community colleges provide preeducation courses for their students during their associate degree experience, and that they emphasize the transfer of minority students to baccalaureate-granting institutions. One example of such an effort is the Teaching Leadership Consortium (TLC) project, which prepares students who transfer from Cuyahoga Community College to Kent State University.

In-Service Training

Although formal in-service training had been a feature of the community colleges throughout their history, calls for expanding that activity reached a peak as institutional expansion subsided, and relatively few new staff members were employed. Who would teach the new students and handle the different technologies? Faculty members already there had their own priorities, based on their expectations when they entered the college and their subsequent experience within it. Administrators had found it much easier to employ new instructors to perform different functions than to retrain old instructors—a procedure that worked well as long as expansion was rapid. But when the rate of change exceeded the rate of expansion, when new priorities were enunciated more rapidly than new funds could be found, the residue of out-of-phase staff members increased—hence the calls for staff development.

Several types of in-service preparation programs have been established. The most common have been discipline-based institutes, released time, sabbatical leaves, and tuition reimbursements for instructors to spend time in a university-based program, as well as short courses or workshops on pedagogy sponsored by single institutions or by institutional consortia. Studies such as those conducted in Iowa (Miller, 1985), Illinois (Wallin, 1982), New York (Winter and Fadale, 1983), and Texas (Richardson and Moore, 1987) revealed these preferences. Instructors sought courses and programs in their teaching field, offered by universities close at hand, so that they could gain further knowledge in their sphere of interest, degrees and credits that would enable them to rise on the salary schedule, and time off from their teaching responsibilities. Administrators, in contrast, preferred workshops and seminars offered on campus for the instructors, with the content centering on pedagogy and community college-related concerns.

Some colleges have developed elaborate, continuing professional development activities. Hoerner and others (1991) found several with exemplary programs for occupational and technical instructors. Roueche, Roueche, and Milliron (1995) describe training for part-timers. Some states—for example, Florida in the 1970s and California in the 1980s—appropriated sizable funds to be used for staff development at the college's discretion. However, evaluations of the effects of such activities have often found inconsistent results, depending on how the colleges allocated the money and the uses to which it was put (Alfano, Brawer, Cohen, and Koltai, 1990).

Work Load, Salary, and Tenure

Faculty work load. The term usually connotes the hours spent in the classroom each week times the number of students enrolled, occasionally with a nod to committee service. No one speaks of the professor's research load, scholarship load, or consulting load. Teaching is the ponderous portion of the profession, the burden to be carried.

Prior to the 1970s the community colleges operated under work rules much like those in the secondary schools. The principal, president, or governing board set the hours and working conditions and hired and fired the staff. Statements made by the American Association of University Professors (AAUP) regarding academic freedom had never quite penetrated. Then, when rules authorizing public employee bargaining units were passed, the rules changed. Collective bargaining spread until it formed the basis of faculty negotiations for around 60 percent of the community college instructors. Its period of rapid growth ended in the 1980s as state legislatures stopped passing laws demanding that the college governing boards recognize faculty bargaining units. But where it was in place, it formed the basis of work load negotiation, with the administrators effectually shunted aside.

Faculty work load varies somewhat among teaching fields, but it has been relatively consistent over time. Koos (1924) reported 13.5 hours taught weekly by full-time faculty in the public colleges of the 1920s, 14.9 hours in the private institutions. Numerous studies conducted since the 1920s have found 13 to 15 lecture hours per week to be the norm; for example, the National Center for Education Statistics (1991) cites 15.2 hours spent in two-year college classroom teaching in 1988.

Class size is more variable than teaching hours. Many negotiated contracts specify the maximum number of students that can be assigned to a class, but student dropout invariably reduces class size before the end of the term. Instructors of physical education, music, studio courses in the arts, and courses in laboratory sections usually have the highest number of teaching hours but the smallest class sizes. In Illinois, for example, in Fall 1987, lecture classes averaged 19.2 students and laboratory classes averaged 12.8 students (Illinois Community College Board, 1988).

There is little difference in faculty work load in states where a majority of the faculty are covered under collective bargaining agreements (California, Illinois, Michigan, New York) and those where the faculty are not so covered (Texas, Arizona, Utah). The major contrast is in administrative involvement in setting the working conditions for the faculty. The negotiations yield contracts that move nearly all decisions to the level of the negotiators, that is, the board and the faculty unit representatives. Attorneys for both groups are involved in interpreting the contracts and in arbitrating the disputes. The choice for the administrators is not whether they approve of such contracts but only of how they learn to live with them. Many of the administrators in states where bargaining began were slow to realize that. It is difficult for people who grew up with a perception of their professional role as one of closely managing staff behavior to realize that the rules have shifted, that the contract negotiated with the staff has become the dominant force. Years after the faculty won the right to bargain collectively, this perception seems quaint, but as the unions were growing, it was high on the list of administrator's concerns.

The relationships between administrators and instructors head the list of changes occasioned by collective bargaining. The contracts spell out the details of class size, hours that the instructors are to spend on campus, conditions of sabbatical leaves, and numerous other aspects of faculty life. But the number of teaching hours and the size of the classes has not changed much in decades. Nor have faculty concerns about work load and committee service changed. Instructors may fight continually for reduced hours in the classroom, but they are reluctant to give up the chance to teach additional hours for extra pay. In California 40 percent of the full-time instructors teach at least one additional class per year (California Community

Colleges, 1989). Even so, the instructors who are active in their disciplinary associations continually call for reduced teaching loads. The pages of *Teaching English in the Two-Year College* and the various disciplinary association newsletters often carry articles commenting on how the community college instructors teach liberal arts classes to freshmen and sophomores just as the university professors do. And they say that the community college instructors have a more difficult job because the students are less well prepared. Why, the argument goes, should the community college instructors teach twice as many hours? Still, few sustained practices are being introduced that would have students taught by paraprofessional aides, or through reproducible media that would reduce live-contact hours.

Except for the part-timers paid at an hourly rate, salary ranges for community college instructors have tended to be higher than in secondary schools, lower than in universities. Eells (1931) reported that the median salary of the best-paid instructors in the 1920s was about the same as that of starting professors in the universities. But most community college instructors were able to reach the top of the salary scale in twelve or fifteen years, whereas in the universities more steps intervened although a higher ceiling was available. The ratio shifted somewhat when collective bargaining made deep inroads and the tops of the salary schedules were lifted, but the university ranges remained greater. In the 1980s, according to tables showing average salaries, community college faculty consistently received lower salaries than faculty in all of public higher education. The differential widened from less than 7 percent at the beginning of the decade to nearly 10 percent in 1985–86 and to 15 percent in 1992–93 (National Center for Education Statistics, 1994j, p. 234).

Tenure patterns in community colleges more closely resemble those in the lower schools than they do the procedures in universities. Tenure is awarded after a single year or, in many cases, after a probation of two to three years; the practice rarely approximates the seven-year standard common in universities. Although tenure rules vary from state to state, in some states tenure is awarded simultaneously with a full-time teaching contract. That is, after a one-year contract has been tendered and the instructor has fulfilled his or her responsibilities, a contract for the succeeding year can be demanded unless the institution can show cause that the instructor is not deserving of it. Often, unless it is included in the state laws governing community colleges, tenure becomes a negotiable item in contract bargaining.

Part-Time Faculty

More so than in the universities, less so than in adult schools and extension divisions, the community colleges depend on a part-time work force. The reasons part-timers continue to be employed in sizable numbers are that they cost less; they may have special capabilities not available among the full-time instructors; and they can be employed, dismissed, and reemployed as necessary.

The ratio of part-time to full-time instructors has changed during various stages of community college development. In the early years sizable percentages of the instructors were part-timers, often from local high schools. As the colleges matured, they were more able to support a corps of full-time instructors; in the late 1960s almost two-thirds were so employed. Then the ratio of part-timers increased, so that by 1986 they had reached 60 percent of the total; but by 1992 the proportion slipped back to 53 percent (see Table 3.2). These ratios depend on growth and decline in various areas of the curriculum, state and accrediting association guidelines, work force availability, and numerous other factors. Overall, though, the colleges have come to depend on low-cost labor to balance the budget. As long as the law or collective bargaining agreements do not stop them, administrators will continue to employ lower paid part-time instructors. Part-time instructors are to the community colleges as migrant workers are to the farms.

Pay rates are the key to employment of part-timers. Taking it strictly on a per class basis, they cost considerably less. In California in 1993, their hourly pay averaged $34.64, or around $1,700 for a

Table 3.2. Numbers of Full-Time and Part-Time Instructors in Two-Year Colleges, 1953–1992.

Year	Total Instructors	Full-Time Instructors		Part-Time Instructors	
		Number	Percentage	Number	Percentage
1953	23,762	12,473	52	11,289	48
1958	33,396	20,003	60	13,394	40
1963	44,405	25,438	57	18,967	43
1968	97,443	63,864	66	33,579	34
1973	151,947	89,958	59	61,989	41
1978	213,712	95,461	45	118,251	55
1979	212,874	92,881	44	119,993	56
1980	238,841	104,777	44	134,064	56
1981	244,118	104,558	43	139,670	57
1982	236,655	99,701	42	137,060	58
1983	251,606	109,436	43	142,170	57
1984	252,269	109,064	43	143,205	57
1985	228,694	99,202	43	127,681	56
1986	274,989	110,909	40	164,080	60
1987	256,236	107,608	42	148,628	58
1992	253,711	118,194	47	135,518	53

Source: American Association of Community and Junior Colleges, 1955–1988; National Center for Education Statistics, 1994l.

three-unit course. The full-timers were earning $50,546 plus fringe benefits of $9,254, for a total of $59,800 for teaching ten classes per year, that is, $5,980 per course, or around three and one-half times as much (California Community Colleges, 1994). Other states showed similar patterns. The nine-month salary for full-time faculty in Illinois in 1989 was $40,434 (Illinois Community College Board, 1991). The part-timers were being paid at a rate about one-fourth as great: $1,059 per three-credit course. The sizable gains in compensation made by community college instructors during the 1980s were granted to the full-timers, whose average salary nationally in 1992–93 was nearly $39,000 (National Center for Education Statistics, 1994j, p. 236).

The sources of part-timers have shifted. The early junior colleges sought secondary school instructors because they were qualified teachers, and they sought university professors because they lent an aura of prestige. However, by the mid 1970s, only two-thirds of the part-timers working in community college academic programs were employed elsewhere. Some part-timers were "volunteers": retired teachers, business or professional people, or other citizens not dependent on the funds they received for teaching. Others were "captives," teachers with no other source of income, most of whom aspired to full-time employment. Fifty-six percent of the part-timers responding to a survey at Pima Community College said they would apply for a full-time position if one were available (Silvers, 1990).

Are the part-time instructors qualified? Do they teach as well as full-timers? Numerous studies have attempted to answer those questions, but the findings are inconclusive. Cohen and Brawer (1977) reported studies showing that the part-timers are less experienced. They have spent fewer years in their current institutions, they are less likely to hold memberships in professional associations, they read fewer scholarly and professional journals, and they are less concerned with the broader aspects of curriculum and instruction and of the disciplines they represent. However, when they are working in the field—for example, when the local minister teaches a course in religious studies or when a realtor teaches courses in real estate— they may be more directly connected to the practical aspects of their work, and they may have a greater fund of knowledge than most full-time instructors. As for the routine aspects of the job, part-timers certainly seem to present few problems; they are just as likely to turn in their grade sheets on time, and their students rate them as highly as they do the full-timers.

The part-timers are difficult to classify because they are only marginally connected with the profession. They may be people highly professionalized in another field, graduate students marking time until they complete their studies, or loosely affiliated teachers who commute from job to job, working when they are called upon.

Although they hold the same credentials as full-timers, they occupy a different status. They are chosen less carefully, the rationale being that because the institution is making no long-term commitment to them, there is no need to spend a great deal of time and money in selection.

The most positive aspects of the part-timers are seen where they are business or professional people conversant with the latest developments in their field by virtue of their concurrent involvement with it. They also enable small colleges to offer courses for which a full-time load could not be mounted: an esoteric foreign language or religious studies course, for example. And they allow the colleges to meet last-minute demand for an extra section of a popular course. The worst features of their use are when the college brings in two or more part-timers to teach similar courses as a way of avoiding employing a full-timer.

A broader issue is related to the part-timers' effect on community college teaching as a profession. Clark deplores the widespread use of part-timers, calling it a "disaster for the professorate . . . nothing deprofessionalizes an occupation faster and more thoroughly than the transformation of full-time posts into part-time labor" (1988, p. 9). Nonetheless, the colleges' reliance on part-timers has been consonant with developments in most other areas of the American work force in the 1990s, where the tendency has been to convert as many jobs as possible to positions for which the employer has minimal responsibility for staff continuity or fringe benefits.

Evaluation

The how and why of faculty evaluation have been considered since the community colleges began. Because of the colleges' roots in the lower schools, early evaluations were often conducted by administrators who visited classrooms and recorded their perceptions of instructors' mannerisms, appearance, attitude, and performance. As the colleges broke away from the lower schools, and as the faculty gained more power, evaluation plans became more complex. Peers and students were brought into the process, and guidelines were established for every step. These procedures often gained labyrinthine complexity; rules specified how often evaluations would be made, how much time they would take, who was to be involved, at what point the instructors would be notified of the results, which people or committees would notify them, how long an instructor's file would be maintained, who would have access to the file, and what steps would be involved in the appeal process.

Superficially, the procedures gave the appearance of attempting to improve instruction. Practically, they had little effect. If an instructor was to be censured, dismissed, or rewarded for exceptional merit, the evaluation records provided essential documentation. But only a minuscule percentage of the staff was affected. Instructors who wanted to improve could act on the commentary of peers, administrators, and students. Those who chose instead to ignore the feedback could do so. Only the instructors who were far distant from any semblance of good teaching—for example, those who failed to meet their classes regularly—could be called to task. In general, the most minimal evidence of classroom performance or student achievement satisfied evaluators.

Faculty associations' intrusion into the evaluation process proved a mixed blessing. Frequently, the contracts mandated that the whole faculty be involved in evaluation at every step of the way. This involvement would be a step toward professionalization because, by definition, a profession should police its own ranks, set standards of conduct, and exercise sanctions. However, faculty bargaining units leaned considerably more in the direction of protecting their members from judgments made by administrators than toward enhancing professional performance. The types of faculty evaluation in vogue at the time the contracts were negotiated tended to be written into the rules. The forms, checklists, and observations remained the same.

Still, faculty evaluation persists because it suggests that the institution and the profession are concerned with improving and policing their ranks. Nearly all institutions engage in it on some basis—from pro forma procedures to satisfy a set of rules, to more genuine attempts to affect instruction. As several studies have shown (for instance, Renz, 1984; Collins, 1986), evaluations related to instructional practices can be useful in enhancing perceived effectiveness; however, evaluations conducted for the primary purpose of satisfying external agencies have little effect and the staff tend to be dissatisfied with them. Attempts to link faculty evaluation with merit pay have been tried numerous times, but with limited success. Seniority remains dominant as a determinant of salary level.

Most colleges evaluate part-time faculty members, often in the context of faculty development programs. The studies usually find that students view part-timers about the way they do the full-timers and that differences in grades awarded (Thompson, 1990), student retention, and student learning cannot be ascribed to their instructors' employment status (Iadevaia, 1991; Osborn, 1990). The part-timers and full-timers respond similarly to faculty development activities; Mattice and Richardson's (1993) study of adjunct faculty who had participated in instructional workshops found them exhibiting a higher usage of good teaching practices.

Burnout and Satisfaction

The term *teacher burnout* entered the literature in the 1970s. It referred to instructors who were weary of performing the same tasks with few apparent successes and a lack of appreciation for their efforts. The term supplanted dissatisfaction, which connoted being a malcontent. *Burnout* suggested people whose fatigue was caused by environmental pressures beyond their control. A reduced rate of institutional expansion had led to an aging faculty, and because most colleges paid increments for years of service, their faculty crowded toward the top of the salary schedules. Many members of that group found few new challenges in their work and despaired of facing a succession of years doing the same tasks for the same pay. They turned to other jobs on their off hours. Always present in some measure, moonlighting became more prevalent. Schuster (1989) estimated that 15–20 percent of all professors in America were burned out.

Actually, faculty satisfaction and dissatisfaction have been traced for some time. For the first half century of community college history, when most faculty members were recruited from the secondary schools, positive attitudes among the faculty were the norm. Moving from a secondary school to a college faculty position offered both higher status and a reduced teaching load. Consequently, most studies of faculty satisfaction found that it was related to the conditions under which the person entered the institution. Older faculty members—those who were appointed from secondary school positions, who entered teaching after retiring from a different type of job, who had made a midlife career change, or who were teaching in career programs after being affiliated with an occupation—showed up as the more satisfied groups. The younger instructors—who may not have thought of themselves as career teachers but who found themselves performing the same tasks year after year with little opportunity for the revitalization that accompanies a new challenge—were the dissatisfied ones.

However, burnout may be a more complex phenomenon. Organizational or external demands have often been related to dissatisfaction, whereas intrinsic attitudes have been considered responsible for satisfaction. Herzberg, Mausner, and Snyderman (1959) postulated a "two-factor theory": that the elements leading to personal satisfaction are related to the content of the work, whereas the environment surrounding the worker leads to dissatisfaction. Several studies of community college instructors have traced this duality. Cohen (1973) found that feedback from students was most likely to lead to feelings of satisfaction, whereas characteristics of the workplace, such as lack of support from administrators and colleagues or institutional red tape, led to dis-satisfaction. Wozniak (1973) also identified interpersonal relations with students and a sense of accomplishment in teaching as deter-minants of satisfaction among the instructors he studied, whereas dissatisfaction stemmed from institutional policies, administrative demands, and similar extrinsic characteristics. Statewide studies of faculty in Pennsylvania (Hill, 1983) and New Jersey (Ryder and Perabo, 1985) have confirmed the thesis.

Overall, the health of the faculty depends more on working conditions than on salaries or threats of dismissal. Bok notes that the professors who do not want to teach anymore "probably suffer from deeper problems of motivation beyond the reach of crude incentives such as money or loss of tenure" (1993, p. 172). People who instruct try to do a reasonable job because it is satisfying for them. Merit pay fails because it cannot penetrate the tradition of instruction as that which leads to unknown effects. All people receive extrinsic rewards in equal proportion. Their motivations are intrinsic.

This attitude of satisfaction coming from personal interaction with students and privacy in the classroom also found its way into the contracts negotiated by faculty representatives and the com-munity college districts. In fact, it may have been one of the bases of the drive toward unionization. If a faculty member's feeling of self-worth depends in great measure on being left alone to fuse content and style of teaching, it follows that faculty members as a group are uniquely qualified to make decisions concerning what and how they shall teach. Thus, one reason for the polarization between the fac-ulty and the administrators and trustees that accompanied the rise in collective bargaining may have been that the faculty sensed that only people who were currently engaged in instruction could under-stand the way instructors feel. "Recommendations about a new teaching method coming from faculty members are more likely to be considered by teachers while information presented by adminis-trators . . . can be ignored" (Purdy, 1973, p. 181).

Many of the changes that have occurred since most faculty members were employed might have been expected to lead to dissatisfaction. An increase in the number of ill-prepared students made it more difficult for instructors to find satisfaction in effecting student achievement. A reduction in the number of specialized courses made it less likely that an instructor would be able to teach in an area of special interest. More students tended to be part-timers, dropping in and out of school; as a result, faculty could not sustain relationships with these students beyond one term. The percentage of students completing courses fell sharply, so that instructor satisfaction in seeing individual students through even a single course was reduced. More formal requests for measures of productivity were installed, along with demands that instructors present evidence of student achievement. And the feasibility of moving from community college to university teaching, never great, has become even less likely.

London (1978) discussed the effects of one community college on its instructors, noting that faculty members did not have a voice in determining the policy of admitting marginal students; they questioned the open-door policies, and the teaching of poorly prepared students adversely affected their morale. Seidman's (1985) broader sample of instructors similarly expressed dismay with their institutions' policies, which seemed to put these institutions in league with the welfare, parole, and mental health services of the state. They resented all activities that make the colleges seem like those agencies, even though they acknowledged that someone has to educate the masses.

Desires

Like members of any professional group, most instructors would like to improve their working conditions. They want more professional development opportunities, sabbatical leaves, grants for summer study, provisions for released time, and allowances for travel. They also want more secretarial services, laboratory assistance, readers and paraprofessional aides, and other support services. They would like better students, too, more highly motivated and with stronger academic backgrounds. They would like better instructional materials. Many of them are not satisfied with the textbooks, laboratory materials, or collections of readings that they are using in their classes. Many want more and better laboratory facilities. Brawer and Friedlander (1979) reported these findings, and Seidman (1985) corroborated them.

Thus, faculty desires seem to have stabilized. Despite the rhetoric surrounding collective bargaining and contract negotiations, instructors were generally satisfied. They wanted to better their working conditions, but they tended not to aspire to positions at other levels of schooling. Some of their desires were much like those articulated by employees in other enterprises: security and a living wage. Continuity of employment and periodic salary increases were the minimum. The faculty felt threatened when enrollment declines or declining budgets boded to strike at those essentials.

But beyond the basics, the instructors seem unrealistic. They want better working conditions, but that translates into shorter working hours, better-prepared students, and smaller classes. Desirable as these might be, they are difficult to obtain because they run counter to college policies and budgetary realities. As long as colleges are reimbursed on the basis of the number of students attending, instructors will have a difficult time achieving more pay for fewer student contact hours. As long as colleges are pledged to maintain a door open to all regardless of prior academic achievement or innate ability, instructors will be unable to satisfy their desire for students who are better prepared.

Even when the desired changes in the workplace are more realistic, one goal is often in conflict with another. To illustrate: faculty members, in general, want more participation in institutional decision making, but they dislike administrative and committee work. They do not aspire to be administrators; they resent the time spent on committees; they see their classroom activities and their meeting with students outside class as the portion of their workday that brings the greatest satisfaction. But administrative decisions are made in the context of committees, memoranda, and persuasion— a context similar to a political arena. Instructors will not easily attain their goal of participation in decision making as long as they shun the mechanisms through which decisions are made.

The matter of support services offers a second illustration of conflict between instructors' desires. Relatively few instructors have paraprofessional aides or instructional assistants available to them. However, Cohen and Brawer (1977) found only about one in eight expressing a desire for more of these types of assistants. Apparently, the ideal of the instructor in close proximity to the students remains a paramount virtue. Instructors seem unable to perceive themselves as professional practitioners functioning with a corps of aides. They want to do it all: interact with students, dispense information, stimulate, inspire, tutor—all the elements of teaching—through personal interaction. They do not realize the magnification of influence that they might obtain through relinquishing some portions of their work to paraprofessionals or assistants.

Through negotiated contracts instructors have tried to mitigate the untoward conditions of the environment and attendant feelings of dissatisfaction. These contracts often make it possible for instructors to be relieved of routine responsibilities and to change their milieu. Provisions for released time to work on course revisions or other projects related to teaching are often written into the contracts. Tuition reimbursement plans that pay instructors to study at universities have been included. Some contracts allow the faculty-student ratio to be spread across the academic department, making it possible to compensate for low enrollments in specialized courses with high enrollments in the department's introductory classes. Funds for travel and for sabbatical leave have also been negotiated.

However, the contracts may not offer enough. No contract can substitute for the feelings of self-worth engendered by the knowledge that one can always escape the current workplace by moving to a different institution. During the 1980s new full-time positions were scarce, and faculty exchange programs were not widespread. Nor could the contracts ameliorate the faculty's feeling that students were poorly prepared and that traditional programs, in which the instructors taught when they entered the institutions, were on the decline. The contracts' provisions for job protection through tenure and elaborate procedures for due process proved of minimal value to people who found themselves forced to teach subjects not of their choosing. The attempts to recruit students to the institution rang like false coin on the ears of instructors, who suspected, with good reason, that these students would be even less interested in affairs of the mind than those with whom they were already confronted. Administrative pleas for retaining students were hardly welcomed by instructors, who felt that students had a responsibility either to pursue the course work satisfactorily or to leave. And few instructors took kindly to calls for grading practices that would not penalize students for failing to perform course work adequately, a policy that had its zenith in the late 1970s and has become less popular since.

Professionalism

The faculty are more nearly teachers than members of a teaching profession. Few of them have access to aides; fewer still rely on them for assistance. Teaching is generally acknowledged to be solo performance; the door to the classroom is jealously guarded. Collective bargaining has brought greater faculty control over the conditions of the workplace but little change in the process of instruction. For most faculty members, the longer they are at the college, the weaker their affiliation with their academic discipline becomes.

Some commentators have reasoned that the community college is best served by a group of instructors with minimal allegiance to a profession. They contend that professionalism invariably leads to a form of cosmopolitanism that ill suits a community-centered institution, that once faculty members find common cause with their counterparts in other institutions, they lose their loyalty to their own colleges. This argument stems from a view of professionalism among university faculties that has proved detrimental to teaching at the senior institutions: that is, as faculty allegiance turned more to research, scholarship, and academic disciplinary concerns, interest in teaching waned.

However, that argument suggests that a professionalized community college faculty would necessarily take a form similar to that taken by the university faculty. It need not. It more likely would develop in a different direction entirely, tending neither toward the esoterica of the disciplines nor toward research and scholarship on disciplinary concerns. The disciplinary affiliation among community college faculty is too weak, the institutions' demands for scholarship are practically nonexistent, and the teaching loads are too heavy for that form of professionalism to occur.

A professionalized community college faculty organized around the discipline of instruction might well suit the community college. The faculty are already engaged in course modification, the production of reproducible teaching media, and a variety of related activities centered on translating knowledge into more understandable forms. A profession that supports its members in these activities would be ideal. Teaching has always been the hallmark of the colleges; a corps of professionalized instructors could do nothing but enhance it. This form of professionalism might also be applied to curriculum construction. Whereas instructional concerns have been left to the faculty, the propagation of curriculum has been more an administrative charge. A professionalized faculty might well direct much of its attention to designing a curriculum to fit an institution that shifts priorities rapidly.

A professional faculty in charge of the essential conditions of its work could also reconceptualize the academic disciplines themselves to fit the realities of the community colleges. As an example, many of the traditional liberal arts courses are ill suited to the students in the career and developmental programs that constitute much of the community college effort. More apposite instructional sequences could be designed for those students. Whether a professionalized community college faculty could succeed in the necessary curriculum reformation is not certain; it is certain that a disparate set of instructors cannot do so and that university professors or community college administrators will not lead in this essential reconstruction. Such disciplinary reconceptualization takes stimulation from peers, the contribution of individuals acting as proselytizers, and the application of thought about the core principles in each discipline as they pertain to the variant teaching roles that must be adopted for the different clients. These activities require a professionalized faculty. As Eaton (1994) has noted, the future of both the collegiate and the general education functions in community colleges may hang in the balance.

Several efforts have been made to assist faculty professionalization. National journals directed toward two-year-college instructors in mathematics, journalism, and English have been established. The faculty in some states—including Hawaii, Connecticut, Ohio, Utah, and New York—have published their own journals. Statewide Academic Senate groups have expressed interest and gained power in curricular affairs. Professional associations, such as the American Mathematics Association for Two-Year Colleges, the Community College Social Science Association, and the Community College Humanities Association, have been formed. Some institutions have fostered professionalism by supporting individual instructors through internal grants for course revision and media preparation. In colleges that employ instructional aides and paraprofessionals, the faculty play a managerial role. The number of foundation and federal grants available to community college instructors has increased, thus offering those faculty members with considerable professional commitment the opportunity to magnify their influence by managing curriculum development projects. In a few colleges the faculty have developed their own projects to modify institutional practices in testing and placing new students. And in a few, as detailed by Parilla (1986) and Vaughan (1988), faculty scholarship and research have been encouraged.

As for burnout, a feasible short-term solution might be to keep the faculty engaged in fulfilling the responsibilities of teaching that reach beyond the classroom. For example, the colleges might provide funds and released time to those who would build better instructional materials or who would conduct research on their programs' effects such as the classroom assessment practices popularized by Angelo and Cross (1993). Instructors may well expand their role beyond that of classroom teachers to become presenters of information through colloquia, seminars, lectures, recitals, and exhibitions offered for both students and the lay public. Most faculty members in the academic areas feel there are too few such presentations at their own colleges and want to devote more time to them. The more sophisticated contracts make provision for instructors to act in such capacities and also to manage learning laboratories, prepare reproducible media, or coordinate the work of the part-time faculty.

Some instructors understand the value of presenting information in large lecture sections. Departments that can generate sizable ratios of student contact hours have often taken advantage of large lectures to support their more specialized courses. Similarly, to enhance flexibility in instruction, college administrators might consider paying instructors from one department to teach short portions of courses in another, or using community service funds to augment instructional budgets. These types of funding arrangements have proved difficult to effect, but formulas that pay colleges for total programmatic emphases might make them more feasible.

Although instructors at two-year colleges may be moving toward the development of a profession, its lines are as yet indistinct. The teaching loads take their toll, but as long as instructors insist on moonlighting and on having close personal contact with students in classes—the smaller the better—the attendant high cost of instruction makes it difficult for colleges to fund the alternatives that could be pursued. The most positive note is that the community college has become a well-known, visible workplace, not only among its own staff but also among the legislators and agency officials who make decisions affecting its directions. And, as a group, faculty members no longer look to the universities for their ideas on curriculum and instruction, nor do they see the community colleges only as stations on their way to university careers. Community college instruction has become a career in its own right.

Issues

Many of the key issues affecting faculty center on the continuing untoward separation of the occupational and the academic; the private world of instruction; the separation of the remedial instructors; and the uncomfortably slow development of a unique professional consciousness. Some of these issues can be feasibly managed; others will persevere because of the nature of the profession and the institution.

Will adversarial relations between the faculty and boards and administrators subside? Are they related primarily to contract negotiations, or are they based in the essence of the institution?

Can teacher burnout be mitigated through deliberate modification of the working environment? Or are moonlighting and psychic early retirement to be permanent conditions?

Will faculties engage in the necessary reconceptualization of their academic disciplines to fit the realities of their colleges? Or will the collegiate programs survive primarily as intellectual colonies of the universities?

Will instructors realize that paraprofessional aides are important for their well-being over the long term? That funds for new media can enhance their satisfaction?

Will administrators continue employing part-timers for the short-term salary savings that accrue? Or will they allow the faculty to build its profession and help it by minimizing the annual influx of teachers?

All these questions relate to the history of the colleges, to the funds available, and, above all, to whether college leaders perceive their institutions as labile structures responding readily to the whims of all comers or as centers of teaching and learning with an ethos of their own.

Governance and Administration
Managing the Contemporary College

The terms *governance* and *administration* or *management* are not discrete. They overlap and are often used interchangeably, not clearly depicting either institutional functions or precise activities. Peterson and Mets (1987) defined them as encompassing both structure and process: governance relates to decision making, management to executing the decisions. Corson (1960) defined governance as though the college itself were a government: "the process or art with which scholars, students, teachers, administrators, and trustees associated together in a college or university establish and carry out the rules and regulations that minimize conflict, facilitate their collaboration, and preserve essential individual freedom" (pp. 12–13). However, he also noted the difficulty of separating the established policies from the practices maintained on their behalf; the act of administering a policy is as much a part of that policy as is the statement of rules or laws on which it is based.

This chapter traces some of the common forms of governance and administration, including state-level coordination, models of district and college organization, concepts of leadership, attempts at efficiency, and processes of planning. These areas change continuously as new ideas for managing the institutions become popular. The one constant is that the colleges are complex entities, and a description of one never quite fits the others.

Categorizing Governance

Numerous attempts to categorize governance and management have been made, most stemming from observations of university systems. Linear, adaptive, and interpretive systems constitute one set of categories. The linear are directly linked, the adaptive are responsive, and the interpretive are more culturally based (Chaffee, 1986). Other models of governance have attempted to separate the collegial from the political, viewing both as different ways of sharing authority. A management science approach views governance as rational, focused on decision making. A different model for college operations uses the term *organized anarchy* as a way of describing an environment in which no individual or group has much influence (Cohen and March, 1986). Weick (1976) popularized the term *loosely coupled systems* to describe colleges as groups of subunits that interact with one another in unpredictable ways.

In general, it seems that most of the excessively analytical models that have been proposed to explain the workings of universities do not aptly cover the less complex community colleges. However, Richardson (1975) suggested that models must be constructed if the colleges are to be understood. He therefore offered three major models to explain why colleges appear as they do. The bureaucratic model presents the college as a formal structure with defined patterns of activity that are related to the functions spelled out in law and policy decisions. The positions are arranged in the shape of a pyramid, and each series of positions has specified responsibilities, competencies, and privileges. This organization is held together by authority delegated from the top down, with persons at the top receiving greater benefits than those at the bottom; the lowest levels of the triangle are occupied by faculty and students. The political model (following Baldridge's 1971 model) postulates a state of conflict among contending forces—students, faculty, administrators, and trustees—each with different interests. In a quixotic plea for the colleges to become shared learning communities, Richardson (1975,

p. ix) postulated a collegial model: "Instead of being at the bottom of a pyramid, faculty and students are part of a community of equal partners. Authority is not delegated downward as in the bureaucratic model; rather, trustees share their authority with students and faculty as well as with administrators. Students and faculty members communicate directly with the board rather than through the president." The model is based on group process, the concept of community, the sharing of authority, and the making of decisions within a framework of participation and consensus.

The bureaucratic and political models seem most applicable to community colleges. The institutions are organized hierarchically, and compromises among contending forces chart their directions. Colleges are social organizations with their own rules. Despite all the rhetoric about satisfying student and community needs, the procedures maintained in community colleges tend toward protecting the staff's rights, satisfaction, and welfare. The collegial or participatory model is a delusion; the notion that students have much voice in college administration has little basis in reality.

Not excessively concerned with theoretical models, community college managers conduct their affairs typically embroiled in the complexities of the moment, perhaps hearkening to a golden era when rules were few and administration was simple. In its early years, when the junior college was often an adjunct of the local secondary school, the institution was usually administered by the high school principal or by a designate responsible to the principal. The local school board took up junior college affairs as part of its regular responsibilities. As the colleges separated themselves from the local school districts, the newly established boards of trustees similarly concerned themselves with budgetary matters and the selection of presidents who would keep the staff content and the college running smoothly, or at least keep the problems from becoming apparent to the public. Yet as long ago as 1931, when Eells wrote his book on the junior college, he noted that the areas of governance and administration were too varied and comprehensive to be treated completely. Although boards of trustees and administrators may have been able to govern without apparent conflict, issues of financing, staff morale, and conformity with state laws have always been present.

Governing Units

Different forms of college control have been popular at one time or another. In the past two decades, the number of private junior colleges has declined, multiunit college groupings have increased, and nearly all colleges affiliated with local public school districts have severed that connection. The public colleges are now arrayed in single independent districts; multiunit independent districts; state university systems and branch colleges; and state systems, some with innovative patterns, such as noncampus colleges. Individual comprehensive colleges may include specialized campuses or clusters organized around curricular themes.

Independent two-year colleges—a category that includes church-related institutions, private nonprofit colleges, and proprietary schools operated for profit—have varying patterns of control. The ultimate control of church-related colleges is vested in the governing board of the church itself. Boards of control for other independents may be associated with the occupations emphasized, or they may be self-perpetuating bodies composed of concerned philanthropists. Directors of development, also known as fund raisers, are also usually prominent in the college's organizational chart. Because many private colleges still maintain residence halls, there may also be a director in charge of campus life. The proprietary schools are organized quite like the business corporations that they are, with sales and marketing as central features of the enterprise.

Regardless of organizational form, size seems to be the most important variable. In study after study—whether the topic of concern is students, curriculum, library holdings, or unit costs—institutional size, more than any other characteristic, differentiates publicly supported institutions from one another. In addition, the significant differences between public institutions and private junior colleges (which are almost all quite small) appear to be related as much to size as to control.

The Local District

Most public colleges in the nation are organized within single districts. A board of trustees, either elected locally or appointed by a governmental agency, establishes policy for the institution and employs a chief executive officer. Vice-presidents or deans manage business affairs, student personnel, academic instruction, and technical education. In most colleges the department chairpersons report to the dean of instruction or vice-president for instruction. However, in larger institutions, as shown in Figure 4.1, assistant superintendents and division deans may be added to manage detailed operations under each of the main functions.

The multiunit independent district dates from the 1930s, with Chicago and Los Angeles as early examples. The multiunit districts typically arose when a college opened a branch campus that eventually grew to a size that warranted an independent administration. As shown in Figure 4.2, these multicollege districts operate with a central district organization headed by a president or chancellor and staffed with research coordinators, personnel administrators, business managers, and numerous others responsible for overall academic, fiscal, and student services. Many multiunit districts, with St. Louis and Miami-Dade as notable examples, operate under a single-college, multicampus format.

Multiunit districts are far more complex, structured, and formalized than single-college districts. Those who advocate centralizing administration generally stress greater economy and uniformity of decisions. After examining forty-five colleges in multiunit districts, Kintzer, Jensen, and Hansen (1969) concluded that highly centralized colleges are characterized by maximum uniformity, impartiality, and efficiency; however, the risk of depersonalization

Figure 4.1. Traditional Organization Chart for a Large Community College.

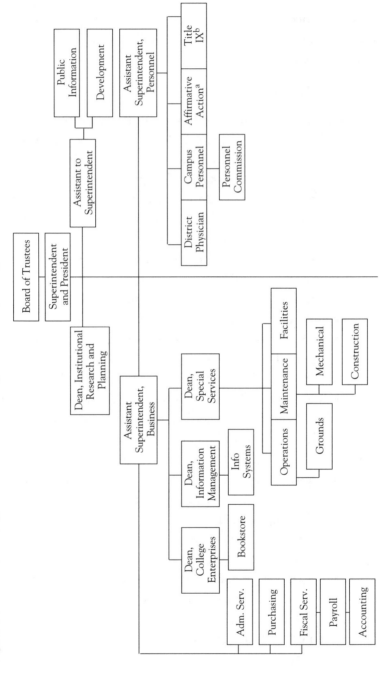

Figure 4.1. Continued.

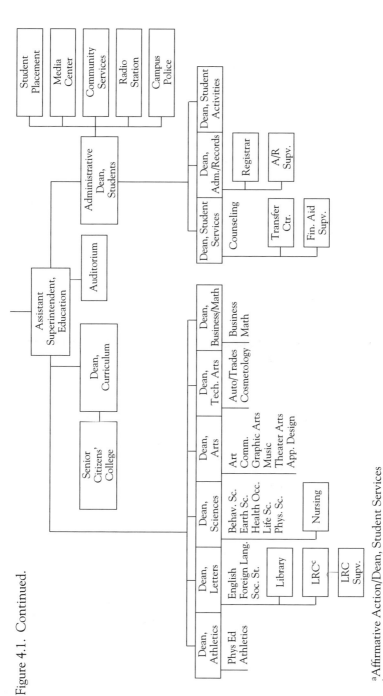

ᵃAffirmative Action/Dean, Student Services
ᵇTitle IX/Dean, Arts
ᶜLearning Resource Center

Figure 4.2. Organization Chart for a Multicollege District.

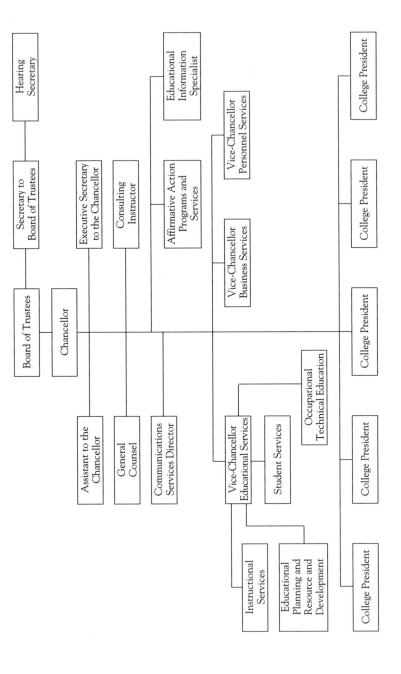

and low morale is increased. Lander (1977) showed that when multiunit districts in Arizona were formed, another stratum of administrators was inserted between the first-line administrators at each college and the district's chief administrator. He concluded that increased size—the major factor contributing to structural differences—forced increases in complexity of function, formality in communication, delegation of responsibility, and centralization of ultimate authority.

A few researchers have examined the specific differences between centralization and decentralization. Chang (1978) reported that centralized structure is supposed to eliminate duplication of purchasing, data processing, facilities planning, personnel, research, finance, physical plant, and contracting; standardize recruiting, fringe benefits, and payroll and affirmative action procedures; provide specialized personnel for collective bargaining purposes; foster the equal treatment of support services, salaries, promotions, grievances, and resource allocation; and minimize rivalry and competition between campuses at the same time that it enhances recruitment campaigns, publicity, grantsmanship, community service, and coordination; facilitates educational program coordination and staff development; and permits the formation of vocational advisory committees for each vocational field rather than one area on separate campuses.

Jensen studied the administration of multiunit districts fifteen years after his original study and found that the central office was largely responsible for curriculum objectives, personnel policies, and finance, while student services and accreditation were handled at the local-unit level (1984). His findings on the centralization of curriculum formation were echoed by Merren (1992), who traced curriculum and course approval procedures in five large multiunit districts. Each had a professional coordinator of curriculum, who sorted through the mechanisms in place that functioned to bring course and program modifications from the individual instructors or departments up to the district level.

Balancing the district's needs to avoid program duplication and to centralize purchasing and personnel functions with the campus staff members' desires for autonomy is a continuing challenge. Ideally, participation in decision making would be shared at all levels from the central office to the various campus departments, but power tends to gravitate toward the central district administration. As an example, in nearly all multiunit districts, budget requests may be generated on each campus, but only within the guidelines and limitations set down by the central authority. The central district offices often also maintain separate legal affairs offices to ensure that all decisions on personnel selection and assignments are made in accordance with the terms of the contracts and laws governing the institution.

The issue of participation is important in an era when empowerment and involvement of all staff members has become a guiding principle of administration. In California, shared governance was mandated in the late 1980s as a way of ensuring that the faculty and the rest of the staff could give input on all decisions. The result has been a flurry of documents that have attempted to sort out responsibilities among faculty associations, academic senates, classified staff organizations, local boards, local and district administrations, and the state board and chancellor's office. Wirth (1991) reviewed these processes and concluded that implementing shared governance is tedious; responsibility still must be maintained; and the appropriate role for faculty, staff, and administrators must be recognized. Nussbaum and others (1990) showed how the effort to encourage student participation in governance matters was being undertaken.

Investigating the extent to which shared governance changed administrative patterns and decision making in California's community colleges after the 1988 state mandate, Flanigan (1994) found that faculty involvement on committees had certainly increased, but that neither the quality of committee meetings and reports, nor the level of trust between faculty and administration, had changed. What had changed was that the decision-making process slowed down because of the necessity for involving groups of administrators, faculty, and classified staff, each with its own special interests.

The State

Publicly supported colleges are under the control of a single authority in numerous states. In 1965, Blocker, Plummer, and Richardson identified twenty states where the community colleges were under the control of a state board of education and six where the colleges reported to a state department or superintendent of education. Separate state junior college boards or commissions existed in only six states; in thirteen others the colleges were under a state board of higher education or the board of a four-year state university. Kintzer (1980a) found fifteen states with boards responsible for community colleges only.

Tollefson and Fountain's 1992 study indicated that community colleges are governed primarily by one of four entities. Of the forty-nine states surveyed, seven states' community colleges were governed by a state board of education, sixteen were governed by a state board of higher education, seventeen were run by community college boards, and seven were controlled by a public university system. Maine's technical colleges are monitored by an appointed Board of Trustees for the Maine Technical College System, South Dakota's vocational schools are run by local school districts, and Vermont has established an independent corporation, in addition to a K–12 grade commission, to govern adult and vocational schools linked with high schools. Several states, including Louisiana, Wisconsin, South Carolina, and New Mexico, have dual systems of governance: vocational or community colleges, along with two-year branches of university systems that are governed by the university boards.

In states where the public community colleges are under state board control, decisions of funding and operation have become maximally centralized. Connecticut, Delaware, and Minnesota, for example, seem to have one community college with several branches, whose presidents report to the state chancellor. Statewide bargaining and budgeting are the norm, although some autonomy in curriculum planning has been reserved for the individual colleges. Figure 4.3 shows the organization pattern typical of such states. However, depending on the authority of the state board and its responsibilities, there is much variation among the states. Hale (1994, pp. 144–149) displays the organization charts for the state offices managing community colleges in Washington, Oregon, and California. Among the differences, highly centralized Washington has an extensive planning and information services unit and numerous budget specialists, whereas the Oregon Board of Education's "Commissioner of Community College Services" has a minimal staff. The California Community College Board's Chancellor's Office has ten vice chancellors in charge of everything from legal affairs and governmental relations to student services and curriculum and instruction.

In many states a combined state university and community college system has been established in order to implement state-level management. More than one hundred two-year colleges, campuses, or institutes affiliated with state universities have been established in eighteen states. Such institutions are prevalent in Ohio and Wisconsin. All public community colleges in Alaska, Hawaii, Kentucky, and Nevada are under the state university system. The university president is the chief executive officer, and the presidents of the colleges answer to the university executives rather than to their own governing boards (see Figure 4.4). The university boards of regents establish policy. The University of Wisconsin system operates more like a statewide multicampus district, with a chancellor heading the system and each campus under the direction of a dean.

Garrett (1992) asked state directors about the extent to which the community college system in their state was centralized or decentralized. Naming twenty-nine issues such as funding sources, accountability, and quality control, he found that the most centralized states

Figure 4.3. Organization of a State Community College System.

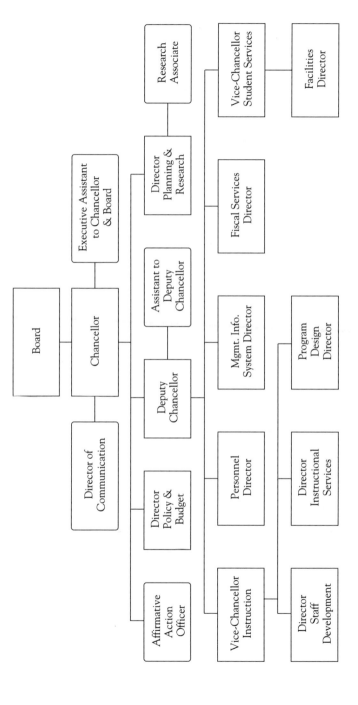

Figure 4.4. Organization of a University-Controlled Community College System.

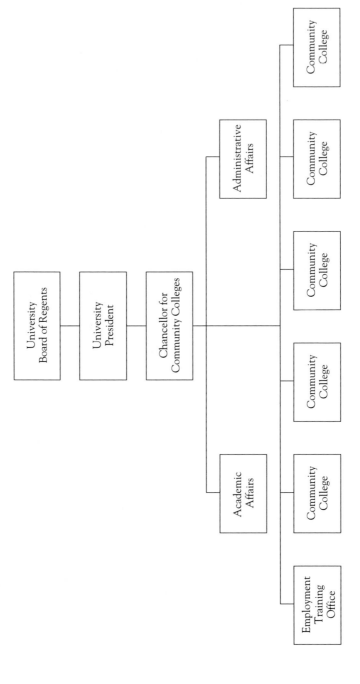

were those where the colleges were under a separate state board or under the university system: Connecticut, Hawaii, Delaware, Nevada, and Kentucky. The least centralized systems were Missouri, Michigan, and Idaho, where the state office had little more than a coordinating and reporting function. He further reported that the level of centralization relates rather closely to the percentage of funds that each college receives locally: "72.9 percent of the variation in the centralization index is accounted for by the percentage of local funding" (Garrett, 1993, p. 13).

A single state community college board that can exert influence on the state legislature, compete with the university for funding, ensure quality education and equal treatment of faculty, and coordinate a statewide college development system seems appealing. If the boards responsible for community colleges were also responsible for all of higher education, a thoroughly coordinated, economical, and articulated pattern of higher education for the state might result. Ideal in theory, this practice has not been universally adopted, and where it has, its benefits have not been uniformly realized. Institutional competition for support defies any organizational plan.

Increasingly, state agencies have assumed control over expenditures and program planning and have promulgated rules for nearly all aspects of college functioning, from the employment of personnel to the space a college should allocate for different functions. Nonetheless, it is difficult to make a case for the greater efficiency that a trend toward larger units was supposed to bring. In fact, numerous authors have documented complaints about duplication, contradictory regulations, and the mass of approvals that must be garnered from various regulatory agencies before college leaders can make a move.

The problem is not merely one of decision-making authority between the colleges and the state board; it relates also to other state agencies. Washington, for example, has a state board and thirty district boards. In addition, executive orders from the governor; directives from the Office of Financial Management; and contractual controls, legal opinions, and audits stemming from numerous state agencies—all "must be taken into account in the decision-making process and in the actual operation of the colleges" (Mundt, 1978, p. 51). Information demands alone are high: "Recently the president of Highline Community College . . . found the college was reporting to twenty-nine outside, third-party agencies in one way or another" (p. 53). Elsewhere, state laws may provide for public hearings to precede any major change in college procedures, from the fees charged to program modifications. College autonomy is continually compromised.

Most commentators believe that state-level coordination has made the college leaders' jobs more difficult and the colleges less responsive to their local communities. Tillery and Wattenbarger (1985) summarize these contentions in their review of the long-standing trend toward state control. However, the advantages of greater state-level coordination have also been documented. Funding has been made more equitable than it was when community college districts depended on local tax revenues and the gap between richer and poorer districts was pronounced. Some states have developed sophisticated management information systems and student information systems wherein all colleges provide data in uniform fashion; the data then can be cross-tabulated for the benefit of planners at individual institutions and can be used to generate reports for other state and federal agencies. Articulation between community colleges and public universities in the same state has also been enhanced when statewide coordination is evident. In addition, a state board is more able to speak to the legislature with a single voice.

The line between statewide coordination and state control is fine. Many educators would prefer that the resources be provided with no strings attached, since state mandates regarding the programs and services to be provided might unduly restrict their efforts to provide the proper services for their constituents. State-level coordination has certainly moved decision making to broader political arenas, and it has fostered the development of administrators whose chief responsibility is to interpret the codes. But it has also yielded more stable funding, more services for certain groups of students, such as people with disabilities, and higher standards of operation; and it has helped to minimize program duplication. The question of whether it has been of general benefit or detriment cannot be answered. We can say only that it has changed the ground rules for institutional operation, the professional outlook of the staff, and the way the colleges are perceived by the public.

It is easy to overestimate the influence of the state. Each community college is a complex organization, and its operations and products depend much more on its staff, students, and community than on state policies. For example, most public officials believe that students should progress through the educational system as far as their abilities will take them. Dropout at any level is seen as a waste. However, state policy is not often translated into specific mandates that would enhance the transfer of students from community colleges to universities. When state policy is directed toward transfer, significant interventions may be made; in the late 1980s the California legislature made several million dollars available to the community colleges for transfer centers and mandated a matriculation plan that sought to identify and place potential transfer students at entry.

Starting a new community college has certainly become a more complex undertaking since state-level coordination became prominent. In the 1920s the local school may have done little more to start a college than to get the state board of education's approval to offer some postsecondary classes. The 1907 California enabling act had stipulated merely that the board of trustees might charge tuition for such classes. Gradually, the criteria expanded to include minimum enrollments, minimum district population, and tax support.

By 1960 the general guidelines for establishing community colleges included "(1) general legislative authorization of two-year colleges, (2) local action by petition, election or action by local board of control, (3) approval by a state agency, (4) a minimum assessed valuation considered adequate for sound fiscal support of the college, (5) a state or local survey to demonstrate the need for the college, (6) a minimum population of school age, (7) a minimum total population of the district, (8) a minimum potential college enrollment, (9) types of educational programs (curricula) to be offered, (10) availability and adequacy of physical facilities, (11) compliance with state operating policies, (12) proximity of other institutions" (Morrison and Martorana, 1960; cited in Blocker, Plummer, and Richardson, 1965, pp. 80–81).

By the 1970s, Evans and Neagley (1973) had authored an entire book showing the various patterns of college establishment. They discussed state regulations, local needs studies, and ways of securing local support; spelled out guidelines for appointing and organizing the board of trustees; and presented sample organizational charts and recruiting and selection procedures for staff.

Federal Funding and Mandates

The federal role in community college management has not differed much from its role in all of higher education. The community college sector has taken advantage of federal funding available for certain programs—for example, programs to train technicians, displaced workers, and various categories of underprivileged people. The colleges have eagerly sought these types of funds and built programs accordingly. Federally guaranteed student loans and other categories of financial aid have affected the community colleges less than they have the higher-cost universities, but they represent an important source of funds for the institutions—and survival in the case of proprietary schools.

The federal government has insisted that minorities, women, and people with disabilities gain access to higher education. As a result, the colleges have had to modify their employment practices in response to affirmative action rulings. However, each state has had a considerably greater influence than the federal government on the policies governing the colleges within its borders.

Nontraditional Organizations

Regardless of the form of institutional control, different organizational patterns have been tried. The "noncampus" college became popular in the 1970s. Because such institutions typically employed few full-time instructors and offered much of their program through reproducible media, often including open-circuit television, their administrative patterns differed. A president would report to a districtwide chancellor, but program directors or associate deans would take responsibility for separate geographical service areas. Further, because of the emphasis on rapid change in course design, instructional planners would be more prominent than department or division chairpersons. Coastline (California), Rio Salado (Arizona), and the Community College of Vermont were notable examples of "colleges without walls," functioning much like the extension divisions of universities.

At the other extreme, the continuing search for ways of bringing the decision-making process closer to faculty and students led to the development of cluster colleges, or small, semiautonomous units. The more freedom the smaller unit has to design its own academic program and to set its own rules of conduct for staff and students, the more it fits the ideal of a subcollege operating under the umbrella of a parent organization that provides budgets, legal authority, and general structure. Advocates of cluster colleges have put them forth as the best system for bringing students and staff into the process of making decisions about the types of programs that should be presented. These subcolleges may create their own distinctive patterns—focusing, for example, on the humanities or on a group of related technologies—while sharing access to a central library, auditorium, gymnasium, and general administrative support services.

Cluster units have been organized in a number of colleges. The units in Cypress College and Evergreen Valley College, in California, centered on academic disciplines. Small units within Los

Medanos College (California) were dedicated to a core of general education based on interdisciplinary studies. Management was effected through a coordinating committee, with deans of the four major areas in general education (behavioral science, humanities, social science, and natural science) managing the programs in their areas. Traditional academic departments have been conspicuously absent in most cluster college plans. Student services are usually decentralized, each cluster having its own set of counselors.

Other special organizational forms have included colleges organized for particular purposes, for instance, technical institutes built as separate colleges in multicampus districts. Some of these, such as the Los Angeles Trade and Technical College, have a long history. San Francisco's Community College Centers were formed in 1970 to coordinate all noncredit activities. Miami-Dade's Medical Center is of more recent vintage and is even more highly specialized. Santa Monica's Emeritus College, designed for and operated by senior citizens, is another form of a college within a college.

Local Governing Boards

The idea of a lay governing board that represents the people is an old concept in American education, and public education has used elected boards to reflect the collective will and wisdom of the people since earliest times. Ideally, the local board is the bridge between college and community, translating community needs for education into college policies and protecting the college from untoward external demands. The degree to which boards do so has always been questioned, some observers saying that their composition is too homogeneous.

The demographics of community college governing boards are similar to those of university trustees. After reviewing several studies of trustee composition and attitude, Piland (1994) reported that whether elected or appointed, the board members are predominantly white male, college graduate, high-income, middle-aged people with professional or managerial occupations, who tend to hold mainstream views on college admissions policies and traditional program functions. But those are national averages; the board members in large, urban districts are increasingly more representative of minority populations.

Community college boards usually consist of from five to nine members elected from the district at large for four-year terms. They may meet once or twice a month or, in some cases, weekly. Their responsibilities include selecting, evaluating, and dismissing the president; ensuring professional management of the institution; purchasing, constructing, and maintaining facilities; defining the role and mission of the college; engaging in public relations, approving programs; determining staff salaries; and contracting for services. But these powers vary between states; the local boards in Illinois, for example, set the student fees, whereas in California they do not.

Because the boards are public corporations, they are legally responsible for all college affairs. This status involves them in legal actions regarding personnel and the purchase of materials (competitive bidding, advertising, special designs). Therefore, as Potter (1976) has shown, a board must have a working knowledge of educational law and be able to recognize potential legal problems before they develop into actual litigation. He offers examples of litigation brought on by students, faculty members, and other parties—for example, suits by students in relation to tuition or over disruptions on campus (which, they contended, interfered with their education) and suits by faculty members, who have usually engaged in litigation because of dismissal from their jobs.

Governing boards are political entities, and the selection of a trustee may be viewed as a political act in which the appointing authority or the voters weigh costs and benefits. As Goddard and Polk (1976) have indicated, a trustee appointment by a governor may be used to mend political forces, but it may also alienate members of the public who are opposed to the appointees. The elected trustee usually has more power or political independence than the appointed one, but only at the price of the financial and emotional rigors of a political campaign. In instances where the faculty union has contributed heavily to a trustee's election campaign, its influence may be palpable—for example, when the newly elected trustee votes immediately to dismiss a chief executive officer who has fallen out of favor with the union.

State associations for community college presidents and trustees have been prominent in about two-thirds of the states. These voluntary organizations typically coordinate statewide conferences and meetings, conduct professional development workshops for various types of administrators, arrange orientation sessions for newly appointed trustees, prepare and distribute newsletters, and monitor legislation. They provide an avenue for chief administrators and trustees from the colleges within a state to meet and discuss topics of common interest. Active associations that cross state lines, such as the New England Junior College Council, operate in similar fashion. Support for these associations most often comes from members' dues, but some have received funds from the state or a philanthropic institution.

The Association of Community College Trustees (ACCT) has also been active in apprising board members of their need to take a prominent role in college affairs. Since the ACCT was organized in 1972, its publications and conferences have been directed toward moving board members away from a rubber-stamp mentality that approves everything the college administration presents. Along with the Association of Governing Boards (AGB), it has also stressed the importance of the board's monitoring the college's fiscal affairs and public relations and the necessity of open communication between the board and the college president. State offices in North Carolina (Dowdy, 1987) and Florida (Florida State Board of Community Colleges, 1990), among others, have also published manuals for trustee guidance.

The way that many board members approach their work has changed during the history of the community college. Certainly, the organizations have become more complex, and board members must respond to more initiatives from personnel organizations in the college and from monitoring and controlling agents outside the college. Furthermore, the notion of trustee liability, well documented by Kaplin (1985), has become more pronounced. Less frequently seen in the literature but nonetheless prevalent are contentions that trustees sometimes go too far in their tendencies to manage the colleges. Greater control seems inevitably to follow greater responsibility.

Administration

All colleges must have administration, although the way this function is organized and staffed differs from one college to another. In the medieval university, even though the students were powerful—often fixing tuition charges and determining the curriculum—the faculty was the controlling wheel of the institution. During the nineteenth century a system of centralized control developed in the United States, and faculty power diminished as the administration took over the university. The professors concentrated on their research, scholarship, and teaching, and professional managers controlled the affairs of administration, thus dividing the ranks between administrators and teachers.

With their roots in the secondary schools, the community colleges usually were managed by former instructors who had become first part-time and then full-time administrators. Monroe described many of them as autocrats who had freed "themselves from the control of their superiors and the general public. They assumed a paternalistic, superior attitude toward the teachers. Administrative decisions of the past have often gone unquestioned by governing boards. The members of the boards rubber stamp administrative policies and decisions so that, in practice, the college's administrators become the decision makers of the college" (1972, p. 305). But he was speaking of a time gone by. In the 1970s the all-powerful president had disappeared from all but the smallest colleges, and the governing boards had become ever more intrusive.

The role of the president changed as colleges grew larger. And as faculty and community advocate groups grew stronger, it became ever more circumscribed. Still, the president was the spokesperson for the college, interpreting it to the public on ceremonial occasions. The president was also the scapegoat when staff morale or funds for a favored program diminished. The average presidential tenure has been eight or nine years, shorter than faculty tenure but certainly sufficiently long to suggest that the job is not particularly precarious.

Primarily, the president carries out general administrative duties and has periodic meetings with the board and with the heads of state agencies. To a lesser extent, the president makes decisions on faculty recruitment and selection; conducts public relations activities; and coordinates the college program with programs of other institutions and community groups. Fund raising, always high on the list of responsibilities assumed by presidents of private colleges, has recently come to occupy more of the public college president's time. In *Managing Community Colleges*, Vaughan (1994) details twelve areas of presidential focus, including mediating disputes, acting as an educational leader, and serving as an institutional symbol; Moriarty (1994) lists the president's tasks under the major headings of Leadership, Management, and Direct Office functions.

Administrative Patterns

So many administrative patterns have been advocated that it is impossible to describe an ideal form. In the line-staff organization recommended by Blocker, Plummer, and Richardson (1965), the president reports to the board of control, and a business manager and a director of community relations report to the president. Underneath the president on the organization chart is a dean of liberal arts and sciences, a dean of technological science, a dean of students for vocational education, and a dean of continuing education. Under the deans are department or division chairs and guidance personnel, and under them the faculty. According to Blocker and his coauthors, such an organization places the major emphasis on college functions.

The college deans are usually line officers in charge of planning and supervising one or a combination of college programs concerned with instruction, student personnel services, evening division, or community services. The larger colleges may also have deans for college development and for admissions, but deans of men and women, prominent in the early colleges, have disappeared from the public colleges. Like the president, each dean becomes involved with legal issues, public relations, intrainstitutional administration and personnel matters, budgeting, and liaison with state and federal agencies. Most deans serve as part of a president's council or cabinet.

Departmental Structure

The academic program in community colleges has usually been provided through departments or divisions organized around a cluster of academic disciplines or related teaching fields. The primary objective in creating academic departments, inherited from the universities, was to create manageable organizational units, not necessarily to interrelate the teaching of certain subjects or to build interdisciplinary courses. The number of departments is often related to institutional size; in small colleges where not more than one or two instructors may be teaching in any subject field, the combination of teaching fields within a single unit may be quite broad. But in the larger institutions, the number of departments has often increased as the number of instructors teaching a single discipline has grown.

The academic department has been a basic building block in the organizational structure in nearly all community colleges. Its influence has been quite marked. As an example, the administration may organize collegewide orientation sessions for new instructors, but true indoctrination takes place when the neophytes begin maintaining their offices in the suite assigned to the academic department of which they are members. And in-service faculty development work-shops conducted on an institutionwide scale pale in comparison with the influence exerted by a senior departmental colleague's pointed comment, "That's not the way we do it around here!"

Departments often have responsibility for constructing class schedules, assigning instructors, allocating funds for auxiliary employ-ees and services—in short, for acting as miniature governmental units within the larger college structure. For this reason many senior administrators have sought to retain control by minimizing depart-mental power; hence the move toward the larger organizational unit of the division. Other administrators have attempted to minimize the power of the department by having faculty members from dif-ferent departments share office space, or otherwise mixing the staff. But the departments have survived in most institutions, probably because the affinity among instructors teaching the same courses or courses in the same academic fields remains strong. Further, some department chairpersons have served the administration well by maintaining certain records, supervising staff, screening applicants for positions, and reconciling conflicts among staff members and between staff members and students that might have been blown out of proportion if they had reached higher levels of arbitration.

Until the spread of collective bargaining in community colleges, the academic department remained the most popular organizational unit. However, as bargaining units were established, the chairper-sons with managerial responsibilities were often designated as administrators and thereby removed from the bargaining unit. At that point the move toward organizing larger units or divisions accelerated, lest a college have thirty or forty administrators, each supervising only a few instructors. However, the distinction was not clear, and department chairpersons were considered faculty mem-bers in some contracts, administrators in others.

Lombardi (1974) reported studies showing lengthy lists of responsibilities for department chairpersons: sixty-nine discrete items in one statement, fifty-one in another. However, he suggested that the duty statements appearing in collective bargaining agreements seldom contained more than fifteen items. Not much has changed. The negotiated contracts of the 1970s circumscribed the chairs' ability to hire and fire instructors, and the shared governance of the 1990s further restricted their powers as it brought the faculty more toward negotiating their perquisites and working conditions directly with the chief administrators. A study of supervisors, chairpersons, and faculty at Delaware Technical and Community College (Winner, 1989) found all three groups agreeing that the chairs had major responsibility for identifying departmental personnel needs, evaluating the staff, establishing departmental curricular goals, evaluating instructional materials, and representing the department to the administration and to the public. But at least forty additional things that chairs should do were also identified, most of them quite generalized.

Hammons (1984), who has studied department chairs extensively, reviewed a great number of studies of chairperson responsibilities and activities and identified at least forty different functions categorized under five major headings: administration, student-oriented, business and financial, faculty-oriented, and curriculum and instruction. Finding a major problem to be that few of the chairs had received any pre-service assistance in learning what their responsibilities were or how to fulfill them, he concluded that the role of the chair is among the most nebulous in the institution. Numerous responsibilities, most of them vaguely worded, are assigned, but few opportunities to learn how to manage them are provided. Portolan (1992) confirmed that the instructional administrators she studied seemed to be experiencing a middle management syndrome of feeling ineffective and powerless. Faced with changing student populations, limited resources, and a range of faculty issues they had not been prepared to handle, they were developing feelings of alienation toward their work.

Collective Bargaining

Collective bargaining swept into higher education on the coattails of legislation authorizing public employees to negotiate. As these laws were passed in various states in the 1960s and 1970s, employee groups ranging from refuse collectors to prison guards gained union representation and began negotiating contracts. Within education, elementary and secondary school teachers were first to take advantage of the legislation—possibly because they were the furthest from professional autonomy (Kemerer and Baldridge, 1975). Community college faculties were next most likely to be represented by a bargaining agent, with the National Education Association and the American Federation of Teachers their two most prominent agents. By 1980, authorizing legislation had been passed in half of the states. The spread of collective bargaining slowed notably in the 1980s as only two additional states passed authorizing legislation, but by mid-decade over two-thirds of the full-time instructors in public community colleges were working under contracts negotiated collectively. The 320-some contracts noted in Table 4.1 actually covered more than 100,000 faculty in over 60 percent of the colleges because many involved multicollege systems.

Because the community college faculty are the most unionized of all in postsecondary education, it is not surprising that most faculty strikes have occurred in these colleges: ninety-five between 1966 and 1994. The ratio has shifted, however. Before 1979, 63 percent of all faculty strikes in higher education were in community colleges; since 1980, only 51 percent were in community colleges (National Center for the Study of Collective Bargaining in Higher Education and the Professions, 1995).

The expansion of collective bargaining brought about a shift in administrative roles. In general, it marked the demise of the concept of paternalism, with the president as authority figure, and opened an era of political accommodation among contending forces. These changes were difficult for many administrators, whose

Table 4.1. Number of Faculty Collective Bargaining Contracts at Two-Year Colleges by Agents, 1964–1994.

Year	National Education Association	American Federation of Teachers	American Association of University Professors	Independent	Combination of Major Unions	Total
1966	1	1	0	0	0	2
1970	6	3	1	10	7	27
1975	71	52	3	23	1	150
1980	141	72	5	16	2	236
1985	171	82	4	25	4	286
1987	172	84	4	27	8	295
1994	184	104	6	30	2	326

Sources: Hankin, 1975; National Center for the Study of Collective Bargaining in Higher Education and the Professions, Vols. 1–20, 1974–1994.

experience had not prepared them for their different roles; but the realities of management within the confines of a negotiated contract so confronted them that they either learned to live with the restrictions or they left the practice.

The scope of the contracts suggests the magnitude of their effect. Contract coverage includes contract management procedures; rights of bargaining agents; governance items, such as personnel policies and grievance procedures; academic items, such as class size and textbook selection; economic benefits; and working conditions, such as parking facilities and office space (Ernst, 1985). Under these broad headings practically everything concerning institutional functioning is negotiable.

Collective bargaining drew a legal line between members of the bargaining unit and those outside it—between faculty, on the one side, and administrators and trustees, on the other. It also expanded the number of detailed rules of procedure. It prevented administrators from making ad hoc decisions about class size or scheduling, faculty assignments, committee structures, budget allocations, funding of special projects, and a myriad other matters, both great and small. It forced a more formalized, impersonal pattern of interaction, denying whatever vestige of collegiality the staff in community colleges might have valued. It brought the role of the legal expert to the fore and magnified the number of people who must be consulted each time a decision is considered.

Swift (1979) studied the effects of the negotiated contract on Minnesota community colleges and found that, although job security and fringe benefits were enhanced, managerial authority, campus communication, and faculty involvement in institutional decision making were impaired. At a California community college, according to a report by Armstrong (1978), administrators felt that collective bargaining had reduced their flexibility in assigning tasks. Ernst (1985) also pointed out that the faculty collectively had gained power in governance but individually had lost freedom in defining their own work roles.

Collective bargaining's effects on staff salaries and morale have been examined repeatedly. Wiley's (1993) review of several compensation studies concluded that a negotiated contract elevates salaries initially, but after a few years the difference between unionized and nonunionized campuses is minimal. Studies of staff satisfaction find only small differences but with a tilt toward greater satisfaction for the faculty on nonunionized campuses in areas such as governance, support, recognition, and work load (Finley, 1991). Still, once the faculty vote to establish a bargaining unit, they hardly ever decide to return to nonunion status.

Collective bargaining seems to have accelerated a move to larger institutional units. In multicampus districts where the faculty bargains as a districtwide unit, the district-level administration aggregates power, weakening the autonomy of the individual campuses. In states where the faculty bargaining unit negotiates a master contract for all the colleges, power gravitates toward the state level. At one extreme, this concentration of power may result in a federal system, in which certain powers are reserved for the individual colleges;

at the other extreme, the colleges may become single statewide institutions, with branch campuses in the different localities.

Lombardi (1979), who traced the effects of collective bargaining on administrators, showed that most accepted it reluctantly, recognizing that it reduced them to ministerial functionaries carrying out the decisions made during the negotiations. Other administrators, however, actually welcomed collective bargaining—some because it enabled them to join forces with the union bureaucracy in controlling the faculty; some because it gave them the opportunity to avoid responsibility for their decisions. It has also increased the administrators' reliance on attorneys whose role is to interpret the contracts.

Under collective bargaining the faculty gained prerogatives in establishing the conditions of the workplace, up to and including a say in institutional governance. Administrators lost the freedom to act according to general principles and were forced to attend to the procedures specified in the contracts. Both parties were restrained from reaching private agreements. In general, an informal relationship of faculty and administration as unequal parties became a formal compact of near equals. And governance and management patterns shifted notably as union representatives, administrators, and various committees and associations composed of people from within and outside the college district made more of the decisions affecting college operations.

Leadership

An apocryphal story about Samuel Bronfman, founder of Seagram's, relates that when he entered a room to negotiate a major corporate merger, an aide suggested that he sit at the head of the table. His response, "Where I sit *is* the head of the table."

Why are some colleges consistently more successful than others in effecting student learning, sustaining staff morale, presenting a positive public image, managing growth, raising funds, and answering every challenge promptly and efficiently? According to many commentators, leadership is the answer. The successful colleges are blessed with the proper leaders: people who know how to guide their colleagues, stimulating each to put forth maximum effort toward attaining the proper goals.

Studies of leaders and leadership have a long history in the literature of higher education. Some analysts have sought the common traits exhibited by people in positions of leadership, usually concluding that effective leaders are flexible, decisive, moral, courageous, goal-directed, scholarly individuals who are willing to take risks and who have a concern for others; Vaughan's (1994) writings cover these concepts for the administrators in community colleges. Others, Richardson and Wolverton (1994) and Fryer and Lovas (1991), for example, consider leadership from a contextual perspective, asking how leaders behave when confronted with situations in various academic cultures. Astin and Leland (1991, p. xv) attempt to merge traits and contexts to describe leaders and leadership in terms of "vision, personal commitment, empowerment, and risk." Together with Bensimon (1994), they relate these characteristics to a feminist perspective that views the college not as a rationally managed, hierarchical organization, but as a collectivity of interacting people.

Several of the broader works on leadership also articulate the necessity of viewing leadership as an interactive process. Burns's classic *Leadership* separates the positions of power from the influence that true leaders have over those who follow them without coercion: "Some define leadership as leaders making *followers* do what followers would not otherwise do, or as leaders making followers do what the *leaders* want them to do; I define leadership as leaders inducing followers to act for certain goals that represent the values and the motivations—the wants and needs, the aspirations and expectations—of both leaders and followers" (1978, p. 19). Wills agrees, saying, "Where coercion exists, leadership becomes unnecessary or impossible to the extent of coercion's existence. . . . Coercion is not leadership any more than mesmerism is. . . . The leader is one who mobilizes others toward a goal shared by leader and followers" (1994, p. 70). In sum, leaders are leaders only if they have others following them; and people are willing to follow only if they feel their goals are being attained.

Leadership is thus a transaction between people, not a quality or set of traits held by a person who is in a position of authority; a leader may not even hold a position of authority. Power is interactive. For a leader to exercise power, the other parties to the transaction must grant it. They must be convinced that it is in their interests or the interests of the organization of which they are members that they strive toward the goals that the leader has articulated. Under the guise of democratic leadership, an administrator in a position of authority may appoint a committee to prepare a position statement or make recommendations regarding a decision that must be made. In such a case the administrator has suspended leadership until such time as the committee's report is received, but the necessity for exercising leadership has not disappeared or even changed. The leader still must assess the committee's findings and convince the rest of the staff that they are worthy of acceptance.

In an institution where the product—human learning—is infinite and the lines of authority not clearly demarcated, one does not issue orders and expect them to be obeyed pro forma. The astute leader knows that delivering broadsides, memoranda, newsletters, and the like has little influence on the way decisions are made or people behave. Face-to-face contact, small group meetings, and one-on-one explanations are the dominant influences. Administrators who exercise leadership interact with the people involved. They personally negotiate among warring factions and talk with those who are instrumental in implementing new methods or procedures. They do not take everyone's advice, or imply that they are going to; but they do ask questions, listen to the answers, and take them into account when it is time to make decisions.

Walker (1979) has characterized less effective administrators as those who need to "defend the sanctity of their office" and who react with "counteraggressive behavior when under attack." They believe that they are supposed to make decisions, even unpopular ones, and see that their orders are obeyed and the rules enforced. "They view decision making as a series of personal acts of courage, will, and purpose" (pp. 2–3). The more effective administrators are those who "accept the privileges and status of their office, but wear them lightly. They separate themselves, as individuals, from their office" (p. 4). They consider administration a process, not a series of discrete events, and they tend to be good politicians. Walker concludes that the personality of the administrator seems the most important ingredient; some administrators have succeeded admirably, others failed terribly, even while adhering to ostensibly similar administrative styles in the same type of organization.

Regardless of concepts of leadership, the context of college management is being reshaped continuously. In order to ascertain compliance with state and federal regulations, the college counsel has become central to decision making. Where a bargaining unit exists, the union must be consulted on all but the most trivial decisions. The organization chart may show a staff pattern, but lines of authority do not follow boxes and arrows. State-level associations of deans, faculty members, and various college officers often take positions on legislation affecting the colleges that may run counter to the position that a member's home institution would prefer. Even though the conferees are staff members at locally governed colleges, they exert a form of state-level management. A shadow government has reduced the local districts' powers.

Attempts at Efficiency

Various efforts to make community colleges more efficient have been undertaken in order to increase student learning and, at the same time, maintain cost-effectiveness. Staff members have attempted to make the college accessible to more students, cut student attrition, and teach more for less money. However, increased production in one area might lead to a decrease in another; for example, success in attracting different types of students to community colleges might increase the costs of instruction. Measuring productivity by the number of students processed through a class in a given time equates the outputs of education with those of a factory. Hence, most moves towards efficiency have been in plant utilization, staff deployment, record keeping, and information processing.

Many administrators have been captivated by innovations in management techniques. Program Evaluation and Review Technique (PERT), Program Planning and Budget System (PPBS), and Management by Objectives (MBO) all were once put forward as the answer to decision making. But all have disappeared, and few college staff remember the enthusiasm with which each was greeted in its time.

Total Quality Management (TQM) has become the most recent talisman that will reform administration. As popularized by Deming (1982), its premises center on intrinsic quality control, removal of adversarial relationships, constancy of purpose, continual in-service training, and attention to consumer preferences. It holds that change is inevitable, desirable, and welcome, and that it must be planned for with participation by the greatest number of staff members and laypeople.

Because TQM focuses on process instead of product, it matches the thinking of process-oriented administrators. Because it holds that the college's customers are not only the students but also the local schools, employers, and public agencies, it suggests the consumer orientation that has been written into community college goals. And because of its process orientation, it differs from PERT, PPBS, and MBO, which centered on outcomes or products.

TQM received a considerable amount of attention in the early 1990s, but it was difficult to ascertain whether it would prove a lasting innovation. It does suggest good-sense management technique and it is a process of continual attention to what is going on in the institution. It builds on individual values, enhancing everyone's sense of dignity, and cooperation across the staff. It is hard to argue with those principles because they have been in place for a long time in most institutions; the flat-profile management style has long been a feature of the community colleges. One thing that seems out of place in TQM's principles is holding customer preferences as the highest virtue and defining quality as the extent to which the customers are satisfied. The forces that assail community colleges are much greater than any amount of attention to the colleges' customers can overcome.

Issues

Several issues swirl around the concepts of governance and administration. Which elements of control should be maintained by state agencies? Which should be reserved for the local institutions? Is multicollege or multicampus the better form?

The college as learning enterprise does not operate well when it is managed as a factory with inputs, process, and outputs as the model. Can anarchical elements of collegiality coexist with contracts negotiated by distant representatives? How will the flat profile of shared governance and interactive leadership change institutional functioning?

Issues of productivity and accountability have been raised repeatedly. How can staff members be held responsible for their actions when most of the decisions that affect them are beyond their control? Does the larger bureaucracy protect the staff from external scrutiny? Will the staff ever seriously consider performance indicators or outcome measures?

As the colleges have grown larger and more complex, administrators, faculty members, and trustees all have had to adjust. The only certainty is that, regardless of the form of governance and the models of administration adopted, these adjustments will have to be made with increasing frequency.

5

. . . .

Finances

Sustaining and Allocating Resources

Trends in financing community colleges follow shifts in institutional purpose and mode of organization. The community colleges have expanded so that they enroll half of the people who begin college; they can no longer be considered merely alternative institutions for students who do not wish to leave their hometown to go to a university. They have become large enterprises, some with budgets exceeding the $100 million mark. This chapter traces the sources and allocation of funds, the implications of tuition and student aid, and the ways that colleges have attempted to balance income and expenditures.

Sources of Funds

When the colleges were small, they made modest demands on public funds. Few people outside the institutions cared where the colleges' money came from or how they spent it. But when they and their budgets grew large and began competing for sizable funds with other public agencies, they became much more prominent. And when inflation and rapidly increasing enrollments drove costs upward at a phenomenal rate, the public colleges' support base came under ever-increasing legislative scrutiny. Now that their budgets total more than $18 billion, they command serious attention.

The public colleges have always had to operate in a political arena. Since 1907, when the first junior college enabling legislation was passed in California, there has been continual legislative activity on their behalf. The colleges had been organized as extensions of the secondary schools, deriving their support throughout the public school budgets, but that changed as soon as independent community college districts were organized. The state helped somewhat —for example, in 1920 when a federal law ruled that money derived from mining, producing oil and gas, and so forth on public lands would be turned over to the states, the California legislature decided to give these proceeds to the junior colleges—but their support continued to come predominantly from local tax funds. The usual pattern was for the local district to provide a fixed sum of money per student in attendance, with state aid minimizing the differences among districts of varying wealth. The proportion of state aid was quite small: Augenblick (1978) reported it at an average of less than 5 percent of all public college revenues in the 1920s. During most of the pre-World War II era, student tuition and fees provided more funds to the community colleges than the states did. Richardson and Leslie (1980) noted that in 1934 local districts provided 84 percent of the colleges' support, with student fees accounting for most of the remainder. But even in those early years, there was much variation among states: Eells (1931) showed that student tuition made up 77 percent of the financial support for the Texas colleges, whereas in California taxpayers from students' home districts provided the colleges with 81 percent of their operating funds.

Over the years, community college funding has been marked by shifting proportions coming from tuition, local taxes, and state revenues. As shown in Table 5.1 and detailed later in this chapter, the trend has been toward increased dependence on tuition as a source of revenue. (State and federal grants and loans to students are included in the tuition line.) The other major trend is for the states to pick up an increasingly larger share than the local districts do. This trend was furthered in the late 1970s when California's Proposition 13 limited property tax to 1 percent of 1975–76 assessed valuation, with a maximum of a 2 percent annual increase. Local community college districts found their major source of funds effectually capped and were forced suddenly to look to the state for their funds. Within two years, the state's share of community college revenues increased from 42 to nearly 80 percent. Several other states—notably Arizona, Colorado, Hawaii, Illinois, and Washington—passed legislation similar to California's Proposition 13.

There is considerable variation in support patterns among the states. According to a survey by Garrett (1993), the colleges in many of the states that have large community college systems receive 75 percent or more of their funds from the state: California, Colorado, Florida, North Carolina, Virginia, and Washington. But several large community college states still get close to half their money from local districts, as for example the colleges in Arizona, Kansas, Illinois, Michigan, and Oregon. Although tuition charges account for one-fifth of the colleges' operating budgets nationwide, the colleges in several states derive more than one-fourth their revenue from their students, whereas students in California pay one-tenth of the cost of their education.

Changes in support vary as well from year to year. Wattenbarger and Vader (1986), in their summary of trends in community college funding, noted that expanded funding in the 1960s had given way to a gradual erosion of the colleges' finances in the 1970s. Overall, for every $100 the colleges received in 1981, they received $95 in 1983 and $108 in 1991 (National Center for Education Statistics, 1994f, p. 338). In short, there was a dip in the middle 1980s that corresponded to a decline in the number of full-time students, but by the end of the decade, the allocations had been restored. During the lean years, the colleges made up for the shortfall by increasing the percentage of the operating budget contributed by tuition and by increasing the funds derived from various individual efforts, such as selling services or renting out land. Local funds were decreasing, and state funds, although increasing, had decreased as a percentage

Table 5.1. Percentage of Income from Various Sources for Public Two-Year Colleges, 1918–1992.

						Year					
Source	1918[a]	1930[a]	1942[a]	1950[a]	1959	1965	1975	1980	1990	1992	
Tuition and Fees	6%	14%	11%	9%	11%	13%	15%	15%	18%	20%
Federal Funds	0	0	2	1	1	4	8	5	5	5
State Funds	0	0	28	26	29	34	45	60	48	46
Local Funds	94	85	57	49	44	33	24	13	18	18
Private Gifts and Grants	0	0	0	0	0	1	1	1	1	1
Sales and Services	NA	NA	NA	NA	12	6	6	3	7	7
Other	0	2	2	2	2	7	1	3	3	3

[a]Includes local junior colleges only.

Source: Starrak and Hughes, 1954, p. 28; Medsker and Tillery, 1971, p. 115; National Center for Education Statistics, 1994g.

of the total operating budget. By way of compensation, the colleges tended to decrease current expenditures by deferring maintenance and equipment purchases, freezing new employment, reassigning staff, and increasing the use of part-time faculty.

Capital-outlay projects have usually been funded differently from operating budgets. Some states require the colleges to present long-term plans on the need for buildings and facilities, plans that have been difficult to defend in an era of rapidly shifting enrollments. And when appropriations become hard to obtain, capital-outlay projects are among the first to be curtailed. Some states require a bond issue to finance college buildings. Although the community colleges in many states occupy handsome quarters, their policies of reaching out to offer classes in a variety of off-campus localities have reduced their need for new buildings for traditional instruction. However, special-purpose buildings, especially for newly evolving technical programs, are in high demand.

Allocation Patterns

Increased complexity in patterns of state reimbursement has accompanied the increased proportion of funds coming from the state. Wattenbarger and Starnes (1976) listed four typical models for state support: negotiated budget, unit-rate formula, minimum foundation, and cost-based program funding.

Negotiated budget funding is arranged annually with the state legislature or a state board. Used especially in states where all or nearly all the community college funds come from the state, negotiated budgets demand a high level of institutional accountability for funds expended. Budgets tend to be incremental; one year's support reflects the prior year's, with increments or reductions based on funds available, changing costs, and the introduction or suspension of various programs.

Under the unit-rate formula, the state allocates funds to colleges on the basis of a formula that specifies a certain number of dollars per unit of measure. The unit of measure may be a full-time-student equivalent (FTSE), the number of students in certain programs, the credit hours generated, or some combination of measures.

The minimum foundation plan is a modification of the unit-rate formula. State allocations are made at a variable rate that depends on the amount of local tax funding available to the institution. The allocation may be expressed either as a set dollar amount minus the local funds available per student, or as a proportion of the approved district budget minus the amount provided by the local contributions. In either case the intent is to provide more state funds to colleges where local support is less. Inequities in local support among community college districts are smaller than those among lower-school districts because community college districts tend to be larger and therefore more likely to include both wealthy and poor neighborhoods, and their students come from a broader range of the population. Still, considerable variation exists because community college attendance is not mandatory, so districts can differ widely in the proportion of the population they serve.

The cost-based funding model provides state allocations based on actual expenditures. In this model, state funds are allocated on the basis of program functions, specifically budgeted objectives, and detailed instructional categories. Local tax funds may or may not be factored into the formulas, and the appropriations vary greatly among institutions, depending on the costs of the programs they offer.

The funding formulas are often complex, and whatever formula is adopted benefits certain institutions, certain programs, and certain classes of students while penalizing others. The common practice of reimbursing colleges on the basis of FTSEs may penalize institutions having higher proportions of part-timers. Although reimbursement for occupational students is made at a different rate than for those enrolled in the lower-cost academic programs, costs vary among all the programs. And because of the differences in facilities used, staff salaries, types of students enrolled, and so on, absolute parity among institutions can never be achieved.

There is no consistent pattern in state funding for special student groups or for students in particular curricula. Some states run
support to the colleges according to enrollment in several different
curriculum categories, each carrying a different reimbursement formula, and provide additional funds for particular groups of students
as well. In twenty-three states senior citizens are given waivers of
tuition or fees, and displaced homemakers or displaced workers in
twenty states get various types of aid. Unemployed students receive
aid in fourteen states, and prisoners receive aid in eleven states
(Center for the Study of Community Colleges, 1987). These incon-
sistencies make generalizing about funding a complicated exercise.
Categories of curriculum and students qualifying for various levels
of aid shift continually.

Over the years the community college funding agents have
attempted to solve several complex problems. The first is for state
aid to be equalized, so that colleges in districts with less of a local
tax base do not suffer excessively from lower funding. Various formulas have been devised, with the result that the proportion of state
aid going to the wealthier districts is reduced and that to the poorer
districts increased. One solution has been to recommend full state
funding, giving all colleges an equal proportion regardless of the
local wealth.

Differential program payments point up another dilemma. Some
programs are of most public benefit and therefore worthy of the
highest support. General education, a low-cost program, falls in this
category. The highest-cost programs, such as some of the techni-
cian-training curricula, demand more money per student, but their
benefit may be more for the individual than for the public. Continuous adjustment of budget formulas in every state points up the
impossibility of reconciling that issue.

Another major issue in funding is the linkage between funding
and enrollment. An enrollment-based funding pattern calculates
allocations by using student head count or FTSE to appropriate
funds. Many efforts have been made to separate funding from this

pattern, because costs of instruction—which are nearly all based on academic staff salaries, libraries, and maintenance—are constant, whereas enrollments fluctuate. If each year's appropriations are based on student enrollment, great distortions in revenues calculated against expenditures can result. However, alternative patterns of funding, such as a certain base rate calculated according to overall district population regardless of enrollment, have never succeeded. The proponents of decoupling, as that is called, have argued that expenditures for the various categories of activities may not be related to enrollments. For example, the expenditures on physical plant depend more on the age of the buildings than on the number of students occupying them. The net result, however, is that the formulas for funding become more complex.

Breneman and Nelson (1981) examined community college funding patterns from an economist's perspective and concluded that no one system can possibly accommodate all purposes. Since the various taxonomies purporting to describe community college funding patterns were not based on mutually exclusive categories, they categorized the several choices that must be made in defining financing plans: funding from the state only, or a combination of state and local funding; tuition as a fixed percentage of costs, or on some other basis; budgets negotiated, or following statutory formulas; financing credit courses only, or funds for noncredit; treating community colleges in isolation, or making their support relative to other segments of higher education; and deriving a proper formula based on recovery costs, average daily attendance, student credit hours, or other measures.

Tuition and Student Aid

Questions of the proper balance between local and state funding are no more controversial than the issues surrounding the tuition and fees paid by students. In an era of annual tuition increases, it seems difficult to recall that many two-year college leaders have advocated a no-tuition or low-tuition policy for their institutions, which they felt were natural extensions of the free public schools. However, their views were not shared by many outside the institution.

After studying the history of tuition charges, Lombardi (1976) concluded that the issue was not whether tuition should be charged but how much. He reported a 1941 survey of a national sample of educators, editors, and other officials that found only a small majority affirming free tuition for public junior colleges. And although the 1947 President's Commission on Higher Education stressed the importance of making public education free through grade 14, nearly all the community colleges organized in the 1950s and 1960s charged tuition. In 1970, the Carnegie Commission on Higher Education urged that students pay a larger share of instructional costs as a way of saving the private sector of higher education. The concept of no tuition was destined to abort early in its development. Perhaps Eells anticipated what was coming when he quoted a speaker at the 1928 annual meeting of the American Association of Junior Colleges, who said, "Many people, including those who are careful students of education finance, share the opinion that when the student has monetary investment, he is going to attack the problem of education more seriously than . . . when it is handed to him for the asking" (1931, p. 123).

The pressure for increasing tuition has usually come from state legislators seeking ways of holding down appropriations. Their arguments have been that the people who benefit from going to college should pay and that students will take their education more seriously if their own money is at stake. The counterarguments are that the entire population benefits when more of its members have been educated and that equity demands that low-income students not be forced to pay the same tuition as the sons and daughters of wealthy parents, because such charges represent a higher percentage of family income for the former group.

The most common type of tuition is a fixed rate for full-time students and a uniform credit-hour rate for all others. When full-time rates are charged, they act as an incentive for students to enroll in more courses per term. Where rates per credit hour are charged, they usually eventuate in the part-timers paying a higher per-course rate.

Whereas tuition usually represents a portion of the costs of instruction, student fees are for special services that may not be required for all students. Optional fees may include use of laboratories or special equipment for certain courses, parking fees, library fines, and special fees for late registration or for changes of program. Some states limit the total amount or the types of fees that colleges may charge, but in others the colleges attempt to collect reimbursements for a wide array of services.

Community college tuition recently has increased rapidly. Whereas the median tuition stayed under $100 per year from the beginnings of the community colleges throughout the 1950s, it moved to $100–$199 in the 1960s and $200–$299 in the 1970s. By 1980 it was over $300; by 1987 it had more than doubled to almost $700; and by 1994 it had increased to more than $1,100, or around 50 percent of the tuition charged by public four-year colleges (National Center for Education Statistics, 1994d, p. 6). The differences between states are enormous: in 1995 tuition ranged from $400 in California to $3,000 in some of the colleges in New York and Ohio. Since books, food, and transportation are roughly equivalent for commuting students in both sectors, the overall cost of attending a two-year college has climbed to three-fourths that of a four-year public institution.

Colleges that derive much of their support locally are usually permitted to establish their own tuition within certain limits. Out-of-state and foreign students usually pay at a higher rate, as do certain categories of part-time, adult and evening-division students. In some states at least a minimum tuition must be charged; in others the legislature establishes a maximum. But state policy almost invariably fixes community college tuition at a lower rate than for the public senior institutions because legislators usually want the community colleges to serve as a low-cost alternative for beginning college students.

In the early years, tuition and fees represented a major source of institutional income. They declined as a percentage of total revenues in the 1950s but then began a steady rise. They have provided a conduit for federal aid that might not otherwise run to the community college. And even though mechanisms for distributing state financial aid to students are imperfect because of the limitations on part-time attendance, problems of assessing the financial condition of students' families, and the difficulty in accommodating adult, independent students—all three conditions more prevalent in community colleges than in other sectors—the states have been able to enhance equity by providing funds to the lower-income groups. This has proved a significant method of equalizing opportunity.

In reviewing the issues of equity and efficiency in tuition charges, many economists argue for higher tuition coupled with higher aid. It is possible for colleges to set tuition at a level that reflects the balance between private and public benefits and still maintain equity by running financial aid to low-income students. The problem of aid systems that penalize students who enroll for only one or two courses can be offset by a state's paying the tuition for anyone taking a course considered of prime use—for example, a person on welfare who takes a course in an occupational program. Increased student aid should properly be used for tuition payments, lest the incentive for students to enroll in college and receive financial aid to paying living costs lead to the system's being viewed as an adjunct to welfare.

By the mid 1980s, federal and state aid to students had become a foundation stone of college funding. By 1993, $34.5 billion was being advanced to higher education in the form of grants to special categories of students and loans to students from middle-income as well as low-income families: $25.4 billion from the federal government, $2.1 billion from the states, and $7.0 billion from the institutions. Table 5.2 depicts the proportions going to each sector of institutions. The national community college associations were united in their support of student aid programs, even though the funds were a mixed blessing because they enabled potential students to matriculate at the higher-cost universities and proprietary vocational schools. Without the availability of aid, the latter group, the fastest-growing sector and the colleges' main competition in many areas, would close their doors.

Breneman's review of federally guaranteed student loans (1991) recounted the difficulty of estimating an exact federal contribution because the students who receive loans are expected to repay them. The contribution appears in the form of interest that is paid while the student is enrolled and if and when the government pays the banks when the students default. By 1990 the interest subsidy to students in school, default payments, and special allowances to leaders reached a total of $4 billion annually. Changing populations and different types of schools involved in the programs led to higher default rates. At traditional two-year and four-year colleges, the highest defaults (35 percent) came from the vocational students and from those with family income of less than $10,000 (21 percent).

Table 5.2. Shares of Pell Grants by Sectors, 1973–1993.

Year	Public Two-Year Colleges	Public Four-Year Colleges	Proprietary
1973–74	24.8%	41.4%	7.4%
1975–76	26.1	39.0	9.0
1977–78	24.3	42.8	8.9
1979–80	21.8	39.6	10.5
1981–82	18.7	40.7	13.5
1983–84	18.5	38.0	18.8
1985–86	18.8	37.0	22.1
1987–88	18.5	34.8	26.6
1989–90	21.1	35.8	23.1
1991–92	24.3	35.5	20.7
1992–93	25.7	36.3	18.5

Sources: Gillespie and Carlson, 1983; Lewis and Merisotis, 1987; Knapp and others, 1993; Phillippe, 1994.

When the loan programs began in the mid sixties, most of the students were of traditional college age, going to traditional colleges. More than one-third of the students were in private institutions. The loan programs were established to head off the demands for tuition subsidies that would have been a benefit to the middle class. After attempting various programs, including state guaranteed loans and means-tested grants and loans, the Basic Education Opportunity Grant program, or Pell Grants, were formed, and the Supplemental Educational Opportunity Grant program was also retained. The Student Loan Marketing Association was supposed to provide funds stemming from private loan capital. Needs testing was introduced and the programs became ever more complicated as older, part-time students began matriculating in ever-greater numbers and as proprietary schools were included. Probably the most significant change was this latter development; by 1988, the students attending the profit-making trade and technical schools received one-fourth of all Pell Grants and one-third of all guaranteed student loans (Breneman, 1991, p. 7).

The rationale for the various grants and loans comes from the theory of human capital, which suggests that an investment in people's health and skills yields an economic return similar to investing in physical plants and infrastructure. Thus college is an investment, and the case for borrowing to finance that investment is clear. The big problem with financing students is that they "offer no collateral, they have no credit record, they cannot make payments easily while enrolled, they have little current income, and many would simply be poor credit risks if standard measures were applied" (Breneman, 1991, p. 3). But from the perspective of higher education, the colleges have become fully dependent on the existence of credit, and from the standpoint of the students, borrowing to go to school is increasingly the norm. Changes making the federal government the direct lender in the early 1990s did not modify those basic characteristics of the program.

Problems in Funding

Increases in tuition and financial aid to students and the shifting of the major source of support from local to state tax revenues were the most dramatic, but not the only, problems affecting community college finance. Sizable salary gains were made by instructors working under negotiated contracts, but staff productivity, by any measure, did not increase. This was no surprise to students of educational structures; in fact, Coombs (1968) had outlined an impending educational crisis worldwide because, since teachers' productivity does not rise along with their salaries, the costs per student must rise. Hence, each year an educational system needs more finances simply to accomplish the same results as the previous year. As he put it, "To assume that costs per student will be held at a standstill by far-reaching, economy-producing innovations still to be introduced is to indulge in fantasy" (p. 51). No innovation can rescue educational systems from serious financial difficulty as costs accelerate in what he called one of the last handicraft industries.

Fiscal problems were accentuated by the different types of students. Many observers had applauded the institutions' attempts to reach "new students," but few considered the added costs that came along with them. "New or expanded functions of the colleges such as community services, career education programs, special programs for disadvantaged and minority students, financial aid, health services, and counseling accompany the increases in enrollment. Instructional innovation generates experiments, new teaching methods, and technical devices that often cost more money and usually increase the unit cost of education" (Lombardi, 1973, p. 13). The extra costs of campus law enforcement, utilities, and theft that resulted from offering night classes for part-timers were rarely calculated. And few colleges could properly fund the small classes and personal attention necessary to teach the less well-prepared students who so swelled enrollments since the 1960s. Even extramurally funded programs added to costs when additional people had to be employed to administer them.

Controlling expenditures has been difficult because education is labor-intensive, but it is not impossible. If it were, expenditures would not differ from college to college as much as they do. The per capita cost, the most common measure, is generally derived by dividing the total cost of operation of a college by the number of FTSEs. Sometimes it is determined by cost per credit hour, that is, total cost divided by the number of credit hours taken by students. This concept of per capita costs nearly always refers to current expense of education and rarely to capital-outlay expenditures. The cost per student varies according to the mix of programs that a college offers; some courses cost more than others. Another element of per capita costs is the price of the instructors. Instructors with long tenure and doctorates cost more than those with shorter tenure and no doctorate.

Bowen (1981) reported considerably less difference in expenditures per student among types of institutions than among different institutions of the same type. Using data from 268 institutions sampled from among those that had reported in the Higher Education General Information Survey in 1976–77, he showed that the median expenditure per full-time freshman or sophomore student equivalent was $2,020 at public research universities, $2,025 at comprehensive universities and colleges, and $1,959 at two-year colleges. But the range for public two-year colleges was from $1,102 to $4,150. Data from each state also revealed wide disparities, although the range within states was not nearly as great. Bowen ascribed these differences among community colleges to variance in the relative emphasis on expensive occupational programs and less costly academic programs.

By 1991, the colleges were spending $5,367 per FTSE, triple the expenses of fifteen years earlier but only a 6 percent increase in constant dollars (National Center for Education Statistics, 1993, p. 338). Where does the money go? Half is devoted to instruction;

22 percent to administration; 10 percent to student services; 11 percent to physical plant operation and maintenance; and around 2.5 percent each to libraries, public service, and scholarships.

Solving the Problems

In order to balance budgets, the colleges have given financial planning a more prominent role and have instituted hiring freezes and made selective cuts in personnel, equipment, courses, activities, and services. Cuts in personnel are the most difficult to effect because of contracts, tenure, and seniority, to say nothing of the personal upheaval they entail. The colleges have tried to foster managerial efficiency by employing efficiency experts and training staff members in budget management. They also have responded to fiscal exigencies by making more effective use of physical facilities, including year-round use of buildings, scheduling patterns that distribute class offerings over more of the day, and the use of rented space.

For decades, numerous commentators have detailed these and other ways of controlling expenditures, including reducing the number of low-enrollment classes; restricting staff leaves and travel; employing more hourly-rate faculty members; offering courses in rented facilities off campus; encouraging early retirement of staff; reducing student support services, such as tutoring, counseling, athletics, and placement; freezing orders for supplies and equipment; and offering students credit for experience. Placing faculty members in contact with more students through larger classes or increased teaching hours has been a perennial recommendation, but that has not been an easily implemented reform because of the tradition equating low teaching load with quality. Most recently, the California Community Colleges' Commission on Innovation reviewed numerous areas of potential cost reduction and postulated great savings if the colleges would develop distance learning and technological infrastructures (Berman and Weiler, 1993). But such major modifications have yet to be seen. For the present, collective bargaining and the demographics of aging (and therefore higher-paid) faculty are inexorable in increasing college costs.

Alternative Funding Sources

Alternative funding sources, or revenue diversification, has been practiced by higher education institutions for decades. Notable examples can be observed in institutions that have sizable properties; Stanford University, for example, earns millions of dollars from its shopping center and industrial park. Brightman (1989) showed how separate corporate organizations can be set up for the ventures that earn income, such as food catering services for other organizations in the community, retail sales, and facilities leasing. He noted also that these are not activities that should be pursued by some fully engaged administrator as an add-on to regular professional responsibilities; rather, they are deserving of specially designated staff members who can ensure that the planned programs do not run afoul of state statutes or tax laws.

Numerous other nontraditional sources of funds have been reported. Some colleges aggregate supplemental funds by selling custom-designed instructional television and by training special groups of professional people, often through interactive media. Teleconferencing can also be a fiscal generator. State funds outside the normal budget sometimes have been retrieved to perform a special function; Belmont Technical College (Ohio) received funds from the state department of natural resources "to reclaim land abandoned by former coal mining companies" (Lestina and Curry, 1989, p. 53). Selling or leasing of college lands is another major source of funds. Some colleges have leased their property to other agencies wishing to stage athletic events, county fairs, swap meets, and horse shows. A college with good athletic or convention facilities is in a position to generate considerable income thereby.

One of the more effective, rapidly expanding ways in which colleges are offsetting increasing costs is to augment their budgets by establishing their own foundations to serve as vehicles for receiving funds from alumni, other donors, and philanthropic agencies. Bailey (1986) reported that, as of the beginning of 1986, 730 community colleges had established foundations, up from 546 in 1978. Angel and Gares (1989) estimated that in 1988 the community college foundation assets totaled $250 million. According to Robison (1982), these organizations are usually holding corporations, which possess and manage assets as their only activity; personality or "old buddies" foundations, which act almost as the personal charity of a community/social leader and his or her friends; structural agents or operating foundations, which, acting as separate legal entities, conduct financial transactions not permitted within public school budgets; special-purpose foundations, which solicit, manage, and disburse funds for a single cause, such as a scholarship fund; or comprehensive foundations, which may encompass features of the other four models. Because the foundation is legally and organizationally independent of the college, it is able to promote the well-being of the college without the statutory limits placed on the college's governing board and staff. Pabst (1989) has reviewed the various uses to which the colleges put foundation money, including among others student scholarships, equipment, special-purpose buildings, and endowed chairs for faculty.

Justifying the Costs

Periodically, after they have exhausted their efforts to reduce expenditures, colleges are forced to make policy changes. For example, the colleges' tradition of taking all who applied and keeping them as long as they wanted to stay came under attack. First of all, state legislatures threatened to impose enrollment ceilings if costs per student were not reduced. In addition, many colleges were required to tighten their standards for academic progress. Gradually, community college advocates realized that their proudly voiced claims of unlimited enrollment growth had become passé.

As Richardson and Leslie stated, "The current practice of accepting all who apply regardless of the funding authorized conveys several messages to legislators, all of them undesirable. The first message is that quality is not an important concern of the community college. . . . A second . . . is that very little relationship exists between the amounts appropriated and the numbers of students served" (1980, p. 7). Richardson and Leslie recommended that college administrators gain prior state approval for specific curricula and services and that they introduce first-come, first-served enrollment procedures—in short, maintaining the open door only to the extent that resources permit and ensuring that quality be a hallmark.

The issue was quite straightforward. The lower schools had no choice in the number of students they admitted; every child not only had a right but by law was required to attend school. Community colleges were different; they could restrict their enrollments by cutting the variety of programs offered, by "marketing" less vigorously, and through numerous other stratagems, including dismissing students who were not making satisfactory progress toward completing a program. The only question was whether colleges would do so voluntarily or wait until the legislatures mandated the changes. Most college leaders waited. By the mid 1990s most legislatures had acted to specify enrollment limits.

Issues of efficiency and equity arise in any discussion of financing. Efficiency relates to the ratio between the benefits deriving from some good or service and the costs of producing it. Equity relates to the extent to which different members of society attain like benefits from public expenditures. In publicly supported education the two obviously overlap: A highly efficient institution would spend its dollars only on the people who would use their training to make substantially greater incomes, thus paying back significantly more in taxes than their education cost. But such an institution would be inequitable because the members of certain social groups would not receive any of its educational benefits.

How do the community colleges fit in? Economists often categorize school expenditures as investments in general human capital, in specific human capital, and in consumption benefits with little investment value. The classifications "academic," "occupational," and "community service" fit these respective categories rather well. Remedial programs help people become productive members of society and thus benefit the public by reducing transfer payments. However, the cost is high because of the high-risk nature of the students. Career programs benefit society because of the increased productivity of the labor force, the higher probability of students' going to work after graduation, and the aid to industries that will stay in an area where a trained work force is available. Thus, although students benefit individually from occupational training, substantial public benefits are also present. Community services are most likely to be of the consumer education type, with benefits accruing only to the individual, not to the public. Accordingly, following the practice in university extension divisions, community colleges should charge the consumers for the full cost of providing these services. However, certain types of community service or noncredit courses, such as courses on child care, family nutrition, or energy efficiency, seem to slide over into the category of public benefits.

Aside from the general issues of efficiency and equity, the schools have always had difficulty in determining how well they do when their actual output is measured against their professed aims. Part of the problem has been their inability, or at least their unwillingness, to set their priorities in operational terms. If they were judged solely by the size of enrollments, the criterion used by many advocates, questions of content and quality would not arise. But the legislator, the economist, and the lay citizen might question what the students have been learning, how much, how well, and how fast. And even then an institution may be at once good and bad: good when judged by internal criteria, such as student performance on examinations; bad when judged by relevance to the needs of its surrounding community.

Some attempts have been made to demonstrate more direct economic effects. Bess and others (1980) studied the economic impact of six Illinois community colleges by tabulating college-related business volume, value of local business property because of college-related business, expansion of the local bank credit base resulting from college-related deposits, college-related revenues received by local governments, cost of local government services attributed to college-related influences, and number of local jobs and personal income of local citizens from college-related activities. They found a sizable positive effect on all indicators and estimated the difference between the positive impact and the costs to local government of supporting the college and its staff as at least $850 million, projected statewide for fiscal 1978. The greatest effects were in business volume created by the expenditures of the college and in the expansion of bank deposits. The difference among colleges in impact per dollar expended was attributed to the percentage of staff members living in the district, amount of salaries spent within the district, amount of college funds spent in the district, percentage of student body that attended full-time, and amount of funds deposited in banks in the district.

Despite the importance of doing so, colleges have rarely attempted to document their accomplishments. The reasons are not clear, but perhaps during periods of rapidly expanding budgets and enrollments college managers believe that the increases themselves speak for the worth of the enterprise; and during periods of decline, they have used marketing techniques and political persuasion in attempts to reverse the trend. Carefully controlled studies of institutional efficiency and outcome seem to fall between the planks of advertising on the one side and lobbying on the other.

The world of politics, public relations, and illusion surrounds all public educators, who recognize the importance of maintaining an institutional image of fiscal prudence. But a public agency must spend all the money available to it; therefore, an educational system will be as inefficient in its use of resources as it is allowed to be, because efficiency leads to reduction in funding. College managers who learned their craft in an era when those statements were true find it difficult to shift away from that concept, the bedrock of public agency maintenance. If cuts become necessary, managers try to keep all programs, services, and functions intact in order to avoid the difficult decisions to drop any of them. If further cuts become necessary, they are made where they will be most visible. And larger units, such as multicampus districts, may give the appearance of fiscal prudence because they have fewer top-line administrators, even though the infrastructure may in fact be more expensive.

Issues

College leaders will be forced to face several issues regarding finance in coming years.

How can costs be managed in a labor-intensive enterprise? Bargaining units will restrict the savings that managers formerly gained by employing part-time faculty members and by increasing class size. Reproducible media demand sizable start-up costs and have yet to yield far-reaching financial benefits.

How can accounting procedures document the additional costs to the institution engendered by categorical aid and demands for special programs stemming from external agencies? More broadly, on what grounds can an institution that has prided itself on offering something for everyone refuse to begin a new service that costs more than the revenues it generates?

Does low tuition make sense in the light of substantial student aid? At what point does tuition without offsetting financial aid reduce equity? What are the actual, as opposed to the conceptual, relations between levels of tuition and institutional efficiency? In brief, can benefits be run to one group without offsetting losses to another?

Remedial studies and high school completion courses seem destined to occupy a major portion of the community college effort. A plausible case can be made for reorganizing many of them along the lines of the 6–4–4 plan that was in effect in some districts in the early years. How can colleges obtain funds to teach the basic education that was supposed to have been completed in the lower schools?

Those portions of career education that benefit certain industries are difficult to justify on the grounds of efficiency. How can the colleges expand the targeted portions of their occupational education and defray the costs by effecting greater numbers of contracts without irreparably damaging the integrity of a publicly supported institution?

What measures of institutional productivity can be introduced so that increased costs can be justified? Answers to that question depend on the results the institution is trying to achieve. Can education be defended in its own right, or must the criterion always be the financial return to the students and the community?

Difficult questions all, but college administrators who would be educational leaders will see them as challenges and set to them with vigor.

6

Instruction
Methods, Media, and Effects

Several perennial issues surround instruction: Who does it? How? With what effect? Undergraduate teaching in the universities particularly has commanded attention recently. Books and articles exhort professors to spend more time with their students even if that means they do less research. Anyone with an historical perspective finds it mildly amusing to see the number of comments deploring the status of undergraduate instruction in the universities; the same contentions have been raised for the past one hundred years.

Because community college instructors have never devoted much time to research or academic discipline-based scholarship, they have been free to address nearly their full attention to instructional processes. The colleges have emphasized the importance of good teaching since their earliest days, and their observers have reported unanimously that teaching was their raison d'être. Eells called the junior college "a teaching institution *par excellence*" (1931, p. 389). Thornton proclaimed instruction the prime function, saying that it had to be better in the two-year college than in the university because the students covered a broader range of abilities and their prior academic records tended to be undistinguished: "It is fair to say that most community college students are able to learn but are relatively unpracticed. Under good instruction they can succeed admirably, whereas pedestrian teaching is more likely to discourage and defeat them than it would the more highly

motivated freshmen and sophomores in the universities." He concluded that either the college "teaches excellently, or it fails completely" (1972, p. 42).

Other writers followed these exhortations regarding good teaching with the observation that it was indeed to be found in the two-
year colleges. Although rarely heard since the colleges grew large,
the pronouncement that instruction was better because of the small
classes was often voiced in an earlier time. In addition, junior college instructors were considered to be better than those in the universities because their pedagogical preparation was more evident
and they were bona fide instructors, not teaching assistants. Koos
reported that "*classroom procedure* in junior colleges is assuredly on
at least as high a plane as is instruction of freshmen and sophomores
in colleges and universities" (1924, p. 219). He pointed to the
"superiority of teaching skill" found among instructors at two-year
colleges because, unlike their counterparts at the universities, most
of them came from the ranks of high school teachers and had their
training in pedagogy (p. 201).

Even the way the colleges are organized suggests a commitment
to teaching. An administrator, typically a dean of instruction or a
vice-president for instruction, oversees the formal educational program and usually chairs a curriculum and instruction committee
responsible for all major changes in those areas. The committee
comprises program heads, department chairpersons, and representatives of the library and counseling services. This allocation of
instructional leadership to the administrators has enabled them to
coordinate the work of the faculty members and offer incentives
through instructional development grants, sabbaticals, and released
time to develop new techniques. The evolution of the library into
a learning resource center and the widespread use of tutors and
reproducible media also attest to an orientation to teaching.

This chapter discusses instructional technology, along with notes
on such instructional techniques as television, computers, writing
across the curriculum, and supplemental instruction. Also included

are notes on mastery learning, the learning resource centers, and competency based instruction. A discussion of the assessment of instructional effects, and its pros and cons, completes the chapter.

Before recounting the usage and effects of some of the many instructional forms in place, note should be taken that traditional classroom instruction, that is, one teacher interacting with a number of students, still dominates. Most students still learn by sitting in classrooms, listening to lectures, watching demonstrations, participating in discussions, reading books, and writing examinations. Class size has varied little over the years. Dickmeyer (1994) reported that one-third of the classes overall had between ten and nineteen students and one-third enrolled between twenty and twenty-nine. The other third was about divided equally between classes with fewer than ten or more than twenty-nine students. The Center for the Study of Community Colleges 1991 surveys found that class size averages had changed hardly at all in the previous fifteen years. Fine and performing arts had the smallest classes, averaging between eleven and sixteen per class, with applied mathematics, foreign languages, engineering, physics, and chemistry also tending to be smaller than the norm. Interdisciplinary classes in the humanities, religious studies, and introductory classes in psychology, sociology, and history were typically larger, averaging thirty or more (Cohen and Ignash, 1992).

The Technology and Discipline of Instruction

One of the most persistent ideas in education is that individualization must be the goal in every instructional program. Numerous articles have begun with the statement "Let's assume that the best ratio of teachers to learners is one to one" and then gone on to explain how one or another instructional strategy might be tailored to fit each student. The most extreme version of individualization was realized when colleges began granting credit for experience gained anywhere. Core courses taught in singular fashion and required of everyone were at an opposite extreme. Each had its proponents and both were seen, often in the same institutions.

A technology of instruction in which goals are specified and a variety of learning paths designed so that most students may reach those goals offered a compromise. A variety of learning outcomes and instructional strategies allowed students to decide whether they wanted to be involved in the programs and, at the same time, enhanced the credibility of the institutions as teaching and learning enterprises. Throughout the 1980s the policies in many community colleges were modified so that students who did not make steady progress toward completing a program might be dropped from the rolls. The colleges also developed a variety of instructional strategies to accommodate different types of learners.

A technology of instruction has made some inroads, but progress has been slow. The definitions of *instruction* that are in use offer a clue. *Instruction* may be defined simply as "an activity that implements the curriculum." This definition assumes a set of courses that must be brought to the students. Another definition of *instruction* is "a sequence of events organized deliberately so that learning occurs." This definition does not depend on a curriculum, but it does include the word *learning,* and it implies a process leading to an outcome. But most instructors seem still to define *instruction* not as a process but as a set of activities (lecturing, conducting discussions, cajoling, and so on) in which teachers typically engage. Such a definition removes both the courses and the learners from the enterprise.

Regardless of the medium employed, the basic model of instructional technology includes clearly specified learning outcomes or objectives, content deployed in relatively small portions, learning tasks arrayed in sequence, a variety of modes of presenting information, frequent feedback on student performance, and criterion tests at the ends of instructional units. The instructors are part of the technology of instruction when they define the objectives, write the tests, select and/or present the media, and in general connect the student to the learning tasks.

The technology of instruction has been important for two-year colleges, typically commuter institutions, in which the environment of a learning community is not available to exercise its subtle, yet powerful, influence on the students. The tools basic to an instructional technology have been available ever since words were first put on paper. The expansion in variety and use of other forms of reproducible media have made additional sets of tools available. However, except for the institutions that have adopted competency-based education and its companion form, mastery learning, the concepts of instructional technology have not been widely adopted. It is as though new types of hammers, saws, and trowels had been taken up by artisans unaware of the shape of the houses they were attempting to construct.

The instructors of remedial courses have been among the leaders in adopting concepts of instructional technology. During the 1970s and 1980s, this group moved steadily from the periphery of the educational establishment toward the mainstream. They became not only teachers of remedial classes but also managers of student flow, and their learning centers became more nearly integral parts of the instructional programs. They expanded their provision of academic support services to instructors in the academic and occupational areas, and they became more deeply involved in measuring instructional outcomes. Because they were not expected to perform traditional classroom instruction, and because remedial classes frequently were assigned to them, they were able to develop different instructional forms. Some of them built programs based on mastery learning, while others focused on computer-managed instruction. They became considerably more aware as a professional group; and this awareness was reflected in their participation in vigorously functioning professional associations, the National Association for Developmental Education and the College Reading and Learning Association. Conceptually, they coalesced around instruction as a discipline. Many of them had begun as teachers of reading, English, mathematics, or psychology; but as they became deeply involved in the learning resource centers and the remedial programs, their connections with their academic disciplines weakened, and they became much more concerned with the technology of instruction.

Eventually the remedial instructors began teaching large numbers of freshmen not only at their own colleges but at neighboring universities. In 1993, 35 percent of the entering freshmen at the University of California at Davis were taught remedial English by instructors from Sacramento City College. Similar arrangements were in place between the University of California at San Diego and the San Diego Community College District. Symbiotically, the university faculty who have never wanted to teach remedial studies contracted with a group who have become experts in the task.

Television

Television, one of the most generally adopted teaching tools, is presented on closed circuit for students in the classrooms and through open circuit for the benefit of the public. Many of the open-circuit televised courses can be taken for college credit, and some institutions generate a sizable proportion of their course enrollments through the use of that medium. Enrollments in the televised courses presented by the Dallas County Community College District alone rose from their beginnings in 1972 to over ten thousand per academic year in eighteen courses in 1978 (Dallas County Community College District, 1979). The City Colleges of Chicago organized a TV College in the 1950s, and several other community colleges also received licenses for the cultural enrichment and entertainment of the public as well as for credit-course instruction.

Interest in television led many colleges to develop their own materials. Video production facilities were constructed in most of the larger institutions, and numerous staff members were involved in program generation. By 1980 two-thirds of the instructors nationwide had access to media production facilities. A few college districts—most notably, Miami-Dade (Florida), Coastline (California), Chicago, and Dallas—became widely recognized for the sophistication of their programming. (Interestingly, whereas a university's prestige often rests on its faculty's scholarship and research discoveries, the export of high-quality television programs provides one of the few ways that a community college can gain a reputation beyond its own district's boundaries.) Interdistrict cooperation in production and distribution of televised courses became common, and several consortia were developed to share programs and production costs.

The use of televised instruction grew steadily throughout the 1980s, with open-circuit courses offered for college credit one of the more popular options. Various surveys found consistently that telecourse students were more likely to be women and older than their counterparts taking courses on campus (Brey and Grigsby, 1984). Students were taking the classes because they did not have time for regular attendance on campus, although their purposes for taking the course were similar to those of people who took regular classes. Most of them learned about the courses through mailings or newspaper advertisements. Televised instruction had become well established.

Computers

The advent of the computer gave the colleges another opportunity for instructional innovation. A Washington State report on the use of computers in instruction (Howard and others, 1978) divided patterns of use into (1) computer-based instruction, the use of specialized computer programs, such as models and simulators, in the teaching of economics, business, and engineering; (2) computer-managed instruction, which supports teaching by maintaining student records, administering tests, generating progress reports, and prescribing the most suitable types of instruction; and (3) computer-assisted instruction, the presentation of linear and branching instructional programs.

In the 1980s, the personalized computer gave considerable impetus to this form of education. In 1994, Cross reported that community colleges have both the highest ratio of student-owned to institutionally owned desktop computers and the highest percentage of classes using computer technology for instruction. According to another survey on campus computer usage, community colleges lead in the percentage of courses reporting classroom computer technology usage, and they use computer-based labs or classrooms in nearly twice as many courses as public university courses. Further, community colleges have an average of 24 students per lab computer while public universities have 28.4 students per computer workstation (Green, 1994).

Some form of computer-assisted or computer-managed instruction has been adopted in practically every institution. The PLATO (Programmed Logic for Automated Teaching Operations) system, originated at the University of Illinois, became popular; for example, Cuyahoga Community College (Ohio) introduced it as a supplement to remedial English and mathematics courses (Smith and others, 1981). The Time-Shared Interactive Computer-Controlled Information by Television System installed at Northern Virginia Community College in 1974 was used to present the entire course material for college grammar, basic algebra, English composition, and certain mathematics courses while scoring tests, presenting instructional modules, and maintaining records of grades (Sasscer, 1977). The computer at the Community College of the Air Force has been used to maintain a file of student characteristics, aptitude scores, indexes of reading ability, and educational background; select and present the best course material for each student, record student responses, and administer tests and supplemental training; predict students' completion dates; and evaluate and revise the course materials (Campbell, 1977). This form of combining diagnostics, instruction, and testing has emerged as a frequent application of computer-managed learning.

Miami-Dade combined computer-managed and computer-assisted instruction. Its Open College allowed students to enroll in classes, buy course materials, and go through the course work at their own pace without going to the campus except for examinations. Interaction between instructor and student was handled through the computer; information was transmitted through television. The system evolved to include a Response System with Variable Prescription (RSVP), a sophisticated mode of individualizing instruction and record keeping. The RSVP package maintained students' records and their responses to various surveys and exams, printed reports informing students of their progress, and provided information to instructors about student performance and collective class data. RSVP also delivered personalized letters to students, prodding them to maintain progress. The program was used to diagnose student writing and to provide corrective prescriptions for various types of errors and explanations of basic writing concepts (Miami-Dade Community College, 1979).

As with all forms of instruction, the use of the computer promotes student learning to a greater or lesser degree, depending on the application. A review of only a few of the many assessments that have been conducted reveals varied results. Computer-assisted instruction in English grammar was less effective than a programmed text method (Lundgren, 1985); was more effective than traditional instruction in business organization classes (Brum, 1983); was less effective in developmental reading (Taylor and Rosecrans, 1986); was no different in an air conditioning/refrigeration program (Houston Community College System, 1986); led to greater improvement in reading skills but higher dropout rates (Kester, 1982); or produced higher grade point averages and higher course completion rates (Penisten, 1981). Most of the applications of computer-assisted instruction continued to be supplemental to the basic classroom structure; although the faculty in nearly all colleges had free access to computers, only a minority of them used it as a substitute for or even as an adjunct to their own teaching. The computer was more widely used in specialized situations—for example, in classes for remedial or learning-disabled students—than in the traditional college-credit classes. Its most effective applications were in combining instruction with testing, providing rapid feedback to students regarding their progress, and in general managing the flow of students through the colleges' programs. However, as more students gained familiarity with personal computers (in 1993, one-third of all entering freshmen said they used a personal computer "frequently"), computer-based instruction found applications in a growing number of situations (Astin, Korn, and Riggs, 1993).

Writing Across the Curriculum

During the mid 1970s, Writing Across the Curriculum (WAC) programs gained popularity in both colleges and universities. Responding to a perceived deficiency in students' writing and thinking abilities, advocates of this approach urged the incorporation of writing into all classes and all disciplines. A number of colleges have implemented WAC into their curricula, with students developing writing assignments in specific classes.

Adams and his associates (Adams, Bodino, Bissell, and Smith, 1985) described writing across the curriculum at Somerset County College (New Jersey); Walter (1984) discussed the approach at Sinclair Community College (Ohio); Preston (1982), at Miami-Dade Community College (Florida); and Landsburg and Witt (1984), at Pima Community College (Arizona). This instructional methodology has students developing writing assignments in specific classes. In some applications, the papers are submitted to a writing instructor who assists in evaluating the products; in others, the students in composition classes work on papers that are related to the content of the subject-specific classes.

Other variations of writing across the curriculum have been implemented. Bullock, Madden, and Harter (1987) examined the effectiveness of pairing a developmental reading class with an introductory psychology course as a means of facilitating students' success in the psychology course while improving their reading skills. At Orange Coast College (California), the general education curriculum has been structured to pair four freshmen composition sections with four different liberal arts courses (Salzinksi, 1987). Los

Medanos College (California) offered a block program, with the same instructors teaching two or three courses to the same students and treating students' writing problems in depth (Missimer, 1985). A 1991 issue of *New Directions for Community Colleges* (Stanley and Ambron) described rather fully the history of WAC and presented various approaches to its implementation.

Supplemental Instruction

Supplemental instruction uses course content as the basis for skills instruction, after identifying high-risk courses rather than high-risk students. Pioneered at the University of Missouri at Kansas City, it is designed to teach students to read the texts and interpret the tests used in the academic classes they are taking. In these programs students work outside of class with tutors who attend all lectures for the targeted course. A reader coordinates the work of the tutors with that of the instructors who have agreed to participate by encouraging their students to take advantage of the tutoring. The concept has spread to many colleges where dropout and failure rates in basic, introductory academic courses have been unconscionably high. Wolfe (1987) has described its application and the results obtained in a history class at Anne Arundel Community College (Maryland), and Craig-Claar (1994) recounted its uses at Maple Woods Community College (Missouri). Its uses in natural science and social science courses at various colleges have been summarized by Friedlander (1982). Supplemental instruction shows promise because it provides community college students with what they most need: additional time spent on learning the skills they must have if they are to succeed in the classes they must take.

Cognitive-Style Mapping

The idea that people learn in different ways and that these ways can be guides to instructional practice is an elusive yet enduring notion. The concept of learning style considers personality, information processing, and social interaction—all with the intention of forming instructional methods that will enhance learning for people whose style matches the classroom emphasis.

Cognitive-style mapping, which generated some early interest in the 1970s and 1980s, continued to concern educators in the 1990s. Some colleges used it as a device to determine their students' best learning mode so that they could be placed in and with consonant courses and instructors. The Canfield Learning Styles Inventory (Gruber and Carriuolo, 1991) and the Myers-Briggs Type Indicator (Roberts, 1975) were favored tools. They were used to identify a student's personality type, relate it to the student's preferred learning style, and match the student with instructors or classroom-learning situations that would be most accommodative. Much of this cognitive-style mapping was based on the work pioneered by Joseph Hill at Oakland Community College (Michigan) early in the 1970s. Mountain View College (Texas) designed a cognitive-style program to determine preferred learning styles for the students and aid them in selecting appropriate courses (Ehrhardt, 1980). Funds from the Elementary and Secondary Education Act and the Vocational Education Act were used to bring information on cognitive styles to community colleges in New York, show instructors how to use it, and arrange programs for cognitive-style mapping for the colleges in that state (Martens, 1975; Rotundo, 1976).

Studies based on the concept continue to be experimental. Marrison and Frick (1994) divided undergraduates in agricultural economics into three groups: multimedia instruction (MI), lecture with MI, and lecture only. Field dependent and independent students did not differ in perceptions of MI or lecture, but independents found MI easier to use and more exciting. Rothschild and Piland (1994) indicated three broad types of learners (cooperative, independent, and competitive) and reported finding significant correlation among personality types and learning-style preferences. Other researchers have also looked at personality types and diversity of learning styles (Price, 1991; Schroeder, 1993).

Mastery Learning

Mastery learning, a technology of instruction in itself, was described and advocated by several educators, especially by Benjamin Bloom of the University of Chicago (see Bloom, 1973). The intent of mastery learning is to lead all students to specified competencies (as opposed to programs that have the effect of sorting students along a continuum of individual ability). In a mastery learning plan, competencies are specified in the form of learning objectives. Practice tests, corrective feedback, additional learning time for those who need it, and a variety of instructional techniques are provided to ensure that all, or at least most, of the students attain mastery of the concepts or skills at the prescribed standard.

Proponents of mastery learning have pointed to sizable cognitive and affective gains made by students—gains on test scores and in personal development—when this strategy is used. The gains have been attributed to any or all of the following: more focused teaching, cooperation instead of competitiveness among students, the definition of specific learning objectives, the amount of class time actually spent in learning, practice and feedback before the graded examinations, and teachers' expectations that most students will attain mastery.

Mastery learning procedures have been adopted in some community college courses and programs, even becoming prominent for a while at City Colleges of Chicago (Shabat and others, 1981), but the concept has not swept the field. Many reasons can be advanced for the failure of this technology of instruction to become more prevalent. Faculty members and administrators who have shied away from mastery learning offer several: it costs too much to develop and operate programs with a sufficient variety of instructional forms; it takes too much of teachers' and tutors' time; outcomes for most courses cannot be defined or specified in advance; allowing students time to complete course objectives interferes with school calendars; students may not be motivated if they are not in competition with their fellows for grades; employers and the public expect the college to sort students, not pass them all through at prescribed levels of competency; and accrediting agencies and other overseers demand differential grades. Froh and Muraki (1980) interviewed forty of the two hundred instructors who had been introduced to mastery learning strategies at workshops sponsored by the University of Chicago and the City Colleges of Chicago. About one-third of these instructors said that they had modified or abandoned the components because it was too time-consuming to construct program specifications and tests and to give necessary feedback to the students.

McIntyre (1991) reported that a combination of teacher overload and a lack of administrative support interferes with the implementation of mastery learning, while Kulik and others (1990) and Slavin (1990) discuss effects of mastery learning, based on 108 controlled evaluations. A synthesis of findings from forty-six studies of group-based applications of mastery learning strategies was reported by Guskey and Pigott (1988). In general, the findings were that mastery learning techniques are rarely installed in pure form but that when they are the effects on student learning are salutary.

Competency-Based Instruction

Competency-based education has also made inroads in community colleges, an approach that depends on the specification of desired competencies to be exhibited by the students but does not include all the specific instructional strategies of mastery learning. The Competency-Based Undergraduate Education Project, sponsored in the 1970s by the Fund for the Improvement of Postsecondary Education, wrestled with defining the outcomes of liberal education. Ewens found a paradox in attempting to convert liberal education to competencies. It was the seemingly insoluble dilemma of converting higher education from an ideal-referenced standard to criterion-referenced or norm-referenced standards. "Ideal-referenced judgments presuppose some notion of the good, the excellent, the higher, the best," but most education now deals with minimal competencies, functioning in an environment, and meeting acceptable standards of behavior (1977, p. 19). There is no room for the ideal when we ask "What is a competent person?" The dilemma appears with force in the tendency of all education to teach job-related skills. One's job is what one *does;* one's work is what one *is*. If education teaches for jobs, ignoring what the person is, it runs the risk of creating a corps of dissatisfied graduates when they find that a job is not enough for a satisfactory life—not to mention the issue of whether they find jobs at a level for which they were trained.

For many years, state-oversight and regional accrediting agencies have requested that the colleges specify and assess the competencies to be learned in all programs, but especially those leading to employment. Numerous colleges have done so, using Developing a Curriculum (DACUM) or another process for defining competencies and developing course syllabi. The Carl D. Perkins Vocational and Applied Technology Act of 1990 brought the federal government into the picture by stating that the programs should include competency-based applied learning in academics, problem solving, work attitudes, and occupationally specific areas.

However, specifying tangible, desired outcomes has never been easy, even in the occupational areas. The span from broadly stated college goals to tasks to be performed by students at the end of a portion of a course is long, and the connections may be difficult to make. The links between "making people better," "helping them cope with society," "training them for jobs," "preparing them for clerical positions," and "students will type seventy words per minute" may be too tenuous. A technology of instruction puts responsibility for learning jointly in the hands of instructors and students; both must participate. Perhaps educators despair of being called to account if they fail. Teaching is not like building a wall; the chances are good that a brick will remain in place, whereas the influences on students, the myriad impressions they receive in addition to their instruction, the predispositions they bring to the task—all can change program results.

Still, the most successful adoptions of competency-based education have been in occupational studies. At institutions such as Gateway Technical Institute (Wisconsin), competency-based education is used in all the classes (Kaprelian and Perona, 1981). The extent to which competency-based instruction has been implemented in postsecondary vocational/technical education throughout Texas was assessed by Lovelace and LaBrecque (1993a, 1993b) who found that although over 90 percent of the responding instructors were using competencies from the workplace when developing their curriculum, fewer than 40 percent were using occupational competency examinations to determine students' achievement of those competencies.

Competency-based instruction has also been used as a basis for articulating secondary school occupational programs with their community college counterparts (Doty, 1985). And it has been employed in high school completion programs (Singer, 1987; Oklahoma State Regents for Higher Education, 1993a; Marlowe and others, 1991). Yet competency-based education has not been widely adopted in general education or liberal arts programs. When it has been adopted for this purpose, it has been most successful where working face-to-face is feasible for a critical number of the entire staff, that is, at small colleges such as Kirkwood Community College (Iowa), where competency-based education has become the foundation of the liberal arts program.

Learning Resource Centers

The community college library has long been recognized as an important instructional service. Johnson (1939) called it the heart of the college and recommended numerous ways it might become central to the instructional process. Although none of the libraries developed collections of research materials, they did provide books and periodicals sufficient for a textbook-oriented institution. In 1992, the median library operating budget was less than $200,000, or under $50 per student, with two-thirds of the money going for salaries. The median number of titles held was around 35,000 (National Center for Education Statistics, 1994b).

Most community college libraries underwent a major transformation when they became learning resource centers (LRCs). In some colleges the library remained intact, with facilities added for individual study through the use of self-instructional programs. But in many colleges totally new LRCs were built to encompass a library; a learning assistance center; audio and video learning laboratories; a center for the distribution of audiovisual materials; and centers for tutorial services, graphic and photographic reproduction, and video production. About one-third of the LRCs also had career information centers and computer-assisted-instruction terminals.

The evolution has continued, with some LRCs now operating learning enrichment, tutorial, or survival-skills centers or labs. Some learning centers have taken on a status apart from library functions, operating chiefly as coordinating agencies for tutoring, remedial instruction, student orientation, and independent study (Platt, 1993). In other applications, members have played a role in providing research, material for grant writing, faculty development, and curriculum design in international education (Bailey, Buchanan, and Holleman, 1990).

The librarians at St. Petersburg Junior College (Florida) note that the LRCs often house production libraries for faculty to develop curriculum media as well as offering services to students. They have expanded to include such electronic formats as on-line services, CD-ROM, and multimedia products. Automation within LRCs includes the conversion of traditional card catalogs to digital data bases that are often accessible to faculty and students through college local area networks, making the LRCs logical gateways to the Internet, other library catalogues, on-line indexes, data bases, and texts (S. Anderson, written communication, November 26, 1993).

The LRCs may also effect cooperative ventures with other agencies, such as museums and regional governmental units (Person,
1984). Prager (1991) urges that LRCs incorporate reinforcement
and enrichment activities for students, assessment testing, instruction in library and research skills, print and nonprint resources for
telecourses, tutorial services, a full range of services for underprepared students, and both supplementary instruction and individualized self-paced learning. More than ever before, the library's
incarnation as a learning center positions it at the center of instructional programs.

Interactive Media

Interactive media is a broad term for several functions and technologies, including video and audio live broadcasts or tapes, CD-
ROMs, and other computer-based forms. The common element is
that the user must be able to control the pace and direction of the
presentation. These media combine several features. They are like
telephones in that it is possible to speak readily to people anywhere
in the world, and to speak with more than one person at a time; like
answering machines with infinite storage capacity; and like teaching machines that allow students to create their own learning paths.
They enable searching of dictionaries, encyclopedias, and all the
data bases, abstracting services, and related information sets. They
enable people to revise form, combining books and artwork, blurring the line between creator and critic. Using these media requires
no special skills. Children play games on interactive machines, and
e-mail is as easy to use as the ubiquitous telephone. Selecting index
terms and surfing across data bases is relatively straightforward.

Many colleges have adopted instructional forms based on inter-
active media. Interactive video programs have been developed at
Miami-Dade Community Colleges (Tross and Di Stefano, 1983); at
Hudson Valley Community College (Lawson, 1994); in the Dallas
County Community College District (Olson and others, 1992); at

Valencia Community College (Florida) (Gianini, 1992); and at Burlington County College (New Jersey) (Pokrass and others, 1992). The staff at Thomas Nelson Community College (Virginia) explored ways in which students in composition and literature classes might use local area networks, using interactive computer tutorials to analyze essays, plots, and characterization (Long and Pedersen, 1992). The uses grow exponentially.

What has changed? With the growth of user-controlled media, the school becomes more important than ever because education, critical thinking, and functional literacy are essential for sorting out the messages. Just as reading a book has always required the intelligence to decode print as well as to differentiate arguments, interactive media require the ability to vet the information, determining which signals are important, which are true, and which are relevant.

The more sanguine proponents of interactive media, Lanham (1993), for example, project the form's effect on freedom, responsibility, and individuality. Heretofore, teachers, editors, critics, and publishers have screened the various products, thereby controlling access to ideas. But by placing the individual in a position of searching all data bases, interacting with everyone on the Internet, interpreting and idiosyncratically reforming all types of emanations past and present, the experts will be circumvented. All to the good, proponents say, because no one should have to suffer the biases of someone else's selection.

Many years ago, arguments in favor of universal literacy centered on the notion that all people should be able to read the Bible for themselves without the interpretation of religious leaders. Applied to education, similar thinking suggests that people should be empowered to learn independently of the schools. The ultimate in interactive media allows the learners to form their own questions, find their own answers, construct their own texts, and develop their own knowledge.

Within the schools, however, interactive media must contend with several traditions that militate against their immediately displacing extant instructional forms. At the heart is the core of instruction itself. Devotees of distance learning, interactive media, and all sorts of reproducible instructional situations have been constantly stymied by the difficulty of duplicating a live learning situation. Whether one-on-one tutorial or small class or large lecture hall, the live learning situation involves more than information transmission on the part of the instructor or responses to student questions. The live instructional situation has nuances of body movement, voice intonation, expression, and cues from the instructors and other students that come through the communally breathed air. What tone is being employed? How important is the message that is being transmitted, as indicated by the speech pattern or body language of the person transmitting it? What needs to be repeated because the respondents indicate by their faces a failure to understand sufficiently?

If these verbal and nonverbal cues were not as critical as they are, the various reproducible instructional programs that have been available for half a century would have made more inroads than they have. True, some people learn through using programmed instructional materials, and these materials have become an important part of education in America, just as the mass media have become important. But the predominant form of school-based instruction is still centered on live people talking with live people, and picking up all the nuances of behavior that human beings have learned to associate with messages ever since the beginnings of speech. Reproducible media hold a continuing allure, a promise of low-cost information transmission, but they do not contain the subtle cues to meaning that emanate from the face-to-face contact of a classroom. A nod, a frown, a smile, the shifting of bodies in chairs, the winks and blinks and nods and twitches all have meaning that cannot be duplicated readily through a medium outside the individual (Farb, 1993).

Trends in Media Use

Over the years, interest in various instructional techniques has waxed and waned. Johnson (1969), who surveyed community colleges around the country, tabulated the incidence of cooperative work-study education, programmed instruction, audiotutorial teaching, television, dial-access audio systems, instruction by telephone, multistudent response systems, the use of film and radio, gaming and simulation, computer-assisted instruction, and a host of other techniques ranging from electronic pianos to a classroom in the sky. Hardly an instructional medium could be identified that was not in place at some community college. The trend has continued. By 1985 the Wisconsin State Board of Vocational, Technical, and Adult Education (VTAE) was able to report seventy-eight electronic technologies in use in twelve VTAE districts. A 1992 national survey found 60 percent of the colleges using video-based instruction for distance learning, predominantly in social science, business, and humanities classes (Lever, 1992).

It is reasonable to assume that in an institution dedicated since its inception to "good teaching," new instructional forms will be tried. However, despite the spread of reproducible media, traditional methods of instruction still flourish. Visitors to a campus might be shown the mathematics laboratories, the media production facilities, and the computer-assisted instructional programs. But on the way to those installations, they will pass dozens of classrooms with instructors lecturing and conducting discussions just as they and their predecessors have been doing for decades. Media are being used widely, but usually in association with or adjunctive to live instruction. Many faculty members continue to believe that close personal contact with students is the most valuable and flexible instructional form that can be developed. Purdy's (1973) in-depth study of the faculty at a college widely known for its audiotutorial laboratories, computer-programmed course segments, videocassettes, and other reproducible media (a national magazine dubbed it "Electronic U") revealed a sizable group resistant to all those media.

The Power of Inertia

Media-based techniques are not the only instructional forms that meet resistance. Why don't the faculty require more writing? Many reasons can be advanced, but the one that the faculty often give is that they have too many students in their classes, that if they require their students to write more, then they (the teachers) are required to read more. In most classes, too few papers are assigned because the instructors cannot accept alternatives to their reading them. Either outside readers are not available to them, or they do not trust anyone but themselves to read their students' written work—probably some combination of both. Nor have the faculty ever accepted the notion that student writing can be sampled, with only every second or third paper read or each paper read only for certain restricted characteristics. They still act as though every practice session must be critiqued, whether the student is practicing the piano, hitting baseballs, or writing compositions.

Anything that lessens direct contact with students or that demands more of the instructors' time stands a good chance of meeting resistance. The ad hoc lecture requires the least preparation time. And innovators must prove the positive effects of their techniques, while traditionalists can usually go their way without question. Teaching as a profession has not developed to the point at which proper conduct in the instructional process can be defined and enforced in the face of individual deviation. Hence, whereas lower teaching loads would allow more time for instructional reform, they would not be sufficient to revise instruction; merely giving people more time to do what they are bent to do does not change the perception of their role. Moreover, few colleges or universities reward or provide incentives to instructors who develop reproducible instructional materials—just 15 percent of the schools, according to Green and Eastman (1993). Reproducible media tend to arise outside the colleges and anything not indigenously created is suspect.

The rapidity with which new media appear and the immovability of the academic culture are at odds. Five hundred years after the introduction of moveable type, the book and the lecture still share the territory of instruction. The inexpensive, readily available book did not displace the lecture in transmitting information; it became an additional form. Each has valuable features that the other cannot duplicate.

In this respect, the academic culture resembles its societal context. Cinema did not replace live performances, nor did television replace radio. For that matter, the ascendancy of science over the past three hundred years has not fully displaced belief in the supernatural, and the vision of authority based on superior training must continually contend with a stubborn reliance on folk wisdom.

Applications of instructional technology in academe confront similar cultural inertia. Geoghegan noted how the revolution in instruction, "where learning would be paced to a student's needs and abilities . . . and where universal educational access, transcending barriers of time and space, would become the norm," has become only a "pedagogical utopia . . . enjoying a sort of perpetual immanence that renews itself with each passing generation of technology" (1994, p. 1). "The problem," he contends, "is that only a very small proportion of faculty are actively developing or using such applications, and that once developed, they rarely find their way beyond the individuals or teams whose innovative efforts brought them into existence in the first place" (p. 3). His conclusions: "The technologically driven revolution in teaching and learning that we have sought for so long is probably nothing more than a chimera" (p. 22).

Short similarly describes the "vision that never materialized": classrooms equipped with multimedia technology; interactive, collaborative learning; the "virtual campus that transcends its geographical boundaries . . . via the information highway"—all "remains a concept rather than a reality" (1994, pp. 1–2). He, too, blames instructional inertia, but he also assails the excessive claims made by the few innovators who have sought "a mythical application that will somehow empower faculty to become superstars of the electronic classroom . . ." even while "most faculty-developed software remains in a state of perpetual development, seldom moving beyond the courses taught by the developer" (p. 4). Short concludes by listing thirteen laborious steps, from targeting core components of the curriculum to exploring the implications of the innovation, that must be taken if the changes are to occur.

Assessing Instructional Effects

No type of instructional technology has been sufficiently powerful to overcome the traditional educational forms against which it has been pitted. With rare exceptions, an institutionwide commitment to demonstrable learning outcomes has foundered on the rocks of inertia and on an inability to demonstrate that it is worth the effort entailed. Assessing student learning is, however, as important a component of instruction as any other aspect of the process.

Is the community college the home of "good teaching"? Information on the effects of instruction is always hard to obtain because of the number of variables that must be controlled in any study: the entering abilities of the students, the criterion tests and instructional procedures used, and the level of the course or learning unit, to name only a few. Comparative studies are especially difficult because of the unfeasibility of matching student groups and instructional presentations (are any two lecture sessions really the same?). Rather than try to compare learning attained, many studies have used student and instructor preferences as the dependent variable. Researchers have measured the value of computer-assisted instruction by asking students whether they preferred it to live lectures. The reports usually indicated that many students prefer the interpersonal contact with instructors, while many others do quite well with the instructional programs presented through the computer. But pre- and postinstructional assessments of student learning rarely yield significant differences between treatments.

An intractable problem with research on instruction is that no method can be shown to be consistently superior to another. Dubin and Taveggia reanalyzed the data from ninety-one studies conducted between 1924 and 1965 and concluded "that there is no measurable difference among truly distinctive methods of college instruction when evaluated by student performance on final examinations" (1968, p. 35). The conditions of instruction are so fluid, the instructors so variant, the students so different that true experimental conditions cannot be applied. McKeachie (1963) reached similar conclusions.

In the 1980s, new efforts were made to assess effects broadly, for example, by measuring student learning through statewide, interinstitutional, and institutionwide studies. Even though such studies are common in most other countries, they are alien to American higher education (where the responsibility for measuring cognitive change in students has been relegated to classroom instructors). Therefore, the efforts to institute such studies have been greeted with little enthusiasm. Leaders in many institutions have given lip service to the importance of student outcomes measurement, but, beyond a flurry of study groups and the usual skittishness displayed by educators who are faced with a potential change in their routine, little has been effected.

In a few states, however, the colleges have been encouraged or mandated to install institutionwide testing programs. Sometimes the encouragement includes a budget supplement. Tennessee has authorized up to 5 percent in additional appropriations to each college that provides information on student learning in general education or in the area of the student's major, or data on the number of students passing licensure examinations. Supplemental funds are also available to colleges that use data from surveys of current students, alumni, and dropouts to improve college programs and services. Other states have used the stick instead of the carrot. In Florida, students must pass an externally designed College Level Academic Skills Test (CLAST) before they can receive an associate degree and/or enter the junior year at a publicly supported university. Georgia and Texas have similar programs. Outcomes assessment in those states has been connected with student progress—a significant departure from the more typical practice of assigning places in higher classes primarily on the basis of student interest, course-taking pattern, and grades received.

The press for assessment has continued. Alarmed at the rapid increase in per-student cost, especially since the public pays most of it, and prodded by constituents who deplore the low success rates for minority students, the legislatures and appointed officials in many states have insisted on more direct measures of college outcomes. What proportion of the matriculants obtain degrees? How many pass licensure examinations? How many are employed in areas for which they were trained? And—most disturbing of all for a professional group that has taken pride in its vaguely defined goals and processes—how much did the students learn? For the faculty especially, this last query cannot be set aside as beyond their purview. Influential outsiders are demanding to know just what is happening as a result of their ministrations.

New Jersey's College Outcomes Evaluation Program offers an example of the direction that assessment was taking. The program was created by the Board of Higher Education in 1985. An advisory committee was appointed to develop a comprehensive assessment program with emphasis on "a sophomore test in verbal skills, quantitative reasoning, and critical thinking" (New Jersey Advisory Committee to the College Outcomes Evaluation Program, 1987, p. iii). The board's action followed from various statewide testing initiatives, especially a basic skills assessment program that had been installed for entering freshmen several years earlier. The New Jersey Advisory Committee recommended that several types of assessment be undertaken, some within the colleges and others external to them. The internal measures were to be the outcomes of general education, student learning in each major course, and retention and completion rates—the standard variables in assessing student progress. The main external measure was to be a "common statewide assessment of general intellectual skills." The program was to coordinate these efforts, "oversee the collection and analysis of the information, and report regularly to the Board of Higher Education" (pp. iv–v). Questions of enforcement and sanctions for noncompliance were not settled and the committee was subsequently disbanded.

The New Jersey plan touched the community colleges just as the Florida College Level Academic Skills program had. Collecting student retention and follow-up data is one thing, but a test of student knowledge administered at the conclusion of the sophomore year is quite another. Complaints about outside control of the curriculum and the demise of academic freedom and similar lamentations have become common. Examinations that reveal student learning to people outside the confines of the single classroom are anathema in academe. Few within the colleges have any notion of how to construct them. Except in rare instances, the staff makes no effort to collect and use such information until the state legislatures tie the process to college funding or to student access.

Assessment changed form again in the 1990s as legislatures in some states mandated that the colleges validate their student placement procedures. To what extent do the entry tests, prerequisite courses, and other student tracking devices predict success in college-level courses and student retention and graduation rates? Efforts to relate placement with outcomes were stimulated, but they typically fell afoul of the same problems that plague the methods-comparison studies. The range of influences on student progress is so vast that trying to predict course grades (as unreliable as they are) and student retention (typically related to matters beyond college control) is a frustrating enterprise.

The Pros and Cons of Assessment

The way colleges are organized leads most staff members to resist outcomes assessment. Students are supposed to learn history, music, and mathematics in separate courses and departments. Some students learn more efficiently than others, and classroom tests have always been used to determine which students are better than their fellows. The national testing organizations that offer subject tests from biology to sociology, used to determine which students deserve entry to further school programs, play into this form of normative measurement. It works well when the purpose is to spread individuals along a continuum, because it emphasizes variation in student ability. This variation is so strong that the difference in scores made by students in a single course will often be as great as the difference between the class average and the scores made by another group of students who have never taken the course.

This normative model, useful for assigning places in a program or grade marks to students within it, is different from the criterion-referenced measures usually employed when a program or an institution is being assessed. Criterion-referenced measurement refers to the learning obtained by individuals as measured against a standard. If all students answer all questions correctly, then the entire group has learned everything that the test asked; and if the test was designed as a sample of all knowledge to be gained in a course, program, or institution, then the instructional unit has been a total success. However, applying criterion-referenced analysis in an institution with a history of normative-referenced testing requires a complete shift in the way the staff view their work. Easy to conceptualize, that form of outcomes assessment bogs down in practice. Rare is the institutional leader with sufficient patience or skill to turn the group away from its traditional way of looking at student-learning measures. Rare is the leader who can explain the value and purposes of population sampling and test development that demands items that are not course specific.

Regardless of the impetus for assessment or the model that is pursued, certain principles should apply:

- The results of an examination should not be tied to a single course or instructor; causal inferences should not be sought, nor should the findings be used to judge an instructor, a department, or a discipline.

- The items used must not be course specific but should cover concepts that might have been learned anywhere.

- Scores on the examination should not be made a condition of graduation for the students.

- The student population should be sampled; universal assessment systems are too cumbersome for most colleges to manage.

- Alternate forms of the numerous entrance examinations should be used as measures of student knowledge at the completion of certain numbers of units.

- The faculty must be involved as much as possible in test selection, design, item construction, and test scoring, but installation of the process should not be delayed until all are in accord.

- Specialists in testing who are sensitive to the staff should be employed, with the understanding that, although assessing is a group effort, staff members will not be forced to participate.

- No one set of measures should be used to provide data for different evaluations. Different measures should be used, for example, to evaluate student progress, college processes, and the college's contribution to its community.

- Measures of student achievement need not be restricted to learning but may also include assessment of employment, transfer, satisfaction with the institution, and retention; measures that relate to academic knowledge are of considerably more interest to educators than they are to legislators or members of the lay public.

- A belief in the value of individualization need not extend to variant curricular objectives for everyone; if shared understandings and values contribute to social cohesion, then some consistency in college goals and in measures of college outcomes should be maintained.

Issues

The major issues in instruction center on the extent to which a technology of instruction will progress. Will more instructors adopt instruction as a process instead of an activity? What types of instructional leadership can best effect this change?

Low-cost personal computers have become widespread. How has their use affected the students' writing and computational skills? How has it affected the teaching of those skills?

Assessing instructional outcomes is an integral part of instructional technology. Will persistent calls for mandatory assessment enhance the development of a technology of instruction?

The consequences of a turn away from print as the primary mode of information transmission have not yet been fully realized. What impact on instruction will be made by students who have gained much of their prior knowledge through nonprint sources? Does an instructional program centered on teachers in classrooms best accommodate them?

Mastery learning has been effected in developmental and career education. Can it spread to the collegiate function?

Although each new instructional medium, from radio to the computer, has forced educators to examine their teaching practices, none alone has revolutionized teaching. A general acceptance of instruction as a process that must, by definition, lead to learning might do more in actualizing the prime function of the community colleges.

. . . .

Student Services

Supporting Educational Objectives

The rationale for student personnel services stemmed originally from the institution's need to regulate its clients' activities: "One of the historical models for the student personnel worker is that of regulator or repressor. The student personnel profession came into being largely because the president needed help in regulating student behavior" (O'Banion, 1971, p. 8). In other words, students need to be controlled for the sake of institutional order, a rationale underlying not only the counseling of students into the proper programs but also the registration, student activities, orientation, student government, and record-keeping functions.

However, the rationale evolved so that student personnel services were presumed to be more positively supportive of student development. Reporting findings of the Committee on Appraisal and Development of Junior College Student Personnel Programs, Collins wrote, "The student personnel program should be the pivot, the hub, the core around which the whole enterprise moves. It provides the structure and creates the pervasive atmosphere which prompts the junior college to label itself as student-centered" (1967, p. 13). Eventually, student services combined elements both regulatory and developmental.

This chapter describes the scope of student services and its various emphases. Of particular note are efforts in recruitment and retention, counseling and guidance, orientation, extracurricular activities such as student clubs, and financial aid. Program articulation with senior institutions is included as well because that is often the responsibility of student affairs personnel.

Scope

Consensus has never been reached on the precise role of student services. How much emphasis should be placed on helping students mature? Should the services specialize in assisting students in navigating the bureaucracy, centering on registration, advising, and financial aid? Dassance (1994) outlines these issues, pointing out how such role ambiguity has not been resolved. He concludes that above all, student services must link all college functions in order to be maximally effective.

Several listings of the categories of services have been published. The League for Innovation in the Community College issued a set of concepts regarding student development. Thirty-one directives organized under seven major headings instructed student development professionals to design processes that would smooth student entry and placement, enhance student interaction with college staff and functions, assist students in gaining support from all types of college services, ensure student learning and development, coordinate with other organizations, maintain student records, and assist in selecting college staff members (Doucette and Dayton, 1989). In 1990, the Board of Governors of the California Community Colleges listed seven categorical responsibilities of student services incorporated in matriculation services: admissions, orientation, academic assessment, counseling and advising, follow-up on academic progress, research and evaluation, and coordination and training of staff (California Community Colleges, 1990).

Recruitment and Retention

Services begin even before students arrive at the institution. Because the community colleges try to serve as many members of the community as feasible, they have frequently engaged in extensive recruitment activities. These activities, which accelerated as the population of eighteen-year-olds declined after peaking in the late 1970s, have been especially vigorous in communities where the percentage of high school students beginning college has decreased.

Sacramento City College provides an example of a coordinated recruitment effort. There, a reentry program was developed to make campus programs visible and attractive to a diverse population of potential students. The program included a video presentation highlighting many questions and concerns commonly faced by reentry students. The video was designed to establish community among reentry students, and to discuss student characteristics, available student services, and strategies for success in college. More importantly, the mission and goals of the college provided the foundation of a positive message for this group: the importance of persistence, and the ability to achieve personal goals (White, 1990). Echoing this thinking, community college administrators have acknowledged the need to impart the colleges' utility not only to potential students but to the broader community as well (Keener, Ryan, and Smith, 1991).

Most community colleges have procedures linking the colleges with their surrounding high schools. The faculty in the technical and occupational programs carry out recruiting activities for their areas, but the counseling staff are responsible for recruitment in general. These activities include administering tests to high school students and then helping them and their parents to interpret the results; providing campus facilities for activities attracting high school students; presenting both videotaped and personal recruitment promotions; offering advanced-placement classes to qualified students; and disseminating radio, television, and mailed information to potential students (not only high school students but also members of the broader community), advising them of campus events.

One example of such liaisons between community colleges and surrounding secondary schools is the Partnership in Action Program sponsored by Butte Community College. Activities in this program include distributing college catalogues to high school students, offering college-level courses on high school campuses, distributing literature and assessment tests to high school students, and offering orientation programs to acquaint students with college life (Butte Community College, 1990).

The drive to attract students has coincided with attempts to retain them, propelled by the quite reasonable notion that it is more feasible to keep the students enrolled than to continuously seek new matriculants. One aspect of retention depends on placing the students in programs commensurate with their interests and abilities. Accordingly, members of the student personnel staff are often involved in admissions testing and cooperate with the instructional staff in using the results of those tests to place students in courses.

State laws sometimes accelerate recruitment and retention processes. In California, legislation has mandated that colleges provide matriculation services to students. Colleges are required to process applications for admission, offer orientation and preorientation services for students, deliver assessment and counseling at the time of enrollment, counsel students regarding their academic and career objectives, assess study and learning skills, advise on course selection, and conduct postenrollment evaluations of students' performance.

Counseling and Guidance

Counseling and guidance have been at the core of student services since the earliest years. Eells (1931) gave guidance a status equal to the "popularizing," "preparatory," and "terminal" functions in his list of the junior college's main activities. The contention has been that community college students need help in moving into the college and out again into careers and other schools, and that individualized instruction through counseling and other nonclassroom-based activities is essential.

Academic guidance has always been intended to match applicants to the programs best suited to their own goals and abilities, and to help students recognize their academic abilities and limitations in an organized and caring manner. Community college counselors try to help students clarify their goals and values. They provide information about educational options, and they assist students in planning educational goals in line with their interests and academic abilities. Spicer offers another goal for those who engage in counseling and guidance: the "commitment to providing all entering and continuing students the direction and support they need to make informed decisions about their future and to develop plans to achieve their goals" (1990, p. 15). All this with a counselor-to-FTSE ratio of one to 382, nationwide (Dickmeyer, 1994)!

The belief that students deserve more than cognitive development in a rigid academic environment has also guided practitioners. The expressions "treating the student as a whole" and "assuming responsibility for the full intellectual, social, and personal development of students" are frequently seen in the student personnel literature. By definition, these professionals try to effect student development in psychic, moral, and physical, as well as intellectual, realms. To student personnel advocates, students are not minds apart from their bodies and emotions; they are whole people, and the college should treat them as such.

As the key element in student development, counseling must be integrated with other campus activities; it must maximize students' chances to reach their potential; it must focus on educational, personal, social, and vocational development; and, being student-centered, it must take into account students' interests, aptitudes, needs, values, and potential. Comprehensive counseling should include goal setting, personal assessment, development of change strategies, strategy implementation, evaluation, and recycling of the whole process for each student.

This therapeutic view affirms the belief that the best way to educate people is to integrate all their objectives and all their ways of functioning—cognitive, affective, and psychomotor. It holds that students are active and responsible participants in their educational growth and process, that with help and support they will make decisions that affect their lives and deal with the consequences of their decisions, and that all professionals on the campus must work collaboratively toward greater integration of their services and their professions. In this approach, counseling is not imposed on students but is initiated and determined by them. It works in partnership with classroom instruction and cocurricular activities. In this student development process, goals are set, the individual's current position in relation to these goals is assessed, and the best strategy for change is implemented. The strategy's effectiveness in meeting the individual's goals is then evaluated, new goals are set, and the process begins all over again.

Assessments of student services' effects are sometimes based on this holistic development model. Measures based on psychological constructs have been applied, and the level of satisfaction that students feel has been a favorite measure. College leaders point with pride to the follow-up studies showing that most students value their college experiences for their contribution to self-understanding, further schooling, social interaction, and job skill training. However, personality development concepts are more applicable in institutions that control most aspects of the person's life. Apparent change in the developing personality is more likely to be revealed in a four-year, residential college than in a commuter institution where most students attend part-time. The character-formation, moral-development thread that appeals to many of the student services practitioners seems fey in a college where half the entrants drop out before completing one term's worth of credit.

Regardless of the concepts undergirding their efforts, counselors face unremitting conflict between guiding students into the programs most consonant with their abilities and allowing them to reach for their own preferred goals. Many students want to go in one direction but seem best qualified to go in another. Guidance counselors have devised procedures for ascertaining student goals and assessing student qualifications, trying all the while to strike the proper balance between goals and abilities. But when students appear without distinct career or study goals, when their goals do not match their abilities, or when the testing instruments do not adequately assess them (and all three often come into play at the same time), the role of the counselor has been blurred. When students have decried discrimination and demanded the right to enter any program, the guidance function has staggered. And when institutional policies allow most students access to all but the programs with limited space or limitations imposed by external accrediting agencies, guidance workers have to adjust.

Some critics have taken guidance counselors to task on broader issues. Gay, for example, argued that

> while student personnel workers have professed themselves to be educators and to be interested in the whole student, they have served essentially as housekeepers, guardians of the status quo, and have been seen by many in the postsecondary education arena as petty administrators or "those people who sit in their office and give warm strokes to students who complain about the system, particularly the teacher.". . . In their present capacities, student affairs workers are clearly providing services, needed services, which contribute to student mobility; but whether or not some of the mundane tasks necessary to the services now rendered are wise use of the skills and talents of counselors and other specialists of student affairs is another question [1977, p. 18].

Brick questioned whether psychological counseling is "an educational function which should be implemented by an educational institution, or . . . a public health function which should be implemented by a public health agency" (1972, p. 677).

Still, counseling and guidance services have been maintained. They are less likely to be questioned now because of their presumed usefulness in maintaining student flow into the programs for which they are best suited and on through to successful program completion. Faculty advisers cannot reasonably be expected to carry the entire burden; in fact, one study found that 21 percent of the students whom the faculty had advised to take certain courses had not met the prerequisites for those courses (Heard, 1987). However, student development theory has become considerably less applicable to the counseling situation because of the high proportion of part-time students who use the college as only one resource in their environment and because of the wide range of student age. It is difficult to apply concepts of adolescent development when at least half of the students are twenty-five or older. In addition, many of the eighteen- to twenty-five-year-olds are responsible for their own behavior and often for that of their dependents. Guidance activities also must be structured differently for the high proportion of part-time students who have been involved in the work force or in other areas of higher education.

Guidance and counseling must also be tailored to special student populations. A great deal of attention has been paid recently to the needs of disabled students on community college campuses. Students with physical and learning disabilities find it extremely difficult to gain employment, establish careers, and remain self-sufficient. Cooper and Michael (1990) note that disabled students are twice as likely to drop out of school as are students with no physical or learning disabilities. One reason for these unfortunate statistics may be the disabled student's limited self-perception, self-esteem, and knowledge of effective studying and job skills (Burns, Armistead, and Keys, 1990).

To curb these discouraging trends, John Wood Community College (Illinois) established the Special Needs Transition Initiative Program, where thirty disabled students were invited to participate in an intensive curriculum in which they learned basic life skills. Students were offered a variety of courses, including financial management, legal rights, study skills, and social and health services.

The students were also introduced to college employment placement services (Burns, Armistead, and Keys, 1990).

Nearly all community colleges provide access for mobility-impaired students and more than 80 percent provide assistance for visually or hearing-impaired students. Around half provide on-campus day care for children of students (National Center for Education Statistics, 1994e, p. 21).

Orientation

Student personnel workers also plan and operate student orientation programs. Tang (1981) described several orientation efforts. Sessions offered during the summer preceding the term, in one- or two-day sessions at the beginning of the term, in classes meeting throughout the first term, and in seminars for special groups of students have all been popular. One college offered a three-day retreat for the first 150 freshmen to sign up with the faculty members who helped in leading the activities. Another maintained a series of weekly lectures on issues of concern to students throughout the term. Orientation in many colleges was the responsibility of the counselors, who set up small sessions to inform students of college policies. Some colleges had orientation committees composed of faculty members, students, and student personnel administrators who planned various events for beginning students.

In determining appropriate formats for these introductory sessions, staff members consider their college's mission statements, campus culture, and student population to tailor an appropriate orientation program for their newest students. Because orientation sessions can be either encouraging and personal or distant and bureaucratic, college personnel recognize the importance orientation plays in helping to retain their new students and to keep them enrolled. What happens to students in their first term is critical to their progress; most of the dropout occurs there, according to numerous studies of entering cohorts. One challenge, as described by Fullerton and Hays (1993), is tailoring orientation programs for a diverse student population. In addition, encouraging students to participate in orientation programs sometimes proves to be problematic.

Upcraft (1984) defines orientation as a program designed by an institution to help new students move more easily from old environments to their new environment, and to guide them towards successful college careers. An effective orientation program is a sustained and coordinated effort, fully supported by the entire campus community, based on sound concepts of student development and knowledge of how much college environments influence students, inclusive of many different resources and interventions, timed and ordered in an organized fashion, evaluated for its effectiveness and influence, and coordinated by a central department or chair.

Specialized orientation programs frequently are offered in the summer before classes begin. At Bronx Community College, student personnel administrators established a program where returning students served as mentors and advisors to new students preceding the beginning of classes (Santa Rita, 1992). Participants subsequently had lower "no show" rates than did nonparticipants. Keeping new students informed and aware of campus events, and fielding their concerns prior to beginning the fall term, helps to maintain enrollment.

Extracurricular Activities

Community college student activities programs are difficult to popularize because many students work part-time, few reside on campus, and many high school leaders elect to attend universities instead of community college. Even though it is not easy to involve students in activities outside their regularly scheduled classes, various types of extracurricular activities have been in place since the earliest institutions organized student clubs and athletic events. Eells (1931) listed numerous student activities in the junior colleges of the 1920s, mentioning in particular Pasadena Junior College (California), in which seventy clubs were active. The most popular were athletic clubs, with literary groups, musical activities, and religious and moral organizations following. Science organizations were most common in the public institutions, but camera clubs, pep clubs, honor clubs, and so on operated throughout the colleges of the day. Today, Pasadena City College involves hundreds of students in clubs such as Circle K International, MECHA, Earthwise, Gay and Lesbian Student Union, Lancer Signers for deaf students, Prelaw Society, and the Women's Network (Pasadena City College, Office of Student Affairs, telephone conversation, October 4, 1994).

Low rates of student involvement in extracurricular activities are evident in the sedate levels of student activism on community college campuses. The student activism that was prevalent on university campuses in the United States, France, Japan, and elsewhere in the 1960s was never as prominent in the American community colleges. The colleges did have their share of antiwar protests, but most of the activism centered on intramural concerns such as student demands for additional financial aid and objections to the way schedules were drawn or instructors were assigned. Protests organized around major social issues were rare.

Community college activism has generally involved student attempts to be free of restrictive rules on their conduct. Student newspapers have often caused difficulty, especially when an editor or staff writer decides to test the boundaries by printing a provocative article, story, or poem. The college's right to guide student conduct thereupon comes into conflict with First Amendment rules governing freedom of the press, and these cases are sometimes taken up by the students at large as evidence of how the school administration tends to treat them as children. Often culturally or ethnically oriented student groups demonstrate at community colleges on behalf of hiring more minority instructors or giving more attention to minority concerns in the curriculum. But in most cases, the activism has not reached the level of disruption that it has taken at the universities.

Student government has many purposes. It may provide student leadership-training programs, with workshops on group dynamics and communications skills; involve students as full voting members of faculty committees; assign responsibilities to student government organizations, including their legal incorporation; assign faculty members to student associations as consultants rather than as advisers; and instruct student government representatives in procedures for polling student opinion on pertinent issues.

As a way of involving more students, some commentators have called for student activities and organizations centering on academic departments. William Rainey Harper College (Illinois) surveyed faculty, staff, and students to review types of programs interesting to each group. The study found that cultural events, musical programs, speakers on current issues, and theatrical productions were favored (Lucas, Pankanin, and Nejman, 1993). Such responses parallel the interests reflected in a survey of faculty, who indicated that there were too few humanities-related colloquia, seminars, lectures, exhibitions, or concerts and recitals offered outside of class (Cohen and Brawer, 1977).

Studies of student athletic activities have found wide variance. Athletic programs are presumptively planned so that student athletes can enjoy the benefits of extracurricular activity along with their academic programs. Most institutions offer intramural sports for interested students, but as the colleges have increased their percentages of older, part-time students, these activities have declined. Student activities have begun centering less on team sports and more on individual pursuits. Clubs and ad hoc groups organized to engage in hiking, cycling, scuba diving, backpacking, and jogging have become widespread. Exercise classes open to staff members as well as students have also sprang up as the concern for physical fitness has grown among people of all ages. Aerobic dancing, swimming, and weightlifting have gained in popularity. In general, though, few colleges have developed programs in which sizable percentages of students participate. At William Rainey Harper College, only 10 percent of the student population expressed interest in participating in intramural sports (Ryan and Lucas, 1992). Their participation was conditional on the level of competitiveness and the types of sports being offered.

Financial Aid

Financial aid for students has become an outstanding feature in higher education. Federal and state funds administered through Pell Grants, Supplemental Educational Opportunity Grants, Guaranteed Student Loans, College Work-Study Aid, and State Student Incentive Grants, to name only some of the programs, have grown so that any shift in their availability has an immediately discernible impact on enrollments. Aid is so much a part of the college system that when the California legislature mandated a $100 per year fee to be paid by community college students, it made $52.5 million dollars available as student aid in the same bill (California State Postsecondary Education Commission, 1984). During the 1989–90 academic year, 45 percent of the full-time and 21 percent of the part-time students enrolled in public two-year colleges received financial aid from some source: federal, state, institutional, or a combination thereof (National Center for Education Statistics, 1993, p. 313).

Federal financial aid to students began with the Servicemen's Readjustment Act (GI Bill) in 1944 and was expanded with the National Defense Education Act (NDEA) in 1958; but the community colleges were slow to seek these funds. Not until after the passage of the Basic Educational Opportunity Grant (now called Pell Grants) program in 1972 did the majority of community colleges organize financial aid offices. Even then, according to Nelson (1976), the presidents of very few institutions felt that they had adequate staff to cover the responsibilities of student aid; some aid officers deliberately understated their requests for aid funds because they felt that it would add to an impossible work load.

One reason for the slow start was the misperception that, because of the comparatively low cost of community college education, students did not need financial assistance. However, students still had to spend money to live, still commuted to classes, and, by attending school, were forgoing income that they could otherwise have earned. Furthermore, since community college students were typically from lower-income groups, their needs were greater even though the cost of college going was less. By the 1980s the financial aid offices in most community colleges had gained the ability to direct grants and loans to students who needed them; one campus office at Northern Virginia Community College was making and maintaining more than fifteen hundred award packages each year (Archer and Archer, 1985).

Still, because of the relatively low tuition costs and because of various aid-program restrictions, such as discrimination against part-time or non-degree-credit attendees, community college students have not received their proportionate share of financial aid. From the mid 1970s through the mid 1980s, the federal scholarship and fellowship funds received by community college students remained at around 16 percent of the total awards, if the proprietary schools were not included, even though the colleges enrolled over 25 percent of all full-time students and an even higher percentage of the part-timers. This proportion varied greatly between states, depending on the percentage of a state's students enrolled in community colleges and on the relative level of tuition charged. Students in community colleges in Arizona, Florida, Mississippi, and Oregon received more than 25 percent of the scholarship funds going to college students in those states, while community college students in Maine, New Hampshire, and Louisiana received less than 5 percent of the grant monies (National Center for Education Statistics, 1986). Students in Maryland community colleges were receiving 21 percent of the total aid awarded to undergraduates in the state; Illinois students received 17 percent of the aid distributed in that state; Texas students received 13 percent. However, the figures for those three states are low compared to the percentage of the students enrolled in community colleges in those states.

Student abuse of the financial aid system has been a persistent problem. The charge has been made that many students enroll merely for the funds available to them and that student aid thus represents another form of welfare payment. Of students who received loans during the 1989–90 academic year, almost 20 percent still had financial debts in 1992. That number was even higher for students in less-than-two-year programs; in this category, about 60 percent of students had outstanding loans in 1992 (National Center for Education Statistics, 1994i, p. 72).

Financial aid availability affects student decisions both in enrolling initially and in maintaining continuing attendance. A series of studies done in California after a mandatory fee was imposed for the first time concluded that the fee contributed to a 7 percent enrollment loss statewide in 1984. Enrollment declines were greatest in districts with the lowest-income populations, but after financial aid procedures were strengthened and publicized, the low-income students returned (California Community Colleges, 1987b; Field Research Corporation, 1986). In addition, California community colleges imposed a surcharge for students who hold bachelor's or advanced degrees. Brinkman (1993) predicted that this fee increase would cause fewer students within this population to enroll in community college classes, and indeed the number of enrollees who reported that they held bachelor's degrees dropped precipitously as soon as the special fee took effect. One community college district reported that in the fall of 1989, almost 10 percent of enrolled students had a bachelor's degree; but in 1994 this number dropped to 5.2 percent (Lee and others, 1994).

Articulation and Transfer

Program articulation refers to the movement of students—or, more precisely, the students' academic credits—from one point to another. Articulation is not a linear sequencing or progression from one point to another. It covers students going from high school to college; from two-year colleges to universities and vice versa; double-reverse transfer students, who go from the two-year college to the university and then back again; and people seeking credit for experiential learning as a basis for college or university credit. The concept includes admission, exclusion, readmission, advising, counseling, planning, curriculum, and course and credit evaluation.

Until recently, articulation with the universities was largely a one-way situation, a series of policies and procedures dictated by senior institutions. But Wattenbarger and Kintzer, who individually and together studied issues in articulation, argued that community colleges should not be bound by university dictates. They found that various senior institution policies discriminate against students who transfer even though transfer students usually perform in a manner similar to their past patterns of accomplishment. They noted that little progress had been made in smoothing transfer relations in the years prior to 1985 and concluded: "At least half of the 50 states continue transfer negotiations interinstitutionally, most on a case-by-case basis" (Kintzer and Wattenbarger, 1985, p. 40). Problems were typically related to the types of courses for which transfer credit should be given, students' finding openings in the academic major field of their choice, and the fact that in most cases the university staff insisted that the evaluation of community college credit should be made by the baccalaureate-granting institution. Cohen, Brawer, and Eaton's 1995 study of policies and programs affecting transfer in eight states reported similar findings.

Where formalized articulation agreements are in place, they are usually brought about through the intervention of state boards of higher education. Agreements on a common core of general education courses are negotiated between the community colleges and universities in several states, but periodic negotiation is necessary to keep them current. Despite many efforts to involve faculty members from community colleges and universities in curriculum articulation, the student personnel staff typically contribute the lion's share of the effort—with counselors, admissions and records officers, transcript analysts, and articulation officers doing nearly all the work. It is one thing to make high-level pronouncements on the importance of articulation, quite another to negotiate the details.

Bers (1994) notes three models for transfer systems in use recently. The student development approach encourages administrators to work with students to plan curriculum, transfer strategies, and financial aid arrangements, and to introduce students to senior institutions to which they could transfer. Second, transfer programs are designed around agreements on course equivalencies, transfer credits, legislative and state policies regarding transfer, and statistics on student transfer rates. Finally, community colleges have designed transfer programs with the participation of faculty, who strive to define course requirements, course content, and academic expectations of faculty at community colleges and senior institutions.

In a pioneering move to stabilize community college entrance and to smooth the way for ultimate transfer, Miami-Dade Community College developed a comprehensive program to screen students into certain courses at entry and to monitor their progress throughout their tenure at the college (Harper and others, 1981). Previous institutional practices had allowed students to take any courses and to stay at the institution indefinitely, whether or not they were proceeding toward program completion. In the new plan, students were advised of the requirements both for graduation from the college and for transfer to various programs in Florida's universities. The system was mandatory; everyone who matriculated, except those who already had degrees and were taking courses for personal interest, was included in it.

The Florida experience was repeated in other states. In California, for example, various efforts to identify and assist transfer students were funded. Several of the state's community colleges built transfer centers to coordinate information about transfer policies and to smooth course articulation, especially for minority and other underrepresented students. Similar centers were built elsewhere— for example, at Cuyahoga Community College (Ohio). These efforts to enhance transfer rates were stimulated not only by state agencies but also by various philanthropic foundations—notably the Ford Foundation, which funded an Urban Community College Transfer Opportunities Program.

Other examples of deliberately designed transfer and articulation activities have been reported. Some colleges select students soon after entry and work to connect them with senior institutions. The Community College of Philadelphia designed a program with Bucknell College centering on two twelve-unit core curriculum programs, Introduction to the Social Sciences and Introduction to the Humanities. The institutions also developed a six-week summer program for small groups of minority students, who study at the Bucknell campus with courses taught by the college and the university faculty (Terzian, 1991). LaGuardia Community College and Vassar have had a similar Ford Foundation-sponsored program (Lieberman, 1991).

Educators concerned with articulation also consider reverse transfers, the students who transfer from universities to two-year colleges. Vaala (1991) noted that one out of five students enrolled in an Alberta community college had previously been enrolled in a four-year institution. Kajstura and Keim (1992) found that the reverse transfers in an Illinois community college left university for financial reasons, academic difficulty, or career changes; 29 percent of the reverse transfers already had the baccalaureate.

Problems of articulation between community colleges and secondary schools have never been as difficult as between community colleges and universities. Nonetheless, as the pool of high school graduates shrank in the 1980s, the community colleges worked to smooth the flow. Sacramento City College (California) issued a report pointing out how community colleges could develop or expand articulation programs with local high schools (Carey, Wark, and Wellsfry, 1986). Various computer-assisted guidance models have been developed so that secondary school counselors can direct students to proper community college programs (Lockett, 1981).

Funding and Effectiveness

Student services to various groups of nontraditional students have expanded. Child care services have become widespread, and offices have been opened to assist students with various types of disabilities. Job placement services, always a feature in community colleges, have grown as the proportion of students seeking immediate job entry has increased. Student services also have been extended to accommodate an increase in entrance testing.

Funds to support these augmented services have been derived from a variety of sources. In some cases special state funds have been made available. In others Vocational Education Act funds, Title III monies, Educational Opportunities Programs and Services funds, and various state and federal programs supporting students with disabilities and those in other special categories have been used. Thus, although the student affairs division might be organized on a line-and-staff basis, the subordinate offices might expand or contract with the availability of funds to support them. For the first time in the history of the community college, the 1980s saw a trend toward funding student services on soft money—that is, extracurricular funds targeted to assist certain types of students.

The effectiveness of student services has been a perennial issue. Typically, evaluation depends on reports from students about how well they perceive the usefulness of one or another aspect of student services. Students at Thomas Nelson Community College (Virginia) indicated that student activities programs were not very good (McLean, 1986). Students at Howard Community College (Maryland) gave high marks to all services except student activities and transfer evaluations (Nespoli and Radcliffe, 1982). Students usually rate job placement services as not very useful.

Evaluation of student services is typically not well conceived. The evaluators often try to assess everything in the student services purview: orientation, counseling, financial aids, student activities, testing—all different forms of service, all different purposes and conceptual bases. Asking the students "How well did each of these services meet your expectations?" is not useful. Most students were never touched by most of the services; for example, studies often find that half the dropouts never saw a counselor.

However, there have been recent efforts at more sophisticated evaluations, particularly attempts to determine how student retention and achievement are affected. The evaluations are made in terms of each service or cluster of services separately. Moorpark College (California) surveyed first-time students who had participated in an orientation program, and those who had not. Students who enrolled had higher retention rates, used services offered to them more frequently, and were more likely to complete assessment and placement tests (Alfano, 1990). Queensborough Community College (New York) found that students who participated in their summer orientation program were only half as likely to drop out of school and were more likely to make better grades (Miller, 1988). Both full-time and part-time students who completed the orientation course at Irvine Valley College (California) had higher retention rates than those students who did not complete the course (Rudmann, 1992). Preregistration counseling and orientation sessions have also been effective in enhancing performance and increasing retention (Alfano, 1990; Spicer, 1990; Rudmann, 1992).

Issues

As a whole, the colleges' services to students have grown faster than the instructional activities, but the various services have shown different patterns. Counseling and guidance declined early in the 1970s in response to students' demands to be admitted to courses of their choice and to the increase in part-time students, but these services increased in the 1980s as tight budgets and competition from other schools forced community colleges into streamlining their procedures for guiding students through the system. Recruitment and retention also became prominent concerns of the student personnel staff, who gradually adopted concepts other than those set down by theorists whose model was the full-time resident student. Articulation has become more important as coordination of all education in each state has developed.

However, not all student services have expanded. Student activities supporters have not been able to convert their programs to fit commuting students, and much of what they formerly did has been adopted by community service directors, a trend in keeping with the expansion of the colleges from campus to community.

The challenge for college leaders has been to maintain a balance among all services and coordinate them with the formal instructional program. But issues of educational philosophy swirl around the questions of student personnel work. How much responsibility does the college have for the lives of its students? How personalized can an institution dedicated to mass education afford to get?

Although between-sector comparisons are precarious because of differences in institutional mission, the question of whether community college students receive as much financial aid as their university counterparts has not been resolved.

Program articulation with the secondary schools will have to be expanded. Can the articulation committee members eventually realize that fitting the college's courses to the senior institution's requirements is not the most important, and certainly not the only, job they must do?

The concepts underlying student activities stem from an era long past. How can programs be restructured to fit the adult, part-time, nonresident student body that predominates in community colleges?

Answers to these questions will determine the future course of student services in the community colleges. As with all other questions about the types of services that community colleges provide, the answers rest on the energy and political skills of the advocates of one or another activity. And that, above all, is why the services vary as much as they do in colleges across the country.

8

Career Education

Occupational Entry, Change, and Development

A group of prominent citizens called together by the American Association of Junior Colleges (AAJC) in 1964 to serve as a National Advisory Committee on the Junior College concluded that "the two-year college offers unparalleled promise for expanding educational opportunity through the provision of comprehensive programs embracing job training as well as traditional liberal arts and general education" (American Association of Junior Colleges, 1964, p. 14). The committee recommended that "immediate steps be taken to reinforce occupational education efforts" (p. 1), a statement similar to those emanating from many other commissions and advisory groups, including the AAJC's own Commission on Terminal Education a quarter century earlier. Its words were notable only because they came at a time when the floodgates had just opened and a tide of career education programs was beginning to inundate the two-year colleges.

The year 1963 marked the passage of the federal Vocational Education Act, which broadened the criteria for federal aid to the schools. Along with the new criteria, Congress appropriated funds generously—$43 million in 1968, $707 million in 1972, and $981 million in 1974—and these funds were augmented with additional monies for occupational programs for the disadvantaged and for students with disabilities. On this surge of monies, occupational education swept into the colleges in a fashion dreamed of and pleaded for but never previously realized by its advocates.

In this chapter we consider various aspects of career education, including the growth, successes, and limitations of courses and programs designed to lead to initial job entry with no further schooling or to modify the skills of people who have already been employed. Also covered are the broader implications of career education: is it a deterrent to baccalaureate seekers? How can its social benefits and individual benefits be disaggregated? How successful are students in obtaining employment in the fields for which they have been prepared?

Early Development

One of the criteria for professionalization is the number of years of schooling that a group can require before allowing neophytes to enter their rank. A major impetus to the expansion of higher education early in the century was the drive toward professional status made by numerous occupational groups. And as these professions developed, a set of auxiliary or support occupations, sometimes called semiprofessional, developed around them. Professional training moved into the university, but the training of the auxiliaries remained outside. The community colleges grew in part because some of their earlier proponents recognized the coming need for semiprofessionals and despaired of the universities' adjusting rapidly enough to provide this less-than-baccalaureate education.

Calls for occupational education in the two-year colleges had been made from their earliest days. In 1900, William Rainey Harper, president of the University of Chicago, suggested that "many students who might not have the courage to enter upon a course of four years' study would be willing to do the two years of work before entering business or the professional school" (cited in Brick, 1965, p. 18). The founders of the junior colleges in California postulated that one purpose of their institutions was to provide terminal programs in agriculture, technical studies, manual training, and the domestic arts. Alexis Lange indicated that the junior colleges would train the technicians occupying the middle ground between manual laborers and professional people, and Koos (1924) described and applauded the occupational curricula in the junior colleges of the early 1920s.

Arguments on behalf of occupational education were raised at the earliest gatherings of the American Association of Junior Colleges. At its organizational meeting in 1920 and at nearly every meeting throughout the 1920s and 1930s, occupational education was on the agenda. Brick traced these discussions and noted that "the AAJC was aware that it had to take a leadership role in directing the movement for terminal education" (1965, p. 120). He quoted C. C. Colvert, president of the association, who, in a 1941 address, had admonished junior college educators for not encouraging the national government to fund occupational education for people of junior college age: "Had not we of the junior college been so busy trying to offer courses which would get our graduates into the senior colleges instead of working and offering appropriate and practical courses—terminal courses—for the vast majority of junior college students, we might have thought to ask for, and as a result of having asked, received the privilege of training these young people" (cited in Brick, 1965, p. 121).

The thesis of Brint and Karabel's book *The Diverted Dream* (1989) is that the AAJC was the prime force in effecting a change in community college emphasis from prebaccalaureate to terminal-occupational education. The extent to which local school boards and college leaders were attentive to the national association is debatable, but there is no doubt that AAJC had been diligent. In 1939 it created a Commission on Junior College Terminal Education, which proceeded to study terminal (primarily occupational) education, hold workshops and conferences on its behalf, and issue three books summarizing junior college efforts in its area of interest. Much had been done, but, as the commission noted, more remained to do: "At the present time probably about one-third of all the curricular offerings in the junior colleges of the country are in the non-academic or terminal fields. Doubtless this situation is far short of the ideal, but it shows a steady and healthy growth in the right direction" (Eells, 1941a, pp. 22–23).

In 1940, terminal programs were offered in about 70 percent of the colleges. The most popular were business and secretarial studies, music, teaching, general courses, and home economics. About one-third of the terminal students were in business studies; enrollments in agriculture and home economics were quite low. Tables 8.1 and 8.2 present data on the numbers of colleges and programs.

Definitions

The terminology of career education has never been exact: the words *terminal, vocational, technical, semiprofessional, occupational,* and *career* have all been used interchangeably or in combination, as in *vocational-technical*. To the commission and the colleges of 1940, *terminal* meant all studies not applicable to the baccalaureate, but programs designed to lead to employment dominated the category. Earlier, *vocational* had generally been used for curricula preparing people for work in agriculture, the trades, and sales. But because it usually connoted less-than-college-level studies, most community college educators eschewed the term. *Semiprofessional* typically referred to engineering technicians, general assistants, laboratory technicians, and other people in manufacturing, business, and service occupations. *Technical* implied preparation for work in scientific and industrial fields. *Occupational* seemed to encompass the greatest number of programs and was used most often for all curricula leading to employment. *Career* education was coined in the 1950s to connote lower-school efforts at orienting young people toward the workplace. The title was applied to several programs sponsored by the U.S. Office of Education after Sidney Marland

Table 8.1. Percentage of Total Curricular Offerings Classified as Terminal or Vocational in Junior Colleges, 1917–1937.

Investigator	All Junior Colleges		Public Junior Colleges		Private Junior Colleges	
	Number of Colleges	% of Offerings Terminal	Number of Colleges	% of Offerings Terminal	Number of Colleges	% of Offerings Terminal
McDowell (1917)	47	14	19	18	28	9
Koos (1921)	58	29	23	31	35	25
Hollingsworth-Eells (1930)	279	32	129	33	150	29
Colvert (1937)	—	—	195	35	—	—

Source: Eells, 1941a, p. 22.

Table 8.2. Number of Students Enrolled in Each Terminal Field, 1938–39.

Group	Number Enrolled in All Terminal Curricula	Gen. Cultural	Agriculture	Business	Engineering	Fine Arts	Health Services	Home Economics	Journalism	Public Service	Misc.
All institutions	41,507	6,205	1,673	14,511	4,449	3,406	1,603	1,387	808	6,500	965
Public	30,261	4,724	1,631	11,278	3,915	2,341	1,029	876	673	3,033	761
Private	11,246	1,481	42	3,233	534	1,065	574	511	135	3,467	204

Source: Eells, 1941a, p. 239.

became commissioner in 1970; it has survived because it is suffi-ciently broad to encompass all the other terms.

Although the college-parallel (collegiate) function was domi-nant in community colleges until the late 1960s, the structure for career education had been present from the start. The community college authorization acts in most states had tended to recognize both. The California District Law of 1921 allowed junior colleges to provide college preparatory instruction; training for agricultural, industrial, commercial, homemaking, and other vocations; and civic and liberal education. The comparable 1937 Colorado act defined a junior college as an institution providing studies beyond the twelfth grade along with vocational education. Mississippi required that the junior college curriculum include agriculture, home eco-nomics, commerce, and mechanical arts. By 1940 nearly half of the states' junior college laws specifically set forth the terminal func-tions along with the college-parallel studies. The national and regional accrediting associations of the time also wrote that provi-sion into their rules.

However, student enrollments did not reach parity. Well into the 1950s, occupational program enrollments accounted for only one-fourth or less of the whole. In 1929, 20 percent of the students in California and 23 percent in Texas were in terminal programs (Eells, 1941a, p. 24), and not all of those were in occupational stud-ies; the figures include high school postgraduate courses for "civic responsibility." Eells reported 35 percent in terminal curricula in 1938, but when nonvocational terminal curricula were excluded, the percentage dropped to less than 25, a figure that held constant until 1960. Although 75 percent of students entering junior college as freshmen did not continue beyond the sophomore year and hence were terminal students by definition, only about one-third of them were enrolled in terminal curricula. "The difference of these two figures shows that *more than 40 per cent of all junior college stu-dents are enrolled in curricula which are not planned primarily to best meet their needs*" (Eells, 1941a, p. 59).

Limitations

Why did the career programs fail to flourish before the 1960s? First, their terminal nature was emphasized, and that tended to turn potential students away; few wanted to foreclose their option for further studies. For most students, going to college meant striving for the baccalaureate, the "legitimate" degree. That concept of collegiate education had been firmly established.

Another impediment to the growth of career programs was the small size of the colleges. Average enrollment remained below 1,000 until 1946. Colleges with low enrollments could not offer many occupational courses; the costs were too high. Eells (1941a) reported a direct relation between size and occupational enrollments. Small colleges (up to 99 students) had 10 percent in terminal curricula; medium colleges (100–499 students), 32 percent; large colleges (500–999), 34 percent; and very large colleges (1,000 and over), 38 percent.

A third reason for limited terminal offerings was the association of many early junior colleges with high schools. In these colleges, administrators favored collegiate courses because they were more attractive to high school students than vocational courses, they entailed no new facilities or equipment, they could be combined with fourth-year high school courses in order to bolster enrollments, and they would not require the hiring of new teachers.

The prestige factor was important. Most of the new junior colleges were opened in cities and towns where no college had existed before. Citizens and educators alike wanted theirs to be a "real college." If it could not itself offer the bachelor's degree, it could at least provide the first two years of study leading toward one. In the eyes of the public, a college was not a manual-training shop. Well into the 1960s, college presidents reported with pride the percentage of their faculty holding doctoral degrees.

Costs were an important factor. Many career programs used expensive, special facilities: clinics, machine tools, automotive repair shops, welding equipment. By comparison, collegiate studies were cheap. The transfer courses had always been taught in interchangeable classrooms. The same chairs and chalkboards, and often the same teachers, can be used for English, history, or mathematics.

And last, the secondary schools of the 1920s and 1930s provided education in shop trades, agriculture, secretarial skills, bookkeeping, and salesmanship. Career education in community colleges could not grow until employers in these fields began demanding some postsecondary experience and until the health, engineering, and electronic technologies gained prominence.

For all these reasons, and despite the efforts of Eells and his commission and subsequent AAJC activities, college leaders did not rally around the calls for terminal occupational studies. In some states—Mississippi, for example, where occupational education was a requisite, and California, where the institutions were large enough to mount comprehensive programs in both occupational and collegiate studies—occupational education did well. But in the smaller institutions in states where the popularizing function, that of promoting higher education, was dominant, sizable career programs were not developed.

Calls for change continued. In 1944, the Educational Policies Commission of the National Education Association published *Education for All American Youth,* a report that stressed the desirability of one or two years of occupational education. In 1947, the President's Commission on Higher Education recommended an increase in the number of community colleges, so that students who might not benefit from a full four-year course of studies could attain an education enabling them to take their place in the American work force. The commission recommended the expansion of terminal programs for civic and social responsibility and occupational programs that would prepare skilled, semiprofessional, and technical workers.

The AAJC-affiliated advocates of occupational education pressed unrelentingly for more vocational curricula and courses and for greater efforts to encourage students to enroll in them. For example, in the chapter "Development of the Junior College Movement" in the second edition of *American Junior Colleges,* Ward devoted twelve lines to the college transfer function but more than a page and a half to the status of technical education. She observed that despite the growing interest in and "the overwhelming need for terminal education . . . the development of these courses generally has been very slow" (1948, p. 15). In fact, she felt it safe to generalize "that effective terminal courses have never been offered in sufficient numbers to meet the need for them—that is, terminal courses which provide education both for an occupation and for personal adequacy" (p. 14). Jesse Bogue, executive secretary of the AAJC, urged the colleges to "strike out boldly, demonstrate that they are not bound by tradition or the desire to ape senior colleges for the sake of a totally false notion of academic respectability." He warned educators that, unless they acted, legislatures would follow Texas's example of setting a minimum of "40 percent of programs . . . in so-called terminal fields [to] qualify for state aid" (1950, p. 313).

Growth

Career education enrollments began growing at a rate greater than liberal arts enrollments in the 1960s and continued to do so for twenty years. This rise is attributable to many causes: the legacy left by early leaders of the junior college movement and the importunities, goadings, and sometimes barbs of later leaders; the Vocational Education Act of 1963 and later amendments; the increase in the size of public two-year colleges; the increase in students with disabilities and part-time, women, disadvantaged, and older students; the community colleges' absorption of adult education programs and postsecondary occupational programs formerly operated by the secondary schools; and the changing shape of the labor market.

The Vocational Education Act was not the first to run federal funds to two-year colleges. The 1939 Commission on Junior College

Terminal Education noted that at least sixty-two junior colleges in fourteen states were receiving federal funds that had been appropriated under the 1917 Smith-Hughes Act and the 1937 George-Deen Act. The federal monies were earmarked for institutions where education was less than college grade: "It does not mean that the *institution* must be of less than college grade—only that the particular *work offered*, for which federal aid is received, must be of less than college grade" (Eells, 1941a, p. 29). The U.S. Office of Education called programs of trade and industrial education less than college grade if college entrance requirements were not prerequisites for admission, the objective was to prepare for employment in industry, the program did not lead to a degree, the program was not required to conform to conditions governing a regular college course, and the instructors qualified under state plans. According to Dougherty (1988), as early as 1937 the AAJC was lobbying for the repeal of the provision restricting support to programs of less than college grade.

The 1963 Vocational Education Act and the amendments of 1968 and 1972 vastly augmented the federal funds available to community colleges. The Carl D. Perkins Vocational Education Act of 1984 modified the guidelines further, primarily to determine state responsibilities for administering the funds and to expand the programs directed to students with disabilities and disadvantaged students. By 1985, the community colleges were receiving around 22 percent of the $791 million allotted under Perkins. In 1993, basic grants to states from Perkins funds reached $973 million. Funding for Tech-Prep education, created as part of the Perkins Act, accounted for $104 million. Other federal programs provided additional funds that the community colleges shared: Job Training Partnership; Job Opportunities and Basic Skills; Omnibus Trade and Competitiveness; Worksite Literacy; Cooperative Education. And for every federal dollar appropriated, state governments and local districts provided five to ten more.

These augmented funds came initially at a time when the colleges were increasing in size, a condition conducive to the growth of occupational programs. Between 1960 and 1965 the number of public two-year institutions increased from 405 to 503, but enrollments doubled. By 1969 there were 794 colleges, with enrollments averaging over 2,000; in the 1980s the average was over 2,500; in the 1990s it was over 5500.

As enrollments increased, so did occupational programs. In Illinois, where many of the new districts were formed on the promise to the electorate of having more than 50 percent of the programs in career education, 1,871 curricula, or 66 percent of all curricula, were occupational (Illinois Community College Board, 1976). In Florida associate degree and certificate occupational programs exceeded 200. The small Hawaii system offered 80 different programs.

Although many individual colleges offered 100 or more different occupational programs, those that led to the greatest variety of career options were the most popular. Programs in business drew the most students because of the breadth of options they presented. The health professions and the engineering technologies drew large numbers of students because of the expanding base of the professions in those areas and the ever-growing need for support staff. Computer science became popular in the 1980s because of the rapidly expanding applications of computers in all career fields. Other programs ebbed and flowed depending on job markets.

The growth in students with disabilities and part-time, women, disadvantaged, and older students also reflected the rise in occupational enrollments. Bushnell (1973) pointed out that although 40 percent of all students enrolled in career programs, only 25 percent of full-time students did so. The proportion of women who chose career programs was 35 percent, while among men it was only 17 percent. Disadvantaged students and students with disabilities were encouraged to enroll in occupational programs through special grants. Reports of numerous such programs are in the Educational Resources Information Center (ERIC) files. For example, Queensborough Community College's (New York) College Science and Technology Program has assisted disadvantaged students (nearly all of whom required remediation) in obtaining Associate in Applied Science degrees (Chapel, 1992). Napa Valley College (California) has had a similar program for vocational nursing students (Zylinski and Metson, 1992). California's Greater Avenues for Independence program has provided around $40 million per year from state and local funds to support community colleges' efforts to help welfare recipients enter the work force (Eissa, 1994).

Some of the enrollment increases resulted from the upgrading of institutions and the transfer to the community colleges of functions formerly performed by other segments of education: secondary and adult schools, technical institutes, and area vocational schools or centers. This trend was most marked in Florida, where fourteen of the twenty-eight community colleges had a department designated as an area vocational education school, and others had cooperative agreements with school boards that operate area vocational-technical centers; in Iowa, where all the public community colleges were merged with area schools; in Nebraska, where the state was divided into technical community college areas; and in North Carolina, where the technical institutes were part of the community college system (Lombardi, 1975). In some states, community colleges expanded their occupational offerings with and without formal agreements with other institutions. Nearly all the publicly supported occupational education in Long Beach, San Diego, and San Francisco was offered by the community college districts. Similarly, in Chicago the adult and vocational education programs were transferred from the city schools to the community college system.

The combination of these forces counteracted to a considerable degree those forces that caused students and their parents to value the baccalaureate over the occupational programs. In its statewide master plan for 1978 to 1987, the Maryland State Board for Community Colleges reported that the "increasing emphasis on occupational programs reflects changing values and attitudes among students and their families as to the level of education required to qualify for desirable employment opportunities. This shift is reflected in national projections predicting that throughout the next decade, 80 percent of available jobs will require less than the bachelor's degree" (1977, p. 34). U.S. Department of Labor data listed as the main areas of job openings in the 1980s retail salesclerks, cashiers, stock handlers, and similar jobs for which a bachelor's degree is not required; "Managers and Administrators" was the only job category in the top fifteen to suggest baccalaureate training (Kuttner, 1983, p. 209).

Stability

The growth in occupational enrollments that began in the second half of the 1960s is revealed in the enrollment figures shown in Table 8.3. Obviously, this percentage increase could not continue indefinitely, and it began leveling off in the 1980s. The 1991 CSCC survey found that 43 percent of the class sections offered nation-wide were in career curricula, with nearly three-fourths of the classes in business and office, trade and industry, technical, and health fields. Enrollment in career programs in Illinois stabilized at 34 percent of the head count in 1983 and was 38 percent ten years later; Florida's stayed in the mid twenties, Washington's in the low forties. By 1992, the ratio of occupational-curricula degrees to all degrees awarded had fallen back to the 1979 figure of just over 60 percent (see Table 8.5).

Because of frequent changes in ways of classifying programs and enrollments, it is perilous to compare data between states or even within the same state in successive years. For that reason the national data shown in Table 8.3 cannot reasonably be updated beyond 1975. However, data available from several states that provide reasonably consistent program enrollment figures can be illustrative (Table 8.4). The wide variation among states results partly because of varying community college missions and partly because enrollment data are not reported uniformly between states: the unit

Table 8.3. Enrollments in Terminal-Occupational Programs in Two-Year Colleges as a Percentage of Total Enrollments, 1963–1975.

Year	Total Enrollments	Terminal-Occupational Program Enrollments	Percentage of Total
1963	847,572	219,766	26
1965	1,176,852	331,608	28
1969	1,981,150	448,229	23
1970	2,227,214	593,226	27
1971	2,491,420	760,590	31
1972	2,670,934	873,933	33
1973	3,033,761	1,020,183	34
1974	3,428,642	1,134,896	33
1975	4,001,970	1,389,516	35

Source: National Center for Education Statistics, 1963–1975.

of measurement—head count, or FTSE—varies, and some reports indicate opening fall enrollments while others report fiscal year enrollments. The data have been unstable also because the higher funding patterns for vocational education encouraged colleges to classify as vocational many programs that had been classified previously as general education or liberal arts. In order to show high enrollment in career programs, educators also may have classified as occupational students those who took one occupational course, even though they were actually majoring in a liberal arts transfer program.

Regardless of data reliability, there is little question of the general popularity of career education. A national study done in response to Perkins legislation reported that 43 percent of the total community college student population and more than half of the disadvantaged and disabled students were enrolled in vocational-education programs. Ninety-three percent of the colleges were providing such programs, and of those, 80 percent were receiving funds appropriated under the Perkins act. The colleges were averaging 27 vocational programs each, with federal funds accounting for 18 percent of the cost. Other support was coming from the

Table 8.4. Enrollments in Community College Career Programs as a
Percentage of Total Enrollment in Selected States.

State	Year	Percent
Florida	1991	28
Hawaii	1992	34
Illinois	1993	38
Kentucky	1990	48
Michigan	1990	41
North Carolina	1993	73
Washington	1992	40

Sources: Florida State Board of Community Colleges, 1992; Hawaii State
Board for Vocational Education, 1993; Illinois Community College Board, 1994;
University of Kentucky Community College System (Tudor, 1992); Michigan
State Department of Education, 1991; North Carolina State Department of Com-
munity Colleges, 1993a; Washington State Board for Community and Technical
Colleges, 1993.

states (47 percent), tuition (19 percent), and local funds (15 percent) (*Vocational Education*, 1993).

Although only a minority of community college matriculants
complete programs, the figures on associate degrees awarded provide a measure of career education's popularity. Tables 8.5 and 8.6
show the percentage of career-related degrees and the fields in
which awards were made.

Much of the growth in the 1980s was related to the process of
certification. A student wishing to enter a career as a health service
worker or a laboratory technician often must present the degree,
whereas for the student wishing to transfer credits to the university,
the associate in arts degree is superfluous; the student need only
show a transcript of courses completed.

In summation, linking data from state reports with national data
on degrees awarded and on program and course enrollments yields
a figure of 40–45 percent for the community colleges' overall
degree-credit effort in areas designed for direct employment. This
ratio has been steady since the mid 1970s, declining slightly as more

Table 8.5. Associate Degrees Conferred by Institutions of Higher Education by Type of Curriculum, 1970–71 to 1991–92.

Year	All Curricula	Arts & Sciences or General Programs	Percentage of Total	Occupational Curricula	Percentage of Total
1970–71	253,635	145,473	57	108,162	43
1973–74	347,173	165,520	48	181,653	52
1976–77	409,942	172,631	42	237,311	58
1979–80	405,378	152,169	38	253,209	63
1982–83	456,441	133,917	29	322,524	71
1983–84	452,416	128,766	29	323,650	72
1984–85	454,712	127,387	28	327,325	72
1991–92	504,321	195,238	39	309,083	61

Sources: Stern and Chandler, 1987, p. 102; National Center for Education Statistics, 1994h, p. 21.

occupational education moves into noncredit offerings and into prebaccalaureate programs in health, high-tech, and law enforcement, increasing slightly when additional funds become available such as those provided through federal programs for special purposes or special populations.

Program Success

Career programs are established with the intention of serving students by preparing them for employment and serving industries by supplying them with trained workers. The college staff presumably initiate programs by perusing employment trends in the local area and by surveying employers there. Program coordinators are appointed and advisory committees composed of trade and employer representatives established. Funds are often secured through priorities set down by state and federal agencies. The entire process suggests rational program planning. Nonetheless, questions have been raised about the appropriateness of certain programs and whether the matriculants are well served, and much research on program effects has been conducted.

Table 8.6. Main Fields in Which Associate Degrees Were Conferred, 1992–93.

Main Fields	Associate Degrees	Percentage of Total
Liberal arts, general studies, and humanities	154,594	31
Business management and administration	93,762	19
Health professions	79,453	16
Engineering and related technologies	35,861	7
Protective services	15,117	3
Visual and performing arts	11,888	2
Education	10,267	2
Mechanics and repairers	10,264	2
Computer and information science	9,290	2
Marketing	8,465	2

Source: National Center for Education Statistics, 1995b.

Most students in occupational programs seem satisfied with the training they receive. Follow-up studies routinely find 80–90 percent of the program graduates saying that they were helped and that they would recommend the program to others. Among the students who do not complete the program, a sizable number usually indicate that they dropped out because they received the training they needed in the courses they took, not because they were dissatisfied with the program.

Students have been less sanguine about the help they received in obtaining jobs. Graduates of a Maryland college listed the weakness of college job placement services as a problem area (Gell and Armstrong, 1977), and similar comments were received in surveys of students in a Pennsylvania community college (Selgas, 1977). Career program graduates from North Carolina's community colleges rated job placement services poorest among all the services provided by the institutions (Hammond and Porter, 1984). Such assistance seemed to be given through the occupational programs themselves rather than through a collegewide job placement service.

Career students' relative success in finding and maintaining jobs in the areas for which they were trained has always been a controversial topic. Depending on the data obtained and the criteria for defining success, different researchers reach different conclusions. Noeth and Hanson (1976) studied a sample of 4,350 students who had been surveyed at 110 community colleges and technical schools in 1970. Half of the graduates and dropouts from the business and marketing programs held business contact jobs (for example, meeting customers and selling products), and a large number held business detail jobs (office work). All who had completed the registered nursing programs were working in nursing, students from accounting programs held business detail jobs and business contact jobs, and so on through the programs, with those from the technology programs holding technology jobs and those from the auto mechanics programs holding trades jobs.

Several statewide data sets are available. Students who graduated from forty career programs in Florida in 1983–84 obtained employment in their major field in varying rates. Those in the health fields, who comprised nearly half of the graduates, tended to be employed at rates of 85 percent or greater, whereas some of the other fields, such as office work and real estate, showed only around 50 percent employment (Baldwin, 1986). Of the 998 graduates from the New Hampshire Technical Institute and Vocational-Technical Colleges in 1987, 81 percent were employed—96 percent of them in their college major or a related field (New Hampshire State Department of Postsecondary Vocational-Technical Education, 1988). Seventy-one percent of the career program graduates in the North Carolina community colleges were working in the field for which they had been prepared (Hammond and Porter, 1984). A follow-up survey of graduates of the Wisconsin system found 93 percent employed after three years, 78 percent in a field related to their training (Wisconsin State Board of Vocational, Technical, and Adult Education, 1985). Fifty-eight percent of Maryland's career program graduates were employed full-time in their area of training (Maryland State Board for Community Colleges, 1987). The Illinois Community College Boards' follow-up study of graduates of selected occupational programs in forty-nine colleges found 94 percent employed, continuing their education, or both, with 89 percent working in positions related to their community college studies (Illinois Community College Board, 1994).

Single-college studies show similar findings. Follow-up studies of graduates of career programs at William Rainey Harper College (Illinois), conducted between 1988 and 1992, found 83–87 percent of them working, 64–70 percent in fields related to their major (Lucas, 1988; Lucas and Meltesen, 1992). Of the 850 students who received Associate in Science degrees at Miami-Dade Community College in 1991–92, 67 percent were employed in related fields and 26 percent were continuing their education (Baldwin, 1993). Seventy percent of the graduates of the career programs in Los Rios Community College District (California) were working in a job related to their curriculum (Lee, 1984); over 80 percent were doing so from Johnson County Community College in Kansas (Johnson County Community College, 1994). The programs were obviously keyed to the employment fields.

Still, the data on program success must be interpreted in light of the programs' features and the students enrolled. The number of students who are already employed and enter career programs only to get additional skills must be factored in, just as the students who obtain job certification but find no jobs available to them must be considered. Students who leave programs before graduation and enter employment in the field for which they are prepared must be considered as program successes. Students who graduate but do not obtain employment because they have entered related baccalaureate programs should not be counted among the unemployed. And it is misleading to categorize career programs as a unitary group, because there are high- and low-status programs. Also, there are programs preparing people for areas of high demand, such as health care and electronics technology, and programs in areas for which the market is not as distinct, such as real estate or data processing. Much depends also on the time that has elapsed since the students were enrolled; the ordinary drift of careers suggests that fewer students will be employed in jobs related to their program several years after they have left college.

Some critics of career education are concerned that the programs do little in equalizing status and salaries among types of jobs. They view with alarm the high dropout rates without realizing that *program completion is an institutional artifact*. Even though the AACJC mounted an "Associate Degree Preferred" campaign in the mid 1980s, urging employers to give preference to graduates, the degree is not as important as the skills that the applicant manifests. To the student who seeks a job in the field, completing the program becomes irrelevant as soon as a job is available. The categories "graduate" and "dropout" lose much of their force when viewed in this light. This phenomenon is not peculiar to community colleges: generations of young women participated in teacher-training programs in universities even though few of them expected to teach more than a few years and fewer than half entered teaching at all. If one merely surveys the career program graduates who are working in that area or places graduates in one category and dropouts in another, the true services rendered by those programs may be lost.

Few critics of career education acknowledge that questions about its value are much more complex than simplistic data on job entry and first salary earned can answer. What is the value of an occupational education program when an enrollee hears about an available job, obtains it, and leaves after two weeks? In that case the program has served as an employment agency of sorts. What is the value of a program in which a person who already has a job spends a few weeks learning some new skills and then receives a better job in the same company? There the program has served as a step on a career ladder. What of the person who enrolls to sharpen skills and gain confidence to apply for a job doing essentially the same work but for a different company? And what of the students who enter occupational programs but then transfer from them to other programs in the same or a different college?

A curriculum is a conduit through which people move in order to prepare themselves to do or be something other than what was the case when they began. Yet for some people the curriculum has served an essential purpose if it but allows them to matriculate and be put in touch with those who know where jobs may be obtained. At the other extreme are the students who go all the way through the curriculum and learn the skills, but either fail to obtain jobs in the field for which they were trained or, having attained them, find them unsatisfying. For them the institution has been a failure. The critics cannot seem to accommodate the fact that for many dropouts the program has succeeded, while for many of its graduates it has failed.

Success may be measured in many ways. A few studies of both graduates and nongraduates of career programs have shown that, although most enrolled to obtain job entry skills, many sought advancement in jobs they already held. Around two-thirds of the respondents to a survey of career students in a Kansas community college gave "job entry skill" as their reason (Quanty, 1977; Tatham, 1978), but around one-third had enrolled primarily for advancement. A somewhat smaller percentage of students enrolled in career programs in California community colleges (34 percent) reported that they sought to prepare for jobs; 11 percent of that group had enrolled to improve skills for their present job (Hunter and Sheldon, 1980). Nearly half of the students in the CSCC's 1986 national survey had occupational intent, and those seeking job entry skills outnumbered those seeking to upgrade themselves in a job they already had by only two to one. Such data often fall between the planks when program follow-up studies or comparative wage studies are made.

Another important finding in studies of graduates and current enrollees in career programs is the sizable number who plan to transfer to four-year colleges and who do eventually transfer. Few institutions or state systems collect these data routinely, but where they are available, the relationship between career programs and further education is well established. In a California statewide study, 25 percent of students enrolled in career curricula said that they intended to transfer (Hunter and Sheldon, 1980), and national data compiled by the CSCC in 1986 yielded a similar figure (Palmer, 1987b, p. 134). Regardless of their intentions when they enrolled, 40 percent of the Los Rios Community College District (California) career program graduates transferred (Lee, 1984); the figures are 36 percent of the William Rainey Harper College (Illinois) career alumni (Lucas, 1988), 11 percent of the graduates of the technical institute and the six vocational-technical colleges in New Hampshire (New Hampshire State Department of Postsecondary Vocational-Technical Education, 1988), 14 percent of the career program graduates in Illinois (Illinois Community College Board, 1987), and 27 percent of the career program graduates in Maryland (Maryland State Board for Community Colleges, 1988). Many of the graduates were employed in their field of study and pursuing further education simultaneously.

Can students from career programs receive course credit when they transfer to baccalaureate-granting institutions? A national study by the CSCC accounted for the percentage of courses in the non-liberal arts that transferred to both research universities and comprehensive colleges and universities. Considerable variation was shown, both in the types of courses that transfer, and among types of universities, with the flagship institutions accepting fewer courses than the four-year colleges that had high numbers of career-related programs of their own; as an example, Illinois State University and the California State University system would give credit for more than 60 percent of the occupational courses whereas the University of Illinois and the University of California accepted only around 20 percent of them. But the overall transferability of the non-liberal arts suggested that, "Except for trade and industry courses, the concept of 'terminal education' should be laid to rest" (Cohen and Ignash, 1994, p. 29).

The Broader Implications

Career education has other implications: to what degree *should* the schools be in the business of providing trained workers for the nation's industries? None, say the academic purists; totally, say many community college leaders. A lengthy list of commentators and educational philosophers would argue that the preparation of people specifically to work in certain industries is not the school's purpose because the school should have broader social aims and because the industries can do the particular job training much more efficiently. And those who take this approach are not necessarily those who plead for a return to an era when higher education was for providing gentlemen with distinctive sets of manners.

The pattern of work-force training in other industrialized nations offers a few insights. Some countries depend on postsecondary institutions to carry the main burden, some on schools in the compulsory sector, and others on adult education that is provided by other than formal educational institutions. For example, postsecondary vocational education in Canada is centered in the community colleges; in France it is in the high schools and apprentice training centers; Germany has a dual system with students pursuing vocational education through the upper secondary schools and in on-the-job training; Italy depends on technical schools and non-school-based vocational programs; Japan has special training schools at the postcompulsory level; and the United Kingdom provides vocational training through institutions of further education and through apprenticeships. The greatest proportions of students in vocational programs in formal postsecondary structures are in Japan, Germany, France, and Italy (National Center for Education Statistics, 1994m).

Is career education primarily an individual or a social benefit? Individuals gain skills that make them more employable and at higher rates of pay; society gains skilled workers for the nation's businesses and technologies. Solmon (1976) argues that community colleges can and should work closely with employers to facilitate students' passage through to the labor market. To the extent that they do, everyone benefits: students, their families, the colleges, business, and the general public. Solmon contends that the costs must be maintained by all. Students forgo earnings while they are in school for the gain of ultimate entry into the labor force with greater skills. Although employers must provide expensive apprenticeships, they can benefit by using cooperative programs to identify students whom they would like to retain. The colleges lose some control over their students when business firms decide whom to involve in cooperative programs, and when those programs become more susceptible to external evaluation. However, they gain by doing a better, more direct job for students and by keeping them enrolled longer.

Nevertheless, other writers in education, and certainly the majority of those who comment on the role of the community colleges, suggest that education is an essential expenditure for economic growth and is not merely a nonproductive sector of the economy, a form of consumption. To the extent that the schools are viewed as investments of this type, educators can make a more effective claim on national budgets. To justify this claim, the schools must be brought in line with the goals of society; if they are to foster economic growth, they must provide trained workers, and the more they provide trained workers, the more they will be looked upon to fit those trainees to the jobs that are available. Hence, they can be criticized to the extent that their graduates do not obtain jobs or are not able to function effectively in the jobs they get. Thus the term *overeducated* can be used to describe those who are prepared for nonexistent jobs or who have jobs to which they do not apply the type of education they received.

Should the colleges get paid on some pro rata basis only when the trainees have been employed? The proponents of payment only for training that results in jobs argue that it would free the public school sector to provide education in the broad sense, leaving job training to the proprietary schools (Wilms, 1987). The notion is seductive but fraught with problems. First, the institutions' managers might be tempted to select at entry only those people who are likely to be employable, leaving behind the difficult ones. Second, depending on the institution to provide data about who is employed and for how long before funds are released begs creative data reporting. Third, employers prefer a larger pool of potential employees rather than the smaller pool that this type of contracting for performance would effect. Still, the specter of institutional accountability looms over the occupational programs.

Eells (1941a) explored the fact that 66 percent of the students were enrolled in programs designed primarily to prepare them for what 25 percent would do: transfer to the upper division. At the time he was writing, there was no great difference between the public and the private junior colleges: "The problem is essentially the same for both types of institutions" (p. 63). However, Eells also noted that "of all groups, only the private junior colleges of the New England states and the public junior colleges for Negroes report an enrollment in terminal curricula which even approximates the proportion of terminal students" (p. 59). Now, there were colleges that knew what they were doing! The private junior colleges of New England could fit the girls for homemaking, sales, and secretarial work, and the public junior colleges for blacks in the South could prepare their students for the manual trades.

Recently the urge to completely vocationalize the community colleges has been strong among some commentators, Clowes and Levin (1989) for example, who are aware of the sizable funds and handsome political support attendant on career education. Their arguments sound plausible: since many students neither transfer nor get an associate degree, they should stop trying to compete academically and obtain a marketable skill before leaving the educational system. Nevertheless, there are risks, too. Breneman (1979) has pointed out that emphasizing the financial return for undergraduate education proved a disservice to the colleges, not because the analysis was wrong but because educational leaders accepted the economists' determination that people who go to college earn more in their lifetime than those who do not, and they used this argument in their presentations to legislatures and the public.

The idea of career education reflects a belief that separate curricular tracks are the best way to accommodate the varying educational objectives and characteristics of the students. However, Palmer (1987a) suggests that the organization of career education as a separate curricular track stems from several viewpoints other than student intentions. The first is a "political agenda" held by state legislators and college planners. According to this agenda, occupational programs are supposed to serve students whose primary educational objective is to gain skills allowing them to enter the work force. Second is the "terminal education" agenda, which sees occupational studies as a way of serving academically less able students, who are not likely to obtain the baccalaureate. Third is the "economic agenda," which holds that occupational studies improve the economy through labor-force development and thus serve society. These three agendas, embedded in the history of the community college, have been put forth by national leaders from Eells (1941a, 1941b) to Parnell (1985). A fourth, the "hidden agenda," has been postulated by other commentators who charge that occupational programs channel low-income and minority students away from academic studies and the upward social mobility attendant thereon.

Palmer's study demonstrates that the career programs in community colleges may have been furthered by leaders who subscribe to those beliefs but that the "agendas" do not accurately reflect what the curricula do. Occupational studies actually serve a much broader diversity of students, students with a wide range of abilities and goals. The programs are not exclusively related to the work force or the economy; they also serve individuals wishing to obtain skills for their personal interest, students who take vocational classes "for their intrinsic value and not necessarily for their vocational import" (1987a, p. 291). Palmer based his assertions on the 1986 CSCC survey of students enrolled in all types of classes in community colleges nationwide. In that survey, 16 percent of the students in occupational classes indicated that they were *not* enrolled in an occupational program, and 26 percent of the students who *were* in occupational classes or programs said that they intended to transfer. He rejects the charge that community college students are counseled into career programs on the basis of their academic ability and hence their socioeconomic status. His analysis shows that the enrollment patterns in high-status and low-status occupational classes deviate considerably from what would be expected if curricular tracking were efficiently carried out. Low-income students enroll in high-status and low-status program areas in almost equal numbers; and highly self-confident students equally tend to enroll in low-status program areas, just as students with below-average self-ratings of ability are as likely to enroll in high-status programs. "Many students clearly go their own way, regardless of whether counselors try to track students by ability" (p. 305).

In summation, an oversimplified view of career education as a track leading away from the baccalaureate gives ground to several errors. It neglects the extent to which occupational classes serve avocational or community service functions. It enhances the confusion of curricular content with student intentions. It suggests that career education serves an ever-changing middle-level portion of the job market, which supposedly requires some college study but not the baccalaureate, thus ignoring the high transfer rates exhibited by career program graduates. And it perpetuates the myth that career studies are the exclusive domain of the low-ability or low-income students.

Whether or not career education is useful or proper, it has certainly captured the community colleges. Its advocates have increased, and more of them are being appointed to administrative positions, mostly in vocational areas but occasionally in positions involving academic program supervision. Upgrading of instructors, which started in the 1950s, was supported by the enlarged appropriations for staff development programs and encouraged by salary schedules that provided incentives for academic degrees. Many of the instructors who formerly had only trade experience have acquired bachelor's and master's degrees, removing one of the most potent symbols of inferiority in the academic community.

All these factors—the 1960s to 1980s enrollment surge; staff upgrading; and financial support from business, industry, and government—have given occupational educators a buoyancy that shows up in new courses, programs, teaching strategies. They have a large reservoir of funds, mostly public but some private and foundation, to undertake studies on every aspect of occupational education: preparing model courses and programs, conducting follow-up studies of graduates, assessing employment trends, establishing guidelines for choosing new courses and curricula, and developing criteria for weeding out the obsolescent and weak courses and programs or for upgrading others to conform to new job specifications. They have been flattered that four-year colleges and universities have been showing greater interest in two-year occupational courses and programs, but they are concerned about losing enrollment to the four-year colleges as well as to the proprietary vocational schools. They worry also about losing the programs themselves if the baccalaureate becomes the requisite degree, as it has become for registered nurses in many states.

Regardless of the curriculum favored, many college leaders view with concern the growth of the proprietary or for-profit schools. This group, the fastest-growing sector of postsecondary education in the 1980s, includes cosmetology and barber colleges, trade schools, and business and secretarial institutes, along with several other less populous categories. According to the Association of Independent Colleges and Schools (1988), they were growing both in the number of students served and the number of institutions. In 1988, 92 colleges and business schools belonging to the association offered Associate in Arts or Science degrees, up from 62 only a year earlier. And 144 additional institutions offered specialized associate degrees in occupational studies, applied sciences, and business, up from 119 in 1987. The National Center for Education Statistics (1993, p. 175) reported a quarter of a million students enrolled in accredited two-year proprietary schools. Supported in the main by students who were receiving federal and state aid with which to pay their tuition, this group was proving a most effective set of competitors in the market to provide vocational training. Their students were much more likely to receive financial aid—75 percent versus 27 percent in the public two-year colleges—and on average they received twice as much money per capita (National Center for Education Statistics, 1995c, pp. 7–8).

Merging Academic and Occupational Studies

The separation between the career and collegiate functions is more organizationally than conceptually inspired. Consider the statement "Students will learn to plan more efficient use of time, analyze written communications, understand interpersonal relations, respond appropriately to verbal directives, evolve alternative solutions, maintain involvement with tasks until resolution, communicate effectively verbally." Are those goals related to occupational or to baccalaureate studies? They are likely to appear in course syllabi from either area.

Some eloquent pleas for merging career and liberal studies have been made. Solmon (1977), who has conducted several studies on the relations between college going and the kinds of jobs that graduates get and the extent to which they are satisfied with those jobs, points to several commonly held misconceptions: that job preparation in college is antithetical to short-term enjoyment of being in college or preparation for citizenship or appreciation of the arts; that students tend to get jobs for which they were specifically trained in a major field or in a job-related training program; and that the more education one receives, the greater the chances of obtaining a good job. On surveying numerous graduates of all types of programs several years out of college, he found them wishing they had had more preparation in English, psychology, and ways of understanding interpersonal relations. He recommended breadth in studies in all programs.

Harris and Grede (1977) predicted a breakdown in the rigid dichotomy between liberal arts and vocational curricula or between transfer and nontransfer curricula in community colleges and foresaw a time when teachers of the liberal arts would recognize the importance of career education, and teachers of vocations the importance of the liberal learning. However, this prediction has not come to pass, not least because of the rigidity of the separate funding channels through which support flows into the career and the collegiate courses. At most, courses in some colleges have been designed so that they incorporate elements of both the liberal arts and career studies. As long as career programs lead to the associate degree, the proponents of the liberal arts will be able to sustain their courses as program requirements.

Of itself, occupational training involves a higher risk for the student than liberal arts education. The costs in tuition and forgone earnings may be the same for both, but occupational training is almost entirely wasted if there is no job at the end. The liberal arts at least hold the person's options open, a perception certainly accounting for at least some of the liberal arts' continuing popularity among students. Since it seems impossible to predict with much accuracy the types of jobs that will be available by the time an entering student leaves school, the problem can be accommodated in two ways. First, the educational system can be made open enough that people may return successively for retraining throughout life. Second, the initial training can be made sufficiently broad that the skills learned are applicable to a variety of situations. The argument can be made that all contemporary education is vocational, since it is designed for people who will one day work. Furthermore, the concept of work is sufficiently broad to accommodate people who are less interested in doing or making things than they are in maintaining jobs for their status, social connection, and the human interaction they provide. Many people define themselves by their role but not by their work; it is easier for them to say that they are the assistant manager of something than it is for them to recount exactly what it is they do.

In the long run, career education usually fails if it is focused narrowly on job skills. Knowing how to produce something is quite different from all of the other requirements for sustaining employment. Functional literacy is basic, along with interpersonal relations and knowledge of how to find the job in the first place. Furthermore, the concept of matching a trained worker to an available job is not as prominent now in the overall picture of employment as it was previously. Entrepreneurship is the place where many new jobs are created. It involves not only skills but knowing how to find capital, knowing about the marketplace, knowing all that it takes to organize a business. A growing proportion of career training has been directed toward helping people create their own jobs through small-business development.

Occupational education has become a major function in most community colleges, but the high growth rates of the 1960s and 1970s have stabilized. Unless more community colleges become exclusively vocational-technical postsecondary institutions—as at least 15 percent of them were by 1980—or unless more proprietary schools are defined as community colleges, enrollments in the career programs will probably remain under 50 percent of the total credit-course enrollment. But this percentage will depend in large measure on the way programs are classified.

The major change in recent years has been that career programs in community colleges increasingly became feeders to senior institutions, which were undergoing their own form of vocationalization. Students were finding that many of the credits they earned in their two-year occupational programs were acceptable for transfer. Thus, the categories "occupational" and "transfer" became inadequate to describe the realities of the community colleges, and "terminal" certainly became obsolete. Sizable percentages of the transfer students sought leisure-time pursuits; sizable percentages of the occupational students desired certification for transfer. A view of the community colleges as terminal institutions and of the universities as institutions for students interested in the liberal arts is woefully inaccurate.

Because many career programs are serving as the first two years of a baccalaureate program, the community colleges must articulate those programs with the programs at senior institutions. They are much more likely to do that than to support program separation or to concentrate on the occupations that do not require the baccalaureate, such as secretarial skills or construction trades. Competition from the proprietary schools for programs in these areas is too great, and to the extent that the community colleges emphasize such trades areas, they become vulnerable to the charge that they channel their clients into low-status occupations.

In his book *The Two Cultures*, the English writer C. P. Snow (1959) posed a distinction between the humanities and the sciences. The scientific culture attempts to describe laws of the natural world and is optimistic that problems can be solved. The other culture, the literary world, is pessimistic about the likelihood of solving major problems and regards members of the scientific culture as barbarians. According to Snow, the literary intellectuals or artists lack foresight, are unconcerned about their fellow humans, and do not understand what science can do. The scientists regard the artists as lacking precision in thought and action, as speaking in phrases capable of a myriad of interpretations.

There are other ways, however, to contemplate a gap between two cultures. Perhaps on one side are those who have a vision of the future; who work with discipline, pride, and rigor; who articulate their ideas through language that has consistent meaning; who value the intellect. On the other side are those who demand quick gratification; who refuse to be told what to do or what to study; who are antiliterate, rejecting language; who deal with feeling, not thinking, with emotions, not intellect. If these are the two cultures, the split is not between the liberal arts on the one hand and career education on the other. That argument is passé, even though community colleges are still organized as though the real distinction were between people who were going to work and those who were not. Work in the sense of vocation demands commitment, planning, delay of gratification, application of intelligence, acceptance of responsibility, a sense of present and future time. As such, it differs less from the concepts surrounding the liberal arts than it does from the antiliterate, language-rejecting, stultified group, who cannot understand themselves or their environment in terms that have common reference.

As though it anticipated later developments, the AAJC's 1964 National Advisory Committee concluded, "Time must be provided, even in a two-year curriculum, for at least basic courses in languages, arts, and social sciences. The technicians of the future must be inoculated against the malady of overspecialization. . . . They must not be forced to concentrate so narrowly on technology that they cannot be useful citizens or cannot accommodate changes in their own specialties" (American Association of Junior Colleges, 1964, p. 14). Nearly a quarter century later, an AACJC-sponsored group reiterated a concern for combining career and general education: "Many students come to the community college with narrow backgrounds, and, for them, career education may mean only gaining skills for a specific job. . . . Through lack of attention to general education, community colleges often exacerbate this tendency toward narrowness. . . . We recommend that the core curriculum be integrated into technical and career programs" (American Association of Community and Junior Colleges, 1988, pp. 17–19).

Some things don't change very much.

Issues

Career education's phenomenal growth in the 1960s and 1970s stabilized in the 1980s. Will its 40–50 percent enrollment share continue? How much will competition from the proprietary schools affect it?

Can career education be effectively merged with the collegiate function? Few prior attempts to integrate esthetic appreciation, rationality, ethics, and other elements of higher learning with programs training people for particular jobs have met with success. Can the staff itself do it? Does the community college leadership want it?

The lines between career and collegiate education have become blurred since more students began transferring to universities from community college career programs than from the so-called transfer programs. Questions of the conceptual differences between occupational and liberal studies have often been raised, but the answers have yielded little to influence program design in the community colleges. What type of staff training, program reorganization, or external incentives might be provided to encourage faculties and administrators to reexamine both programs in the light of the practicalities of their own institutions?

Programs designed to prepare students to work in particular industries should be supported, at least in part, by those industries; many examples of this type of support have been set in place. But how can industry be assigned its proportionate share of all training costs? What channels can be opened to merge public and private funds so that an equitable share is borne by each?

The full effects of career education as the prime function have yet to be discerned. The public's view of community colleges as agents of upward mobility for individuals seems to be shifting toward a view of the institutions as occupational training centers. This narrowing of the colleges' comprehensiveness could lead to a shift in the pattern of support.

9

Developmental Education
Enhancing Literacy and Basic Skills

Nothing is easier to decry than the ineffectiveness of the
schools. One observer of American education noted:

> Paradoxical as it may seem, the diffusion of education
> and intelligence is at present acting against the free
> development of the highest education and intelligence.
> Many have hoped and still hope that by giving a partial
> teaching to great numbers of persons, a stimulus would
> be applied to the best minds among them, and a thirst
> for knowledge awakened which would lead to high
> results; but thus far these results have not equaled the
> expectation. There has been a vast expenditure . . . for
> educational purposes . . . but the system of competitive
> cramming in our schools has not borne fruits on which
> we have much cause to congratulate ourselves.

The sentiments in this passage, written in 1869 by the American
historian Francis Parkman (p. 560), have been echoed countless
times since.

Numerous critics have taken the position that the schools may
teach people to read and write, but they fail to teach them to think.
Parkman himself felt that the school "has produced an immense
number of readers; but what thinkers are to be found may be said to

exist in spite of it" (p. 560). One hundred years later, the American poet and critic John Ciardi complained that "the American school system has dedicated itself to universal subliteracy. It has encouraged the assumption that a clod trained to lip-read a sports page is able to read anything. It has become the whole point of the school system to keep the ignorant from realizing their own ignorance. . . . An illiterate must at least know that he cannot read and that the world of books is closed to him" (Ciardi, 1971, p. 48). Similarly, H. L. Mencken asserted that "the great majority of American high school pupils, when they put their thoughts on paper, produce only a mass of confused puerile nonsense. . . . They express themselves so clumsily that it is often quite impossible to understand them at all" (cited in Lyons, 1976, p. 33). And a more contemporary writer, the novelist Walker Percy, has offered this devastating critique: "Our civilization has achieved a distinction of sorts. It will be remembered not for its technology nor even its wars but for its novel ethos. Ours is the only civilization in history which has enshrined mediocrity as its national ideal" (Percy, 1980, p. 177).

The charge has been raised that students not only fail to become well educated but also do not learn even the rudiments of reading, writing, and arithmetic. The title of Copperman's 1978 book reflects one indictment: *The Literacy Hoax: The Decline of Reading, Writing, and Learning in the Public Schools and What We Can Do About It.* Copperman reports studies showing that over twenty million American adults, one in every five, are functionally illiterate—that is, incapable of understanding basic written and arithmetic communication to a degree that they can maneuver satisfactorily in contemporary society. The popular press has repeatedly carried articles about the tens of millions of adult Americans who cannot read or write well enough to perform the basic requirements of everyday life or who are only marginally competent.

A steady outpouring of books has continued the critique. Bloom complains that "our students have lost the practice of and the taste for reading. They have not learned how to read, nor do they have the expectation of delight or improvement from reading" (1987, p. 62). Hirsch begins his best seller with the words, "The standard of literacy required by modern society has been rising throughout the developed world, but American literacy rates have not risen to meet this standard" (1987, p. 1). Harman's examination of illiteracy describes how "more and more working members of mainstream America are found to be either totally illiterate or unable to read at the level presumably required by their job or their position in society" (1987, p. 1).

Not all commentators blame the schools alone. However, although each generation's cohort of criers-with-alarm has had its favorite target, most of them eventually disparage the public schools. But none of this is really new. Comments on students' lack of preparation may be found as early as the beginnings of the colleges in colonial America. Rudolph noted, "Because the colonial colleges were founded before there existed any network of grammar schools . . . most entering students were prepared privately, often by studying with the local minister" (1977, p. 52). So many colleges were built in the first three decades of the nineteenth century that they could not find enough students who were prepared for higher learning. Hence, "college authorities, defining their own course of study, learned to restrain their expectations in deference to the preparation of the students who came their way" (p. 60).

This chapter is concerned with several aspects of developmental education, especially the difficulty in assigning standards and definitions and assessing program outcomes. The conventional belief is that literacy has declined. But how much? And by what measurement? Certainly the colleges are deeply involved with remedial studies, but at what cost to their image? And to what effect? The several dilemmas surrounding the tracking of students into less-than-college-level courses are explored, along with some of the practices in which the colleges are engaged.

Decline in Literacy

Broad-scale denunciations are one thing, accurate data quite another. Information on the literacy of the American population over the decades is difficult to compile, even though data on the number of people completing so many years of schooling have been collected by the Bureau of the Census for well over one hundred years. Intergenerational comparisons are imprecise because different percentages of the population have gone to school at different periods in the nation's history and because the United States has never had a uniform system of educational evaluation. Still, the concern about the importance of literacy, its decline, and the need to do something about it has reached the level of a major national priority.

Eight National Education Goals were set into law on March 31, 1994, when President Clinton signed the *Goals 2000, Educate America Act*. One of the eight goals is that every adult would be literate, possessing the knowledge and skills to compete in the workplace and to exercise the responsibilities of citizenship. Since the various commissions that had been working on the *Goals 2000* project for several years prior to the legislation recognized that defining literacy was a key to determining whether the goal had been reached, they developed standards, norms, and instrumentation so that measures of literacy in all age groups could be reported according to common referents.

Concerns about literacy came as no surprise to educators who have reviewed the scores made on nationally normed tests taken by people planning on entering college. The available evidence suggests that the academic achievement of students in schools and colleges registered a gradual improvement between 1900 and the mid 1950s, an accelerated improvement between the mid 1950s and the mid 1960s, and a precipitous, widespread decline between then and the late 1970s, before stabilizing in the early 1980s. The Scholastic Aptitude Tests taken by high school seniors show mathematical ability at 494 in 1952, 502 in 1963; it dropped as low as 466 in 1979 but by 1994 had climbed back up to 479. Verbal ability went from 476 in 1952 to 478 in 1963, then dropped in 1980 to 424, where it stabilized; it was 423 in 1994 (The College Board, 1994).

The scores made by students who participated in the American College Testing Program between 1967 and 1989 reveal a similar pattern. In those two decades math scores declined from 20.0 to 17.1, and social studies from 19.7 to 17.2. English showed a dip in the early 1980s but in 1989 was within one tenth of a point of where it had been in 1967. Natural science scores were stable and actually registered a small increase. The overall composite went from 19.9 to 18.6 (National Center for Education Statistics, 1993, p. 130). Declines in academic achievement during the 1970s and subsequent stabilization in the late 1980s were confirmed by the National Assessment of Educational Progress (NAEP) studies of seventeen-year-old students. For the decade following 1983, students' performance in math declined slightly, reading and writing showed little change, and science improved (Mullis and others, 1994, p. 7). These changes are depicted graphically in Figures 9.1, 9.2, and 9.3.

No one can say with assurance which social or educational condition was primarily responsible for the decline in student abilities that apparently began in the mid 1960s and accelerated throughout the 1970s. Suffice it to say that numerous events came together: the coming of age of the first generation reared on television, a breakdown in respect for authority and the professions, a pervasive attitude that the written word is not as important as it once was, the imposition of various other-than-academic expectations upon the public schools, the increasing numbers of students whose native language is other than English, and a decline in academic requirements and expectations at all levels of schooling. This last is worthy of elaboration because it is the only one that is within the power of the schools to change directly.

Figure 9.1. SAT Scores: 1953–1994.

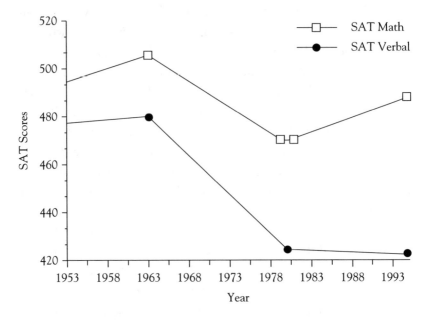

Figure 9.2. ACT Scores: 1975–1992.

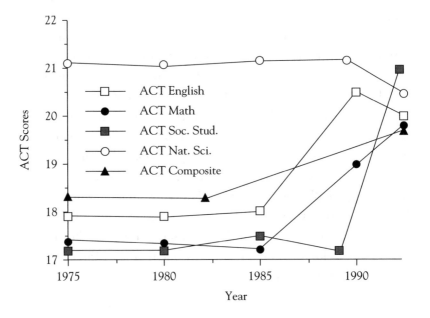

Figure 9.3. NAEP Scores: 1971–1990.

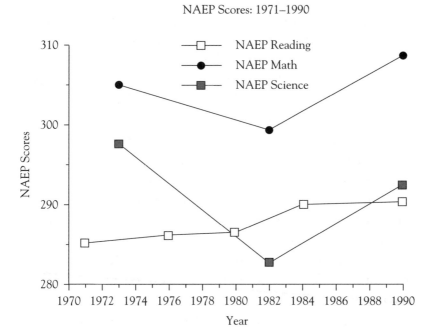

School Requirements

Several premises underlie schooling—for example, that students tend to learn what is taught, that the more time they spend on a task the more they learn, and that they will take the courses required for completion of their programs. Hence, when expectations, time in school, and number of academic requirements are reduced, student achievement, however measured, seems certain to drop as well. In its 1978 report on *The Concern for Writing*, the Educational Testing Service noted: "The nub of the matter is that writing is a complex skill mastered only through lengthy, arduous effort. It is a participatory endeavor, not a spectator sport. And most high school students do not get enough practice to become competent writers" (p. 4). In the 1960s and 1970s, the schools put less emphasis on composition, and even in composition courses "creative expression" was treated at a higher level than were grammar and the other tools of the writer's trade.

Copperman (1978) recounted the depressing statistics regarding deterioration of the secondary school curriculum. Specifically, the percentage of ninth- through twelfth-grade students enrolled in academic courses dropped between 1960 and 1972, from 95 to 71 percent in English courses and proportionately in social studies, science, and mathematics. In other words, the average high school graduate had taken four years of English in 1960 and only three years in 1972. And the curriculum in English shifted from sequential courses to electives chosen from courses in creative writing, journalism, public speaking, classical literature, science fiction, advanced folklore, composition, mass media, poetry, and a host of other options. Not only were students taking less science, math, English, and history, but in the academic classes they did take, the amount of work assigned and the standard to which it was held deteriorated as well.

Further, the texts used in secondary schools and two-year colleges became more simplistic, written at a level that the average twelve-year-old could understand. Richardson, Fisk, and Okun (1983) showed how in one representative community college the requirements for reading and writing in all courses, including general education and the liberal arts, had been reduced. Students were expected to read little but the textbook; even in that, they were reading not for content or ideas but only for the minimal amount of information needed to pass quick-score examinations. The expectations for student writing had dropped so that students wrote at most a few pages in any course.

Attempts to reform the elementary and secondary schools so that they can better effect student learning have been made periodically for most of their history. Early in the century reform centered on professionalizing school personnel. In the post-World War II era, equal opportunity and access were primary. During the 1980s school reform shifted toward educational excellence and outcomes assessment. During the latter years increased requirements for high school graduation and state-centered student testing programs became prominent. By 1990 most states had changed their curriculum requirements for graduation, with the majority of changes directed toward increases in the number of math and science studies (detailed in Chapter Eleven). Student testing had increased as well, with more than one-third of the states requiring a minimum competency test for high school graduation (National Center for Education Statistics, 1992c). But as the SAT, ACT, and NAEP results show, overall gains in literacy have come slowly, if at all.

College Admissions

Because each college set its own standards, and because the founding of colleges preceded the development of a widespread secondary school system, the early colleges displayed a wide variety of admission requirements. By the latter part of the nineteenth century, most of them were operating their own remedial education programs. In 1895, 40 percent of entering students were drawn from preparatory programs operated by the colleges and universities themselves (Rudolph, 1977, p. 158).

Numerous attempts to stabilize college admissions have been made. In 1892 the National Education Association organized a Committee on Secondary School Studies, known as the Committee of Ten, which was to recommend and approve the secondary school curriculum for college matriculation. In 1900, the College Entrance Examination Board began offering a common examination for college admission. Nonetheless, the wide variety in types and quality of colleges in America made it impossible to devise uniform admission standards. There has never been a standard of admission to all colleges in the United States. The Educational Testing Service and the American College Testing Program offer uniform examinations across the country, but each college is free to admit students regardless of where they place on those examinations.

Of all postsecondary educational structures in America, the public community colleges have borne the brunt of the poor preparation of students in the twentieth century. When sizable cohorts of well-prepared students were clamoring for higher education, as in the 1950s and early 1960s, the community colleges received a large share of them. But when the college-age group declined and the universities became more competitive for students, the proportion of academically well-prepared students going to community colleges shrank. Thus, the colleges were dealt a multiple blow: relaxed admission requirements and the availability of financial aid at the more prestigious universities, a severe decline in the scholastic abilities of high school graduates, and a greater percentage of applicants who had taken fewer academic courses.

The community colleges responded by accommodating the different types of students without turning anyone away. They have always tended to let everyone in but have then guided students to programs that fit their aspirations and in which they have some chance to succeed. Students who qualified for transfer programs were never a serious problem; they were given courses similar to those they would find in the lower division of the four-year colleges and universities. Technical and occupational aspirants were not a problem, either; career programs were organized for them. Internal selectivity was the norm; failing certain prerequisites, applicants were barred from the health professions and technology programs. The students who wanted a course or two for their own personal interest found them both in the departments of continuing education and in the transfer programs.

The residue, the poorly prepared group of high school pass-throughs, has been the concern. What should the colleges do with marginally literate people who want to be in college but do not know why? How should they deal with someone who aspires to be an attorney but who is reading at the fifth-grade level? Shunting these students to the trades programs was a favored ploy, giving rise to Clark's cooling-out thesis (1960). Another ploy was to offer a smattering of remedial courses where students would be prepared, more or less successfully, to enter the transfer courses—or entertained until they drifted away. But the decline in achievement exhibited by secondary school graduates—and dropouts—in the 1970s hit the colleges with full force. The problem of the marginal student became central to instructional planning.

The Magnitude of Remediation

Data on entering students who need remedial help in their studies suggest the magnitude of the problem. Since New Jersey began giving its College Basic Skills Placement Test in the early 1980s, one-half and more of the students entering the county (community) colleges have needed remediation in verbal skill, computation, and algebra. In 1991 the percentage of test takers lacking proficiency in verbal skills reached a ten-year low (New Jersey Basic Skills Council, 1991) and had not improved by 1993 (New Jersey State Department of Higher Education, 1994). In Washington, well over half the students entering community colleges were deficient in English, reading, and/or mathematics (Washington State Board for Community College Education, 1985). In Oklahoma the figure was 44 percent (Oklahoma State Regents for Higher Education, 1993b). A Texas statewide study found 40 percent of the students needing remedial reading and writing (Skinner and Carter, 1987).

Many single-college studies have found similar or higher percentages. More than 40 percent of the entering students at Rockland Community College (New York) were directed to the developmental studies department (Brown and others, 1989), and 88 percent of the first-time students entering Shelby State Community College (Tennessee) were placed in remedial and developmental studies courses (Hobbs, 1988). At Hudson County Community College (New Jersey), 30 percent of the 1989 entrants began in developmental education and 50 percent in English as a Second Language courses (Fujita, 1993b). Clearly, curriculum revisions, enhanced standards, and high-school graduation examinations had yet to effect substantive change in student abilities.

Remedial, compensatory, and *developmental* have been used as more or less interchangeable terms for courses designed to teach literacy— the basics of reading, writing, and arithmetic. Students have been advised to enroll in those courses on the basis of entrance tests or prior school achievement. The courses are usually not accepted for credit toward an academic degree, but their funding comes through the regular academic instructional budget, sometimes augmented by special state or federal program appropriations to assist disadvantaged students.

Even though the decline in student ability stabilized in the 1980s, developmental education grew. The rise in remedial course enrollment occurred because student ability had sunk so low that college staff members, legislators, and the staff of the universities to which the students transfer had had enough. The dropout and failure rates were unconscionably high. When the population was expanding and an ever-increasing number of new students showed up each year, the problem was not as acute and few colleges did anything about coordinating developmental education. In the late 1970s, however, the attitude shifted as the college staff realized that it was more feasible, not to say socially and educationally defensible, to keep the students enrolled than to let them drop out as a result of academic failure.

All public two-year colleges have had developmental or remedial courses. The Center for the Study of Community Colleges (1978) tallied the sections offered in a national sample of public and private colleges in 1977–78 and found that about three in eight English classes were presented at below-college level; in nearly one in three mathematics classes, arithmetic was taught at a level lower than college algebra; and remedial classes accounted for 13 percent of the enrollments in chemistry. In 1991, CSCC again tracked credit courses and found developmental studies continuing their prominence; 31 percent of the scheduled class sections in English and 16 percent in math were so designated. (The lower percentage in math was the result of a greatly expanded effort in math labs or nonscheduled developmental activities.) These data were corroborated in state studies: 18 percent of the credit-course enrollment in Illinois and in Washington community colleges was in remedial courses (Illinois Community College Board, 1994; Washington State Board for Community College Education, 1993).

Revised Practices

Developmental courses and programs can be built within the colleges, but several questions remain: is developmental education effective? How does it affect the college staff? How can it be conducted in the context of an open-admissions institution without jeopardizing the college's standards and its legitimacy in higher education? How can segregated developmental education programs respond to charges of racism and class-based tracking? How many times should the public pay the schools to try to teach the same competencies to the same people?

Placement testing and integrated developmental education services have dominated recent efforts in remedial studies. Beginning in the late 1970s, the nation's community colleges moved toward a system of placement testing, restricted admissions to many courses and programs, integrated remedial programs complete with counseling and tutorial services, and assessment of the efficacy of these procedures. In the 1980s state-mandated placement testing was installed, first in Florida and Georgia and subsequently in Texas, California, and New Jersey, among other states. These requirements affected all the publicly supported institutions.

Since 1988, students wishing to enter the Georgia university system as regular-placement freshmen must have completed a prescribed college preparatory curriculum (CPC) in high school. If not, they make up the deficiencies in English, foreign language, mathematics, science, or social science by completing additional prior coursework. In Fall 1989, 39 percent of the students in Georgia's two-year colleges were enrolled in one or more remedial courses; this compares with only 8 percent at the state universities. The Georgia experience, though, is that "merely completing the CPC in high school does not guarantee success in college, rather it is the quality of the experience as measured by the SAT scores and high-school averages that seems to make the most significant contribution to subsequent success in college" (Hamilton, 1992, p. 154). The CPC's predictive value "is weak in comparison to scholastic aptitude test scores and high-school averages . . . " (p. 152).

In their study of students enrolled in remedial writing classes, Alfred and Lum (1988) reported that individual demographic characteristics and placement policies paled as predictors in comparison with the grades earned in the remedial classes. In brief, a grade earned in a remedial class coupled with a grade earned in a composition course "was a more effective predictor than any of the ten independent variables" (p. 116). As decades of research in education have shown, the best predictors of grades earned in subsequent courses are grades earned in prior courses. Generally speaking, if students complete their remedial coursework successfully, they go on to succeed in the regular college program. However, less than half the students entering the remedial courses complete them.

Another prominent move in developmental education has been the integrated program, combining instruction in the three Rs with counseling, tutoring, study skills seminars, and a variety of special interventions. Students participate voluntarily or, more often, are placed in the program on the basis of scores made on an entrance test. Special counseling procedures are established, and each student's attendance and progress are monitored. The courses may include remedial reading and writing, and adjunct classes centering on certain content areas also may be provided. The students may be tutored individually by professionals or peers. The programs frequently include reproducible instructional sequences presented through learning laboratories. In some of the more sophisticated developmental programs, remedial classes are offered through the English and mathematics departments, adjunct courses or study programs are offered through the learning resource center, study skills activities are presented by members of the counseling staff, and tutorials are coordinated by any of the aforementioned divisions. The intent of all developmental activities is to keep students in school and to help them improve their basic skills so that they can complete an academic or vocational program satisfactorily.

In summation, how to guide and teach students who are unprepared for traditional college-level studies is the thorniest single problem for community colleges. Some institutions seem to have given up, as evidenced by their tendencies to award certificates and degrees for any combination of courses, units, or credits—in effect, sending the students away with the illusion of having had a successful college career. Others have mounted massive instructional and counseling services especially for the lower-ability students, stratagems designed to puncture the balloon of prior school failure. But in most programs in most institutions, expectations for student achievement have declined. The weight of the low-ability student hangs like an anchor on the community colleges.

Program Effects

Hundreds of studies reported in the published literature and in the ERIC files suggest that student placement procedures are valid and that students learn to read and write in the remedial classes. The integrated developmental programs, designed to effect retention as well as learning, similarly show positive results. These effects are not surprising; when staff members are involved in a comprehensive program, they pay closer attention to students, integrate teaching with counseling, provide a greater variety of learning materials than ordinary students receive, and motivate their enrollees to devote more time to their studies. In short, when special treatment is applied, when students are given supplemental counseling, tutoring, and learning aids, when they are singled out for additional work, they tend to remain in school. Special treatment of any sort yields special results.

How do college faculty members who face students daily feel about massive compensatory education efforts and the poorly prepared students in their classes? Students' abilities exert the single most powerful influence on the level, quality, type, and standard of curriculum and instruction offered in every program in every school. Other influences—instructors' tendencies, externally administered examinations and licensure requirements, the entry levels imposed by succeeding courses in the same and other institutions—are of lesser importance. Nothing that is too distant from the students' comprehension can be taught successfully. All questions of academic standards, college-level and remedial courses, textbook readability and coverage, and course pacing and sequence come to that.

Students are part of the instructors' working conditions. Except for faculty members recruited especially to staff developmental programs, most feel that their environment would be improved if their students were more able. In the CSCC's 1977 national survey of science instructors at two-year colleges, respondents were asked, "What would it take to make yours a better course?" Over half of them noted, "Students better prepared to handle course requirements" (Brawer and Friedlander, 1979, p. 32). That choice far outranked all others in a list of sixteen.

If students cannot be more able, at least they might be more alike, so that instruction can be more precisely focused. Teaching groups of students whose reading or computational abilities range from the third to the thirteenth grade is demoralizing; everything is more difficult, from writing examinations to showing group progress—hence the unremitting pressure for ability grouping, remedial courses, and learning laboratories that serve to remove the poorer students from the classrooms.

As integrated developmental programs grew in the 1980s, separate divisions combining faculty members, counselors, and support staff were formed to accommodate them. As noted in Chapter Six, this separation of the developmental education staff from the academic discipline-centered faculty has led to an increased level of professional consciousness among members of the former group. They publish their own journals, which carry articles on peer tutoring, the pros and cons of mandatory testing, ways of organizing reading and writing laboratories, and the various treatments they apply to students who come within their purview. In some colleges the academic instructors still treat them as pariahs, but they have their own colleagues and support groups.

Developmental educators are responsible for a sizable proportion of the studies conducted on the effects of various instructional treatments. Baker (1982) compared the effectiveness of remedial classes with that of traditional courses by examining students in the two groups according to the scores they made on standardized writing tests. Suter (1983) and Johnson (1985) compared grades earned in other classes and retention rates for students who had been through a developmental studies program. Marcotte (1986) used graduation rates as the dependent variable and tracked the students who graduated back through the developmental education program to determine its effects. A study at Broward Community College (Florida) found combined persistence and graduation rates among students who scored below college level in reading, writing, and mathematics to be highest among those who completed at least three college preparatory classes (Gabe, 1989). Students who took advantage of tutorial services at Los Medanos College (California) were more likely to earn higher course grades and complete their classes (MacDonald, 1987). In a California statewide study, students who participated in services especially designed for matriculants with low entering skills achieved higher grades and were more likely to persist in college (Scott-Skillman and Halliday, 1991). All of these studies describe the treatments applied and track their effect on student learning, as measured by grades earned in other classes, persistence and graduation rates, and scores made on various testing instruments. In general, when students are left to their own volition, relatively few participate in remedial activities, but when they are barred from taking college-level courses or strongly urged to take advantage of the services provided for them, they tend to do better.

Legitimacy

The question of legitimacy is one of image in the eyes of the public, the potential students, the funding agents, and the other sectors of education. Like any other public agency, an educational institution must maintain its legitimacy. The community colleges have strived to maintain their claim to a position in the postsecondary sector through numerous stratagems. In the 1950s and 1960s, for example, they sought people with doctoral degrees to serve as staff members and rewarded current staff members when they obtained the higher degree, even though possession of a doctorate bore little or no relation to a faculty member's professional activities. The doctorate was a way of saying, "We are as good as the senior institutions." Similarly, they segregated their developmental programs in an attempt to regain the legitimacy lost when the colleges accepted adult basic studies and job-training programs that could in no measure be considered college level.

Actually, a school's legitimacy rests on its academic standards and the definition of its guiding principles. Academic standards certify that a student holding a certificate or degree has met the requirement for employment or for further study at another college; they are the basis for the reputation of institutions and the people who work in them. Even though community colleges typically maintain open-admissions policies, they must still attend to these concerns. Their students must be certified; their instructional programs, testing and counseling services, course content, and course requirements must all relate to a shared vision of desired competencies and outcomes. Their certificates or degrees must evidence some set of proficiencies achieved at some minimum level.

What are the standards in developmental education? Here the special programs exhibit several problems in common with the traditional. One of the main problems is the difficulty in setting fixed *exit* criteria (grading standards) for courses and programs that have no set *entry* requirements. If anyone may enroll regardless of ability, a wide range of students will be attracted. Accordingly, either the exit criteria must be fluid, with a different standard for each student, or the time and type of instruction must be greatly varied, or the instructors must maintain exceedingly modest expectations. All three options are at play in practically all programs.

Standardized expectations of accomplishment, or exit criteria, suggest social norms as contrasted with standards for individuals. Social norms suggest that people who would function adequately in particular social settings (the workplace, school) must act to a certain standard. The alternative, relating accomplishment to the desires or entering abilities of individuals, suggests that any accomplishment is satisfactory and that the institution has succeeded if any gain in individual ability can be shown. This conflict between social and individual standards is an issue of the absolute versus the relative, and it strikes at the heart of developmental education.

Different groups take different positions on the issue. Community college instructors tend to argue in favor of absolute standards. The Academic Senate for California Community Colleges (ASCCC) (1977) has studied the problem extensively, surveying its members and sponsoring state conferences on the issue. The ASCCC deplored some of the pressures to lower standards: students entering the college with inadequate basic skills but with expectation of passing the courses, as they have done throughout their prior school careers; ill-prepared students insisting on enrolling in transfer courses rather than remedial courses; the virtual elimination of D and F grades and concomitant wider use of passing grades; reduction in the number of required subjects; and the cult of growth afflicting community colleges, as evidenced by aggressive student recruiting drives. The ASCCC Academic Standards Committee recommended that standards should be maintained through the use of diagnostic and placement testing, directive counseling, academic prerequisites for courses, and proficiency testing before awarding academic degrees. These recommendations were in no small measure responsible for California's adopting matriculation standards in the 1980s.

Advocates of the concept of lifelong learning often provide an opposing view. To them, any seeker of knowledge should find the institution a resource to be used for an infinite variety of purposes. Cross, for example, has argued that substantial changes in school forms are needed, so that anyone may learn anything at any time: "My concern is that in our exuberance for recruiting adults and certifying that *their* learning projects meet *our* standards, we will corrupt independent, self-directed learners into learners dependent on someone else to determine where, when, and how people should learn. Visions of a learning society with people of all ages enthusiastically pursuing learning that interests them could so easily turn into a joyless learning society with people grimly fulfilling requirements and seeking legitimacy for every conceivable variety of learning" (1978, pp. 19–20).

These opposed positions suggest differing views of present and potential students. Some see them as lethargic illiterates; others, as humanistic knowledge seekers.

The Dilemma of Tracking

Segregating the less well-prepared students has much appeal. Classes can be made more homogeneous; the bright students are not forced to wait for the less able to catch up; and, most important, the instructors whose classes have been relieved of the poorer students can retain the attitude that they are teaching in a true college. However, the practice of shunting students to remedial classes is based on tenuous assumptions, especially the assumption that student performance standards are immutable, when nearly all school programs are actually based on shifting norms. The concept of functional literacy provides an example.

Definitions of Functional Literacy

One definition of functional literacy is "the level of reading, writing, and calculating ability that people need to succeed in the public realm in which they choose to operate." Under this definition the level of literacy required to function as a citizen, taxpayer, or homemaker, or merely "on the street," serves as a criterion. A second definition is "the level of reading, writing, and ability to send and receive messages that it takes to obtain and maintain a job." Obviously, different levels of literacy are required for performance in different types of jobs. A third definition of functional literacy is "the level required to perform successfully in a college program." Here again, different types of programs require different levels of competency. Harman cited a 1956 omnibus definition: "A person is functionally literate when he has acquired the knowledge and skills in reading and writing which enable him to engage effectively in all those activities in which literacy is normally assumed in his cultural group" (1987, p. 4). All these definitions, then, can be subsumed under the statement, "Functional literacy is the ability to communicate in the symbolic language of reading, writing, and speaking that is adequate for people to maintain themselves in the context of particular situations," or, as the NAEP defines it, "using printed and written information to function in society, to achieve one's goals, and to develop one's knowledge and potential" (Kirsch and Jungeblut, 1986, p. 3).

So defined, functional literacy is related to the milieu in which people find themselves. It is relative; there are no absolute minimum standards of competence. A functionally literate person in some school settings may be functionally illiterate in certain jobs. And a person who is quite able to communicate within the confines of certain jobs may be functionally illiterate for purposes of a college program.

Hence a dilemma. Institutional legitimacy and faculty predilections rest on standards, defined outcomes, and certifiable results. But the definitions guiding staff efforts and the precepts of continuing education or lifelong learning are relative. Each person brings idiosyncratic backgrounds and aspirations to the institution; each finds a separate set of experiences. How can the two be reconciled in an open-admissions institution? The question is not limited to developmental education, but the influx of students with low academic ability brought it to the fore. In addition to providing a more useful learning experience for the poorly prepared students, many of the developmental education programs have segregated them into separate enclaves, thus protecting, at least temporarily, the legitimacy of the other portions of the college.

Imprecise Criteria

Selective admission to any program is as discriminatory as it is justifiable. Regardless of the yardstick applied, the people who are shut out of the programs in which they wanted to enroll have been discriminated against. Yet, with accrediting agencies, state licensing boards, and senior institutions looking in, program directors feel justified in admitting only a select few, particularly if the field of endeavor for which the program prepares people can take only so many graduates or if college facilities allow for only so many matriculants.

Should the colleges restrict admissions to certain programs? If some applicants cannot gain admission to a program because their level of literacy is lower than a cutting score, the issue is resolved for them. But if applicants *are* admitted to the program, then program operators have the responsibility to teach the skills required for them to succeed in it. The pattern of allowing all to enter and using the program itself to screen out the unworthy should be discounted, first because one cannot at the same time teach and judge, and second because it is too expensive, both in terms of public funds and concern for people, to allow sizable numbers to enroll with the expectation that many of them will not complete the course of study.

The pressures for selective admission to various programs have grown in recent years. In the 1950s, most colleges screened students into remedial programs if their prior high school grades or their scores on entrance tests suggested that they might not be able to succeed in the transfer programs. In the 1960s, the pressure to allow anyone to enter a transfer program grew, the reason being that remedial programs were seen as catchalls for the less worthy, as holding tanks for students who must be "cooled out" of higher education. In the 1970s, the pendulum swung back, with many institutions building developmental programs, screening students into them, moving away from the attitude of letting students try everything and fail if they must. That trend accelerated in the 1980s as state mandates spread.

However, it is quite possible to teach functional literacy in the transfer program. Some notable efforts at mainstreaming—that is, allowing lower-ability students to take the regular college classes even while they are being assisted supplementally—have been made. Many of these efforts involve the use of learning laboratories. As examples, in the Developmental Studies Program at Penn Valley Community College (Missouri), the Learning Skills Laboratory (LSL) was used as an extension of the math and English classroom. Students could complete LSL instructional activities, as prescribed by faculty members, before progressing to the course or concurrently with it (Ford, 1976). Sacramento City College (California) initiated a Higher Education Learning Package (HELP) to promote the success and retention of students with basic skill deficiencies while mainstreaming them into regular courses. Students who were reading at a sixth-grade level worked with instructors and tutors in small groups and on a one-to-one basis (Bohr and Bray, 1979). Introducing concepts of mastery learning into the regular courses in City Colleges of Chicago resulted in student achievement and retention superior to those obtained in remedial courses or in the regular courses taught in nonmastery fashion (Chausow, 1979). A series of one-hour study skills courses coordinated with the regular academic courses in Dutchess Community College (New York) led to better grades and retention not only in the related courses but also in other classes (Weeks, 1987). Thus, remediation does not have to come in the form of segregated remedial courses.

It is likely that most students can succeed in the collegiate and occupational programs if they are required to supplement their courses with tutorials, learning labs, special counseling, peer-group assistance, and/or a variety of other aids. *Required* is a key word in the foregoing sentence; left to their own choice, few students who need assistance will seek it out. Several surveys have found that, of their own volition, students tend not to take advantage of the support services that the college provides for them. Yet mandating support services means that additional funds must be found. The question is how much effort the colleges are willing to put into the extra treatment required by students who enter programs that overwhelm them. Given a choice between an admissions screen to keep students out of the programs and the allocation of sizable funds to ensure students' success if they are admitted, many institutional managers faced with static budgets opt to keep the less well-prepared students out of the transfer courses by placing them in remedial courses or segregated compensatory education programs.

But denying students admission to programs of their choice is difficult to justify. The open-door philosophy of the community college implies that these students should not be denied. The fact that some can succeed also suggests that they should not be denied. And the fact that students who are denied access to collegiate programs are typically denied exposure to the humanistic and scientific thought on which these areas are based mandates that they *must* not be denied. Community colleges have succeeded in opening access to all; if that access is limited to a developmental program that offers primarily the same type of basic education that failed the students in the lower schools, then students have been cruelly

denied access to higher learning. The colleges cannot afford to operate separate programs for the less qualified unless those programs are
verifiably supportive of the collegiate and career programs.

Those who would impose standards for programs at any level
face difficulties stemming from lack of consensus on institutional
purpose, antagonism to the idea of group norms, and, in secondary
schools and community colleges, the inability to impose entrance
requirements. Selective screening into the collegiate programs could
not be maintained in an earlier era because students demanded and
got the right to fail, and that contributed to the unconscionable
attrition figures of the 1970s. Selective admission into the collegiate
programs has been tried again because it is easier to screen students
out *en bloc* than to establish criteria for functional literacy course
by course. Yet unless those criteria are defined, selective admissions
will again be unsuccessful. Even though it is impossible to bring all
students to the point at which they can succeed in the courses and
programs of their choice, the community colleges must continue
trying. As the Commission on the Future of Community Colleges
pointed out, "Literacy is essential both for the individual and society. . . . Community colleges must make a commitment, without
apology, to help students overcome academic deficiencies and
acquire the skills they need to become effective, independent learners" (American Association of Community and Junior Colleges,
1988, pp. 16–17).

Reconciling the Dilemma

Three options are available to colleges that would reconcile the
conflict between maintaining standards and allowing all students
to enter the programs of their choice. First, they can define the specific competencies required to enter and succeed in each course.
"College level," "program proficiency," and "academic standards"
are not sufficiently precise. There is too much variation among
courses in the same program—indeed, among sections of the same

course—for these criteria to hold. Standards are too often relative instead of absolute. Screening tests can be used at the point of entry to each class. And precise exit criteria—also known as specific, measurable objectives—can be set.

The second option is to allow all students to enroll in any course but to limit the number of courses that poorly prepared students can take in any term and require that they take advantage of the available support services. Thus, students might take only one course at a time and participate in tutorial and learning-laboratory sessions on the basis of three hours for each credit hour attempted.

The third option is for the colleges to abandon the pretext that they offer freshman- and sophomore-level studies. They could enroll high school dropouts, adult basic education students, job seekers, and job upgraders, offering them the services they need outside the "credit hour" structure.

All three options are now in play to some extent. The colleges that are involved in mastery learning and other techniques that rely on precisely specified measures of student progress have built their programs on absolute standards. Those that monitor student progress and insist that students participate in auxiliary instructional exercises have moved well toward building the kind of collegewide instructional effort that teaching poorly prepared students demands. And those that have erected separate institutes that concentrate exclusively on adult basic education and career-related studies have abandoned collegiate studies de facto.

At least two options are *not* acceptable: allowing sizable percentages of students to fail, and reducing academic standards so that those who do get through have not been sufficiently well prepared to succeed in the workplace or in further education. High failure rates have led to numerous charges that the community colleges are a dead end for many of their matriculants, especially the minority students. By reducing standards, as detailed by Richardson, Fisk, and Okun (1983), the colleges were merely pushing the problem off to the students' employers or to the academic institutions in which they subsequently enrolled. In the 1980s the numerous state man-dates designed to improve student progress reflect a decided unwill-ingness to allow either of those options to continue.

As community colleges become involved more heavily in devel-opmental education, they have to reconcile their relations with the secondary schools, from which they broke away. Education at any level depends on prior preparation of the students. The decline in the secondary schools during the 1970s was one of the most notable events of the decade in education. Why it happened is not relevant to this discussion; reduced school budgets, the coming of age of a generation reared on television, the assigning of noned-ucative tasks to the schools, and numerous other causes have been cited. But much of the blame can be placed at the colleges' doors. The dearth of communication between college and secondary school staff members, the lack of articulation in curriculum, the failure to share teaching materials except on the basis of a random encounter, all must be mentioned. Concerns for social equity replaced a prior concern for admission standards. In their haste to expand access, the colleges neglected to assist the secondary schools in preparing the people who would be coming to them and even, in many cases, to recommend the secondary school courses that the students should take. Reconciling the dilemma will force them to rectify this omission.

Issues

Whether or not the community colleges pick up the seventeen-year-olds who have left high school early, and whether or not they serve as a bridge between schooling and work for their older stu-dents, developmental education fits within their mission of con-necting people with opportunities. They will be involved in remedial studies in one form or another, and their career education programs have already enrolled half of their students. Linking the two may be a natural next step. Can the colleges do it?

The colleges need more information about the effects of the developmental education in which they are so heavily engaged. Do segregated remedial programs lead to higher standards in other courses? Do the faculty members outside the programs add content to the courses from which the lesser-ability students have been removed? Do they pass students through the courses more rapidly when they are relieved from having to wait for the slower students? If so, all these results should be tabulated as benefits of the separate programs. If not, the better students have not gained from the absence of the poorer ones. So far, studies of these effects have been almost nonexistent.

Several attempts to engage instructors in defining the outcomes of their courses in specific, measurable terms have failed. What forms of staff development would be successful? What incentives could be used?

Would allowing instructors to test the students who sought entry to their classes and bar those who did not pass the test suffice to encourage them to become accountable for passing a specified percentage? No moves in this direction are apparent.

Required support services increase instructional costs. Can the colleges find sufficient funds for the necessary tutors, counselors, learning-laboratory technicians, and paraprofessional instructional aides? Can the faculty be encouraged to work with these aides, so that classroom and auxiliary instruction lead to parallel objectives?

What patterns of learning are demanded of students in the courses currently in place? Finding answers to that question demands analyses of classroom tests and teaching techniques, a form of research rarely seen in the contemporary college. Will the faculty and administrators demand it?

The overriding issue is whether community colleges can maintain their credibility as institutions of higher education even while they enroll the increasingly less well-prepared students. If they can, they will fulfill the promises of their earliest proponents.

10

· ·

Community Education
Extending College Services and Training

Community education, the broadest of all community college functions, embraces adult and continuing education, along with numerous other services to the local community. It may take the form of classes for credit or not for credit, varying in duration from one hour to a weekend, several days, or an entire school term. Community education may be sponsored by the college, by some other agency using college facilities, or jointly by the college and some outside group. It may be provided on campus, off campus, or through television, the newspapers, or radio. It may center on education or recreation, on programs for personal interest or for the good of the entire community.

The various forms of community education usually are fully supported by participant fees, grants, or contracts with external organizations. Participants tend to have short-term goals rather than degree or certificate objectives. They are usually older than the traditional eighteen- to twenty-one-year-old students, and their range of prior school achievement is more varied: many of them already hold baccalaureate or graduate degrees, and many more have never completed high school. They usually attend the courses or activities intermittently and part-time. They have their own reasons for attending, and program managers design activities accordingly.

Found in the earliest community colleges, these activities were carried along for decades on the periphery of the career and collegiate functions. They expanded greatly in the 1970s, slowed in the 1980s as college services came under closer scrutiny from external budget allocators, and grew again in the 1990s as college leaders continually sought new avenues for funding services to particular community groups.

This chapter reviews the rationale for and scope of community education, emphasizing the most popular activities: continuing education and contracted services. It considers also the perennial problems of funding, assessing effects, and validating these services that fall outside the traditional collegiate offerings.

Rationale

Beginning with Jesse Bogue, who popularized the term *community college* in the 1950s, and culminating with the Commission on the Future of Community Colleges' report, *Building Communities* (American Association of Community and Junior Colleges, 1988), the leaders of the AACJC were vigorous in their support for community education. Edmund J. Gleazer, Jr., president of the association from 1958 until 1981, wrote extensively in favor of education for direct community development, the expansion of the colleges beyond their role in postsecondary education, and continuing education as the main purpose. He emphasized the "community," rather than the "college," in the institution's title. To him, the institution was a resource to be used by individuals throughout their lifetime and by the general public as an agency assisting with community issues.

One of Gleazer's prime contentions was that "the community college is uniquely qualified to become the *nexus* of a community learning system, relating organizations with educational functions into a complex sufficient to respond to the population's learning needs" (1980, p. 10). He thought the institution capable of serving as a connector by virtue of its students and staff members, who frequently work at other jobs in the community. The college would be a link among all community organizations that provide learning activities. "Among these are radio and television stations, newspapers, libraries, museums, schools, colleges, theaters, parks, orchestras, dance groups, unions, and clubs" (p. 10). As for the money to pay for all this, Gleazer made repeated calls for fiscal formulas that would recognize the diverse programs presented by community colleges. However, he recognized that "a kind of riptide exists between the interest in lifelong education and the apparently limited financial resources available for conventional education for traditional students" (1976, p. 6).

Numerous other commentators have favored community education as a dominant function for community colleges. Myran (1969) traced the community education concept through university extension services and the adult and continuing education that has been offered by the public schools for the past century. These institutions were thereby able to provide educational services to individuals and groups without being wed to traditional academic forms, such as credits, semesters, and grades. In Myran's view, the community-based college is eminently equipped to provide such services because of its ability "to coordinate planning with other community agencies, its interest in participatory learning experiences as well as cognitive ones, the wide range of ages and life goals represented in its student body, and the alternative instructional approaches it arranges to make learning accessible to various community groups" (p. 5). Martorana and Piland (1984) similarly promoted the concept; Cross has furthered it in many of her writings, such as *Adults as Learners* (1981); and it is thematic in the numerous issues of *Community Services Catalyst*, published since 1970.

Its intentions are noble. Harlacher and Gollattscheck recommended a college that would be a "vital participant in the total renewal process of the community . . . dedicated to the continual growth and development of its citizens and its social institutions" (1978, p. 7). Such a college would offer the kinds of education community members want, not the kind that pedagogues think is good for them, and at locations where the learners are, not where the college says they should be. Harlacher and Gollattscheck urged community colleges to cooperate with social, governmental, professional, educational, and neighborhood agencies in mutually supportive advisory relationships and in joint ventures.

Most recently, the AACJC-sponsored Commission on the Future of Community Colleges has urged the colleges to coalesce around the community education concept:

> The community college, at its best, can be a center for problem-solving in adult illiteracy or the education of the disabled. It can be a center for leadership training, too. It can also be the place where education and business leaders meet to talk about the problems of displaced workers. It can bring together agencies to strengthen services for minorities, working women, single parent heads of households, and unwed teenage parents. It can coordinate efforts to provide day care, transportation, and financial aid. The community college can take the lead in long-range planning for community development. And it can serve as the focal point for improving the quality of life in the inner city [American Association of Community and Junior Colleges, 1988, p. 35].

This seems a large order, but the commission is dedicated to fostering the colleges as centers of community life. Its report begins with the premise that "The term *community* should be defined not only as a region to be served, but also as a climate to be created" (p. 3), and many of its seventy-seven recommendations follow from that theme.

What has stimulated these calls for completely revised structures? What has made these advocates so concerned with community building and noncampus forms? One clue is provided by the nature of community colleges' political and fiscal support. The colleges draw minuscule funds from private donors and have few foundation-supported research contracts. Instead, they depend almost entirely on public monies awarded in a political arena. And here they have difficulty competing with the more prestigious universities for support in legislatures dominated by state university alumni. They seem to be turning to their local constituents, seeking links with taxpayers at the grass roots—seeking support from the business community, for example, by providing customized job-training services for local employers.

Community education proponents foster activities different from the traditional courses taught by regular faculty members, saying that these are archaic, restrictive, discriminatory, and narrowly focused. They seem to feel that doing away with the traditional forms in which education has been conducted will necessarily lead to a higher quality of service. In their desire to eschew elitism, they articulate populist, egalitarian goals. The more diverse the population served, and the less traditionally based the program, the better.

The overarching concept of community education is certainly justifiable; few would quibble with the intent of an institution to upgrade its entire community rather than merely to provide a limited array of courses for people aged eighteen to twenty-one. However, the total seems less than the sum of its parts. The components of community education must be addressed separately in order to understand its scope and effect. Are all segments of equal value? Who decides what shall be presented, and who shall pay for it?

Categories

The terms most commonly used in definitions of community education include

- *Adult education:* instruction designed for people who are beyond the age of compulsory school attendance and who have either completed or interrupted their formal education

- *Continuing education:* the learning effort undertaken by people whose principal occupations are no longer as students, those who regard learning as a means of developing their potential or resolving their problems

- *Lifelong learning:* intermittent education, whether or not undertaken in school settings

- *Community services:* the broadest term; whatever services an institution provides that are acceptable to the people in its service area

- *Community-based education:* programs designed by the people served and developed for the good of the community (Brawer, 1980)

Respondents to a nationwide survey of directors of continuing education defined it as "courses and activities for credit or non-credit, formal classroom or nontraditional programs, cultural, recreational offerings specifically designed to meet the needs of the surrounding community and using school, college, and other facilities" (Fletcher and others, 1977, p. 12). "Community-based" education was more related to community problem-solving activities.

Not content with a definition centering on the participants' age, proponents of adult and continuing education refer to it as learner-centered education, with the learners participating "actively at every stage of the educational process. . . . The content and the methodologies should draw heavily upon the learner's life and work experience." The instructors are "facilitators of learning," concerned more with process than with content (Freedman, 1987, p. 63). As with most concepts in education, continuing education is more an ideology than a theory.

Conceptually, community education includes elements of career, developmental, and collegiate education. Career education is organized around programs that prepare people for the job market, whereas community education includes short courses offered for occupational upgrading or relicensure. Collegiate education is directed toward preparing people for academic degrees, whereas community education may include regular college courses taken by adults, the awarding of college credit for experience, and noncredit courses actually taught at the college level—for example, conversational foreign languages. Developmental education is designed to remedy the defects in student learning occasioned by prior school failure, whereas community education may include adult basic studies that focus on literacy, high school completion, and general education development. Some elements of community education—programs for people with disabilities and for prison inmates, for example—may cut across all three of the other functions. However, other elements in community education relate more to providing noneducative services to the community than they do to the educational dimension itself. In this category would fall the opening of college facilities for public functions and a variety of recreational services—the community service notion.

Practically, the source of funds tends to divide community education from the other functions. Community education activities are more likely to be self-supporting, fully funded through tuition or with money provided by an outside agency on the basis of a contract for services rendered. State and federal funds earmarked for special groups are often used in community education programs. In some cases local tax monies and categorical grants are used for community education, whereas career and collegiate education are funded by the states through various formulas, usually based on student enrollment or credit hours generated.

Enrollments

The variations in definition and categories make it difficult to estimate the magnitude of community education. Enrollment figures, especially, are unreliable; they are usually understated except when being pronounced by advocates intent on showing that the colleges serve nearly everyone in their district. Because degree-credit courses are funded at higher, more consistent levels than most of community education, the tendency was to classify as much as possible as degree credit, thus inflating those numbers at the expense of community education enrollment figures. However, as the states placed limits on the number of credit hours for which they would reimburse the colleges, that practice was curtailed. Actually, the total community education enrollment would far exceed the combined enrollment in the career-certificate and collegiate-degree programs if people who enrolled in college-credit classes but without degree aspirations were classified instead as adult education students. But enrollees in noncredit courses and participants in community service activities are those typically counted.

The enrollment figures that are available are worth recounting. Community education enrollments (in-service, recreational, and life enrichment programs that are not part of for-credit, academic programs) were reported in the AACJC *Directory* between 1974–75, when they were 3,259,972, and 1984–85, when they totaled 3,651,225. For the decade they ranged between three and four million. However, the introduction to the 1980 *Directory* states that "because these programs vary in length, with no clearly defined registration periods, it is difficult to get a clear picture. . . . Some institutions do not routinely collect enrollment figures from community education students" (p. 3). Extrapolating from the 877 institutions that did report student head count in noncredit activities in 1984–85, the compilers of the *Directory* estimated that 4,848,065 participated nationwide, with 99.3 percent of them in public colleges. The AACC has since stopped reporting these data in its *Directory* because of the imprecision of the figures.

Data difficulties make it impossible to compare community education enrollments between states as well. Some state reports include adult basic education and/or participation in recreational activities, and others do not. Further, head-count enrollments in community education usually include duplicate enrollments occasioned when the same person participates in more than one non-credit course or activity during the year. Nonetheless, state enrollments are useful as an estimate of the magnitude and types of functions included in the community education definition.

For example, the AACJC *Directory* reported 153,086 participants in community education in 1979 in California, compared with a total enrollment of 1,101,648 students in degree-credit programs. This relatively low ratio reflects the predominance of the California secondary schools in adult education. In the three community college districts that had jurisdiction over adult education, more than half of the students were classified as adults. Community education enrollments in California plummeted after the passage of Proposition 13 in 1978 cut off the local funding base for community services, but enrollments rose again when the courses were reinstated on a student-fee basis.

The total varies as well in other states. In Florida the community colleges have major responsibility for offering courses to individuals aged sixteen and older who had legally left the lower schools. In 1985–86, 119,936 were enrolled in adult general studies and 122,711 in community instructional services, totals comparable to the enrollments in collegiate and career programs (Florida State Department of Education, 1987). The North Carolina Community College System's 1992–93 *Annual Statistical Report* said that 60 percent of the students in the state were enrolled in programs that do not lead to college degrees. These included occupational, adult basic education, and avocational areas (North Carolina Department of Community Colleges, 1993b). In Washington, 33,662 students were enrolled for such reasons as preparing for retirement and developing parenting and homemaking skills. An additional 11,396 students sought basic skills training, including English as a second language (Washington State Board for Community and Technical Colleges, 1992). The Mississippi Public Community and Junior Colleges *Enrollment Report* for Fall 1993 showed that 36 percent of the students were in "non-credit" courses, including adult basic education

(ABE), graduate equivalency diploma (GED) programs, literacy programs, and training in various industries (Mississippi State Board for Community and Junior Colleges, 1993).

There is no question that the demand for non-degree-related courses is high across all segments of the population. A 1991 National Household Education Survey found that one-third of all employed adults had enrolled in some type of job-related, part-time educational activity in the prior year. Managers and professionals were much more likely to participate, but employed people in all categories were taking courses in professional development, technical or skilled job training, and several additional areas. The modal enrollee was aged thirty-five to forty-four (National Center for Education Statistics, 1994c).

Scope

The scope of community education is reflected in documents emanating from colleges around the country. Continuing education alone covers a broad area.

Continuing Education

A Ford Foundation Study reported by Gittell (1985) found that many low-income adults are involved in community education and concluded that community-based colleges provide an important option for many people who are not served elsewhere. Whatever the financial circumstances, many groups of people are involved because community education addresses a wide variety of concerns, including child care, substance abuse, senior citizen services, student achievement/school effectiveness, community pride/support for schools, unemployment and underemployment, literacy/diploma and degree completion, and community economic development.

Programs for special groups are provided, usually when sufficient funding can be obtained. Programs for displaced workers, gerontology programs for both the general public and providers of direct services to older adults, women's programs, retired persons' programs, and programs for single parents or displaced homemakers are directed toward particular groups. Several hundred community colleges participate in the Servicemembers Opportunity Colleges program, which allows members of the armed forces and their families to enroll in college-level programs at community and state colleges and universities. This program, founded in 1972, helps to "strengthen and coordinate voluntary college-level educational opportunities for Service members" (Servicemembers Opportunity Colleges, 1995, p. 1). The program advocates flexible access to higher education for members of the armed forces and strengthens the liaison and communication between the military and higher education.

Credit for Experience

The awarding of college credit for experience is a component of community education. A survey of Texas community colleges (Golemon, 1979) revealed that 76 percent awarded credits applicable to an associate degree. The learning was validated by examination, a verified experience record, personal interview, or combinations of these and other methods. In Sinclair Community College's (Ohio) Credit for Lifelong Learning Program, students are awarded credit for prior experiences that match or are equivalent to college level courses (Mann, 1993). Whatcom Community College (Washington) developed a handbook for students to help them gain credit for prior learning experiences (Deiro, 1983). Orange Coast College's (California) Assessment of Prior Learning (APL) program included an assessment procedure used to award credit for demonstrated competencies (Snow and Bruns, 1982). A similar program in Texas was described by Lindahl (1982).

Special Services

Several types of cooperative endeavors between community colleges and other community agencies may be found. The AACJC's Policies for Lifelong Education project surveyed cooperative relationships between colleges and community groups in 1978 and reported an average of fifty-nine cooperative arrangements serving 8,781 people at each of 173 colleges. Arrangements between the colleges and local and state clubs and organizations as well as other educational institutions dominated the list. Cooperative arrangements were also found with county and municipal government agencies and private enterprise, including industrial concerns. These joint ventures ranged from sharing facilities to offering mutually sponsored courses. The majority of funds came from tuition and fees charged participants, but many of the programs were supported by college community service funds, often generated by local taxes (Gilder and Rocha, 1980).

Although not included in the community education figures, the many programs that fine arts and humanities departments sponsor in cooperation with local agencies, such as arts councils and museums, are properly a part of the concept. Some colleges have developed community-based forums in which the participants discuss subjects reported in the local newspaper. The community forum procedure has been used to bring the humanities to participants through lectures, panels, debates, dramatizations, films, and radio broadcasts.

Community education often involves providing special services to other publicly funded institutions, prisons for example. Since 1967, Arizona community colleges have provided basic skills and vocational training to inmates within their expanding prison system. Hagerstown Junior College (Maryland) began its prisoner education program in 1969. J. F. Ingram State Community College (Alabama) and Southeastern Illinois College have also been prominent in inmate education. In 1976, more than 260 community colleges provided services to approximately 26,000 inmates (Wolford and Littlefield, 1985). (A more recent study estimated there are approximately 22,000 inmate students; see Cvancara, 1994.) Community colleges in Canada have organized similar programs; Snowden (1986) has described the New Brunswick Community College program in a maximum-security facility.

These programs for prisoners seem to be effective. In 1990, between one hundred to two hundred associate degrees were awarded to Arizona's prison inmates (Bennett, 1991). The largest inmate education program in Virginia, in existence since 1984, operates in Mecklenburg Correctional Center, through Southern Virginia Community College. In 1990, 30 percent of the inmates were enrolled. The program's intentions are to enhance a sense of accomplishment, self-esteem, and practical training for life after prison (Gendron and Cavan, 1990). The J. F. Ingram program claims a 2 percent recidivism rate for its graduates, as compared with 35 percent in the rest of the Alabama prison system (Cvancara, 1994). However, legislation in 1994 cutting federal funds for prison education depressed these involvements.

Continuing education programs also serve other special groups. Adult basic education, centering on basic skills development for functionally illiterate adults, has been provided by community colleges in areas where that activity is not well coordinated by elementary and secondary schools. A study of adult basic education in Washington community colleges (Seppanen, 1991) found that most of the students who had been enrolled in programs designed to make up for high school deficiencies cited personal interest goals for themselves. The Adult Basic Education Program at Rio Salado Community College (Arizona) served more than 5,700 students in numerous locations (Vanis and Mills, 1987). Milwaukee Area Technical College (Wisconsin) helps migrant and seasonal farm workers and their dependents obtain GED (graduate equivalency diploma) degrees and either gain employment or continue their education in postsecondary institutions outside the agricultural setting (Martinez and Gonis, 1992). The success of such programs is evident in enrollment patterns. In 1991, about 2.5 million adults were enrolled in adult basic education programs across the country; more than one million more were enrolled in adult secondary education programs.

A review of other activities conducted under the heading of continuing education's special services reveals little change in scope over the past decades. Many colleges offer job fairs to help connect people who need jobs with businesses that need people; recreational activities in senior citizen's centers (Heinrich, 1991); parenting classes (Hare and others, 1987; Witmer, 1990); child care training programs (Campion and Kyle, 1990); and drug and alcohol abuse workshops (Mellander and Hubbard, 1990).

Contracted Services

Contract training refers to instruction that is provided for specific occupational purposes, usually outside the college-credit program. It falls into three categories: training designed specifically for the employees of certain companies; training for public-agency employees; and training for specific groups such as unemployed people or people on welfare. Funds for the contract training may come from the companies or public agencies that benefit or from state or federal funds.

Surveys conducted by the League for Innovation in the Community College (Doucette, 1993) and the National Center for Research in Vocational Education (Lynch and others, 1991) suggest the magnitude of contract training. Practically all the community colleges in the nation provide work force training. The programs designed for specific companies include job-specific and computer-related training, management preparation, and workplace literacy. Although the employers who benefit provide a significant portion of the cost of these programs, college funds are often used as a supplement. Because the programs are only tangentially connected with the college-credit curriculum, some faculty groups have complained that they are employing instructors who do not pass review by the regular faculty, and that they are bypassing the traditional channels of curriculum development, thus weakening the overall college program (Stanback-Stroud, 1993). But these are minority voices; contract training has become a significant portion of the community college's overall educational effort. And in some colleges it was big indeed; in 1991, sixteen selected community colleges reported that they had generated over $42 million through contract training during the previous years (Updike, 1991). Roueche, Taber, and Roueche (1995) describe many other types of collaborations with community agencies.

Community colleges have long taken advantage of various federal programs designed to retrain technologically displaced workers and other unemployed people, using funds provided by the Manpower Development Training Act of 1962, the Comprehensive Employment and Training Act of 1973, and the Job Training Partnership Act of 1983. These programs assisted the colleges in designing activities in accordance with local job needs and in cooperation with employers in their region. In 1985 the Sears-Roebuck Foundation gave a sizable award to enhance collaboration between community colleges and local employers. Through the award the AACJC and the Association of Community College Trustees established a Keeping America Working project (American Association of Community and Junior Colleges, 1986).

Labor union leaders also have supported community education programs—for example, by negotiating tuition aid packages with employers, serving on advisory committees for the colleges' occupational programs, and helping to establish cooperative apprenticeship training programs and programs to assist union members in studying for leadership roles. Some union-sponsored activities assist members in studying the liberal arts (Berger, 1988). Others are designed to help working people deal with personal problems or problems with employers.

Several examples illustrate contract training's effectiveness. The Chancellor's Office of the California Community Colleges describes the working and educational relationships between five community colleges and the public sector (California Community Colleges, 1993). Included is a program Southwestern College has implemented along with the U.S. Navy in which students participate in internships located at the command posts. Orientations to work responsibilities and military guidelines accompany the training. At the end of the internship, students are given 120 days in which they can be hired by the navy into full-time positions. IBM's program with Illinois Valley Community College and forty-seven other colleges trains employees about new technologies associated with computer integrated manufacturing (Andrews and Allen, 1992).

Entrepreneurship Training

Establishing a small business has always been a natural sequence for some graduates of community college career programs. In 1980, a congressional act created Small Business Development Centers (SBDCs), a venture funded jointly by the federal government, the U.S. Small Business Administration, and state and local public and private agencies. These centers, in many cases housed in community colleges, were designed to help individuals interested in starting a business, and those who already had businesses but required management assistance.

Carmichael (1991) discusses the steps involved in establishing SBDCs in community colleges and describes Lane Community College (Oregon), with the first community college-based network in the nation, and Bergen County Community College (New Jersey), with one of the first pilot programs funded by the SBA. Other exemplary programs include Montgomery Community College (Maryland) and several other colleges in the Washington, D.C. metropolitan area.

The difference between entrepreneurship training and small-business development on the one hand, and work force training on the other, lies both in program centers and in people for whom the programs are intended. Designed to assist people starting their own businesses, entrepreneurship training's content ranges from developing a business plan to obtaining licenses and loans and to employing other people to operate a successful business.

The CSCC examined the scope and magnitude of entrepreneurship training in the nation's community colleges and found that most of the large-city colleges had some such involvement, usually provided through their continuing education division or through a center for economic development or small-business development institute. The programs were organized on an ad hoc basis when state, federal, foundation, or local-agency funds could be acquired. Typically, the people toward whom the training was directed could afford to pay little or no tuition (Center for the Study of Community Colleges, 1994). Several other reports describe both statewide and local efforts to promote entrepreneurial competence in California (Carvell, 1988), Kansas (Gainous and others, 1987), and Clackamas Community College in Oregon (Borquist, 1986).

In sum, because the concept of community education describes an area of service that knows no limits on client age, prior educational attainment, interest, or intent, the scope of offerings is limited only by staff energies and imagination and by the funds available. According to Coastline Community College (California) administrators, "The community is its campus, both physically and philosophically. The college nurtures the community and is, in turn, sustained by it. . . . Virtually any course may be offered if it is approved by the state, can attract sufficient enrollees to make it cost-effective, and if suitable instruction is available. Considerable latitude in programming decisions devolves upon the college, which, as a result, is encouraged to adopt a fairly aggressive marketing posture" (Luskin and Small, 1980–81, pp. 25–27).

Effectiveness

Are the programs effective? Assessing the outcomes of community education is difficult because, with the entire community as the client, effects are diffuse and subject to contamination from innumerable sources. One way of measuring the effect of continuing education courses has been to ask the participants how they liked them. The 4,631 students enrolled in community service courses in ten Florida community colleges were asked why they enrolled and the extent to which their expectations were met. Among the twenty-two choices, the major reasons for enrolling were "to improve my chances of employment" (42 percent), "to further my cultural or social development" (39 percent), and "to learn a certain hobby" (34 percent). The only areas in which expectations were not met by at least 60 percent of the respondents were "to help with an alcohol-or-drug related problem" and "to learn about family planning" (Nickens, 1977, p. 269).

Other evaluations typically are process-related. The Maryland State Board for Community Colleges has specified that continuing education courses, in order to be eligible for state funding, "must illustrate the skill or knowledge to be developed and the student outcomes expected" (1988, p. 13). McGuire (1988) has provided a set of criteria by which entire community-based programs might be measured. But these again are process criteria: the extent to which community members were involved in program planning, the linkages that were built between the college and other community agencies, the feedback received from community leaders and clients, and similar subjective measures that are dependent on an observer's interpretation. All of community education seems to be assessed as though it were continuing education for individuals raised to the level of the broader group. If the clients define the goals and the processes, success is measured by their saying that they achieved those goals. Independent ratings based on measurable change seem as scarce as is advance determination of the change to be effected.

Organization and Funding

The organization of Coastline Community College in California, as a noncampus institution devoted primarily to community education, and similar institutions in Arizona and Washington stimulated the development of a new form of professional community college educator. The managers of these institutions not only must be curriculum and instructional designers, the role played by practitioners in all colleges, but also must interact with community advisory committees, find agencies to bear the cost of their programs, advertise for students, employ part-time staff members continually, produce varieties of new instructional media, and resolve jurisdictional disputes with other agencies. Even though such roles are not as well defined in the more conventional community colleges, those with sizable community education efforts have, of necessity, a number of people acting in those capacities.

Separate administrative entities have also been organized in several individual colleges. Valencia Community College (Florida) began an Open Campus in 1974 to coordinate all continuing education, community services, and functions that the college was providing away from the campus. Headed by a provost reporting directly to the president, the Open Campus was organized as a unit equal in autonomy to the other branch campuses of the college (St. John, 1977). The off-campus learning center operated by Lansing Community College (Michigan) included a director of continuing education, a formal contract between the college and the local school districts, a broad selection of courses, and the same basic support services that were provided at the central campus (Herder and Standridge, 1980). The Extended Learning Institute at John Tyler Community College (Virginia) used television, radio, and newspapers as media for the instruction of a wide variety of students in its district (Adams, 1986). These types of organizations—which coordinate the noncredit courses, distance learning, and related community education activities—have been built in many colleges. They typically have their own staff, budget lines, and funding sources.

Myran (1969) identified five organizational patterns for community service programs operating within traditional college structures. In the *departmental extension* pattern, community service programs are located in and generated through the departmental structure. The other four patterns consist of differentiated administrative structures. In the *college centralized* pattern, professional community service staff members divide their time between assessing community needs and coordinating programs. They are located in a separate department or division. Staff members in the *community specialist* model are located in the community rather than on the campus. In addition to semipermanent advisory committees that may be coordinated by a college staff member, the *community advisory group* arrangement includes ad hoc committees dealing with critical issues. Administrators in the *college affiliate* pattern have direct responsibility to organizations in the community and an affiliate relationship with the college.

Haynes and Polk (1991) note that a college should have a reason for establishing a separate department for continuing education. This rationale will help organizers construct the program's mission, goals, and specific services to be offered and will help in assessing the impact of these services. However, some of the goals created in the development of community education may be counterproductive if faculty and staff are not involved in designing them. The authors conclude that careful development of community education services will result in positive financial gains.

The ways that community education has been funded reflect its growth and variety. Some community education activities receive no direct aid; all expenses are borne by the participants themselves or by an agency with which the institution has a contract. Others are funded by enrollment formulas that tend to be lower than the formulas used for the career and collegiate courses. Funding for the recreational and avocational activities within the community education definition is the most difficult to obtain because those activities seem least justifiable for support at taxpayer expense.

Some states have funded adult basic education at the same rate as career and collegiate programs. Others have funded them well but under different formulas. In Florida, developmental and community instructional services received nearly as much state money per FTSE as the career and collegiate functions. However, continuing education courses in Iowa were not eligible for state aid. Oregon reimbursed colleges for remedial and continuing education courses at approximately the same level as for collegiate and career programs. Maryland funded continuing education courses that met certain criteria, especially if they focused on occupational, developmental, and consumer education; recreational courses were not eligible for reimbursement (Maryland State Board for Community Colleges, 1988). Once again, it is important to note that between-state comparisons cannot accurately be made because the definitions of the courses and programs included in the different categories vary widely.

There is no best plan for financing community colleges in every state, and disputes over financing often disguise disagreements over the community college mission. Haynes and Polk (1991) pointed out that continuing education units designed to keep an institution viable during periods of decline were self-serving and less likely to succeed than those that identified and served a community's educational needs. State officials certainly accord lower priority to financial support of these programs, compared with the traditional academic and occupational functions. Historically, community services have been funded by local sources, and as community college finance shifts toward the state level, funding becomes more precarious. In Virginia, a survey was taken of the forty members of the state senate, and the presidents of the state's twenty-three community colleges, to see how well these two groups agreed on which programs could be appropriately funded by state taxes. While the senate and presidents agreed upon the majority of goals, these two groups ranked "providing general interest courses and activities for senior citizens and other community members" twelfth out of fourteen categories (Ashworth and Vogler, 1991).

The precarious base of funding for community education was revealed during the 1978–1981 period, when tax-limitation legislation was passed in several states and a national administration pledged to reduce taxes was elected. Soon after the 1978 passage of Proposition 13 in California, the average community services budget was cut by at least 50 percent. These cuts resulted in a 76 percent increase in courses for which fees were charged and a 24 percent decrease in courses funded through college budgets. Kintzer detailed the cuts, showing that 20 percent of the 4,600 noncredit courses were eliminated and 10 percent were placed on a fee basis. Recreational noncredit classes were reduced by 60 percent, and senior citizen programs were halved statewide as twenty-one colleges deleted their community service budgets. Overall, since Proposition 13 "eliminated the five-cent permissive property tax that had protected community services activities, including programs, personnel, and some capital construction, for nearly fifteen years, the fiscal basis for this function was destroyed" (1980b, p. 7).

However, the programs not only survived but actually expanded. In 69 percent of the colleges surveyed by Harlacher and Ireland, the community services directors said that "the status of their community services and continuing education programs had increased during the past five years. Another 21 percent said that the status had been maintained" (1988, p. 3). The prime programmatic emphasis was on work-force training and retraining, with leisure-time education and economic development the secondary areas of emphasis. Despite the strength of these programs, the growing mandate for self-support by community services and continuing education programs posed a major threat to their continued expansion. The regulations most commonly cited by their respondents were state rules regarding self-support for noncredit offerings, community instructional service, and leisure-time courses. Other notable threats to expansion were lack of instructional support and integration, and competition from the private sector and community-based organizations.

Much of community education transfers the costs of certain programs from one public agency to another. The training programs conducted by community colleges on behalf of police and fire departments that are too small to operate their own academies offer an example. Where the departments pay the college to do the training, little changes except that the college coordinates the training. But in some instances, law enforcement programs are converted to degree- or certificate-credit programs, thus qualifying them for support through the state's educational funds. The cost of these programs is therefore transferred from the local to the state government budget. Similarly, some industries contract with community colleges to train their workers, paying for the services. But in numerous instances, targeted training programs are given for credit, thus shifting the cost from the industrial concern to the state budget.

College managers tread carefully when developing training programs for the employees of local industries. The programs are often presented at the plant site, using the company's equipment. There is no problem if the company pays all expenses, including the instructors' salaries, on a flat rate or cost per head. But if the programs are offered for college credit and the usual state reimbursement procedures are in effect, they must be open to all applicants, thus potentially compromising the company's work rules. In many cases existing courses offered at the college have been modified to fit a major employer's requirements, thereby maintaining intact the faculty contracts and preexisting course accreditation. The company may provide new equipment, paying in kind for the special service. Program development costs may also be charged to the company, but the accounting procedures occasioned by the charge-back can be difficult to effect.

Contracts to train military personnel are particularly intricate. They specify the site, the curriculum, and the tuition that may be charged. They are overseen not only by the college accrediting agency but also by the military officials, the Veterans Administration, and other federal agencies. Difficulties arise when, for example, the college faculty is covered by a union contract but the military does not recognize union membership for its employees. Such involvements also add greatly to the college's administrative costs because of the complexities of arranging the contracts and maintaining elaborate files for the auditors.

In sum, the variety of activities within the scope of community education provides an opportunity not only for serving new clients but also for manipulating the funding to the institution's advantage. If a course can be designated as a degree-credit course and thus become eligible for state aid, it may be moved to that category. If a program can be offered on a contractual basis, with a different government agency or a private industrial concern paying for it, it may be so arranged and thus not drain the college's operating funds. Although administrative costs may be high, community education offers opportunities for creativity in program planning and staff deployment to college managers who find their efforts in the traditional programs hamstrung by external licensing bureaus and negotiated contracts with the faculty.

Program Validity

Advocates answer questions of validity by saying that through community education they can serve the entire populace. To them, community education is a natural extension of the open-door policy and the egalitarian impulses that gave rise to community colleges in the first place. The idea of community uplift has also been presented as a purpose. To those subscribing to that idea, the development of a sense of community is the goal. The college serves as the focal point for community pride. The events that it sponsors enhance a sense of community in the district; the act of planning, teaching, and participating in recreational programs and personal-help workshops fosters community spirit. By this line of reasoning, any activity that brings people together—health fair, senior citizens' day, hobby course offered in a convalescent home, or college-sponsored trip to a foreign country—will suffice.

Less noble, but nonetheless prevalent, is the intent to aggrandize the institutions or at least to maintain their current size. Decline is painful. College leaders who peruse the demography charts, consider the competing institutions in their area, and study the potential market for their own programs may wonder about sources of students. Enrollment of older students enabled the colleges to avoid severe declines when the population of eighteen-year-olds dropped in the 1980s. Much of community education acts as a marketing device, not only for the activities offered within it but also for the traditional college programs. The awarding of credit for experience offers a prime example. As many as 80 percent of the people who receive such credit go on to take additional courses at the college. The term *changing markets* is frequently used by those who exhort the institutions to move into new service areas lest they suffer the fate of once-prosperous industries that failed to adapt to changing conditions.

Community education seems also a way of blunting charges of failure in other areas. In the 1950s and 1960s there were widespread contentions that community colleges would enable the disadvantaged to move upward on the socioeconomic ladder and would teach skills of citizenship and literacy to people whom the lower schools had failed. College spokespersons also promised to provide an avenue to the baccalaureate for students of lesser ability and lower income. All these goals prove more elusive than their proponents expected. It is easier to propose new roles for the colleges than to explain away their inability to fulfill old ones.

The issue of institutional credibility must also be addressed. Is the community college a true college? Most community education advocates and most of those who make fervent calls for a "new mission" make light of that question, but it has been posed both by members of the public and by professional educators. Faculty members trying to maintain collegiate standards in their courses certainly take a dim view of most community education activities. Correspondingly, most community education proponents find little place for the regular faculty members in their programs, preferring instead to staff them with part-timers working ad hoc with little or no commitment to the institution itself. Community education has thus fostered internal dissension. Administrators may perceive the traditional faculty members as anchors dragging at an institution that would propel itself into a new era; the faculty tend to cast a jaundiced eye on the recreational activities and the contract programs that use instructors as interchangeable parts to be dismissed when the particular programs for which they were employed have ended.

To those whose memories of college center on courses in the liberal arts taught on a campus, community education threatens to debase the institution. Their perception of college is as a place of mobility for individuals who, through exposure to higher learning, take their place as productive members of society. To them, community uplift is an alien dimension; its aspects seem to be frills or peripheral functions at best, anti-intellectual at worst. They question the standards in the noncredit, open-circuit, and continuing education programs; and they wonder about quality control in an institution lacking a corps of full-time professional scholars. They reject contentions that an institution serving up a pastiche of uncoordinated functions bears any relation to an institution of higher learning. Community education advocates may try to dismiss these critics as anachronisms nostalgic for the ivy-covered college for an elite group, but the ranks of the critics include sizable percentages of the public, who want their community college to serve as an avenue of mobility for their children, not as a purveyor of circuses and illusions.

Future Development

The future for community education rests on its funding base and the way it is organized within the colleges. The people served through community education do not fit typical student categories. They seldom enroll in programs leading to degrees; they may not even be enrolled in formally structured courses but, instead, may be participating in events especially tailored for their interests. Therefore, any attempt to fund community education on the basis of average daily attendance, FTSE, or some other category that suggests students attending courses leading to degrees or certificates on a campus is at variance with the intent of the program and the pattern of student participation.

To the extent that community education activities are merged even conceptually with the collegiate and career education functions, they all are weakened. Community service activities cannot flourish when they are presented by people with traditional views of instruction and when they are funded ad hoc. The collegiate function is weakened when it coexists with community service activities in which people get college transfer credit for participating in courses and events even when they are not intending to gain degrees. And the career education function suffers when the figures on the number of people gaining employment in the areas for which they were trained are reduced by the number of students upgrading their skills in jobs they already hold or transferring to senior institutions instead of going to work.

Community colleges that want to maintain successful community education operations should be reorganized. Ideally, community education would be funded programmatically; that is, a college would be awarded a fixed sum each year to provide cultural, occupational upgrade, recreation, personal interest, community health, and semiprofessional retraining programs to the people of its district. Or the colleges could maintain their open-access policies— with students taking courses that may or may not lead to degrees —but should build a transfer or honors college within such a structure. The main funding pattern would be for individuals participating in courses with reimbursement on an attendance basis; but the transfer or honors college would be operated separately, with a variety of specially funded enrichment opportunities and work assistance or scholarship monies made available. Another way of separating community education efforts might be to maintain the college's collegiate and career functions but to offer all the community education services through an extension division, as many universities have done. This would put all community education on a self-sustaining basis, since those who take the short courses or participate in the activities offered would pay for them ad hoc. Still another way of maintaining the traditional college with a community education component would be to place the community service work, along with the remedial and adult basic education function, in a separate center, where staff members might not have credentials. Unlike the regular faculty, who are paid on a class-hour basis, they would be paid for working a forty-hour week. None of these models is likely to enjoy widespread adoption. Community education will continue as adjunctive, supported by participant fees, contracted services, and special-purpose grants.

The education of youth in the sixteen-to-twenty age group may well be a fruitful area for expanding community education services. In the late 1970s the Carnegie Council on Policy Studies in Higher Education conducted several studies pointing to the importance of revised educational forms encompassing both schooling and work for sizable percentages of youth. This area of study was pursued in the 1980s by the U.S. Department of Education, which published a number of reports on the topic, for example, *Education and Training of 16- to 19-Year-Olds After Compulsory Schooling in the United States* (Stacey, Alsalam, Gilmore, and To, 1988). Special funds from state and federal governments and philanthropic foundations will be run to this area in increasing volume.

Expansion of community colleges' activities to include special services for youth would be consistent with their tradition. Throughout their history they have been the recipients of technical and vocational functions that previously had been assigned to trade schools affiliated with the public school districts; the flowering of career education in the community colleges was merely the most recent development in that trend. The increasing number of arrangements whereby the colleges take responsibility for high school graduates at grade 11 suggests a move in that direction. Lieberman (1988) details many such programs. The federal government's interest in programs that assist students in moving from school to work provides an incentive.

Adult basic education is another area for the possible expansion of community education. In almost every state special funds have been made available for literacy training for adults, and in many states this responsibility has been shifted from the lower-school districts to the community colleges. The Goals 2000 target for adult literacy suggests an expanded federal government interest in this area.

It seems, then, that the areas of community education most promising for further development are those that have taken the community colleges away from their higher education affiliation. But this redefinition in the direction of career and literacy training differs markedly from the idea of the community college as an agency of direct community uplift. It is the community college as latter-day secondary school, not as social welfare bureau. It is the community college as educational structure rather than as purveyor of recreational activities and quasi-educative services.

The prognosis for other forms of continuing education is less clear. It is certain to vary in different institutions, depending mainly on the directors' vigor in attracting funds and publicizing offerings. The large market frequently noted by proponents of lifelong learning is composed, in the main, of people teaching themselves to play tennis, make furniture, cope with their families, understand their own physiology, and deal with cyclical changes in their lives. Those who need the discipline afforded by structured, institutionally sanctioned activities may be enticed away from their self-help books and informal study groups. But it is doubtful that they will greet eagerly the intervention of an agency that would coordinate all their learning efforts.

The issue of social versus individual benefits looms large in connection with community education. Most economic theorists would contend that funds collected from the taxpayers at large should be used to benefit society; hence, if a program is more beneficial to the individual than to the broader community, the person receiving that benefit should bear the cost. This is the basis for the legislative antagonism toward supporting courses in macramé and ceramics. And, indeed, many community education advocates were caught with their premises down when those human "needs" for activities that were provided by the college during the period of liberal funding dried up as the recreational programs were put on a pay-as-you-go basis, and enrollments declined to the extent that tuition advanced.

However, much of community education cannot be neatly categorized into services that benefit individuals rather than the broader society. When people complete a program in nursing at public expense and go on to work as trained nurses in the community, who benefits more, society or the individuals? Society gains trained nurses; the individuals gain access to a profession in which they can earn many more dollars than they could without the training. At the farther extreme are those forms of community education that assist society most clearly. One example is provided by community forums that explore patterns of energy use, quality of life, the effects of zoning, and the environment in the local community. Citizens are provided with information important to their making decisions within the social unit.

Those who would expand community education might do well to articulate and adhere to certain principles underlying its structure. The programs most defensibly supported by public funds are, first, those that tend toward the socially useful, as opposed to the individually beneficial, end of the continuum—for example, the forums instead of the self-help programs. Second, they are the verifiably educative programs, as opposed to those that are predominantly recreational, which provide credentials offering the illusion of learning, or which are thinly disguised contributors to transfer payments. Third, they are programs that provide services that are not readily available elsewhere for the people they serve. Thus, the better-integrated businesses would manage their own employee training programs while the colleges concentrated on assisting workers in less well-organized industries, such as restaurant workers in their area, who might benefit from periodic refresher courses in health care and sanitation. Heretofore, members of these latter groups have been the least likely to participate in education of their own volition, but the true community service institution would bend all effort to serve them. Unfortunately for the concept of social utility, programs in which the colleges effect training relationships with Fortune 500 companies are much more common than those that support farm workers or the homeless.

The advocates might also reduce their claims that community education has the potential for solving community problems. As Talbott observed, the college is confusing its ability to take on the whole community as its province with its ability to take on and solve all of the community's problems: "To take on the role of an omniscient social welfare agency strains the credibility as well as the resources of the college. It is not set up to revamp the courts, to change the traffic pattern, to purify the water, to clean the air of smog" (1976, p. 89).

Gottschalk (1978) also noted the dissimilarities between serving individuals and society by differentiating between problems and issues. Problems are individual; issues are broad enough to affect the community. Individuals who are unemployed have problems that the community college can mitigate by training them sufficiently so that each may obtain paid employment. But massive unemployment is a community issue, over which the college has little control. Attempting to solve community issues would require political action, which the colleges cannot afford to undertake because the risk of offending important public support groups is too great. The colleges sometimes get involved in low-risk community issues, offering forums on safe topics such as energy conservation. But a forum on the history of a local labor dispute would be risky. Most college leaders opt for the safe course. The local arts council may often meet in a college building that is never made available as a dormitory for the homeless.

Issues

Community education has not reached parity with degree- and certificate-credit programs either in funding or in internal and external perceptions of the college's main mission. For the foreseeable future, the community college as nexus for all the area's educational forms is an even less likely eventuality. How can an institution funded predominantly by the state respond appropriately to local needs?

Cultural and recreational activities conducted as part of community service programs have declined in the face of limited budgets and concomitant conversion of these functions to a self-sustaining basis. Should colleges try to maintain their recreational functions? Can cultural presentations be offered as part of the regular humanities programs and thus be absorbed into their funding packages?

How can quality be controlled in community education programs that do not come under the scrutiny of any outside agency or under internal curriculum review?

Any public agency ultimately can be supported only as long as the public perceives its value. The educative aspects of community education—its short courses, courses for institutionalized populations, and courses offered on job sites—are the colleges' strengths. Each noneducative function may have a debilitating long-term effect because it diffuses the college mission. Each time the colleges act as social welfare agencies or modern Chautauquas, they run the risk of reducing the support they must have if they are to pursue their main purpose.

11

Collegiate Function

Transfer and the Liberal Arts

The collegiate function encompasses two concepts: student flow and the liberal arts curriculum. Student flow refers to providing education at the thirteenth- and fourteenth-grade levels for students who are moving through the American educational system, which reaches from kindergarten through graduate school. The liberal arts curriculum includes education based on the humanities, science, and social science, the basic studies for most college students.

In this chapter, we marry the two. The discussion of the liberal arts is followed by the way that these studies affect student transfer to senior institutions. Curriculum details are included. The reasons for the decline in the collegiate studies in the 1970s, and their subsequent stabilization, are examined, along with the faculty as a liberal arts support group. Also included are discussions of the academic disciplines, transfer rates, ways of assessing student learning in the liberal arts, and the possibilities for merging the various curricular strands.

Liberal Arts

Originally, the liberal arts embodied the collegiate function. They were the main and, in some cases, the only curriculum in the early American colleges. Codified in the medieval European universities, they were brought into the colleges as reflecting the best in human thought. From ancient grammar, rhetoric, logic, music, astronomy, geometry, and arithmetic, all considered essential for the learned person, the humanities gradually came to include classical languages, philosophy, and natural science. By the end of the nineteenth century, the physical and social sciences had also shouldered their way into this curriculum.

In the late nineteenth century, the universities gained dominance over the liberal arts colleges and, together with them, assumed responsibility for defining the educated person. Before that time, people studying the liberal arts were as likely to do so in their own home, in a society of amateurs, in a church or monastic setting, or in an independent laboratory as within a school. But the universities institutionalized the teaching of science and those aspects of the humanities that had not theretofore been part of the curriculum—modern foreign languages, literary criticism, art, and history—and made the study of them tantamount to being educated.

This institutionally based definition of education was fostered by an intramural revolution: the ascendancy of scholarship. The universities were grounded on the assumption that they would sustain the work of contemplative scholars advancing the frontiers of knowledge. For their part, the scholars felt they could best pursue their work by organizing themselves into academic disciplines. Thus, along with all other areas of intellectual endeavor considered worthy of inclusion in higher learning, the liberal arts took disciplinary form. One who would be ennobled by them studied them from the viewpoint of the disciplines as defined by the scholars. The organization of the curriculum became ineluctably associated with the form of the discipline.

This conversion of the liberal arts predated the advent of the community colleges. By the time these new institutions came on the scene, the collegiate function had already been so codified in terms of the academic disciplines that no college, no legislature, no educator's call for a "student-centered curriculum," no student's cry for "relevance" could shake it. All attempts to tailor the students' studies to their own interests produced little more than rearranging the number or sequence of courses required for graduation, wide varieties of course distribution requirements, or laissez-faire elective systems. The liberal arts were captives of the disciplines; the disciplines dictated the structure of the courses; the courses encompassed the collegiate function.

Ideally, the liberal arts provide contexts for understanding, rather than the knowledge that some bit of esoterica is true or false. If the definition of education depended on knowledge of certain data, facts, or the modes of discourse in any academic discipline, then no one prior to the nineteenth century was liberally educated, because the concept of the academic discipline did not exist. The liberal arts can be useful only as they help people evaluate their society and gain a sense of what is right and what is important. This sense is not inborn; it is nourished through studies in which the relations among forms and ideas are explicated—the "general education" ideal. The conversion of the liberal arts from these precepts to academic disciplines reflected a major shift away from the individual to the organization as the arbiter of learning.

Transfer Courses

Thus structured, the collegiate function was adopted in toto by the community colleges. In their drive for acceptance as full partners in higher learning, with their faculty trained in university departments, they arranged their curricula in the university image. The terms *college parallel, college transfer,* and *college equivalent* were (and are) used to describe their academic programs. Their collegiate function, their part in the acculturation of the young, was embodied in the transfer courses. The more closely those courses resembled university courses, the higher their status.

The most pervasive and long-lived issue in community colleges is the extent to which their courses are accepted by the universities.

Articulation agreements (sometimes written into state education codes), interinstitutional standing committees, and policy statements that date from the earliest years of the community colleges to the most recent all attest to the importance of transferability. For all the rhetoric emanating from community colleges about their autonomous curriculum for special students and purposes, the universities have dominated the collegiate function by specifying what they accept for transfer credit, what they require for the baccalaureate degree. Major or sudden changes in community college courses can often be traced to a nearby university's changing its graduation requirements and/or its specifications for the courses that must be on the transcripts of incoming transfer students.

The community colleges rarely articulated their curriculum with that of the secondary schools, where courses in the various disciplines developed inconsistently. United States history, American government, literature, biology, and modern foreign languages were included in the secondary school curriculum; but philosophy, anthropology, art history, Western civilization, religious studies, and interdisciplinary sciences and humanities were rarely seen. Community college practitioners of those disciplines, as well as all the other disciplines in the liberal arts, have looked to the universities for guidance in forming their courses. There has been minimal flow-through from the lower schools and a paucity of give-and-take of ideas, course patterning, or texts.

In the earliest community colleges, most of the offerings were transfer courses in the liberal arts. Koos (1924) studied the curriculum in fifty-eight public and private junior colleges during 1921 and 1922 and found the liberal arts totaling three-fourths of the offerings. Ancient and modern languages alone accounted for one-fourth of the curriculum. English composition was taught, but literature courses accounted for more than half the courses in English. Agriculture, commerce, education, engineering, and home economics, along with all other occupational studies taken together, came to less than one-fourth of the whole (see Table 11.1).

Table 11.1. Average Number of Semester Hours and Percentage of Total Curricular Offerings in Junior Colleges by Subject, 1921–22.

Subject or Subject Group	Number of Semester Hours	Percentage of Total Offering
English	17.1	7.9
Public speaking	2.9	1.4
Ancient languages	16.9	7.9
Modern foreign languages	40.0	18.6
Mathematics	15.9	7.4
Science	29.9	13.9
Social subjects	22.3	10.4
Bible and religion	2.3	1.1
Philosophy	2.1	1.0
Psychology	3.0	1.4
Music	6.2	2.9
Art	4.2	2.0
Physical education	2.5	1.2
Agriculture	3.0	1.4
Commerce	10.9	5.1
Education	7.9	3.7
Engineering and industrial	13.1	6.1
Home economics	12.5	5.8
Other occupational	1.9	0.9

Source: Koos, 1924, p. 29.

This emphasis on the liberal arts continued well into the 1960s. All observers of the community colleges were aware of it. In 1960, Medsker discussed the prestige value of "regular college work." In 1966, Thornton wrote that transfer "is still the function on which the junior colleges expend most effort and in which most of their students express interest" (p. 234). Even after the flowering of career education, Cosand reported, "Community colleges were, are, and will be evaluated to a major degree upon the success of their transfer students to the four-year colleges and universities" (1979, p. 6).

However, the 1970s saw an extreme narrowing of the collegiate curriculum. Except for political science, history, and literature, many two-year associate-degree-granting institutions
effectually abandoned the humanities. Cultural geography, religious studies, and ethnic studies were found in fewer than one-
third of the colleges. Cultural anthropology, art history and
appreciation, interdisciplinary humanities, theater history, and
philosophy were offered in one-third to two-thirds of them. The
greatest number of humanities courses was seen in the older institutions, a legacy of the days when the colleges fed from one-fourth
to one-third of their students to senior colleges. The trend was
decidedly toward introductory courses for the transfer students and
specialized courses for adults taking them for their own interest,
not for degree credit.

Tables 11.2 through 11.6 display data on the magnitude of community college offerings in each discipline in the humanities, sciences, and social sciences. Laboratory sections in the sciences are
not included. The information has been compiled from several studies conducted by the CSCC between 1975 and 1991. Detailed
descriptions of the survey procedures, along with additional information on instructional practices, may be found in *The Collegiate
Function of Community Colleges* (Cohen and Brawer, 1987); "Art
Education in American Community Colleges" (Center for the Study
of Community Colleges, 1988); and Cohen and Ignash (1992).

Curricular Variety

Beneath the stultifying sameness of a curriculum comprised primarily of introductory courses, a notable variety can be perceived. Specialized courses flourished where instructors with a bent toward
designing and marketing those courses were found. Nearly every college in the CSCC samples had one or a few instructors concerned
with presenting something of particular interest, determined to do
something different for the different students with whom they were

Table 11.2. Percentage of Total Credit Curriculum by Major Discipline Areas in 164 Community Colleges: 1991.

Discipline	Percentage of Total Curriculum by Class Section
Humanities	13.42
English	12.75
Math and computer science	10.69
Business and office*	10.67
Personal skills/avocational**	8.27
Trade and industry	8.05
Technical education	7.87
Sciences	7.68
Social sciences	6.66
Fine and performing arts	5.42
Health*	4.44
Marketing*	1.46
Education*	1.10
Engineering technologies*	0.85
Agriculture (non-liberal arts)*	0.51
Home economics*	0.10
Other	0.07

*Indicates career courses.

**Includes courses in freshman orientation, career and life planning, and physical education.

Source: Cohen and Ignash, 1994.

confronted. The oft-heard contention that the curriculum cannot be centered on the collegiate function because the pragmatic students would not attend the courses and because the transferring institutions would not force them to attend did not hold. Exciting, active, lively engagements with ideas, tastes, and values did attract audiences, just as in the broader society the cinema and the stage have survived commercial television. Faculty members who have determined to break away from their transfer-credit, lecture/textbook course offerings have been able to do imaginative college-level work with their students. Unfortunately, their ideas typically were uncoordinated and unexported and had to be reinvented afresh by their counterparts in other colleges.

The collegiate function has tended to center on courses based on reading and writing, textbooks and examinations. In the 1970s that function suffered a dual assault from students oriented toward careers and from students who were ill prepared in the lower schools. However, it tended to thrive in the continuing education component of community education, just as it did in university extension programs within the senior institutions, which themselves faced the same types of shifts in student desires and capabilities. A true picture of the collegiate function is obscured if it is perceived only through the filter of the transfer-credit courses.

Some of the ways that the transfer-credit curriculum has been modified can be discerned. Community colleges offer relatively few

Table 11.3. Liberal Arts Class Sections by Subject Area, 1986 (N = 95 Colleges) and 1991 (N = 176 Colleges).

	1986	1991		1986	1991
Agriculture	1.2%	0.1%	History	4.0%	4.8%
Anthropology	0.6	0.8	Interdisciplinary		
Art history	1.0	1.0	social sciences	0.1	0.9
Biology	5.0	5.3	Interdisciplinary		
Chemistry	3.0	2.3	humanities	0.1	1.0
Earth and space	1.0	1.1	Literature	2.0	1.9
Economics	2.5	2.2	Mathematics	20.0	18.9
Engineering	5.0	2.5	Music		
English	21.0	22.5	appreciation	0.8	0.8
Environment	0.2	0.1	Philosophy	1.0	1.8
Fine and			Physics	2.0	1.6
performing arts	13.0	9.6	Political science	2.0	3.0
Foreign			Psychology	6.0	5.4
languages	5.0	8.5	Sociology	3.0	2.9

Sources: Cohen and Brawer, 1987, p. 36; Cohen and Ignash, 1992, p. 52.

Table 11.4. Percentage of Community Colleges Offering Humanities Courses During Spring Term, by Subject Area.

Humanities Subject Area	1975 (N = 156)	1977 (N = 178)	1983 (N = 173)	1986 (N = 95)	1991 (N = 164)
History	90%	92%	93%	92%	91%
State and local	28	26	31	25	30
Western world	82	83	76	71	74
United States	87	88	85	83	86
Other world regions	28	23	26	25	25
Special groups	29	30	26	23	36
Social history	25	28	20	23	9
Political science	89	94	90	86	90
American government	75	82	71	75	80
Local/city/state	40	40	35	40	38
Comparative	23	20	28	25	24
Tools and methods	26	26	15	3	5
Specialized (topical)	18	15	43	26	12
Jurisprudence	30	34	33	36	61
Literature	91	92	93	87	91
Introduction/survey	84	87	80	74	54
Genre	38	36	35	41	36
Authors	20	17	24	23	15
Group	24	22	22	22	71
Bible	6	6	12	6	9
Popular	15	16	11	9	6
Classics	10	9	10	3	15
Foreign languages	82	80	82	78	86
French	60	56	57	59	62
German	40	38	45	41	36
Italian	11	12	17	16	14
Russian	9	7	4	5	11
Spanish	70	68	72	68	77
Career-related Spanish	6	10	6	1	3
English as a second language	26	33	27	38	41
Classics	4	5	5	5	5
Other	8	11	15	15	24

Table 11.4. Continued.

Humanities Subject Area	1975 (N = 156)	1977 (N = 178)	1983 (N = 173)	1986 (N = 95)	1991 (N = 164)
Miscellaneous	50	51	61	69	47
Interdisciplinary/survey	28	28	38	52	45
Theater	24	26	34	26	32
Film	12	16	21	17	23
Specialized	19	18	16	12	4
Philosophy	66	64	68	76	74
Introduction/history	56	56	54	58	61
Ethics	25	23	29	37	37
Logic	26	26	39	38	43
Religious	21	18	21	34	20
Specialized	15	19	20	13	9
Art history/appreciation	70	68	76	76	80
History/appreciation	69	67	84	77	78
Specialized culture	3	6	6	13	15
Other specialized art	7	7	12	6	15
Music history/appreciation	74	70	69	63	71
Introduction/survey	73	68	75	62	70
Jazz	3	6	9	8	10
Specialized	7	7	4	13	12
Cultural anthropology	44	46	44	48	46
Introduction/survey	39	42	41	45	44
American Indian	4	5	8	7	3
Folklore/magic/ mythology	1	2	1	NA	7
Other specialized	12	11	6	14	5
Social/ethnic studies	22	21	10	(included	15
Ethnic	15	15	6	in	9
Women	3	3	4	history	3
Individual	1	1	2	and	1
Other	12	11	4	literature)	4
Religious studies	26	28	24		22
Introduction/survey	12	14	15	(included	15
Specialized	10	11	8	in	4
Texts	16	17	12	philosophy)	8
Cultural geography	26	22	34	NA	24
Introduction/survey	26	21	32		22
Specialized/regional	3	1	5		3

Sources: Cohen and Brawer, 1987, pp. 37–38; Cohen, 1991.

Table 11.5. Percentage of Total Humanities Class Sections by Subject Area.

Discipline	1977 (N = 178)	1983 (N = 173)	1986 (N = 95)	1991 (N = 164)
Cultural anthropology	3.2%	2.1%	2.7%	1.5%
Art history/appreciation	3.8	4.2	5.7	4.2
Foreign languages	20.5	27.7	28.4	35.8
History	23.0	19.9	21.5	19.4
Interdisciplinary humanities	7.2	7.3	5.7	6.2
Literature	11.4	11.2	10.0	8.2
Music appreciation	3.3	3.4	4.8	3.5
Philosophy	6.4	6.2	7.8	7.1
Political science	16.6	14.7	13.5	12.6
Religious studies	1.5	1.4	(included in philosophy)	0.6
Social and ethnic studies	3.1	1.9	(included in history)	0.7

Sources: Cohen and Brawer, 1987, p. 38; Center for the Study of Community Colleges, 1991.

courses in the history of any world region other than the United States, comparative or specialized political science, literature of a single author, languages other than Spanish and English as a second language (ESL), ethnic and women's studies, and cultural geography. However, courses in social history, Spanish, film appreciation, and the history of art in certain cultures have increased. Most of these changes have attracted students to areas in which enrollments were diminishing. A decline in introductory classes in music appreciation has been offset by increased enrollments in jazz and other specialized forms.

These changes may be traced through most of the disciplines. Art history instructors capitalized on student interest in certain cultures by presenting the art of Mexico or Asia to students who might not have studied the art of Europe. New courses in folklore, magic, and mythology attracted some students who would not have enrolled in anthropology courses dealing with kinship systems.

Students who would not take classes in climatology signed up for "The Living Desert" or "Preserving the Prairies." Specialized courses in problems of the city replaced introductory sociology, just as courses in family life took students from introductory psychology. An interest in ecology drew students who were not interested in or qualified for courses in physics or chemistry to "The Oceanic Environment." Although precise figures cannot be obtained, taking all categories of students together, these specialized, current-interest courses accounted for around 20–25 percent of enrollments in the liberal arts.

Although student interest in careers took enrollments away from the traditional transfer programs, the collegiate function was

Table 11.6. Percentage of Total Classes Offered in the Fine and Performing Arts in 1987 (N = 109) and 1991 (N = 164).

Subject Area	1987	1991
Visual arts		
Design	6%	7%
Graphics	6	6
Handicrafts	16	20
Painting/drawing	14	24
Special projects	1	1
Dance	6	6
Drawing	6	6
Music		
Instruments	24	17
Theory	9	7
Voice	10	8
Special projects	1	2
Theater		
Acting/drama	4	4
Production/directing/ stagecraft	3	2
Special projects	1	0.5

Source: Center for the Study of Community Colleges, 1988, 1991.

maintained in a different form. Courses in political science and jurisprudence were found in every program for law enforcement officers. Students in social welfare programs took specially modified courses in sociology. The allied health programs in numerous institutions included medical ethics and Spanish. And the faculty in some institutions built such courses as "The Humanities in a Technological Society" for career education students, so that they might meet general education requirements without taking the traditional history and literature courses. There was some overlap, too, in liberal arts course work presented to students who were planning careers in liberal arts-related fields. Although 22 percent of the students in fine arts and performing arts classes reported that their most important reason for attending college was "to satisfy a personal interest (cultural, social)," 38 percent anticipated that within five years they would be involved in the arts to the extent of making a career and a significant proportion of their income therefrom (Center for the Study of Community Colleges, 1988).

The breadth of curriculum is moderated by institutional size. Even though practically all the colleges offer the basic classes, specialized courses are found in few small-enrollment institutions. Table 11.7 displays some of these relationships.

Table 11.7. Percentage of Colleges Offering Certain Liberal Arts Classes.

	Colleges with More Than 6,000 Students	Colleges with Fewer Than 1,500 Students
Art history	91%	57%
Cultural anthropology	83	15
Cultural geography	40	6
Interdisciplinary humanities	71	26
Dance	40	6
Earth/space science	81	19
Statistics	98	50

Source: Cohen and Ignash, 1994, p. 19.

The most rapid change in the collegiate curriculum in recent years has been in English as a second language (ESL), which expanded from 30 percent of the foreign language enrollment in 1983 to 43 percent in 1986, and 51 percent in 1991. Together with Spanish, it accounted for 75 percent of all the foreign language credit-course sections. Approximately 250,000 students were taking ESL for credit and nearly as many were in noncredit courses (Cohen and Ignash, 1992). The decisions behind offering or not offering credit, investigated in six large ESL programs in six states, were found to be based on issues of state funding and financial aid policies; where the programs were placed (adult or continuing education); and whether ESL was classified as less-than-college-level work. If the greater proportion of a college's curriculum were devoted to credit, then ESL also tended to be offered for credit (Ignash, 1994).

The collegiate function also thrived elsewhere in noncredit and in noncourse formats. In approximately three of every eight colleges, numerous concerts, recitals, and musical events were presented each year, and around one-fourth of the colleges mounted art exhibits. The colleges were also deeply involved in theatrical productions, film series, and lectures and seminars open to the public. These events were funded typically by the participants or by the colleges themselves, although a few colleges were successful in obtaining funding from external sources. In many cases the colleges participated with community drama or musical groups, local art councils or museums, and secondary schools in presenting these events.

Articulation Agreements

The tendency of many community colleges to develop a pattern of courses and events tailored particularly for their own students is reflected in the types of articulation agreements maintained between community colleges and senior institutions in their area.

Community college representatives almost invariably try to encourage senior institutions to accept for transfer credit the special-interest and interdisciplinary courses designed apart from adherence to traditional concepts of the academic disciplines. Although changes in university requirements affect enrollments in individual courses in community colleges, their effect on overall enrollments is less clear. Frequently, a community college responds to a change in, say, history requirements by no longer requiring its own students to take a survey of American history but maintaining a three-hour history requirement for the associate degree and allowing students to choose a course in local history or the history of a particular culture.

The effort to avoid penalizing baccalaureate-bound students who begin in community colleges occurs at the state level as well. Many state systems of higher education have standing articulation committees with detailed procedures for gaining course approvals. Course equivalency guides are maintained and common course numbering systems are pursued. Articulation agreements often specify the courses that the two-year colleges may *not* offer, rather than those they must offer; junior- and senior-level courses offered by the senior institutions, particularly, are out of bounds. In some states articulation boards review noncredit offerings as well as credit courses and act, for example, to discourage conversational language offerings in two-year colleges' community education programs because those courses are considered the province of the senior institutions.

Paradoxically, there still is little articulation between community colleges and secondary schools. Community college instructors rarely speak to their counterparts in high schools. They tend not to accompany counselors on their annual visits to the high schools to advertise their offerings, and they make little attempt to recruit promising students of the liberal arts from secondary schools. Counselors seem more inclined to emphasize the job-related features of the community college than to advertise the collegiate function as such.

Curricular Stability

The articulation agreements attest to the tenacity of the idea that the liberal arts are still important and that community colleges are a major port of entry to higher learning. However, in addition to persistent assaults from devotees of immediately and obviously job-related studies, the collegiate function has been assailed as being irrelevant to the students. The study of history came under particular attack in the 1970s because many American social institutions and traditions were similarly under attack. The belief in social progress and in a nation that allowed opportunity for all its citizens was weakened. Allegations about racism, sexism, and unjust wars came together as criticisms of American society. Hence, requiring students to study a bland history that emphasized the social justice and democracy of America was condemned. Similar accusations were leveled at literature, fine arts, and other cornerstones of the liberal arts. Even language symbolized oppression because it denied the person's individuality, and bilingual studies received intramural support accordingly.

Because numerous educators agreed that their curriculum was unworthy, the terms *relevance* and *individualism* replaced the calls for teaching values and a common heritage. Accordingly, supporters of the liberal arts had little defense against demands for occupational education. Consumerism became the hallmark of education, a consumerism whereby the client-consumers dictated the terms under which they would study, what they would study, and what they expected to obtain from their efforts. Under these conditions an education that demanded commitment, adherence to traditions, intensity of scholarly inquiry, examination of alternative value systems —the bases of the liberal arts—could not sustain itself. It had few adherents within or outside the academy.

The cult of relevance, of meeting student needs, of allowing every student to define a particularized curriculum came to be considered the highest form of schooling. An institution that could adjust most suitably to an infinite variety of student desires was the ultimate in responsiveness. Relevance was interpreted as providing job skills to the young, who, save for the intervention of the schools, might be unemployed. As Hurn summarized, "Lacking any consensus as to the content of liberal education, and lacking confidence in their prescriptive authority—as the catchphrase puts it, 'to impose their values upon others'—educators were in a weak position to mount a defense of anything other than an educational supermarket, where customer preferences, in the middle and late 1970s at least, were clearly for the more immediately utilitarian and basic items on the shelf" (1979, p. 632).

Attempts were made to sweep the collegiate function out of community colleges. Numerous legislators and institutional trustees were lauding the colleges as places designed to prepare workers, whose training had no space for liberal arts courses. And liberal arts devotees, who remained convinced that traditional academic transfer courses were the sole vehicle for transmitting the liberal arts, inadvertently fed these contentions. The more successful the colleges became in their mission of providing trained workers for the community, the more precarious became the idea of liberal education within them.

However, reports of the demise of the collegiate function were greatly exaggerated. Enrollments in liberal arts classes stabilized in the 1980s at just over 50 percent of total credit-course enrollment. By 1991, enrollment in liberal arts classes had climbed back up to 56 percent. Granted that a sizable proportion of this enrollment was in science, social science, English, and mathematics courses in service to occupational programs, and that much of it was directed toward students attending for their personal interest or fulfilling distribution requirements for the associate degree, the collegiate function was tenacious. Career education enjoyed widespread support and handsome funding. But because of the efforts of the community college liberal arts instructors, the effects of state or locally mandated graduate requirements, university transfer expectations, and, in general, the place of the community college in higher education, the collegiate function proved resilient.

Faculty and Academic Disciplines

The collegiate function survives not least because of the faculty, who have been its staunchest supporters. When the liberal arts were brought from the universities into the community colleges, the ethos of academic scholarship did not accompany them. The colleges were not supportive of scholarship, and the university training that instructors received was not, in itself, adequate to foster teachers who would attend to the reflections and meanings of their disciplines. Further, too few instructors have banded together to build interdisciplinary courses in the sciences, social sciences, and humanities. The argument that the universities would not accept new types of course for transfer credit is spurious; practitioners in two-year colleges have not pursued them with sufficient diligence.

The idea that the faculty, as independently functioning practitioners, should have the power to define the curriculum stems from the turn-of-the-century university model. The concept of academic freedom, of instructors teaching what they want within the confines of their own classrooms, was not accepted by the secondary schools. But the community colleges adopted it even though few of their instructors developed courses that fit the institutions' broader social purposes. Within the liberal arts especially (but not exclusively), the departmentally designed and administered examination is often resisted. Common textbooks for courses taught in multiple sections by different instructors are more the exception than the rule. Although community college instructors ostensibly work from common syllabi, on file in the dean's office for display to visiting accreditation teams, those documents typically serve only as general outlines for course construction.

If the liberal arts exist within an anarchy, if scientists and humanists work within different frameworks of ideas, the curricula that they articulate will be diverse. In universities, however, the expectation is that instructors will be affiliated with the academic disciplines and that the curriculum will reflect the tenets of those disciplines. In community colleges, where disciplinary affiliation is much weaker, the unseen hand of the academic discipline is much less strong as an influence on the form of courses or on instructors' activities. Accordingly, the innovation and flexibility so prized by community college spokespersons derive less from educational philosophy than from the fact that the curriculum is without a rudder. One instructor's whim will change the pattern, emphasis, and direction of a course and hence a curriculum. Whereas the university organizes the intellectual world in a division of *intellectual* labor and necessarily accommodates a plurality of diverse intellectual stances, the community college organizes its world in a division of *faculty* labor and necessarily accommodates a plurality of diverse instructor stances. Amorphous, sporadic monitoring of instructors by department chairpersons, deans of instruction, accreditation teams, and peers is of little consequence. Instructors' work is influenced by the writers of textbooks they use, the speakers at conferences they attend, the new information they learn in in-service programs or on their own. But the enterprise is chaotic, directionless.

An example is provided by contrasting the modes of teaching the liberal arts and the occupational courses. Traditionally, the liberal arts have been taught by a teacher in a room equipped with chairs and a chalkboard. Instructors have acted as though contact between the students and themselves is the key element, as though all that is necessary for a person to learn is to engage in dialogue and to read and reflect in a solitary fashion. Career educators, in contrast, have taken the position that they need laboratories, shops, equipment, and links with the business and industry community in order to teach people a trade. They say their students must practice the craft, not merely talk about it.

What if the faculty in the liberal arts took similar views? Music instructors might allege that students cannot properly learn to appreciate music unless the college provides each of them with a compact disc player and recordings of a couple of hundred classics. Instructors teaching art appreciation would say that students cannot learn unless they are provided with slide viewers, sets of slides showing all the principal art in the Western world, and funds to travel to museums. Anthropology instructors might insist that students be paid to work at archeological digs, so that they can learn the ways of thinking in earlier cultures. Political science instructors would have students serving as apprentices to politicians and bureaucrats in all types of government agencies, so that they can learn how decisions are really made. And certainly the best way to learn a language is to live in a country where that language is spoken, with the colleges sponsoring such trips. But liberal arts faculty members rarely advocate such views, whereas nursing educators insist that they must have laboratories, equipment, and on-the-job training. It would not occur to them to try to teach nursing in a room equipped with nothing more than chairs and a chalkboard. They get the clinics and the funds they need to maintain their small student-teacher ratios. The liberal arts instructors get chalk dust on their clothing.

These variant attitudes stem from the different ways that the career and collegiate functions were taught before they came into the colleges. Career preparation evolved from a history of apprenticeships in work settings, the traditional mode of learning a trade. The liberal arts were the province of a group inclined toward contemplation. Thus, it costs more to teach the occupations because the workplaces are duplicated or at least simulated on site. Liberal arts educators in community colleges do not even have the benefit of sizable library collections. And they do not act in concert to modify the conditions.

The collegiate function in community colleges has been characterized by a reduction in emphasis on the academic disciplines. Community college instructors tend not to conduct scholarly inquiry, not to belong to disciplinary associations, not to be excessively concerned with disciplinary purity. All to the good for faculty members who are instructed to teach in areas of current student interest and who must often cross disciplinary fields; the instructor whose work load comprises one course in anthropology, another in sociology, and two in American history does not have the luxury of maintaining currency in all fields. However, the turn away from disciplinarianism has had some untoward effects. Many courses appeal to immediate relevance and focus excessively on the person, to the detriment of making intellectual demands. Under the guise of presenting a student-centered curriculum, courses that reflect the popular literature of self-help books on coping, gaining singular advantage, and other personal concerns are often built within the liberal arts framework.

All curriculum must, in the end, be based on knowledge. No matter what the ultimate intent of a student-centered course, that course cannot maintain its collegiate character unless something is being taught. That something is the subject; that subject stems from the discipline. Without the anchor of the humanistic and scientific disciplines themselves, the basis of the academic tradition, the collegiate function would be adrift. Even if the liberal arts were not a curriculum in themselves, they would still have to be maintained as the foundation of the liberal education that is provided through all the other curricula.

The demise of the academic disciplines as the organizing principle of collegiate courses has both reflected and served to limit faculty members' awareness of recent trends in their academic fields. Such an awareness is important even for such a seemingly simple task as evaluating the new textbooks that appear. But it is important for more than that; the academic disciplines need reconceptualizing to fit remedial and career education, the institution's dominant functions in addition to transfer. This reconceptualization cannot be made outside the colleges themselves. For the sake of the collegiate function, community college instructors must reify their own disciplines. It is difficult for a group that has severed connection with its disciplinary roots to accomplish that.

Student Ability and the Curriculum

No curriculum exists in a vacuum. The decline in the collegiate function in the 1970s and its subsequent stabilization are revealed in the liberal arts courses detailed in this chapter and in the student transfer rates documented in Chapter Two. It relates also to the changes in the academic ability of the entering students and to the curriculum in the high schools from which they come.

The figures in Chapter Nine illustrate the decline and subsequent improvement in NAEP, SAT, and ACT test performances by high school students during the 1970s and through the early 1990s. In 1975, when average SAT scores had been declining for over a decade, Willard Wirtz, former secretary of labor, chaired a commission that sought to explain and resolve the lowering of educational standards. The commission found that students were taking fewer courses in general English and math and were enrolling in more vocational courses such as driver education and home economics. School days had become shorter and course textbooks weakened in quality (Ravitch, 1985). Data collected by the National Center for Education Statistics (1993) further illustrate high school students' reluctance to enroll in math, science, and English classes. In 1982, students completed an average of 3.80 courses (Carnegie units) in English, 3.10 courses in history, and 2.54 courses in math (p. 132). Not surprisingly, as more students stopped enrolling in English and math courses, their performances on verbal and math ability tests dropped as well.

Attempts to rebuild the high school curriculum were widespread. In 1983, the National Commission on Excellence in Education published *A Nation At Risk* (Gardner and others, 1983), in which it highlighted the importance of education for the civic well-being of our nation. This report suggested that states adopt a curriculum, known as "the New Basics," to include four years of English; three years of mathematics, science, and social studies; one-half year of computer science; and two years of foreign language for students who wish to go to college. Ravitch notes that "by late 1983, a national survey found that forty-six states had either raised their graduation requirements recently or were debating proposals to do so" (1985, p. 67).

A notable shift in high school course enrollments occurred. Table 11.8 displays the changes between 1982 and 1992. All academic areas showed an increase, with mathematics, sciences, and foreign languages showing the most notable gains. In 1992, 56 percent of students took chemistry, as compared with 32 percent in 1982; 70 percent took geometry in 1992, versus 48 percent in 1982; 22 percent took biology, chemistry, and physics, compared with 10 percent in 1982. Overall, the high school curriculum was rebuilt to the levels of the 1950s. The effect of the strengthened requirements was a reduced number of vocational education classes (bookkeeping, typing, shop) and an increase in the totality of courses taken by graduates (National Center for Educational Statistics, 1993, pp. 144–148).

In sum, students coming to the colleges in the late 1980s had taken more academic courses, and their academic abilities had begun to climb. In the broadest fashion, the foundations of educational practice had been verified: students will take the classes that they are required to take, and those who take classes in a particular area of study are likely to learn something about that area.

Table 11.8. Average Number of Carnegie Units Earned by Public High School Graduates in Various Subject Areas: 1982 and 1992.

	1982	1992
Total Carnegie units	21.44	23.75
English	3.87	4.18
Social studies	3.16	3.58
Total math	2.55	3.39
Total science	2.16	2.87
Foreign language	.96	1.67

Source: National Center for Education Statistics, 1994j, p. 133.

The General Academic Assessment

The latter truism has been demonstrated in community colleges. In one such application in 1983–84, the CSCC administered the General Academic Assessment, a survey and content test that would reveal student knowledge in general education and in the liberal arts. The test included representative items in English usage, the humanities, mathematics, sciences, and social studies and was given in five forms to over eight thousand students in twenty-three colleges in Chicago, Los Angeles, Miami, and St. Louis.

Tables 11.9 and 11.10 present some of the findings, which suggest two major outcomes: (1) students who complete more college courses tend to know more; and (2) students know what they know; the best predictor of the students' scores on one of the subtests was to ask them, "Compared with other students at this college, how would you rate your ability to [various discipline-related questions]?"

The Transfer Function

One of the community college's primary purposes has been to accept students from secondary school, provide them with general education and introductory collegiate studies, and send them on to senior

Table 11.9. Means on Scales by Number of Completed College Units.

Total Units	Math	Literacy	Social Science	Humanities	Science	Total Liberal Arts
0–14	4.45	4.73	4.64	3.02	4.89	21.73
15–29	4.84	4.84	4.80	3.13	5.05	22.65
30–44	4.88	4.90	4.88	3.31	5.25	23.23
45–59	5.18	4.96	5.13	3.54	5.27	24.07
60 or more	5.51	5.55	5.58	4.24	5.84	26.71
Total sample	4.85	4.92	4.92	3.35	5.17	23.21

Source: Riley, 1984.

institutions for the baccalaureate. An associate degree usually qualifies the recipient to enter the university as a junior. In many states,
the degree guarantees junior status. However, certain courses may
not be acceptable, some university departments may require alternate courses, and transfer may not guarantee entry to the particular program a student desires.

One of the thorniest problems is that of determining which
community college courses are acceptable for graduation credit in
which university. Practically all the liberal arts classes qualify, but
the courses in the trades and technologies are variable. As an example, the University of California accepts only 29 percent of the non-
liberal arts classes offered in that state's community colleges, but the
California State University will award credit for 62 percent of them.
Course transferability rates similarly vary at the University of Illinois, Urbana, and Illinois State University, with the former taking
16 percent and the latter 80 percent of the non-liberal arts. The
University of Texas, Stephen F. Austin State, and Southwest Texas
State are much more uniform; 35 percent of the non-liberal arts
classes are acceptable at the junior level at UT Austin and 42 percent at the state university branches. In all three examples, the differences seem to relate to the correspondence of programs in
particular fields. The University of California and the University of
Illinois have no undergraduate majors in marketing, trade and
industry, or engineering technology, and few in health or technical

Table 11.10. Means on Scales by Self-Rating on Scale-Related Skill.

Self-Rating	Mathematics	Literacy	Social Science	Humanities	Science
Poor	3.82	4.16	4.22	2.66	4.44
Fair	4.49	4.58	4.0	2.99	4.81
Good	5.16	5.08	5.17	3.48	5.25
Excellent	6.17	6.28	5.82	4.22	6.34
Total sample	4.85	4.92	4.92	3.35	5.17

Source: Riley, 1984.

education, whereas those fields can be found in the California and Illinois State University systems. Majors are more evenly distributed across the university types in Texas (Cohen and Ignash, 1994).

The collegiate function is intact. The decline in liberal arts studies and student transfer rates that was manifest in the 1970s and 1980s has been stemmed. In 1991, liberal arts enrollments were a few percentage points higher than five years earlier. In 1994 the transfer rate also had been stable for the previous six years. Collegiate and career studies stood together as the college's primary functions.

Even so, the proponents of one or another function have not slackened their efforts. The notion that career studies should be primary has been advanced repeatedly by those who view the community college's main role as helping people prepare for the workplace. They usually neglect to acknowledge that cultural and basic literacy, the ability to communicate in context, understanding societal conditions, and similar goals of a liberal arts education are essential for practically every job. Those who advocate the liberal arts often ignore the realities of their students' lives; all of them are or will be in the work force, and most will require some form of specialized training.

The waves of fashion, trends in funding, interests of students, and imaginativeness of the faculty all affect the prognosis for collegiate studies in community colleges. Several trends favor the expansion of these studies. Aspects of finance favor collegiate studies because they are less expensive than the career and developmental programs. Tradition is on their side; they have been present since the first days of the institutions, and tradition (or inertia) plays an important role in education. Those who would abandon collegiate studies must answer to charges that they are thereby denying opportunity to the great numbers of students who still see the community college as a stepping stone to higher learning.

For the collegiate function to reach its full potential and involve all students, it must not be sequestered away from the career programs. Instead of depending exclusively on graduation requirements to attract career education students to their classes, the faculty might integrate the liberal arts with career education through a merger of principles stemming from both the humanities and the sciences. Technology is ubiquitous; students would have little difficulty understanding generally how the history of politics, ethics, sociology, and philosophy of science and technology affect their world. Those who would be more than job holders would attend to the fundamental assumptions undergirding what scientists and technologists do. In general, literature and art in the community colleges have not dealt sufficiently with technology, but a fully integrated course could be required in all career programs. Similarly, portions of the liberal arts could be designed especially for key courses in the career programs, a pattern described more fully in the next chapter.

If the collegiate function weakens, it may be a result of continuing high levels of funding for career programs without sufficient intramural concern for general literacy and social awareness. Furthermore, students reared on a diet of instant information presented through electronic media may find the reflectiveness and self-discipline basic to the collegiate function difficult to master. Although some imaginative efforts at integrative courses presented through television have been made, the long-term effects of a turn away from print have not yet been fully appreciated. Communication through nonprint images is pervasive. The spoken word is carried across distance not by a courier with a packet of letters but through wires and waves. The ubiquitous handheld calculator has done for arithmetic what the invention of moveable type did for story telling. Supermarket checkers rely on bar codes; restaurant cashiers, on pictures of the product superimposed on a register key that records the cost of an item and the amount of change to be tendered. Why, then, should educators be concerned about teaching the liberal arts? Advocates of the collegiate function would argue that the failure to do so only perpetuates social-class divisions and increases the benighted individual's reliance on authority. Any educator with less than a totally cynical view of society would agree.

Issues

The overriding issue is whether the community colleges should maintain their position in higher education. If they should not, no deliberate steps are necessary. Continued deterioration in course requirements will suffice. But if they should, what can they do?

Can the collegiate function be expanded beyond the college-parallel courses? Can it be made part of the career programs? What can the liberal arts say to students who want nothing more than job upgrading or new skills?

Must the collegiate function decline along with the decline in students' tendency to read and write? Can the liberal arts be offered in a manner that fits less well-prepared students' ways of knowing?

Advisory committees comprising concerned citizens, labor leaders, and employers have been influential in connecting the career programs to the world of work. Can lay advisory committees for the liberal arts similarly help connect those programs to the broader society?

The collegiate function has many advocates within and outside the colleges. The future of the community college as a comprehensive institution depends on how they articulate its concerns.

12

· ·

General Education
Knowledge for Personal and Civic Life

Confronted on the one side by universities wanting better-prepared students and on the other by secondary schools passing through the marginally literate, captives of their own rhetoric to provide programs to fit anyone's desires, the community colleges erected a curriculum resembling more a smorgasbord than a coherent educational plan. What else could they do? Their policies favored part-time students dropping in and out at will, whose choice of courses was often made more on the basis of convenience in time and place than on content. Their funding agents rewarded career, transfer, and continuing education differentially.

Most colleges responded by abandoning any semblance of curricular integration, taking pride instead in their variety of presentations for all purposes. Except in career programs monitored by external licensing agencies and accreditation societies, the idea of courses to be taken by every student pursuing a degree diminished. Disintegration of the sequential curriculum was not confined to community colleges. The universities have been plagued with course proliferation since the turn of the century, and a similar, if less pronounced, phenomenon affected the secondary schools when the number of electives that might be taken to fulfill graduation requirements increased. Yet the belief that some studies are important for all students dies hard. Pleas for core curricula have been sounded from innumerable platforms, where secondary schools and universities alike are chided for allowing students to pass through them without enjoying any experiences in common.

This chapter considers the history, rationale for, and status of general education, emphasizing the problems in defining it. It makes a plea for advancing general education in community colleges and presents a model for so doing.

Background

Those who call for an integrated curriculum frequently use the term *general education*. General education is the process of developing a framework on which to place knowledge stemming from various sources, of learning to think critically, develop values, understand traditions, respect diverse cultures and opinions, and, most important, put that knowledge to use. It is holistic, not specialized; integrative, not separatist; suitable more for action than for contemplation. It thus differs from the ideal of the collegiate function. The liberal arts are education *as*; general education is education *for*.

General education received widespread publicity in 1977, when the Carnegie Foundation for the Advancement of Teaching published *Missions of the College Curriculum*, indicating the imminence of the first curriculum reforms in higher education in thirty years. The Carnegie Foundation said the time was right because the test scores of students entering college were down, and it was obvious that much was wrong in precollegiate education. Further, students seemed to be learning less in college, and even though remedial education had been tried by all types of colleges, it was difficult to show the efficacy of these efforts. The foundation proposed a reform toward integration in a curriculum that had become fractionated, toward education in values in a curriculum that had purported to be value-free. It sought a return to general education.

The Carnegie Foundation report was followed by several reports on the same theme emanating from other agencies. *Involvement in Learning*, a report by the Study Group on the Conditions of Excellence in American Higher Education (1984), formed under National Institute of Education auspices, advocated a liberal education that would enhance shared values and involve students in the learning process. A National Endowment for the Humanities report, *To Reclaim a Legacy* (Bennett, 1984), called for a general education centered on traditional texts and curriculum. Another report, *Integrity in the College Curriculum*, sponsored by the Association of American Colleges (1985), called for a basic curriculum that would teach students to think about subject matter in the manner that academic specialists approach it. And a subsequent Carnegie Foundation report, entitled *College: The Undergraduate Experience in America* (Boyer, 1987), advocated a general education that would extend throughout the college experience and integrate specialized education across disciplinary fields.

So it is one more time around for general education. What happened to it the first time it flourished, in the early nineteenth century? And the second time, between 1920 and 1950?

General education can be traced to the moral philosophy courses found in American colleges during their first 200 years. These integrative experiences often were taught by the college president and presented to all students. Remnants of the integrated courses pulling together knowledge from several areas may still be seen in the capstone courses required of all students in a few contemporary institutions. However, that type of general education broke apart in most colleges in the second half of the nineteenth century, to be replaced by the free-elective system. No longer were there to be courses that all students would take; no longer would the colleges attempt to bring together threads of all knowledge in a unified theme. Blame the rise of the academic disciplines, the professionalization of the faculty, the broadening of knowledge in all areas, the increased numbers of students, each with his or her own agenda—all these accusations have been made. But, for whatever reason, the elective system took over. The old classical curriculum died out, taking with it the idea of the curriculum as a unified whole to be presented to all students. By the turn of the twentieth century, most American colleges had come down to an irreducible minimum in curriculum: faculty members with academic degrees teaching courses of their choice to those students who elected to study with them or whose goals required that they be there.

All curriculum is, at bottom, a statement a college makes about what it thinks is important. The free-elective system is a philosophical statement quite as much as is a curriculum based on the Great Books or one concerned solely with occupational education. It is an admission that the college no longer has the moral authority to insist on any combination of courses, that it no longer recognizes the validity of sequence or organized principles of curriculum integration. The system was not without its critics. The early-twentieth-century Carnegie plan—assigning units of credit for hours of study—was introduced in an attempt to bring order out of the free-elective curricular chaos. It had the opposite effect. That is, by ascribing units of credit of apparently equal merit, it snipped to pieces whatever unity was left in the academic subjects themselves. Three credits of algebra had the same meaning as three credits of calculus; a three-credit introductory course in a discipline was of equal value to an advanced seminar in the same field. When a student may accumulate any 120 credit hours and obtain a baccalaureate degree, when all credits are the same, all unity of knowledge falls apart.

The initial reaction against the free-elective system gave rise to distribution requirements—curriculum defined by bureaucratic organization. Groups of courses were specified in a process of political accommodation among academic departments. In order that the history department would vote a six-unit English requirement, the English department was expected to reciprocate by voting a six-unit history requirement. Protecting departmental territory became the curriculum organizer. Placing a disintegrated mass of free-elective courses into a set of distribution requirements gives the appearance of providing the curriculum with a rationale. Thus, the noble truths of general studies arose post hoc to justify the politics of distribution—whence the popular statements that colleges provide a breadth of studies, ensuring that their students leave as well-rounded individuals. In the 1970s the Carnegie Council found that students spend about one-third of their time in undergraduate school taking distribution requirements, the other two-thirds going to the major and to electives. Gaff (1983) found that distribution requirements accounted for half of the units needed to complete an associate degree in the community colleges he studied; the other half went to electives or, especially in occupational programs, to major field requirements. The political accommodations among departments were in equilibrium.

The success of distribution requirements as an organizing principle for curriculum did not stop those who advocated curriculum integration. Their early attempts to return order were founded in survey courses; Columbia University's "Contemporary Civilization" course, first offered in 1919, is usually seen as the prototype. These courses give the overview, the broad sweep, in history, the arts, the sciences, and the social sciences. The academic discipline is the organizing principle of the course, but the course is supposed to show the unity of knowledge, to integrate disparate elements from many disciplines. Survey courses became quite popular during the 1920s and 1930s. Surveys of social sciences, for example, were built into the "Individual in Society" courses. The humanities surveys became "Modern Culture and the Arts." Separate surveys of natural, physical, and biological sciences were also attempted, but with less success.

Advocates of survey courses constantly struggled to maintain the integrity of their offerings against the faculty tendency to convert each course into the introduction to a discipline, to teach concepts and terminology in a particular academic specialization as though all students were majors in that field. The faculty objection to the survey courses was that they were superficial, trying to encompass too many different portions of human knowledge. As each course slid away from a true interdisciplinary orientation to become the first course in an academic discipline, it tended to lose its general-education characteristics.

Nonetheless, many interdisciplinary courses survived. Much seemed to depend on the level of specialization within the discipline. Social science instructors had little trouble putting together political science, sociology, economics, and anthropology into a general social science survey. Science instructors, however, may have believed that they were teaching a general survey if they integrated molecular and organismic biology into one course. It was difficult for them to include the physical and earth and space sciences. In 1935 most of the college survey courses were in social science, followed by natural science, physical science, and biological science; only a few humanities surveys were offered (Johnson, 1937).

General education suffered originally from the free-elective system and the broadening of knowledge that was properly a part of the college curriculum. In his history of the undergraduate curriculum, Rudolph traced the concept into the 1970s and concluded: "Where highly publicized general education requirements reshaped the course of study in the 1940s and 1950s, less publicized erosion of those requirements took place in the 1960s and 1970s" (1977, p. 253). What happened to it this time? According to Rudolph, general education fell victim to faculty power, lack of student interest, increased demands on faculty time, difficulties in integrating the disciplines, and, most of all, its own lack of demonstrated value and the superficiality of the presentations. General education has remained a noble idea but a practical backwater in most of American higher education.

Definitions

A good part of the difficulty with general education rests with its definition. The term has been in use for more than seventy years and has been defined innumerable times. Sometimes it has been defined narrowly, for instance, as the trivium and quadrivium, the discipline of the medieval scholars; and sometimes broadly, as that education which integrates and unifies all knowledge. It has been confounded with the liberal arts, and it has been connected to the human developmental cycle. It has been defined as what it is not. Following are some of the definitions.

On the side of breadth, the 1939 Yearbook of the National Society for the Study of Education saw general education as concerned with the "widest possible range of basic human activities." It was to guide the student "to the discovery of the best that is currently known and thought." It was "dynamic," "democratic," "systematic." The student was to gain "a real grasp of the most widely ramifying generalized insights—intellectual, ethical, and esthetic" (p. 12). The Harvard "Red Book," *General Education in a Free Society*, also announced that general education was to bring all knowledge together (Committee on the Objectives of a General Education in a Free Society, 1945). Hutchins (1937) defined general education as an interdisciplinary undertaking centered on great books and ideas, and he recommended that high schools and junior colleges devote their curriculum to such studies. (This definition was promulgated fifty years later by William Bennett, then the U.S. secretary of education.)

General education has also been defined as that which everyone should know. The Executive Committee of the Cooperative Study in General Education said that it should provide "the basic understandings and skills which everyone should possess" (1947, p. 17). Mayhew said it should establish "a common universe of discourse—a common heritage" (1960, p. 16). In the proceedings of a 1959 Florida junior college conference on general education (Florida State Department of Education, 1959), the idea of commonality, those learnings that should be possessed by all persons, was articulated repeatedly. Boyer and Kaplan argued for a common core that should be taught to all students. They spoke of a need for "comprehensive literacy" and "an awareness of symbol systems" that everyone in contemporary society must have (1977, p. 67). This definition has staying power: the subtitle of Hirsch's book, *Cultural Literacy*, was *What Every American Needs to Know* (1987).

General education has also been defined by what it is not. It is nonspecialized, nonvocational; it is not occupational education; it is not learning to use the tools of a discipline or learning a specialized language. A report of a conference held at a community college in Florida in 1976 offers a wondrous example of definition by exclusion:

> At the operational level, general education . . . is not special; that is, it is not designed for specific groups of people or special activities. . . . It is *not* an introduction to disciplines as the first step in specialization. It is *not* content for its own sake. It is *not* the development of skills or the acquisition of knowledge precisely for their applicability to a job, a career, or another specialization. It is *not* a collection of courses. It is *not* simply a rearrangement of content, like an interdisciplinary program or course for the sake of being interdisciplinary. It is *not* so abstract and future-oriented that it can only be hoped for, wished for, or assumed to happen somewhere, sometime. It is *not* merely being able to read, to write, and to do arithmetic [Tighe, 1977, pp. 13–14].

General education also has been contrasted with liberal education. Educators have always agreed that education should be useful for something (all curricula are justified for their practical value). Apologists for liberal education have held that it frees people from such external tyrannies as caste biases, societal constraints, and professional experts, as well as from the internal tyrannies of ignorance, prejudice, superstition, guilt, and what the Thomists might call "the appetites." Having to do with the virtues, it has been rationalized as affording knowledge for its own sake. In general education, by contrast, knowledge is power—the power of coping, understanding, self-mastery, and social interaction. It must lead to the ability to do, to act: gaining rationality alone is not enough. People who have had a general education are supposed to act intelligently. This view grounds the construct in the everyday affairs of a person: dealing with supervisors and co-workers, choosing associates, coping with family problems, and spending leisure time in socially desirable and personally satisfying ways. To be successful, a general education program not only explicates the skills and understandings to be attained but also relates those competencies to external referents, to what people are doing when they have gained them.

According to Miller, "It is especially ironic that general education, which was originally formulated as a reaction to what were perceived to be the serious shortcomings of liberal education, should today be confused with the latter. Indeed, the two terms are often used interchangeably, despite the fact that the two forms of education have fundamental conceptual differences" (1988, p. ix). Liberal education is centered in the past, with knowledge historically viewed as an end in itself and the curriculum merely a vehicle for the acquisition of knowledge; general education holds that knowledge is hypothetical and should be regarded as the means to the end of a better personal life and a better society. The generally educated student would use knowledge as needed to solve human problems.

Accordingly, general education is often defined in terms of the competencies to be gained by those whom it touches. A group studying general education in California community colleges in the early 1950s offered a list of twelve competencies to be exercised by a person who is generally educated (Johnson, 1952, pp. 21–22):

- Exercising the privileges and responsibilities of democratic citizenship

- Developing a set of sound moral and spiritual values by which he guides his life

- Expressing his thoughts clearly in speaking and writing and in reading and listening with understanding

- Using the basic mathematical and mechanical skills necessary in everyday life

- Using methods of critical thinking for the solution of problems and for the discrimination among values

- Understanding his cultural heritage so that he may gain a perspective of his time and place in the world

- Understanding his interaction with his biological and physical environment so that he may adjust better to and improve that environment

- Maintaining good mental and physical health for himself, his family, and his community

- Developing a balanced personal and social adjustment

- Sharing in the development of a satisfactory home and family life

- Achieving a satisfactory vocational adjustment

- Taking part in some form of satisfying creative activity and in appreciating the creative activities of others

This list, or portions thereof, was duplicated verbatim in many community college catalogues because it gave the appearance of being competency-based even though it was sufficiently broad to justify any course or program.

The Variant Rationalizations

Given the plethora of definitions, the failure to maintain general education consistently is easily understood. General education is prey to any group with a strict view of curriculum. Throughout this century the same forces that splintered knowledge into academic disciplines have continued their antagonism to a general or unifying education. The academic profession was departmentalized in its specializations, thus posing a contradiction for the integration of learning. The academic departments insisted that students pick a major—the earlier the better. Courses were built as introductions to disciplines, with their own logic, terminology, goals, organizing principles, and modes of inquiry; adding distribution requirements while leaving the internal organization of the course intact did not enhance knowledge integration, common learnings, or competencies. In short, the academic discipline, with its hold on the faculty and the organization of the college, was the first and most pervasive deterrent to general education.

The definition itself has been part of the problem. If general education is defined by what it is not, instead of what it is, it is open to any type of course or experience. Constantly denying the restrictive organization of occupational and discipline-based education has propelled general education into the areas of unstructured events, counseling activities, courses without content, programs with broad goals impossible of attainment—the anticurriculum.

The breadth of the positive side of the definition hurt too. The most specialized course in Elizabethan literature might lead students to "understand their cultural heritage." The most trivial course in personal habits and grooming might assist students to "maintain good mental and physical health." Guidance and orientation programs could assist students to "develop a balanced personal and social adjustment," and so on throughout the list of competencies and throughout the range of activities and services provided by colleges. Where anything can be related to general education, it falls victim to the whims of students, faculty members, and administrators alike. Positive or negative, none of its goals has been specific enough to have more than rhetorical value. Even when college staff members meeting in conference agree on them, the agreement usually dissipates when each instructor develops course content and methodology to be displayed in an individual classroom.

Despite its superficial appeal, defining general education as "that which everyone should know" has fared no better as a curriculum organizer. It has never been easy to codify, and recently two additional forces have afflicted it. One set of contentions holds that no knowledge is basic to everyone because everyone has a different background that gives rise to a unique outlook; a man cannot understand a woman's perspective, a person whose forebears came from Africa cannot understand the viewpoints held by one whose ancestors were European, and books written by members of one group are thus irrelevant to others. The second antagonistic force is that language, values, and understandings evolve so rapidly that no reference is more relevant than another, none has permanence, none survives a new season's TV shows. See, for example, the parenthetical definitions sprinkled throughout our daily newspapers; no knowledge of the Bible, the works of Shakespeare, Aesop's Fables, or any other works that have given rise to the English idiom is assumed.

General education was tainted early on. The phrase *terminal general education* was in use in the 1930s, suggesting that it was an education for the student who would never go on to higher learning. In some senior institutions, separate colleges were devised as holding tanks for students deemed unqualified to enter the regular programs. Here they would get the last of their formal education, nondisciplinary, nonspecialized, and—according to many professors—of dubious merit. If general education was seen as a curriculum for students unable to do real college work, it was doomed to suffer. Perhaps it was an extension of high school general education, but then what was it doing in a real college? And how could a self-respecting faculty member have anything to do with it? Credit the idea of terminal general education as one of the factors leading to the failure of general education to hold the attention of the academy.

Another clue to the unstable history of general education can be found in its emphasis on individual life adjustment. Early proponents of general education fostered guidance activities. B. Lamar Johnson, a spokesperson for general education during much of his half century in higher education, said in 1937, "Uniformly colleges committed to general education stress guidance. This is reasonable, for if general education aims to help the individual adjust to life, it is essential to recognize that this adjustment is an individual matter—dependent upon individual abilities, interests, and needs. Upon these bases the colleges assist the student to determine his individual objectives and mould a program to attain them" (p. 12). But if the individual is to "mould a program" based on his or her "abilities, interests, and needs," then anything may be seen as general education for that individual. The person may take the most specialized courses or no courses at all. Such a definition dooms the idea of integrated courses—indeed, of all common courses. Thus, general education in the 1930s was so fractionated that it included everything from the Great Books curriculum to life-adjustment courses and student guidance.

The idea that the student should be led to a "satisfactory vocational adjustment" was also common in definitions of general education at midcentury. Occupational education has achieved great success in American colleges and universities, but for different reasons. It was built on an alliance of educators seeking support, students seeking jobs, and business people seeking workers trained at public expense; it has capitalized on legislators who are pleased to assign schools the task of mitigating unemployment; it has been enhanced by parents who want the schools to teach their children to do something productive. It has done well, and if it is a part of general education, then general education has done well, too. But when general education is defined as leading students to understand relationships between themselves and society, to gain a sense of values and an appreciation for cultural diversity, and to fulfill the other broader aims of the program, occupational education is left out.

Credit its inclusion with blurring the image of what general education is or could be.

The expansion of higher education to include more than three thousand colleges has also added to the difficulties with general education. Free from the imposition of state-level requirements throughout much of their history, the colleges were able to develop an indigenous curriculum. When institutions could define their own patterns of study, it was possible for a strong president to leave a mark, for an institution to develop its own philosophical set. Some colleges were reorganized around specific curriculum plans when their prior offerings proved inadequate to attract a sufficient number of students to keep the college going. But in nearly all cases, it was the strong central figure who articulated the philosophy and used it to install a specialized curriculum and particular course requirements. Rarely did a group of local-campus faculty members and second-line administrators put together a viable curriculum. Rarely did a state legislature or a federal agency design integrated general education programs. At best, the states mandated distribution requirements, thus ensuring some form of curriculum balance; at worst, through their reimbursement schedules, they encouraged the expansion of occupational programs and courses to fit special student groups, thus stultifying indigenous curriculum development.

One more contributor to the instability of general education is the decline in literacy, which forced developmental education into the colleges. When faculty members are concerned with teaching basic reading, composition, and computational skills, they often think they must abandon instruction in critical thinking, values, and cultural perspectives. The influx of what were euphemistically called "nontraditional students" led to a failure of will even among some of the proponents of general education, who proposed warmth, love, and counseling, instead of curriculum, for that group. General education was shunted aside by those who failed to understand that it could be taught to everyone.

Except for an excessive concern with the academic disciplines, all these problems were more pronounced in community colleges than in universities. The lack of strong educational leadership, a failure to define general education consistently, the rise of occupational education, and adult literacy training affected the community colleges markedly. The colleges were so busy recruiting "new students" that they forgot why they wanted them; the idea that they were to be generally educated was lost. Student demands for relevant or instant education, for something pragmatic or useful, were interpreted as a need for occupational training. And the colleges' place in statewide networks of postsecondary education allowed them to excuse their curricular shortcomings by saying that true general education would not be accredited or would not articulate well with the senior institutions' curriculum.

Public support for a curriculum that would teach students to think critically and participate in the polity has not been easy to generate. There is too much suspicion of authority, too ready an acceptance of political candidates offering a negative agenda. Not only has faith in the schools wavered, but also faith in government, in business corporations, and indeed in the authority of adults. The students' cry of the 1960s, "You have no authority to tell me what to study!" was accepted as valid by educators, who themselves were members of a community that had lost faith in its institutions. They had come to expect, even to welcome, corruption in government and business because governments were by definition oppressive and business rapacious. The evidence was all around; Nixon's derelictions, congressional peccadilloes, top officials in Reagan's administration shipping arms to Iran clandestinely, corporations bribing government officials—all of this was "normal." The crime was in getting caught.

The disaffection with the institution of government was revealed further in local, state, and national elections in the 1990s. Some candidates ran for office promising to introduce no legislation because "we already have too many laws." Others had no platform except to say, "I'm not an incumbent." Term-limits legislation passed in numerous states. It was easy to visualize an election in which "None of the above; leave the office vacant" would win a plurality. Thus the same forces that should lead people to cry out for a curriculum of unification militate against its pursuit.

Still, general education survives. Is it relevant? Pragmatic? Pertinent to community needs? Legitimate in the eyes of the public? General education in community colleges will rise or fall in answer to those questions. It will depend also on the definitions accorded to it and to the terms *education* and *curriculum*.

We define *education* as "the process of learning," of change in attitude or capability. It may take place in school or outside; it may be guided, monitored, or haphazard; but it is something that happens to the individual. *Curriculum* is "any set of courses." This definition excludes those aspects of schooling that take place outside a structured course format. It should not be difficult for community college staff members to accept; as participants in a commuter institution, they have always been uneasy about ascribing value to student activities, clubs, dormitories, and other appurtenances of the residential college. The definitions connect education and curriculum with organized sequences—hour-long, week-long, year-long—designed to lead individuals from one set of abilities or tendencies to another; in short, to instruction.

Why General Education in Community Colleges?

Statements on behalf of general education have been advanced not only by educators as far back as the earliest writers on community colleges—Lange, Koos, and Eells—but also by groups outside the academy. In 1947, the President's Commission on Higher Education noted the importance of semiprofessional training but contended that it should be "acquired in an environment that also cultivates general education, thus offering the student 'a combination of social understanding and technical competence'" (Park,

1977, p. 57). Ten years later, President Eisenhower's Committee on Education Beyond High School also articulated that combination, viewing it as the particular responsibility of the community colleges. Subsequently, an American Council on Education task force recommended that any institution offering an associate degree should attest that its students have become familiar with general areas of knowledge and have gained "competency in analytical, communication, quantitative, and synthesizing skills" ("Flexibility Sought . . . ," 1978). The degree should state not only that the students gained their training in a college but also that the training included a general education component.

Numerous forces prevent excess in any curriculum for too long. Accrediting agencies, student enrollments, institutional funding sources, and the professional intelligence of the staff all act to maintain curriculum balance. The trend in community college curriculum was decidedly toward career and developmental education in the 1970s; the 1980s and 1990s saw a cessation of that trend, and succeeding decades may see it swing back toward preparing the generally educated person. Career education can be too specialized; students learn job entry skills, but they may not learn how to continue to advance within the job. Career educators have also run the risk of frustrating trainees who cannot find the jobs for which they were specifically trained. The career programs are not automatically relevant or valuable; they can be as meretricious as the most esoteric discipline-based course. Without the breadth that accompanies general education, the colleges would be occupational schools undifferentiated from industrial training enterprises or proprietary schools. Developmental education is limited in scope because it does not accommodate human needs for self-expression, social interaction, and understanding of the world. The slogans "salable skills" and "back to basics" are not sufficient for mounting a program in higher education.

Curiously, the idea of lifelong learning, the same phenomenon that excused the abandonment of general education, may be the best argument for maintaining it in community colleges. Hutchins (1937) took issue with the idea of lifelong learning that would train and retrain people for occupations, saying that anything to be taught to young people should be useful to them throughout their lives, that successive, ad hoc retraining in specific skills would not lead them to understand anything of importance about their own lives or the world around them. But it is precisely the older students who perceive the need for general education, even while they seek upgrading within their own careers. They know that employment depends less on skill training than on the ability to communicate and get along with employers and co-workers. They know that a satisfying life demands more than production and consumption. They know that they must understand the ways institutions and individuals interact, that, for the sake of themselves and their progeny, they must understand and act on social issues. They know that they must maintain control over their lives, that what they learn assists them in maintaining individual freedom and dignity against a society that increasingly seeks to "deliver" health care, information, and the presumed benefits of living. That is why they come to the colleges with interest in the arts, in general concepts in science, understanding the environment, relations with their fellows, questions of personal life crises and developmental stages—all topics in a true general education curriculum. As Miller concluded, "It may well be that adult or continuing education has already become the cutting edge of general education. Continuing education programs, by force of economics if nothing else, tend to be student centered, future oriented, and change oriented programs. The methods of adult education are especially sympathetic to the goals of general education" (1988, p. 176).

Inherently, the community colleges are neither more nor less able to offer a distribution of courses that would satisfy a general education requirement than are the universities or secondary schools; it is a matter of labeling and packaging. However, their students are less likely to accept distribution requirements because the associate degree has little value in the marketplace and the universities will allow students to transfer without it. Integrated general education courses, however, could find a home in community colleges if faculty members and administrators believed in their value. Instructors are not closely tied to the academic disciplines, nor do they typically engage in research and specialized writing. Many of the colleges have formed divisional instead of departmental structures. The colleges have some advantage, too, in developing problem-centered courses in general education through their ties to the local community.

For which of the many students coming to community colleges shall general education be provided? The answer is that the college should provide general education for all its enrollees. The college must guarantee the availability of general education throughout a person's life. Lifelong learning is more than the opportunity for successive retraining as one's job becomes obsolete; it is access to the form of general studies that leads to an understanding of self and society. General education must not be optional, lest the gulf between social classes in America be accentuated as members of the elite group learn to control their environment, while the lower classes are given career education and training in basic skills. The colleges must provide general education for young students, whether or not they intend to transfer to senior institutions, and for adults, who see the world changing and want to understand more about their environment.

A key question in general education is "How?" The question must be resolved in the context of the open-access institution. "Open access" means "open exit" as well. If a student may enter and drop at will, the ideal of curriculum as a set of courses is severely limited. There can be no continuity of curriculum when a student takes one course, goes away for a number of years, and comes back to take one more. This casual approach is unprecedented in higher education and requires special planning if general education is to be effective. At the very least, each course must be considered a self-contained unity, presented as though the students will never consider its concepts in another course.

Those who would plan general education must take care that they not repeat the cosmic rationalizations offered by early-day apologists for general education, who saw the students becoming imaginative, creative, perceptive, and sensitive to beauty; knowing about nature, humanity, and culture; acting with maturity, balance, and perspective; and so on. The colleges are simply not that influential. However, general education must not be debased by tying the concept exclusively to reading, writing, calculating, operating an automobile, using appliances, consuming products, practicing health, preparing income tax forms, borrowing money, and so on. Important as these tasks are, they can be learned elsewhere.

The rationale for general education in the community college is the freedom enjoyed by the informed citizen. Only when people are able to weigh the arguments of the experts are they truly free. These experts may be discussing issues of the environment, whether to put power plants or oil docks in or near cities. They may be advising on governmental questions. Or they may be deciding who may be born, who has a right to live, what it means to be healthy, and how, where, and when one should die. People need to understand how things work—social systems and persuaders, artists and computers. General education is for the creation of a free citizenry, the Greek ideal of the citizen participating in the polity. Because we are embedded in families, tribes, and communities, we must learn to be free-thinking citizens, learn the literacy necessary for life in a civil society, the competence to participate in the broader community, the ability to think critically.

Freedoms gained through a general education extend from the person to the society. The ability to place one's own problems in broad perspective, to make informed choices about the conduct of one's own life, is the cornerstone of freedom for the individual. The idea of freedom is different now than it was in an earlier era. To be free economically does not mean setting up one's own farm; it means having alternative ways of working within the modern corporate system. To be free politically does not mean going to town meetings and deciding on local issues; it means understanding the consequences of actions taken by bureaucrats and the ways of influencing or countering those actions. Being free morally and personally does not mean abiding by community mores; it means having the ability to understand and predict the consequences of one's actions for self and fellows in the context of a higher order of morality.

The cross-currents that affect community colleges generally affect their involvement with general education. It is possible to be optimistic about the future of general education because there is an irreducible minimum in curriculum and instruction below which the college ceases to be. The curriculum must be educative; staff members must act like educators; students must learn. A publicly supported college cannot operate indefinitely with a curriculum perceived as a set of haphazard events; with a corps of part-time instructors who have no commitment to the institution in general, let alone to the planning of curriculum in particular; and with students who drop in casually if they have nothing better to do that week. Such an institution may continue functioning, but it has lost its guiding ethos. A general education that leads to the ways of knowing and the common beliefs and language that bind society together is offered in every culture through rituals, schools, apprenticeships. The community colleges are responsible for furthering it in the United States.

General Education in Practice

Many community colleges have attempted to devise general education patterns. The integrated course has its own history, and several descriptions of interdisciplinary survey courses have been reported. Course outlines have been reprinted, ways of organizing the courses have been detailed, and problems in maintaining course integrity have been discussed. As an example, interdisciplinary courses in the humanities have been prominent, but activity in other areas has been undertaken as well. Courses for general education have been centered on contemporary problems: race relations, drug use and alcoholism, ecology and the environment, social controversies, and world peace. In the 1930s such courses were often built on political problems—at that time fascism versus democracy; in the 1950s it was communism versus democracy. In the 1960s political problems gave way to issues surrounding the individual, and courses on "The Individual and Society," "Understanding Human Values," and "Intergroup Relations" became more prevalent. But the ideal of education for civic responsibility would not die. Several colleges—Broome Community College (New York), for example—continued seeking ways of educating students for democratic participation (Higginbottom, 1986).

Many colleges that tried such courses subsequently returned to distribution requirements based on a variety of courses. Santa Fe Community College (Florida) opened in 1966 with common courses in science, social science, and humanities. In 1972, the integrated courses were dropped and distribution requirements installed.

A few colleges maintained integrated courses. When Miami-Dade opened in 1960, instructors were hired especially to develop and teach an integrated humanities course. Over the years, however, the course became eight weeks each of art, philosophy, music, literature—a mosaic pattern. The social science course remained integrated but evolved into popular psychology, human relations, and the quest for the self. The college did not build an integrated science course, and by 1977 students could satisfy the general education requirement in science by choosing two courses from a given list, the communications requirement by taking one course in English composition plus a literature elective (Lukenbill and McCabe, 1978). However, the pendulum swung again, and by 1978 Miami-Dade had developed a core of five multidisciplinary courses—"Communications," "The Social Environment," "The Natural Environment," "Humanities," and "The Individual"—that were still viable sixteen years later.

Los Medanos College (California) also installed integrated courses successfully. At its inception in the mid 1960s, it built a core of six generic courses in behavioral, social, biological, and physical sciences and in language arts and humanistic studies, a plan notable less for its content than for the way it was organized. First, there was administrative coordination of the curriculum. Second, each course was required for all degree-seeking students. Third, the college employed a full-time staff development officer to work closely with the faculty in preparing the common course outlines. The result was that about one-third of the college's total enrollments were in the general education basic courses, although by 1988 the percentage had dropped as the college expanded into numerous other curricular areas. All this occurred in a college that drew its student population predominantly from a community of low socioeconomic status with a high proportion of ethnic minorities (Collins and Drexel, 1976; Case, 1988).

Various other interdisciplinary combinations have been applied. Valencia Community College (Florida) developed an interdisciplinary studies program centering on a two-year core curriculum organized chronologically (Valencia Community College, 1984). In this program, four courses—each including concepts from the arts, philosophy, religion, English, mathematics, social sciences, and physical sciences—were developed, and distinct guidelines for instructional methodologies were provided. Saint Petersburg Junior College (Florida) also established an interdisciplinary studies program incorporating a thirty-six-hour requirement in humanities, history, ethics, composition, speech, American government, and natural science into a comprehensive package (Wiley and Robinson, 1987). Monroe Community College's (New York) interdisciplinary program centered on human ecology (Harrison, 1987). Several other programs have been described in a volume edited by Higginbottom and Romano (1995).

The examples cited are prominent but not widespread. Across the nation, in the Spring 1991 term, 94,200 students took a class in

Interdisciplinary Humanities; 43,400 took an Integrated Science class; and 30,100 a class in Interdisciplinary Social Science (Center for the Study of Community Colleges, 1991). Compared with the 1.25 million students who entered the community colleges for the first time that year, those enrollments are quite small.

In most community colleges the pursuit of general education is equated with sets of distribution requirements. In the typical institution, students can meet these requirements by taking courses from a list arranged by department or division. The programs in liberal arts, business administration, general science, pre-engineering, accounting, architectural technology, and so on state various numbers of minimum semester hours to be taken outside the main field. The social science electives may be selected from courses in anthropology, economics, political science, psychology, sociology; the science electives, from courses in physics, chemistry, biology, astronomy; the humanities electives, from courses in music appreciation, art history, literature, philosophy; and the courses in communication, from composition, speech, journalism, or writing. That is the most prevalent pattern. It satisfies the accrediting agencies, comfortable with it because of its familiarity, and the universities because it fits their own curricular mode. Few within the colleges question it. Their rationale is based on freedom of choice for the students. But the result is curricular chaos, mitigated hardly at all by the numerous attempts to specify which courses shall constitute a core of offerings acceptable to the senior institutions in a state. California's efforts are illustrative. The university's Academic Senate approved a "transfer core" curriculum but assured the faculty on each campus that it did "not affect prerequisites for majors, or such upper-division courses as are prescribed by differing campuses or programs" ("'Transfer Core' Curriculum . . . ," 1988, p. 59). This kind of qualifying statement has destroyed general education transfer plans repeatedly in one state after another.

A Model General Education Plan

A general education pattern for all community college students can be devised if the staff adhere to certain premises. Curriculum is not put together in a vacuum; it is not the responsibility of each professional person acting independently. A general education curriculum needs a faculty working together, a group coordinated by a dean or division head or program manager. This leads to the first premise: *faculty role definition is essential.* General education cannot be considered only—or even primarily—classroom-centered. The faculty member who wants to hide behind the classroom door and develop courses and instructional strategies independently cannot beneficially participate in a general education program. The part-time instructor with only a casual commitment is of limited value as well. The general education program demands a corps of professional staff members who know how to differentiate their responsibilities.

The leadership for a general education program must come from a staff person whose sole responsibility is to further it. The president can set the tone for general education but is limited in influence on curriculum. Deans of instruction formerly dealt with general education, but in most colleges they have become senior-grade personnel managers. Assigning responsibility to the faculty in general is not sufficient; someone must be in charge. *A general education program must have a program head.* Chair, dean, or director, the title is not important.

Third, the general education program should be *vertically integrated*: a program head and faculty members with designated responsibilities. Several technological programs have adopted this model. Wherever there is a program in nursing, for example, there is a director of nursing with staff members who attend to curriculum, student recruiting and admissions, student placement, and the instructional aspects of the program. General education must be similarly organized.

Next, the general education program should be *managed at the campus level*. Each campus in a multicampus district should have its own philosophy and operational definition to guide the general education requirements because, apart from the managerial problems in trying to coordinate instructional programs on many campuses from a general office, the same type of program does not fit all campuses within a district. Although powerful forces are leading toward more homogeneity among campuses—and, indeed, among all colleges within a state—this trend can be turned around. But campus instructors and administrators must understand the importance of taking the leadership in curriculum development if they would avert centralized curriculum decision making.

A utopian model for effecting general education is offered here. The faculty would be organized into four divisions: Culture, Communications, Institutions, and Environment. Faculty members in these divisions would separate themselves from their academic departments or the other divisions into which the rest of the faculty was placed. The general education program would have its own budget. The faculty would prepare and operate the integrated courses, course modules, course-exemption examinations, student follow-up studies, and relationships with high schools and senior institutions. Funding such divisions would not be a problem; they would generate enough FTSEs to pay for all their efforts. They would do their own staff development as well.

Although each campus or each college would develop its own programs, it is possible to trace an outline of how the programs would operate. Begin with general education in the career education programs. First, a delegate from each of the four divisions would examine those programs to determine whether intervention might be made. Course modules—portions of courses to be inserted into the occupational programs—would be sought. As an example, in a fashion design program, the faculty from Institutions might prepare a short unit on the role of fashions in society; the Communications staff might do one on advertising copy and another on distribution, ordering, and inventory control; the Culture group would do one on fashion as folk art and another on traditional symbolism in fashion. For the allied health programs, general education modules presenting the process of grieving around the world and dealing with the terminal patient might be prepared by the Culture faculty; the faculty from Institutions would do a unit on medical ethics. A program in automotive maintenance and transport would be offered modules on energy utilization by the Environment staff; the laws governing highway construction and use, by the Institutions group; the automobile in American culture, by the Culture faculty.

These types of course sections, or modules, would be arranged in consultation with the career program faculty. They might start with one lecture only, tying the occupation to the broader theme, and eventually work into entire courses, depending on the success of the module and the apparent desirability of continuing it. The faculty can attend to the meaning of work, to concepts surrounding the occupation at hand, to the values undergirding particular vocations. They can suggest options for the portion of the students' lives that is not involved with work. And they can expand students' capabilities within the occupation itself by examining the derivation of that function and how it is maintained in other cultures. Some instructors in the health fields have welcomed a unit of a course taught by an anthropologist that considers the puberty rites in various cultures around the world or a unit on the ethics of euthanasia presented by a philosophy teacher. Course modules on the Greek and Latin roots of medical terminology taught by instructors of classical languages have been successfully introduced. Some occupational programs have accepted entire courses in medical ethics or the rise of technology, courses that encompass the dynamics of the occupation and the themes and problems associated with it. Such courses could be pursued vigorously, and the career programs should pay the costs for such courses and course modules.

The four general education divisions would build their own courses for the students enrolled in the collegiate and developmental programs. Each would do one course only, to be required for every student intending to obtain a certificate or a degree. The courses would be organized around themes, not around academic disciplines. The intent of each would be to point up how contemporary and past, local and distant peoples have dealt with the problems common to all: communications, energy use, social institutions, the search for truth, beauty, and order. The courses would be prepared by the general education staff, specialists in that curriculum form. Their goal: a free people in a free society, thinking critically, appreciating their cultural tradition, understanding their environment and their place within it.

The general education faculty on each campus would build its own four required courses, and, depending on local conditions, there would be great variation among them. The Communications staff might do a course called "How We Communicate," dealing with propaganda, advertising, interpersonal communications, and literary criticism—not criticism of Joyce, Steinbeck, and Salinger but of such contemporary literary forms as administrative memos, radio talk shows, and televised news reports. How do the meanings of "affirmative action," "multiculturalism," and "diversity" vary in different contexts? Students would learn to read the language behind the words.

The Institutions staff might build a course around "People and Their Institutions." This would not be a "Survey of Social Science" or a "History of Western Civilization" course; it would emphasize how people have had to grapple with social institutions throughout the history of civilized society. How did the English kings impinge on the lives of their people? How were the pharaohs able to organize the populace into tremendous labor gangs? What is the grip that modern China has on the minds of its people? How must we deal with our own bureaus and commissions? Here, too, knowledge of the terminology in academic disciplines, the jargon of the specialists, would not be the proper goal.

The Culture staff might do a course on "People and Culture." The theme would be how people have attempted to come to grips with the ultimate questions of all humanity: who are we? Where did we come from? What mark can we leave? The content would be the types of self-expression, through art, music, literature, and dance. Comparative religion would be part of this course only if it were based on the question "Why religion at all?" The way novelists have tried to speak to the human condition would be explored.

The course on "The Environment" could incorporate elements of astronomy, biology, physics—all the earth, life, and physical sciences. It would be concerned with the effects of substance abuse; patterns of energy consumption; shifting concepts in earth and space sciences; how agricultural engineering can be used to mitigate the problem of famine; what can be known through empirical science and what can be known only through intuition, introspection, or revelation.

The pattern of each faculty group having responsibility for one large theme-centered course would allow general education to have its own organizing principles. The course would not offer a few weeks of instruction in each academic discipline, lest it fracture along disciplinary lines. If provision were made for a student to exempt or test out of the course, the general education program staff would develop and administer its own examination or other measure of knowledge sufficiency.

Nothing in this type of reorganization would do away with the specialized courses; the college would still teach "Spanish for Correctional Officers," "General Chemistry," "Introduction to Music," and the hundreds of other discipline-based courses that make up a full curriculum. However, the four theme-centered courses might supplant most of the general or introductory courses now offered.

The general education staff would build modules and specifically designed courses for the occupational students, theme-centered courses for the transfer students, and yet another type of course for the large and growing number of continuing education students.

These students, attending the institution part-time, picking up courses that strike their fancy because of current interest or because of the social interaction that the college offers, deserve something different. Naturally, they would be invited to enroll in the major theme-centered courses; however, they need special problems courses, an extension of the problems touched on in the broader themes courses.

A model for this group is afforded through current practice in community college adult divisions and university extension divisions, in which around one-fourth of the courses are for general enlightenment. Here is where the specialized course of local interest comes into play. If sufficient interest in the history of a local labor dispute or the latest theories about astronomical black holes can be found, the general education faculty would take part, either by offering such a course or by enlisting the ad hoc assistance of other staff members. The important point is that these courses be offered and their availability advertised. It would be incumbent on the general education faculty to tap community interest in, set up, and promote these courses. The common characteristic of the courses is that they must be educative; they must not be presentations of unknown effect.

The instructional forms used in these courses can be as varied as necessary. Members of a general education faculty of the type described may find that they need to write their own extensive syllabi and text materials. They would probably find it expedient to divide responsibilities, some of them lecturing, others building reproducible media, others writing and administering examinations. But they must stay together as a group organized to provide integrated general education.

The community colleges are in a better position than ever in their history to articulate and defend their general education offerings. The senior institutions cannot be excessively stringent in their interpretation of what qualifies for credit at a time when nearly half of college freshmen begin in two-year institutions.

To conclude, this form of general education can and should be constructed. The greatest impediment to it is within the institution itself. A sufficient number of college leaders—trustees, administrators, and instructors—must see the urgency of this pattern of curriculum development. The conflict is between pluralism as a goal and the use of curriculum as an aid to social integration. If individualism is raised to such heights that the common themes underlying the free person in the free society cannot be perceived, it will be impossible to devise a core curriculum.

In 1927, the following words were inscribed atop a public building in Minneapolis:

> *Participation in the rights of citizenship presumes participation in the duties of citizenship.*
>
> *The highest expression of life is cooperative service for the common good.*
>
> *Every citizen owes his city constructive interest in his city's affairs.*

Gender-specific language aside, who now would put such words, the essence of general education, on a public monument? Who now would even write them in a college's statement of purpose?

Issues

Building a general education program in the community colleges will be no easier in the future than it was in the past. The same centrifugal forces operate to fractionate the curriculum.

How can faculty members, each trained in a particular discipline, become competent in constructing interdisciplinary courses? What are the implications for staff development?

Will career education faculty and advisory groups feel that general education requirements have usurped their prerogatives?

If so, how can they be convinced that general education benefits their clients?

Can college leaders display sufficient will and political force to insist that the universities give full credit to transferring students who have taken unique general education courses?

Can the staff in all higher education accept the definition of general education as providing basic understanding for people to act as citizens, rather than as practitioners in narrowly based professions or academic disciplines?

The threat to the academic content of community college education did not come from career education; the technical programs often made rigorous demands on their students. It came from the colleges that offered a few presentations on television, a sizable number of community service programs, and credit courses in hundreds of locations with noncredit options, all with no attempt to ensure that the presentations were educative. The threat came also from the colleges' proudly stated policies that encouraged all to drop in when they want, take what they want, and drop out when they want—the ultimate in curriculum disintegration. A curriculum centered on general education could restore institutional integrity while promoting the form of social cohesion that derives from shared beliefs and people making informed decisions.

13

· ·

Scholarship

Research In and About the Colleges

The amount spent for research in social-service institutions is low in comparison with research and development in the commercial sector. Research in education commands a minuscule proportion of education expenditures and, in fact, has decreased as a proportion of overall budgets since the early 1970s. A major reason for this meager support is that few legislators, members of the lay public, or education practitioners think that research about education is useful, that it has anything to contribute to the productivity or efficiency of the schools.

Like other schools, the community colleges conduct little research, and even less attention is paid to them by extramural research agencies. Data about the colleges are sometimes embedded in reports of postsecondary education in a state or in the nation. But despite the American Association of Community Colleges' efforts to codify a set of "Core Indicators of Effectiveness" (1994), there is no generally accepted national research agenda for community colleges, no consistently funded national agency charged with studying the institutions as unique entities, and few educational researchers directing their attention toward them. The words *community college, junior college,* and *two-year college* do not appear in the index to Feldman and Newcomb's two-volume compendium of research on *The Impact of College on Students* (1969), and only a scant handful of studies that include community college student data are among the more than twenty-five hundred reports cited by Pascarella and Terenzini in their successor volume, *How College Affects Students* (1991). Thus, according to those who study the effects of postsecondary schooling, nearly 40 percent of America's college students, the proportion enrolled in the community colleges, are not even important enough to tabulate.

Even so, some studies of community college functioning are undertaken, and as abbreviated as this research effort is in comparison with the magnitude of the enterprise, it is worthy of note. The research is conducted by university-based analysts; by national organizations, primarily federally sponsored; by state agencies concerned with postsecondary education; and by researchers within the colleges. It takes several forms: historical and sociological analysis; state and national data compilation; data that set norms for interinstitutional comparisons; and information such as program review, student satisfaction, community relationships, and student placement validation that may be used for intramural planning. Much of it is driven by external mandates. This chapter reviews the groups that conduct these studies, the types of research they report, and a few of their findings and persistent problems.

Sources of Research

Except for the college-based institutional research officers, nearly all of the researchers who study community colleges are affiliated with universities or state agencies. An occasional report written by a private, nonprofit corporation or an ad hoc commission may appear, but most of the extramural studies are conducted by university professors and students in the social sciences, most of them in schools of education. Fewer than one hundred university professors are exclusively concerned with teaching and writing about community colleges. Perhaps one hundred more have some interest in the institutions and occasionally conduct a study or prepare a commentary. However, these researchers are responsible for the lion's share of the analyses that appear as published documents. Graduate students working under their direction collect original data or write theses based on existing data sets; many of the reports written by community college practitioners about their own institutions are prepared while they are concurrently enrolled in graduate programs. The professors further stimulate study of the colleges by seeking research grants for special topics, serving on extramural commissions, and advising local, state, and national agencies regarding research directions. Some manage series of research projects; two prominent examples are the National Center on Postsecondary Teaching, Learning, and Assessment and the Center for the Study of Community Colleges.

In recent years, several state agencies have gained the capacity to conduct research on community colleges. Their efforts vary, depending on state-governance structures. Some states (for example, Illinois and Washington) have sophisticated research offices as arms of their governing or coordinating boards. Where the community colleges are part of the state-university system (as in Kentucky and New York, for example), reliable data collection and analysis may result. In other states, such as Colorado, Oklahoma, and North Carolina, the university and the community college systems cooperate closely in compiling and reporting data about both sectors. However, in half the states, cross-institutional research on community colleges is sporadic or effectively nonexistent. A major reason is that state office staffs are small and assign low priority to compiling systemwide information that necessarily masks single-institution accomplishments.

Research on the national level centers in the U.S. Department of Education. Its National Center for Education Statistics sponsors the Integrated Postsecondary Education Data System (IPEDS), the most comprehensive compilation. The center reports annually on the number of community colleges, institutional services provided, revenues, costs, expenditures, enrollment, degrees conferred, and staff composition and salaries. In recent years it has expanded its efforts far beyond IPEDS to assess school dropout, academic progress, literacy development, national goals, and a host of interrelated issues; it publishes separate reports of those data.

Other agencies extract the community college-related data from the NCES reports and publish their own compendia; see Phillippe (1995b), for example. The Education Department also funds the ERIC Clearinghouse for Community Colleges, not a research agency but, since 1966, a collector, indexer, abstractor, and disseminator of research reports. The Clearinghouse has added fifteen thousand documents to the ERIC database, providing an easily accessible archive and resource for everyone studying the institutions.

Various national professional and institutional membership associations conduct a few specialized studies: the National Association of College and University Business Officers collects financial data; the American Association of University Professors collects salary data. Many of the other professional and institutional associations serve the research enterprise by encouraging philanthropic foundations and governmental agencies to sponsor studies of community colleges using paradigms that fit the colleges' mission and role. Some collect information of a type that supports their lobbying efforts.

Institutional Research Offices

Institutional research (IR) in the colleges manifests a pattern ranging from the sophisticated to the rudimentary. Except in a few colleges, it has never been well supported. A study coordinated by the ERIC Clearinghouse for Junior Colleges (Roueche and Boggs, 1968) found full-time research coordinators in only about one in five community colleges, usually the larger institutions. In two of five colleges, responsibility for institutional research was assigned to an administrator who also had other duties, and in two of five, no regular staff member had responsibility for coordinating institutional studies. Knapp (1979) found institutional research offices typically staffed with only one or two persons. In 1987 the community colleges of Southern California averaged only 0.67 full-time-equivalent (FTE) institutional researchers each—hardly enough to fill out the data-request forms that flowed in from the governmental agencies (Wilcox, 1987).

Little has changed in recent years. Miami-Dade Community College's research office boasts eleven staff members, but that is far beyond the number found elsewhere; less than half of its sister institutions in the south employ as much as a half-time institutional researcher (Rowh, 1990). In the late 1980s, state after state generated demands for outcomes assessment but the institutional research offices have not grown nearly so much as the demands for additional information would warrant. In most states, a centralized research effort still depends on someone at the community college level to provide the basic information. And the less able the state office, the more the colleges must do in collecting baseline information according to their own definitions and criteria. Many colleges assign specific research tasks ad hoc to certain staff members who may be released temporarily from their other duties.

Calls for assessment assail the colleges relentlessly: state-level mandates, federal reporting regulations, accrediting-agency requests. First come the requests for data, then the suggestions for how the data should be arrayed, and finally the requirements—do it, or else. These requests and demands seek a variety of types of information: program accountability, outcomes assessment, transfer rates, employment placement validation, graduation rates, evaluation criteria, satisfaction measures, job performance, and assessment—there is no end to the types of information sought. The research office must have ready access to all the information banks in every college office: personnel, admissions, student records, and the like. The task is easier now because of the greater data processing capability that has become economical and readily available in recent years. But the community colleges with research offices averaging one or two FTE staff members per campus can barely keep up with the demand.

Various ways of organizing institutional research offices were reported by MacDougall and Friedlander (1990), who identified, as examples, a centralized model on campus; a central district office but with research coordinators at each of the campuses; voluntary consortia for conducting institutional research; research offices maintained at the state level with college-level partners; and various hybrids such as part-time institutional researchers whose activities were guided by college-level research committees. Huntington and Clagett's (1991) survey found research directors concerned that the position of their office in the college's organization mitigated their ability to obtain data from other college offices. In some colleges, the IR office was linked to the development office, putting data together to assist college staff members who were preparing grant proposals. Many were providing information for college public-relations releases. Most were supplying data to satisfy state or federal directives. Noting the magnitude of state requests, King (1993) reported that each community college in North Carolina was required to submit nearly 200 reports a year to the state department of community colleges, on topics ranging from enrollment in basic skills classes to library accession lists to evaluations of the Visiting Artists Program.

Understaffed as they are, the institutional research offices produce a sizable number of reports useful not only to their own colleges but also to the analyst seeking fine data about program effects. Relating student progress to *placement and testing procedures* is popular. The IR offices also occasionally design *community surveys*, asking, "How many of our district's high school graduates attend our college?" They conduct studies of *student aspirations,* attempting to link them to program design and student success: "Why did the students enroll? Did they get what they were looking for?" They do *program review,* often under the impetus of an external agency's request: "Is this program properly staffed? Does it attract students? Is it cost effective?" They include *comparative* studies: "How do other colleges in our state organize their orientation programs?" They conduct *aca-*

demic validation studies: "Which tests best predict course grades?" And they do *attainment* studies: "How many of our graduates obtained jobs or went on to further education?"

The audience for these reports varies. The state agencies that have requested the data receive copies, as do the college's senior officials and board members. The institutional researchers' state and national associations publish selected documents. Some institutional researchers condense their reports into short memoranda that they distribute to everyone on the campus. The general availability of desktop publishing equipment has made the production of these types of quick releases feasible. They usually include a bar graph or pie chart or some eye-catching artwork and an amount of information sufficiently abbreviated so that the casual reader might still find something of use. The computer has simplified this aspect of the institutional researcher's work, but office support and staffing still lag.

Although most IR reports circulate only within the college, some are distributed to a broader audience. ERIC collects, indexes, and abstracts hundreds every year. Several state and national faculty associations organized along disciplinary lines publish journals in which their members report on studies of their own; the Community College Social Science Association, the Community College Humanities Association, and the American Mathematical Association of Two-Year Colleges are prominent. The journals *Community College Review, Community College Journal of Research and Practice, Journal of Applied Research in Community Colleges, Community College Journal,* and *New Directions for Community Colleges* carry articles by practitioners. Various state groups, including two-year college trustee, administrator, and faculty associations, report their members' studies in their own publications. Several national forums welcome presentations of research. Among the more prominent: Association for Institutional Research; Society of College and University Planners; Association for the Study of Higher Education; National Council for Research and Planning;

American Association of Community Colleges; and Division J of the American Educational Research Association.

Forms of Research

Taken together, the university-based, national, state, and institutional research efforts provide a comprehensive view of institutional functioning. Their agendas overlap somewhat, but each has a tendency to use certain methodologies to study particular issues.

Historical and Sociological Studies

Several treatments of the formation and development of the junior (later community) colleges have been written from the viewpoint of history or sociology. Those with an historical bent look for documentation and details of the founding of individual institutions, hoping that when such examples are strung together, a picture of nationwide institutional formation will emerge. The sociologists usually work from the top down, seeking to link institutional formation with broad social forces and with theories of institutional formation. Interesting also are the biographies of early leaders, attempting to place the great person at the center of institutional development.

Much of the sociological and political-science-based research linking college development to broad social forces is reviewed in the following chapter. A few of the recent historical treatments include books by Eaton, Vaughan, Dougherty, Frye, and Witt and others. Shorter papers have been prepared by Gallagher, Murray, Plucker, Wagoner, and Pedersen. Some trace college genesis to the influence of local officials, such as school superintendents and university presidents, or of business and community leaders. By showing how these actors brought about the community colleges in their areas, the authors rebut the arguments that the colleges were products of a national agenda. If university leaders wanted to give a boost to undergraduate education (Gallagher), if business leaders wanted a precollegiate structure as an ornament of civic pride (Frye), and if school officials built the colleges despite reluctance on the part of state legislators (Dougherty; Pedersen), then the thesis of response to directives from a national association breaks down. Whether these local leaders were acting from noble or base motives seems irrelevant.

The contemporary dominant historical view is that prior to the 1950s the colleges were formed as local institutions in which recent high school graduates could get a start at a collegiate career. Most of the colleges were organized in small towns, far from universities; if the intent had been to form colleges for terminal students, the presence of a university would not have been a limiting factor. Furthermore, if vocational education were the guiding reason for establishing the colleges, they would have been organized first in the big industrial states, not in Iowa, Missouri, Texas, and California. After the 1960s, when sizable funds for occupational education were made available, and when large numbers of poorly prepared students sought college entry, the vocational and remedial functions became prominent along with collegiate studies.

These analyses have served to fill a gap in the research on the community colleges. Several of them have contributed to the ongoing debate over the motives of the early promoters and leaders of the institutions. Were the institutions formed because of the pleadings of national organizations, or did they develop in response to local enthusiasts? Did they arise in response to broad social forces, or to the determination of individual opportunists? Do they evidence a capitalistic society's conspiracy to keep the lower classes in their place? Are they a major democratic force, assisting people in moving toward the American dream of higher-status jobs and social position? Depending on the author's biases, the colleges are either the greatest invention of the twentieth century or the social tragedy of the era. Still, it has been refreshing to see the institution analyzed, even if the analysts range from neo-Marxists to Chamber of Commerce-type promoters.

Descriptive Analyses

Even though large-scale compilations obscure information about single colleges, they provide useful overviews. The U.S. Department of Education's National Center for Education Statistics collects data on all sectors and publishes numerous reports; more than two dozen are cited in this volume. Beyond its routine, census-style reports of enrollments, its data reflect Congressional concerns. Because of the various forms of federal aid awarded to postsecondary students, NCES summarizes data on college revenues, expenditures, and tuition. Federal affirmative action rulings require the colleges to report data on the gender and ethnicity of college staff, students, and graduates, and NCES compiles them. Federal regulations regarding discrimination against, or special funds available for, disabled students have led to various data on special services provided.

Recent legislation is adding to the types of information compiled. In an effort to reduce loan default and abuse of financial aid, regulations such as Student Right-to-Know have brought forth calls for data on student success in the various programs. The Carl D. Perkins Vocational Education Act instructed the colleges to provide data on student job attainment and maintenance. The Goals 2000 legislation has stimulated attempts to develop national curriculum standards, along with information on student literacy and other capacities.

These national data are an essential beginning point for any community college studies. But various types of information useful for a more complete picture of community college contributions are not being compiled routinely. The American Association of Community Colleges (1994) pointed to some of these gaps by citing several core indicators of effectiveness, including student persistence, satisfaction, and goal attainment; transfer and job placement numbers and success ratios; literacy and citizenship skill development; and college relationships with the community. The League for Innovation in the Community College listed sixty-nine measures of "institutional effectiveness" that could be reported (Doucette and Hughes, 1990). Gradually, these types of measures may insinuate themselves into a national research effort. But absent a consistent funding base, such as that enjoyed by NCES, routine collection of such data across all institutions is not likely to develop.

The ad hoc, sporadic approach to data on college outcomes might change if the U.S. Education Department were to continue its early 1990s efforts to draft specifications for a national collegiate assessment system. The purpose of the system was to develop procedures for continuous monitoring of access and outcomes, the rate at which students entering colleges complete their programs, and indicators of the graduates' ability to think critically, communicate effectively, and solve problems. Primarily, the group was looking for uniform reporting formats and some set of indicators beyond accreditation standards that could be readily understood and generally accepted. Along with the National Education Goals, this activity marked a notable departure from the American tradition of leaving goal setting to state and local authorities. But such changes were not to be easily affected. Despite some acceptance of the idea by a public concerned about its schools, many politicians and college officials opposed what they characterized as a usurpation of authority by the federal government.

The types of data that state agencies compile vary widely because of the variant place of community colleges in state higher education systems and because each state legislature and governing board enacts different regulations. State agencies typically receive data from the colleges and publish statewide aggregates regarding college expenditures, graduation rates, staff salaries, student ethnicity and age, etc. Some of these "fact books," such as those published annually in Illinois, North Carolina, and Washington, are useful in making interinstitutional comparisons. But comprehensive data are available in only a few states and, because of variant definitions, interstate comparisons are not warranted.

Ideally, each state agency would collect data across institutions according to consistent definitions, the way that NCES functions for the nation. Then the data would be made available to college-level researchers so that they could download information about their own institutions and cross-tabulate it with indigenously collected data. This would assist the colleges in answering all sorts of idiosyncratic questions about the success of particular student types who received certain instructional treatments. In practice, few such cooperative arrangements are in place.

More often, the state agencies act as NCES does in responding to legislative mandates. The law directs the colleges to initiate a program, student matriculation, for example, and directs the state agency to collect data on program effects, whereupon the agency draws guidelines for the colleges to use in assessing students at entry. The colleges define their procedures and validate their tests in accordance with student access in the programs in which they were placed. Whether the colleges are allowed to select their own instruments, as in California, or uniform tests are administered statewide, as in New Jersey, the IR office has had a portion of its research agenda defined for it. Supplemental state funding for these procedures rarely accompanies the mandates.

Qualitative Studies

A few qualitative studies appear in the literature each year. Some are book-length treatises; others are short reports of less-detailed investigations. The more useful studies provide information on the peculiarities of college functioning through participant observation or interview techniques in which the students and staff members talk about institutional and personal issues. Some studies report the responses verbatim while others contribute detailed analyses. Focus-group summaries are another technique in this genre.

In the hands of skilled researchers, the qualitative studies can be quite insightful. Studies of faculty, from Garrison (1967) to Purdy (1973) to Seidman (1985), tell more about how instructors address their work than can ever be learned from tables displaying the number of hours taught per week or faculty use of computers in the classroom.

Issues, Dilemmas, and Possibilities

> We often think that when we have completed our study of *one* we know all about *two,* because "two" is "one and one." We forget that we have still to make a study of "and." [Eddington, 1958, p. 103]

Whatever the source and the forms it takes, research on the community colleges suffers several limitations stemming from imprecision in the language of the social sciences and from the relationships between researchers and practitioners. Additional difficulties center on the nature of reportage and on the way that support for the colleges is generated and sustained. These problems are prevalent in other sectors as well, but in this section they are related to the literature about the community colleges.

The historical and sociological treatises are evidence that there is no such thing as unbiased scholarship. The choice of community colleges as an area of study, the attempt to link institutional formation and development to sociological theory, the premise that either broad social forces or individual initiative gave rise to the institutions, and the conclusion that society is well-served or betrayed by the existence of these open-access, postsecondary structures all argue that the term "objective inquiry" is an oxymoron. The findings are as stylized and predictable as those reached by quantitative researchers who discover that *only* 20 percent of the entering students transfer. (How many transfers would it take for them to remove the qualifier "only"?) The researchers who demonstrate (once again) that students who matriculate at a community college are less likely to obtain the baccalaureate than those who start at a university have offered nothing new. Their conclusions, "The colleges should begin offering the B.A.," or "The colleges should abandon their collegiate function," reveal their prejudgments.

Survey research has its limitations. Even NCES sometimes provides ambiguous information. For example, the question "Which of the following services does your institution provide?", addressed to all the colleges, listed services for students with various types of disabilities. It yielded the finding that 837 of the nation's 1,020 public two-year institutions offer "assistance for the visually impaired" (National Center for Education Statistics, 1994e, p. 21). But the reader of the report has no way of telling whether that assistance is a full-scale curriculum or a set of braille markers on the campus's elevator buttons.

Assessing Institutional Effects

Research is merely a way of answering questions. Various members of the college community and of the broader community have different questions that concern them. The answers that research can yield, the data that must be gathered, the analyses that can be made, and the reports that are distributed all have different configurations depending on the nature of the questions, who asked them, and the type of response that will satisfy the petitioner. The way the information is used to influence programmatic decisions varies similarly.

To give an obvious example, questions are frequently asked about the college and about the benefits that its students receive. The answers are available through data on community demographics and college enrollment patterns and through follow-up studies of students who matriculated and then either dropped out, completed programs, or went on to further pursuits. When a legislator or a newspaper reporter calls and asks, "How many students who entered your college have gained employment?" the researcher should deliver a number based on a valid analysis of the available data. The questioner will not be satisfied by a reference to a lengthy report in which the data are manipulated by an endless array of categories of students and programs, types of jobs sought, student abilities and aspirations, and the like. Difficult for many data base managers to realize, some questions deserve straightforward responses, even though the data base could yield an incredible array of permutations. The analogy is with a parent who, when asked how old the child is, can simply give a number expressed in years (or in the case of infants, in months). The number given does not fully describe the child's weight, height, gender, IQ, eating habits, favorite toy, or any of the other characteristics that combine to tell a more complete story of the individual. Even though the parent is fully aware of the child's other characteristics, to report them is to miss the essence of the transaction. One number suffices to answer the question, "How old is your child?" just as one number can be given in response to "How many students gain employment?"

One complication in accountability measurement is in assigning responsibilities for student learning. The directives demanding program review if certain outcomes are not attained bump into this problem. Whose fault is it, the colleges' or the students'? Always an issue, it has become even more unwieldy as most students transfer among institutions several times before completing a degree. When a student matriculates at one college, attends for a term, enrolls concurrently at a second institution in the next term, abandons both of those and takes classes at a third institution in a subsequent term, and eventually completes a degree at yet a fourth institution, which one is most accountable for the student's progress?

The premise that institutional effects can be separated from the students' tendencies is flawed. Some residential colleges may have been able to demonstrate their value to students who enrolled and stayed for four years straight. But such cohorts are in a minority among students in bachelor's degree-granting institutions and practically nonexistent in the associate degree-granting colleges. Stop in, stop out, take classes here or there, amass credits, get a degree eventually; where and how did learning occur? Assessing students at entry and at graduation, the traditional way of estimating the cognitive or affective change, loses its power in an institution where relatively few students graduate; too few of the entrants are there to take both halves of the measurement.

Research on the contemporary colleges confronts the realities of the institutions. On the one hand, teaching and learning are open-ended. We can always do better: graduation rates can be higher; the students can be more satisfied. On the other hand, the professional staff have only limited incentives to improve what they do. Their welfare does not depend on their institution's performance as measured by student outcomes. They do not get paid more when the students learn more, nor does anyone get dismissed if they learn less. Therefore major gaps appear between goals (however derived), the research that is supposed to measure attainment of the goals, and the extent that the institution will change according to the findings. Each is a separate advent. No externally generated mandate for institutional accountability can affect a hyper-rational, tightly coupled system.

This disjuncture is revealed in the types of goals that are set. Because they cannot penetrate the boundaries separating the different roles of the practitioners, they usually are stated in a way that does not lend itself to straightforward measurement. Admonishing the faculty to set measurable objectives attacks their unwillingness to put forth targets for which they can be held accountable. State-level pressure for outcomes data confronts the administrators' need for positive findings exclusively. Because institutional support depends on image, not data, the quest for valid information may be self-defeating.

Therefore, the goals that intrainstitutional committees pronounce usually relate to process ("The computer lab will upgrade its equipment"; "The college will offer more classes in the evening"), and only occasionally to outcomes ("Our graduation rates will increase by 5 percent"; "The percentage of area employers who report they are satisfied with our students' job performance will average 80 across all programs"). Process goals are acceptable because they suggest that the staff are trying harder. Product goals are suspect because too many uncontrollable variables may act to diminish the results, and failure to achieve the objective may generate untoward criticism.

In intramural research the people studying the phenomenon are included in the complexity being studied. This characteristic sets intrinsic educational research apart from research in other fields. It is the Heisenberg Effect squared; examining a phenomenon changes it, and when the analysts are themselves the object of examination, the paradigms of traditional research are hopelessly distorted. Few practitioners dare to organize studies that have the potential of making them look ineffective; they fear being compared with other institutions or losing credibility. And because the colleges and their clients have multiple purposes, they know that no single outcomes measure captures the institution's complexities. Since we can't measure everything we do, some say, why measure anything?

Unfamiliarity with assessment is a central issue. Ewell (1987) has discussed many of the problems in implementing assessment programs, showing that often no one on campus knows what assessment is for or what its consequences will be. He has also noted the organizational problem of assessment, which, like any innovation, may disturb many long-standing formal and informal relationships. Adelman's (1986) collection of essays on the assessment of college students' learning includes arguments for and against assessment in higher education, descriptions of practices, and critiques of instruments and techniques. Bers and Mittler (1994) report on the status of state and local assessment efforts pertaining to community colleges.

Many other reasons why assessment has not been widely adopted have been advanced, including the uncertain feasibility of measuring important outcomes, the limited time or money available to implement a testing program, the tendency for the faculty to teach primarily what the test will measure, the risk of outsiders' misusing the information gained, and the students' unwillingness to cooperate in a process that has no relevance to them. But all these objections can be overcome if an institution's leaders and at least a portion of its faculty want to pursue the process.

Why should the staff members in any institution measure the learning attained by their students? Such measurement in the abstract is an exercise not likely to gain much staff support. The colleges are not funded according to student learning; budgets are fixed in a political arena. The data can be used for institutional public relations, but only if a skilled leader knows how to weave them into statements of institutional worth. Appeals to professionalism are of little use because the staff perceive information on student learning gathered by outsiders as irrelevant. Information on student outcomes might be used to bolster staff morale, but only if sizable learning gains are demonstrated: like the children of Lake Woebegone, all one's students must be above average. Attempts to feed student-learning data back to instructors, so that classroom practices can be improved, usually prove ineffectual because few instructors will accept data about their students from anyone else.

Even so, assessment can be used for several purposes. Students can be tested at entry so that they can be directed into proper courses. The scores can be used to establish a baseline against which students' learning can be measured periodically as they progress through the programs in which they are enrolled. Students' achievement on licensure examinations, their rate of placement in jobs, their graduation success, and their movement into further education can also be measured, along with their satisfaction with their education. Any type of standardized or locally developed instrument may be applied.

A longitudinal study can be initiated, with the entire cohort of students who are entering for the first time in any term as its subjects. However, this procedure is limited because of the magnitude of the data that must be collected. It works best where a percentage of students is sampled. Each term these students can be asked about their aspirations and course-taking patterns. Different forms of the placement exam or other measures can be used to test the students at entry and at various points along the way. When a small group is sampled, follow-up becomes much more feasible.

An alternative form of outcomes assessment is based on a cross-sectional model, where content measures are included along with items asking about student satisfaction, course-taking behavior, use of support services, and other information about intrainstitutional concerns. An item bank can be developed, with items categorized by skills, such as critical thinking, reading, and writing; by content, such as history, chemistry, and mathematics; and by response type, including multiple- and free-response. The items can be as specific or as general as desired. Tests can be constructed and administered to students in classes, and certain demographic information can be solicited at the same time. After the tests have been taken, groups of students can be classified according to aspiration, number of units taken, prior school experience, or any other measure that seems of interest.

The longitudinal model works best in a college where students matriculate with the intention of participating in programs organized sequentially and where the college's processes are designed to ensure that they do. The cross-sectional model should be used if the college leaders are serious about providing an institution where students can drop in and out at will, the lifelong learning ideal. It skirts the problem of student retention and the difficulty of follow-up because it generates new cohorts each time it is administered. The level of knowledge displayed by the students *collectively*, first at entrance, then after they have completed a certain number of units, and at graduation, can be compared. Any available demographic information can be used to make further differentiations.

Astute college leaders straddle the spaces between the misguided search for comparative numbers that purport to describe institutional value, staff familiarity with process goals and their attendant mistrust of measurable objectives, and their own need for positive findings. They do this by centering their designs on the institution itself over time, never seeking interinstitutional comparisons, never concealing the findings behind obfuscatory irrelevancies or untoward caveats, never attempting to confound the college's various purposes and objectives.

Each area of the college deserves its own set of measurements. For example, an area of inquiry dating to the behavioral objectives movement pioneered by Ralph Tyler in the 1950s has been promoted vigorously in recent years by Angelo and Cross (1993). Each instructor is to set objectives and assess the effects of different techniques, using the findings as the basis for instructional modification. No comparing one instructor's outcomes with another; no attempt to relate the outcomes to other college purposes. With intrinsically designed goals, each classroom is its own object of study, each instructor a researcher.

Extending this concept of the self-contained study to other areas is just as feasible. Only a few, easily understood principles of research need control the process, for example, where surveys are employed, population sampling and nonrespondent bias checks are basic. Most important is that no comparisons be sought between institutions or between programs in the same institution. Each area is discrete. The presidents should limit "We're number one!" to their speeches to athletic booster clubs.

Each of the community colleges' main missions of transfer, job entry, career upgrading, literacy and general education development, and personal satisfaction can be assessed separately and regularly, with results communicated routinely. The measurements could yield periodic reports arrayed as follows:

> *Transfer*: X percent of the students who entered our college with no prior college experience four years ago completed at least four courses here. Of those, Y percent have transferred to an in-state, public university. We anticipate an increase to a Z percent transfer rate within the next two years because of our emphasis on recruiting full-time students and because we have recently concluded new articulation agreements for three of our basic programs with our major receiving university.

> *Job Entry*: X percent of the students who enter with no prior experience in the field and who complete three or more courses in one of our office skills or sales training programs

obtain full-time positions in their field of study within one year, and 6X percent are working part-time. This suggests that our clerical and sales programs serve predominantly as a route to part-time employment and hence can be modified to address that clientele more directly. During the coming year we will organize job placement and training sessions in Y sites to accommodate these job seekers.

These examples display how the definitions and methodologies are revealed in the report along with the study's purposes, projections, and actions to be taken based on its findings. This process would also yield the data that state and federal agencies are determined to acquire. Unless each college controls its own research agenda, a mentality of compliance develops in response to these external demands, and research in and about the colleges cannot reach the potential it deserves.

Issues

The meager support for research on community colleges is not surprising because research in education does not nearly reflect the schools' importance in American life. However, much information about the colleges is available, even if it must be sifted from a mass of reportage that includes self-congratulatory commentary, data compiled with little regard for relevance, unwarranted criticism based on selected statistics, and incomplete compilations.

Few colleges have developed their own research agendas. Can they continue providing data according to external-agency definitions without distorting public views of individual college accomplishments?

Will state-agency and accrediting-association demands for accountability lead to institutional betterment? Or will the colleges treat them as no more than mandated compliance activities?

Can college and state-level researchers sustain a proper balance between adherence to social science research standards and the need to report in journalistic style suitable to a broad audience?

More than anything else, answers to these questions rest on the extent to which the college staff themselves become critical consumers of the research that is produced about their institutions.

14

The Social Role

A Response to the Critics

F̲ew serious scholars have been concerned with the community
colleges, even though they enroll more than one-third of all students in higher education. The scholarly community has tended to
allow institutional spokespersons free rein. Marshall McLuhan is
said to have observed, "If you want to learn about water, don't ask
the fish." Yet people who have wanted to understand the community colleges of America have had little choice; few other than
those within them spoke up.

When the community college is examined by outsiders, the
commentary usually takes the form of criticizing the institution in
its social role or the institution as a school. In the first of these criticisms, the college is often seen in a negative light. It is an agent of
capitalism, training workers to fit business and industry; it is a tool
of the upper classes, designed to keep the poor in their place by
denying them access to the baccalaureate and, concomitantly, to
higher-status positions in society. When it is criticized as a school,
questions are raised about its success in teaching: do these colleges
really teach the basic skills that the lower schools failed to impart?
Can they provide a foundation for higher learning? Here, too, the
answers are usually negative; since the community colleges pass few
of their students through to the senior institutions, they are said to
have failed the test.

This chapter reviews the allegations made by the analysts who contend that the community colleges are negative influences in American society, and it provides a counterpoint to their assertions. It discusses the allocative function, necessary in every educational system, the colleges' real contributions, and possible alternatives to the role that the colleges play.

Criticizing the Role

Several distressingly similar papers have taken community colleges to task for their failure to assist in leveling the social-class structure of America. Karabel (1972) asserted that the community college is an element both in educational inflation and in the American system of class-based tracking. The massive community college expansion of the 1950s and 1960s, he said, was due to an increase in the proportion of technical and professional workers in the labor force. This increase caused people who wanted any job other than the lowest-paying to seek postsecondary training, thus contributing to a heightened pressure for admission to higher education in general. Hence educational inflation: an increased percentage of people attending school and staying longer. But the system of social stratification has not changed: "Apparently, the extension of educational opportunity, however much it may have contributed to other spheres such as economic productivity and the general cultural level of the society, has resulted in little or no change in the overall extent of social mobility and economic equality" (Karabel, 1972, pp. 525–526). Students yes, equality no.

Ever class conscious, Karabel cited data showing that community college students were less likely to be from the higher socioeconomic classes than were students at four-year colleges or universities. They were more likely to be from families whose breadwinner was a skilled or semiskilled worker, had not completed grammar school or had not completed high school, and was not a college graduate. (Not incidentally, these facts had been noted by Koos, the first analyst of junior colleges, fifty years earlier.) Karabel added that most community college students aspired to higher degrees but rarely attained them and that students of lower social-class origins were more likely than others to drop out.

Some years later Karabel argued that the research conducted since he put forth his thesis had confirmed his perspective: "With a far greater body of empirical evidence now available, the fundamental argument may be stated again with even greater confidence: Far from embodying the democratization of higher education and a redistribution of opportunity in the wider society, the expansion of the community college instead heralded the arrival in higher education of a form of class-linked tracking that served to reproduce existing social relations. . . . The overall impact of the community college has been to accentuate rather than reduce prevailing patterns of social and class inequality" (1986, p. 18).

Extending these contentions, Karabel and his coauthor concluded that "the community college has become a vocational-training institution, more and more divorced from the rest of academia, with potentially serious consequences for the life chances of its students" (Brint and Karabel, 1989, pp. 12–13). The authors contended that students who originally desired access to baccalaureate programs at four-year institutions were "diverted" in their goal orientation as community colleges continued to foster their own goals of vocational training. In addition, they continued the argument that community colleges perpetuate the social structure of racial segregation; community college students, often belonging to minority groups, are filtered into vocational and career education, rather than into transfer programs.

Zwerling echoed the thesis that the community college plays an essential role in maintaining the pyramid of American social and economic structure: "It has become just one more barrier put between the poor and the disenfranchised and a decent and respectable stake in the social system which they seek" (1976, p. xvii). The chief function of the community college is to "assist in channeling young people to essentially the same relative positions in the social structure that their parents already occupy" (p. 33). The institution is remarkably effective at controlling mobility between classes because its students come primarily from the lowest socioeconomic classes of college attenders, its dropout rate is the highest of any college population, and dropouts and graduates alike enter lower-level occupations than the equivalent students who attend higher-status colleges. This dropout rate is "related to a rather deliberate process of channeling students to positions in the social order that are deemed appropriate for them" (p. 35).

Zwerling was consistent. He contended that the expansion of occupational education in the community college was "an ingenious way of providing large numbers of students with *access* to schooling without disturbing the shape of the social structure" (p. 61). He showed that in states where the community colleges were at the bottom tier of the postsecondary education hierarchy, they received less money per student than the senior institutions. Hence, the lowest-income-level students had the least spent on them.

Ten years later Zwerling extended his argument about the limitations of class mobility, asserting that continuing education also acts as "a regressive force in our society" (1986, p. 55). He found adult education classes populated by the wealthier people, who use them to enhance their employment credentials and to solve individual life crises. In the interests of equity, the colleges should be more accessible to low-income students. Lifelong learning should "contribute to social change and to a society where merit, not privilege, is rewarded" (p. 59).

Pincus, another writer in the same genre, also discussed the community colleges in terms of class conflict, with a particular emphasis on their role as occupational education centers. He traced the development of the occupational function, showing how it fit everyone's needs exactly: "Corporations get the kind of workers they need; four-year colleges do not waste resources on students who will drop out; students get decent jobs; and the political dangers of an excess of college graduates are avoided" (Pincus, 1980, p. 333). And he alleged that "business and government leaders—those at the top of the heap—regard postsecondary vocational education as a means of solving the political and economic problems created by the rising expectations of the working class" (p. 356).

Pincus deplored the unemployment rates for college graduates, saying that "between one fourth and one half of those graduates who found jobs were 'underemployed'; that is, they held jobs that did not require a college degree" (p. 332). And he cited Clark's cooling-out thesis: "These two-year colleges screen out students who did not have the skills to complete a bachelor's degree and, instead, channel them toward an appropriate vocational program" (1960, p. 333). He showed that nonwhite and low-socioeconomic-status students were more likely to attend community colleges than senior institutions and were more likely to be enrolled in the occupational programs than in the transfer programs. In justice to Pincus, he did conclude that "capitalism in the United States cannot always deliver what it promises. There are a limited number of decent, well-paid jobs, and most working-class and nonwhite young people are not destined to get them. Vocational education does not and cannot change this" (pp. 355–356). His argument, then, was less with the schools than with the system itself. One of his major contentions was that students who enter community college occupational programs are not told the full story about the chances of their obtaining employment in the field for which they are being prepared. If they were, they would probably enter the transfer programs, because the rewards for obtaining the baccalaureate are all out of proportion in comparison to those that a student in a career program might expect.

In 1994, Pincus again purported that "community colleges are part of a stratified system of higher education that reproduces the race, class, and gender inequalities that are part of the larger society" (pp. 624–625), noting that these colleges emphasize terminal vocational programs while transfer programs are secondary to the

colleges' goals. "Rather than encouraging students to limit aspirations, community colleges should teach students why the current
labor force often works against them and what more egalitarian
alternatives exist" (pp. 630–631).

Other commentators have also contended that the career programs divert students from lower-class backgrounds away from baccalaureate studies. Levine postulated a cabal, based in the colleges
themselves: "Faced with a potential student body increasingly large
and diverse in socioeconomic backgrounds and interests, . . . educators encouraged the formation of a new type of postsecondary
education devoted to semi-professional vocational training" (1986,
p. 183). It was easy for him to conclude, then, that "the interests
and needs of the many who attended the junior college to prepare
for the university were frustrated by educators' elitist intentions"
(p. 184). Richardson and Bender, in their treatise on minority
access and achievement, pointed out that, despite increased college attendance rates, "there has been little change in economic
and social class mobility for minorities because their curriculum
choices have been so concentrated in the career and vocational
areas" (1987, p. 1). They argued further that "concentrating occupational offerings on campuses serving the highest proportion of
minorities while concurrently permitting transfer programs to
decline in availability and quality" leads minority students to
"become vocational/technical majors because no viable alternatives
are provided to them" (pp. 44–45).

Data to support the arguments regarding class-based tracking are
easy to find. After examining patterns of college going in Illinois,
Tinto (1973) concluded that low-socioeconomic-status students who
go to community colleges are more likely to drop out than their
counterparts who attend senior institutions. Astin showed that even
when students were equated for entering ability, parental income,
and aspirations, those entering community colleges were more likely
to drop out. He concluded, "For the eighteen-year-old pursuing a
bachelor's degree, the typical community college offers . . . decreased

chances of completing the degree" (1977, p. 255). (However, he subsequently qualified his comment, acknowledging that the regression analysis statistics that he used accounted for only around 25 percent of the variance in degree attainment, with the remainder probably due to some unquantified combination of institutional environment and student characteristics.)

Dougherty pursued a similar line. He saw the community college both as "democratizing access to higher education" and "hampering attainment of the baccalaureate" (1994, p. 21). He stated that these colleges do allow more students to enjoy the benefits of higher education, but that they are not successful at propelling students toward the baccalaureate. Instead, they attract students away from universities because tuition is less, the colleges are often conveniently located to students' homes, and students do not pay for on-campus housing. They accommodate less able students by offering vocational training, but they inherently discriminate against the lower class because community college students tend to drop out of college at a high rate.

Pedersen stated that many "neo-conservatives" have helped to promote the opinion that community colleges should serve the training and education of potential members of the work force. Rather than focusing their attentions on perceived distractions such as training students to become culturally aware and prepared for various life opportunities, the community colleges' "real task" is to narrow the curriculum to work-force training only (1994, p. 4).

And last, in their examination of state systems of higher education as they relate to bachelor-degree attainment, Orfield and Paul (1992) aligned themselves with those who disparage the community colleges. They concluded that the states with a greater commitment to community colleges have lower levels of baccalaureate completion, and neither higher state expenditures per student nor lower tuition increases the completion rates. The institution itself is the stumbling block.

These jeremiads are more politically inspired than empirically founded. At bottom, those who pronounce them are less antagonistic to the community college than they are to what they perceive as a pernicious American social-class system, which they wish were more equitable. The arguments are decades old, different now only in that they name the community college as the villain. Schools at all levels have long been criticized for failing to overturn the social-class system. In 1944, Warner and his colleagues asserted that Americans were not sufficiently conscious of the class structure and the place of the schools in it. They felt that lack of understanding of the class system would lead eventually to a loss of social solidarity. Their concern was for equality of opportunity, for curricular differentiation, and for teaching people to accept the idea of social status.

More recently the belief in the inevitability of the class structure has become less pronounced, confounded now with social justice, equality of opportunity, cultural deprivation, and a determination to correct the abuses historically heaped onto certain peoples. The fact that African-Americans, Hispanics, and other identifiable ethnic groups tend to be overrepresented in the lower socioeconomic classes has contributed to this confusion. Americans historically have had as a common belief a distinct distrust of anyone who preaches class consciousness. That distrust now is manifested as an abhorrence of anyone who suggests the idea of class, because the suggestion is tantamount to racism. Therefore, those who say that the number of people with qualifications for top jobs is quite small, that by definition not enough high-status jobs are available for everyone, and that people are not born equal but instead have diverse potentialities are termed racists endeavoring to maintain their privileged positions by keeping the lower classes in their place. By extension, an institution that predominantly serves the lower classes becomes a racist institution, a tool of the capitalists.

Criticizing the School

A second set of criticisms pertains to the community colleges as schools. Can they really teach the basic skills that the lower schools failed to impart? Do they provide a foundation for higher learning? Do their students learn the proper skills and attitudes that will enable them to succeed on jobs or in senior institutions? Stripping away the rhetoric and social implications reduces these questions to the following: how many occupational education students obtain jobs in the field for which they were trained? How many students transfer to the senior colleges?

The few large-scale studies that have been conducted provide some clues. After reviewing several comparative studies, Pascarella and Terenzini (1991) concluded that the two-year colleges have a moderate negative effect on their students' subsequent occupational status. In addition, they found that there is "about a fifteen % or greater disadvantage in likelihood of bachelor's degree completion during a specified time period" for community college students (p. 591). Part of this may be attributed to the difficulty of transferring from a community college to a senior institution. In addition, the social-psychological climate of community colleges, including peer groups, instructional rigor, student activities and opportunities for on-campus involvement influence how well students will succeed after college. "Providing equal access to participation in the postsecondary educational system is only half of the solution to educational inequities. The other half requires equal access to opportunities to enjoy the full benefits of postsecondary participation" (p. 641).

The U.S. Department of Education's longitudinal study of high school graduates from the class of 1972 reported on the role that the community college had played in their lives (Adelman, 1994). The findings lent evidence to the contention that this cohort of students used the community college to achieve their own personal goals and not necessarily to earn degrees. Comparing students who attended community colleges, those who attended other educational institutions, and those who did not continue their education after high school, data showed that the community college functioned in a variety of "occasional" roles (p. 152) in the lives of these students; the students could engage in learning on their own terms, and in their own time. More students attended community colleges than did students who discontinued their education after high school or who attended only four-year institutions. Community college attendance was more representative of minority students, students who served in the military, and those of moderate to lower socioeconomic backgrounds. Only 20 percent of those who attended a community college earned an associate degree, but earning any kind of degree still made a difference. More students who completed an A.A. degree earned professional jobs than did students who attended a four-year institution but failed to earn a baccalaureate degree.

What does this information tell us? Adelman suggested that we use postsecondary institutions for "utilitarian purposes"; once school is no longer mandatory, we use it when we want to and on our own terms. In addition, we are more interested in learning, gaining new skills, and in completing a basic general education than we are in earning more-advanced degrees. Finally, Adelman states that "our youthful aspirations and hopes exceed what actually happens to us, no matter what we do in between." These hopes and aspirations usually translate into effort, believes the author, which "makes something better than what it otherwise would have been" (1994, p. 167).

Data on the numbers of students who transfer from community colleges to four-year colleges and universities are scattered because the ways of counting transfers vary greatly from system to system and from state to state. Patterns of student flow have never been linear; they swirl, with students dropping in and out of both community colleges and universities, taking courses in both types of

institutions concurrently, transferring from one to another frequently. Among the students in junior standing at a university may
be included some who took their lower-division work in a community college and in the university concurrently, some who started as
freshmen in the university but who dropped out to attend a community college and subsequently returned, some who took summer
courses at community colleges, some who attended a community
college and failed to enroll in the university until several years later,
and some who transferred from the community college to the university in midyear. However, as reported in Chapter Two, when the
data are compiled uniformly across the nation, the transfer rates are
consistent from year to year. In numerical terms, of the 1.25 million
students per year whose initial higher education experience is in a
community college, 250,000 eventually transfer to universities.
Whether this rate verifies the community colleges as contributors
to social mobility or as agencies displacing the hopes of the underprivileged depends entirely on the viewers' perceptions.

Responding to the Critics

The community colleges are not selective, residential collegiate
institutions. The data about their matriculants may be interpreted
in various ways, but it is certain that *in the aggregate* students prepared in community college career programs earn less over a lifetime than those who receive baccalaureate or graduate degrees. It
is also certain that *in the aggregate* students who begin collegiate
studies in community colleges are more likely to drop out or, if they
do go on to the baccalaureate, to take longer in obtaining it.

What else can we say to the critics? They are on firm ground when
they present data showing that many community college matriculants
do not transfer; that the community colleges enroll sizable percentages of minority students and students from low-socioeconomic-status
background; and that, of those students who do transfer, the smallest
percentage is among students from the minorities and lower-income

groups. But their conclusions are not always warranted. Several of the commentators suggest elevating the class consciousness of community college students so that they become aware of the social trap into which they have been led. Zwerling (1976) recommends that students should be shown how they are being channeled within the social-class structure; they should know that the school is an instrument of power, so that they can act to resist it. Pincus similarly seeks to elevate class consciousness: "If community college educators want to help working-class and minority students, they should provide them with a historical and political context from which to understand the dismal choices they face. Vocational education students might then begin to raise some fundamental questions about the legitimacy of educational, political, and economic institutions in the United States" (1980, p. 356).

Other critics reach different conclusions. Some want to make the community colleges equal to the universities, so that the low-socioeconomic students who attend them will have an equal chance at obtaining baccalaureate degrees and higher-status positions. Zwerling (1976) suggests converting all two-year colleges into four-year institutions. Dougherty (1994) also contended that the community colleges should undergo complete organizational reconstruction and become four-year institutions. He would start with the two-year branch campuses that are effective in helping students transfer to the parent four-year institutions.

Astin suggests equating funding so that the community colleges and universities get the same number of dollars per student. He further suggests that "states or municipalities that wish to expand opportunities for such students should consider alternatives to building additional community colleges or expanding existing ones. Although community colleges are generally less expensive to construct and operate than four-year colleges, their 'economy' may be somewhat illusory, particularly when measured in terms of the cost of producing each baccalaureate recipient" (1977, p. 255). Karabel (1972) admits that the colleges are caught in a dilemma. If they increase their occupational offerings, they increase the likelihood that they will track the lower-class students into lower-class occupations, and if they try to maintain comprehensives, they increase the likelihood that their students will drop out without attaining any degree or certificate.

Clowes and Levin seek a different solution because, as they maintain, the community college is coming close to a position "outside graded education and at the penumbra of higher education" (1989, p. 354). They propose that the colleges should deemphasize baccalaureate education and focus instead on the vocational/career education of their students. In this way, they would be able to offer strong programs leading to immediate employment but, by connecting with university-based programs, would also maintain their place within higher education. Kinnick and Kempner (1988) reached similar conclusions.

And so the critics skirt the notion of the community college as an agency enhancing equal opportunity. Faced with the unreconcilable problem of social equalization, they present draconian solutions. Suppose all two-year colleges were converted into four-year institutions. Would all colleges and their students then miraculously become equal? There is a pecking order among institutions that even now are ostensibly the same. Harvard and Northeastern University, the University of California and Pepperdine University, the University of Chicago and Northern Illinois University all offer the doctorate. But in the eyes of the public, they are not equivalent. Authorizing the community colleges to offer the bachelor's degree would not change public perceptions of their relative merit; it would merely establish a bottom stratum of former two-year colleges among the senior institutions.

Suppose funding were equalized. Would the colleges then contribute less to the maintenance of a class structure? Perhaps two-year colleges would teach better if sizable funds were diverted from the universities and run to them. Perhaps they would not. But one thing is certain: the major research universities would be crippled.

That eventuality might well satisfy those critics who are obsessed with the idea of social class. They would argue that the power of the schools to maintain the social-class structure could be reduced quite as effectively by chopping down the top-rank institutions as by uplifting those serving the lower groups.

As for the centrality of career education, *all* higher education, including graduate and professional school, is career oriented. The poverty-proud scholar, attending college for the joy of pure knowledge, is about as common as the presidential candidate who was born in a log cabin. Both myths deserve decent burials.

The Mythology of Schooling

The truism that the further one goes in school, the greater one's earnings has been modified in favor of a myth, that the *type* of school that people attend determines their future success.

The various rulings designed to mitigate discrimination based on a person's gender, religion, or ethnic identification were designed to facilitate access. Young people from every social stratum were to enter college and train for lucrative careers. But the more the goal of equal opportunity was approached, the greater the importance of schooling became. The most marked measure of that importance is the gap in earnings between college graduates and people who have not finished high school, something on the order of three to one. Thus, an anomaly: when the standards for who entered college were set on the basis of wealth, race, intelligence, etc., the arguments for equal opportunity centered on the notion that we were wasting talent by depriving qualified young people of an education. As the doors swung open, as civil rights legislation, state and federal grants for students, and institutions with open-admissions policies became prevalent, issues of segregation within higher education came to the fore. The opportunity to go to college was not enough. Which college was available? Which program? What were the achievement rates for certain members of certain groups? The target kept shifting.

Another myth is that equal opportunity to attend school leads to equal outcomes. America is still comprised of people with unequal status and income, even though the community colleges have equalized access; the colleges must be at fault.

Jencks (1972) offered one response when he explored the socially constructed notion of inequity and concluded that educators confound equal opportunity for education with equalizing income in the population. Rather than demanding that all persons receive the same education, a better way to decrease the gaps in income is to change such public policies as the tax structure. He believed that even if a college education were as easy to obtain as an elementary education, not everyone would attend and inequalities would persist. People work at different paces; they have different abilities and are of different value to their employers. The type of school they attend or the cognitive ability they manifest has little to do with equalizing those traits in the general population. If society really wanted to equalize outcomes, a system would be erected whereby those who attend school and those who do not would receive the same or similar benefits.

Another response might be that the community colleges are no more able to overturn the inequities of the nation than the lower schools have been, that all schools are relatively low-influence environments when compared with other social institutions. But the critics' fundamental error is that *they have attempted to shift the meaning of educational equality from individual to group mobility*. If equal opportunity means allowing people from any social, ethnic, or religious group to have the same chance to enter higher education as people from any other group, the goal is both worthy and attainable. And few would question the community colleges' contribution to the breaking down of social, ethnic, financial, and geographical barriers to college attendance. But when that concept is converted to *group* mobility, its meaning changes, and it is put beyond the reach of the schools. Ben-David put it well: "Higher education can make a real contribution to social justice only by effectively educating properly prepared, able, and motivated individuals from all classes and groups. . . . Higher education appears to have been primarily a channel of individual mobility. . . . It can provide equal opportunities to all, and it may be able to help the disadvantaged to overcome inherited educational disabilities. But it cannot ensure the equal distribution of educational success among classes or other politically active groups" (1977, pp. 158–159). In sum, neither the community colleges nor any other form of school can break down class distinctions. They cannot move entire ethnic groups from one social stratum to another. They cannot ensure the equal distribution of educational results.

Suppose the figures on the percentage of students who transfer to universities were doubled? Would it matter to the critics? The colleges still would not be doing their part in the critics' fanciful dream of class leveling. Warner and his associates said: "The decision to be made by those who disapprove of our present inequality and who wish to change it is not between a system of inequality and equality; the choice is among various systems of rank. Efforts to achieve democratic living by abolishing the social system are utopian and not realistic" (1944, p. 145).

Ordinarily, it serves neither education nor society well when the schools are accused of misleading their clients by making promises they cannot keep. Such charges can have the effect of generating public disaffection on the one hand and, on the other, intemperate reactions by educators. Many commentators, past and present, have been guilty of exaggerated claims that the community college would democratize American society if only all geographical, racial, academic, financial, motivational, and institutional barriers to attendance were removed (witness the title of Medsker and Tillery's 1971 book on the community colleges, *Breaking the Access Barriers*). But criticizing the rhetoric is one thing; criticizing the institution itself is quite another. Although there has been no public outcry against the community colleges, should one arise it will be difficult to tell whether the reaction is directed against the institution itself or toward the image that its advocates have fostered and the claims they have made.

Using the data from the National Longitudinal Study of the High School Graduating Class of 1972 and subsequent surveys sponsored by the U.S. Education Department, some researchers have found that where a student begins college has an important effect on baccalaureate attainment and that students who reside or have jobs on campus are much more likely to persist. However, although the conclusions are logical, the statistics are questionable. Putting variables in a regression equation assumes equivalency at the outset. The NLS data assume that all people in the sample had an equivalent chance to enter the university as freshmen, that the universities had classroom space and residence halls available to accommodate everyone—clearly not so.

Students who start at a community college instead of a university are less likely to obtain bachelor's degrees. Much of the difference relates not only to the differing environments but also to the logistics of moving from one institution to another. The phenomenon may be similar to that experienced by people who have to change planes en route to a destination, as compared with those who have nonstop accommodations. Those who must change may miss their connection because of flight delays or cancellations, or they might get diverted because they have met friends in the connecting airport. But no one accuses the airlines of attempting to subvert their clients' intentions.

How do the analysts interpret the data regarding the University of California's freshman class? Each year, more than 10,000 *qualified* applicants cannot be accommodated; many of them have to begin their higher education careers in one of the state's community colleges. Undoubtedly, for them, baccalaureate attainment will be slightly less likely. Is the selection process the result of an elitists' plot, or was it instituted because of lack of space? The critics' conclusions that the community college is the manifestation of an insidious conspiracy against the poor are not warranted.

The Inevitability of the Allocative Function

Granted that the community colleges are part of an educational system within a larger social system in which numerous institutions sort, certify, ticket, and route people to various stations, what are the options? We could say that society should not be structured along class lines, that it should not support institutions that tend to allocate people to status positions. Those who hold to that view would do well to seek to change the social structure by modifying some considerably more powerful influences—the tax structure, for example. But as long as there are hierarchies of social class (and all societies have them), some social institutions will operate as allocative agencies.

Clark analyzed the allocative function in community colleges and in 1960 applied the term *cooling out* to describe it. He showed that the process began with preentrance testing, shunting the lower-ability students to remedial classes and eventually nudging them out of the transfer track into a terminal curriculum. The crucial components of the process were that alternatives to the person's original aspirations were provided; the aspiration was reduced in a consoling way, encouraging gradual disengagement; and the students were not sent away as failures but were shown the relative values of career and academic choices short of the baccalaureate degree.

Twenty years later, Clark reexamined his thesis, asking whether the cooling-out function might be replaced by some other process and whether the roles of community colleges could be altered so that the process would be unnecessary. He named six options: preselection of students, to take place in the secondary schools or at the door of the community college; transfer-track selection, which would bar the students from enrolling in courses offering transfer credit; open failure, whereby students who did not pass the courses would be required to leave the institution; guaranteed graduation, which would have the effect of passing everyone through and depositing the problem at the doorstep of the next institution in line; reduction of the distinction between transfer and terminal programs, which could be done if the community colleges had no concern about the percentages of their students who succeed in universities; and making the structural changes that would eliminate the two-year colleges' transfer function, convert all two-year institutions into four-year ones, or do away with community colleges entirely.

Clark rejected all those alternatives. Preselection "runs against the grain of American populist interpretations of educational justice which equate equity with open doors" (1980, p. 19). Limiting the number of people who can take courses for transfer credit would shatter the transfer program at a time when students are in short supply. Open failure is too public and is becoming less a feature in four-year colleges as well as in community colleges because it seems inhumane. The dangers of guaranteed graduation have already been realized in the secondary schools ("Everyone is equally entitled to credentials that have lost their value," p. 21). Reducing the distinction between transfer and terminal courses "has limits beyond which lies a loss of legitimacy of the community college *qua* college . . . (auto repairing is not on a par with history or calculus as a college course)" (p. 22). And doing away with the community colleges is unlikely because of the reluctance of senior college faculties to esteem two-year programs and because of the continued and growing need for short-cycle courses or courses such as those offered in university extension divisions.

Clark concluded: "The problem that causes colleges to respond with the cooling-out effort is not going to go away by moving it inside of other types of colleges. *Somebody* has to make that effort, or pursue its alternatives" (pp. 23–24). He pointed to examples in other countries, where the longer the higher education system held out against short-cycle institutions and programs, the greater the problems when educators tried to open the system to wide varieties of students coming for numerous purposes. The trend there is toward greater differentiation of types of institutions and degrees, but "the dilemma is still there: Either you keep some aspirants out by selection or you admit everyone and then take your choice between seeing them all through, or flunking out some, or cooling out some" (p. 28). As he put it, "Any system of higher education that has to reconcile such conflicting values as equity, competence, and individual choice—and the advanced democracies are so committed—has to effect compromise procedures that allow for some of each. The cooling-out process is one of the possible compromises, perhaps even a necessary one" (p. 30). In sum, even if the college only matches people with jobs, providing connections, credentials, and short-term, ad hoc learning experiences—even if it is not the gateway to higher learning for everyone that some commentators wish it were—these functions must be performed by some social agency.

What the Colleges Really Provide

The real benefit of the community college cannot be measured by the extent to which it contributes to the overthrow of the social-class system in America. Nor can it be measured by the extent to which the college changes the mores of its community. It is a system for individuals, and it does what the best educational forms have always done: it helps individuals learn what they need to know to be effective, responsible members of their society. The colleges can and do make it easier for people to move between social classes. As long as they maintain their place in the mainstream of graded education, they provide a channel of upward mobility for individuals of any age. Those who deplore the colleges' failure to overturn inequities between classes do a disservice to their main function and tend to confuse the people who have looked on them as the main point of access to, exit from, and reentry to higher education—the lungs of the system.

There is a difference between social equalization and equal access, between overturning the social-class structure and allowing people to move from one stratum to another. The college that teaches best uplifts its community most. People must learn in college, or what is it for? More learning equals a better college; less learning, a poorer college; no learning, no college. The fact that the community colleges serve minority students, marginally capable students, and other groups never before served by the higher education establishment does not mean they have abandoned their commitment to teach.

A person who receives a degree or certificate and who does not work in the field in which that certificate was earned does not represent an institutional indictment unless no other programs were available to the person. If the community college were a participant in an educational system that said to potential matriculants, "You may enter but only if you are particularly qualified and only in *this* program," subsequent failure to obtain employment in that field might be cause for dismay. But the community college does not operate that way; most of its programs are open to all who present themselves. When programs do have selective admissions, as in dental hygiene, nursing, and some of the higher-level technologies, most entrants graduate and obtain positions in the fields for which they were trained. When programs are open to everyone, as in most of the less professionalized trades, the chances that a matriculant will complete the curriculum and begin working in that field are markedly reduced. "Dropout" is a reflection of the structure of a program. An institution, or a program within that institution, that places few barriers to student matriculation cannot expect a high rate of program completion. The students use the collegiate and the career programs alike, as though each were providing a single set of courses that they might take depending on their goals at the time. The elitists and conspirators may have hoped to divert the masses into vocational studies, but the students are remarkably resilient.

What Are the Alternatives to Community Colleges?

It is possible to sketch the outlines of alternative institutions that would perform the tasks now performed by community colleges. Yet there is no point in taking an ahistorical approach to postsecondary education. Tempting as it is, a view of higher education, of what students need, of what would be good for society, without a corresponding view of the institutions in their social context is not very useful. To start with the questions of what individuals need or what society needs is nice; but, regardless of the answers, the current institutions will not disappear. Institutional needs are as real as individual and social needs; in fact, they may be more valid as beginning points for analysis because they offer somewhat unified positions that have developed over time, whereas "individual" and "social" needs are as diverse as anyone cares to make them. And despite the rapid growth of the Internet and its counterparts, it is thoroughly out of line to pose a view of society with no educational institutions but with everyone learning through the electronic media. The desire for social interaction is too strong; the demand for institutional certification is too great.

Any imagined institution must be postulated totally. That is, what changes will be made in funding patterns, institutional organization, the role of the professionals within the institution, people's use of their time? The institution's goals must be stated realistically; we have for too long suffered the open-ended goals of those who would break all access barriers; would see all citizens enrolled successively throughout their lifetime; would envisage the community college taking on functions previously performed not only by the higher and the lower schools but also by welfare agencies, unemployment bureaus, parks and recreation departments, and community-help organizations.

Can we develop a learning community? Some evidence suggests we can. People are enrolling in university extensions and taking classes in the community colleges for their own interest. A sizable cohort will attend school without being compelled. In addition, the number of ways that individuals gain information and that society stores and transmits it has grown enormously.

On the negative side are the individual needs for structured learning situations, the discipline of learning, the sequence that learning demands. Many forms of learning simply do not lend themselves to instant apprehension and immediate applicability; they build one on the other, and a disciplined situation is necessary to hold the learner in the proper mode until the structure is complete. It would also be difficult to fund the infinite variety of learning situations that would be required. Most of the voluntary learning situations now are funded either by the individuals partaking of them or as adjuncts to more structured institutions.

It is possible to pose alternatives to the community college and stay within the context of existing social institutions. In 1968, Devall offered five such alternatives: proprietary trade schools; on-the-job training; universal national service; university extension divisions; and off-campus courses under expanding divisions of continuing education operated by the universities. However, in the intervening decades, the proprietary trade schools are the only set of alternatives that have grown extensively. And they do not enjoy a history unmarred by excessive claims, inflated costs, fraudulent advertising, and marginally useful instruction. These schools appear as shining lights only to those who feel that the for-profit sector invariably does a better job than the nonprofit institutions do.

The other options would also lead to unintended consequences. On-the-job training would narrow educational opportunity by focusing the learner's attention solely on the tasks to be performed, and it would shift the burden of payment to business corporations that might not benefit therefrom if the trained workers chose to take positions with competitors. Universal national service suggests compulsion; it would extend the grip that public agencies have on individuals and, in effect, prolong the period of mandatory school attendance. Expansion of university extension divisions would have the effect of turning program monitoring back to the universities. But it would also place the programs on a self-supporting basis and would thus deny participation to people with limited discretionary funds. And expanding the university divisions of continuing education would place adult basic education, literacy training, and similar lower-school functions under the aegis of an institution that through-out history has attempted to divest itself of them.

The percentage of community college matriculants who go on to the baccalaureate varies greatly between institutions. It depends on the vigor with which students interested in other outcomes are recruited and on an institution's relations with its neighboring uni-versities. And although the colleges provide career, remedial, and community education, they are certainly not going to surrender the university-parallel portion of their curriculum. If they did, they would be denying access to higher education to those of their stu-dents who do go on, particularly to the minorities and other stu-dents from families in which college going is not the norm. They would betray their own staff members, who entered the institution with the intent of teaching college courses. They would no longer serve as the safety valve for the universities, which can shunt the poorly prepared petitioners for admission to these alternative col-leges and which would otherwise be forced to mount massive remedial programs of their own or face the outrage of people denied access.

Some states have multiple college systems and so separate the collegiate from other functions. The Wisconsin Vocational, Tech-nical, and Adult Education Centers perform all community college functions except for the university lower-division courses; Wiscon-sin has a university-center system with numerous branch campuses of the state university doing the collegiate work. In South Carolina, state technical colleges coexist with branch campuses of the uni-versity. The North Carolina system operates both technical insti-tutes and community colleges. These and other alternative structures can also be found in large community college districts. Coast Community College District (California) has two full-ser-vice, comprehensive community colleges along with one institution devoted exclusively to short-cycle education, open-circuit broad-casting, and community services. In sum, the institutional forms adapt, but all functions are maintained.

We do not necessarily need new structures. Many forms of reorganization in our existing community colleges can be made to accommodate the changing clientele. Some of the more successful adaptations have been made in occupational programs in which the liaison occasioned by the use of trades advisory councils and other connections between the program and the community have fostered continual modifications in curriculum and instruction. The community service divisions engage in their own forms of modification by slanting their offerings toward areas in which sizable audiences can be found. On-campus media forms are introduced to accommodate the different modes of information gathering exhibited by new groups of students. The list could be extended; the point is that adaptations within existing forms are continually occurring.

The list of potential changes can also be extended by accommodations that are rarely made. Long overdue is a reconception of the liberal arts to fit the occupational programs: what portions of traditional liberal arts studies are most useful for students in occupational programs, and how might they best be inserted into those areas? Modular courses have been tried in several institutions, but much more work needs to be done there to build bridges between these two central college functions. Advanced placement for high school students has been authorized in several states and could be encouraged through supplemental legislation.

The community colleges' potential is greater than that of any other institution because their concern is with the people most in need of assistance. President Clinton referred to that characteristic when he described the community colleges as functioning on the "fault line" of American education (Bourque, 1995). If the community colleges succeed in moving even a slightly greater proportion of their clients toward what the dominant society regards as achievement, it is as though they changed the world. They are engaged with people on the cusp, people who could enter the mainstream or who could fall back into a cycle of poverty and welfare. That is why they deserve the support of everyone who values societal cohesion and the opportunity for all people to realize their potential.

Issues

The community college has been criticized for its failure to move sizable proportions of its matriculants to the baccalaureate. But these effects are not uniform. Why do different students go through at different rates? How do institutional and personal factors interact to affect progress?

Even though some of the critics have recommended major changes in institutional structure and functioning, few suggest closing the colleges. However, what would happen to a community if its local college's budget were halved?

Nearly everyone has access to the telephone system. It is a passive, instantly responsive tool that allows people to interact with one another at will. What is the value of the human contact fostered by community colleges?

A television network is another form of passive tool. One turns the television on or off at will, seeking entertainment or diversion. How much is the entertainment provided by the colleges worth?

Museums offer both entertainment and education. A museum may be compared with another museum according to the strength of its collection, the appeal of its exhibitions, and the number of people who participate in its programs. What would be the value of assessing the colleges along those dimensions?

Government agencies are social institutions designed to provide services. They are successful to the extent that they enhance the quality of life in a community by maintaining order and providing public places where people may conduct their own affairs. Can the colleges be so assessed?

Because few scholars are concerned with community colleges, there is no true forum. The colleges' own spokespersons do not help much. Either they do not know how to examine their own institutions critically, or they are disinclined to do so. They say the colleges strive to meet everyone's educational needs, but they rarely acknowledge the patent illogic of that premise. They say the colleges provide access for all, but they fail to examine the obvious corollary question: access to what? The true supporters of the community college, those who believe in its ideals, would consider the institution's role on both educational and philosophical grounds. Democracy's College deserves no less.

15

$\bullet$ $\bullet$

Toward the Future

Trends, Challenges, and Obligations

Just as historians like to play with the past, educators enjoy speculating on the way the future will affect their institutions. It is tempting to believe that the future is manageable, that an institution can be set on a course that ensures its efficiency, relevance, and importance for the community it will serve.

The imminence of a millennial year stimulated an abundance of commissions organized to assess trends in community college functions and support. State-level groups in Alabama, Connecticut, Maryland, and North Carolina, among others, were active in the 1980s, along with a national Commission on the Future of Community Colleges, empaneled under the auspices of the Carnegie Foundation for the Advancement of Teaching and the AACJC. The flurry continued into the 1990s, with California establishing a Commission on Innovation, designed to advise the community colleges on how to accommodate increasing populations with limited resources. On the national level, the *Goals 2000: Educate America Act* was concerned with participation, literacy, and graduation rates in all of higher education as well as with outcomes in other sectors.

The commissions based their studies on apparent population trends, especially age and ethnicity, and on changes in the economy. Predictions were that the growth of the ethnic minority population would accelerate and the proportion of middle-aged workers would decline as the post–World War II baby boomers aged. The economy would continue shifting away from manufacturing and toward service functions as the dominant form for the United States. This postindustrial or information age would require a more literate work force and fuller participation by groups heretofore excluded or consigned to the no-longer-prevalent assembly line. Competition from newly industrialized countries would force us to take a global perspective toward production. America would remain a dominant force, but only if we worked more intelligently.

Each of the commissions issued reports predicting the need for enhanced educational services and emphasizing the importance of maintaining comprehensive, high-quality community colleges that would serve a broad range of clients. Each was optimistic that these institutions were well suited to act in the best interests of the population. None suggested reducing the scope of the colleges. None suggested major departures from contemporary patterns of service. But all warned that the colleges would be expected to serve more students with fewer resources.

In common with similar studies in prior decades, all reports stressed the importance of career education, open access, partnerships with industry, excellence in teaching, and cooperative relationships with other educational sectors. But a new emphasis on outcomes assessment appeared in these commissions' reports. The importance of valid information on college effects has become so evident that the commissions—which might not have been expected to give more than a passing reference to this issue—put it high on their list of essential institutional and state activities. As an example, the *Goals 2000* activities centered directly on national and state-by-state assessment and began issuing periodic report cards based on data collected uniformly across the nation.

This chapter merges information from the commission reports with trend data emanating from other literature to yield a picture of community colleges in the coming years. It deals with the students and the faculty, organization and structure, and curriculum and instruction. The chapter also discusses outcomes assessment, a concept that continues to grow and gain acceptance from educators at all levels of schooling as well as among the laity.

The Institutions

Projecting the future for the community colleges of the early twenty-first century involves projecting the future for the nation in general: its demographics, economy, and public attitudes. The demographics are apparent; population trends are predictable and the potential college students are in the lower schools, but the number who will attend community colleges is uncertain. The national economy is even less certain. However, the United States is a great economic engine, with a highly trained cadre of professional practitioners able to adjust to shifting influences in the workplace. Barring a major social upheaval such as a war, depression, or severe inflation, the nation will be able to continue educating its youth and sustaining lifelong learning for its adults. The community colleges will play a role in this process similar to that which they have developed over much of this century: prebaccalaureate, occupational, remedial, and adult education provided to a broad spectrum of the local population.

Public attitude, always mercurial, influences the colleges. Periodic disgruntlement with taxation and the rise of other priorities such as prisons and the criminal justice system sometimes translate into lower support for education. But as long as college degrees are perceived as the route toward personal advancement, people will demand access and will eventually agree to paying for it. None of the fiscal crises in any of the states has led to serious calls to close down the higher education system.

The number of public community colleges will hardly change; practically all the colleges necessary had been built by 1975, when a college could be found within commuting distance of nearly all the people in all but a few states. The number has remained constant ever since, reaching stasis at just over 1,000. Change in this group will occur only to the extent that public universities organize additional two-year branch campuses or community colleges upgrade satellite centers to full campus status.

The business colleges, specialized training institutes, and proprietary trade schools are a different sector entirely. They thrive on public funds administered through state and federal student aid, but their programs, purposes, governance, and decision-making processes set them quite apart. Since many are accredited to award associate degrees, they appear in the tabulations generated by NCES and the Carnegie Foundation, around 420 of them in 1994. Several thousand are in existence, and no one can predict with certainty how many will attain degree accreditation and be classified as two-year colleges in coming years.

The independent or private junior colleges seem destined to cling to a small territory, similar to that held by the four-year, private colleges in relation to the massive public universities. Woodroof's (1990) analysis found them shouldered aside by the public colleges. His data were sobering: in contrast to NCES, which reported 175 private junior colleges in the late 1980s, he found half that number operating as distinct, separate, liberal arts institutions, with one-third single sex and three-fourths of them east of the Mississippi. But his conclusion was overly somber: "There may come a time in the near future when there are simply too few resources, too few students, and too few faculty members willing to work at poverty income levels . . ." (p. 83). Although the independent junior colleges passed their prime decades ago, they will not disappear.

The form of the community college will not change. The institution offering career, collegiate, developmental, and continuing education has become well accepted by the public and by state-level coordinating and funding agencies. The college staff also are familiar and comfortable with it. Modifications will be in emphasis, not in kind. Some institutions will drive toward expanded community services, as in contract education, building separately funded and managed programs that may grow to be as large as the traditional college services. Where the state universities build numerous branch campuses and otherwise make it easy for students to matriculate, the community colleges will emphasize career studies and continuing education. Where the community colleges serve largely as feeders to the universities, the collegiate function will remain strongest. But all current services will continue to be provided, with growth or shifting emphases depending on funding and shifting population bases, not on educational philosophy.

The Students

Projecting the number of college students in general is precarious because various factors—such as employment possibilities, financial aid availability, and the demands of the military—affect the rate of college going. Estimating the numbers who will attend community colleges is further complicated because of unknowns such as the attractiveness of competing institutions. Even a seemingly straightforward projection of the magnitude of the population in general is subject to variability because of immigration patterns. One factor is certain: as long as the economic benefit of going to college remains high, there will be a demand for collegiate studies.

There will be plenty of students to share among all postsecondary sectors. The absolute number of eighteen-year-olds in the United States peaked at 4.3 million in 1979, bottomed at 3.3 million in 1992, and is projected to rise to 4 million by 2004 (Table 15.1). Anticipating less school dropout, NCES (1995a) predicts that the number of high school graduates in 2004 will surpass 3 million, the same as the number that graduated when the population of eighteen-year-olds was at its peak in 1979.

Despite the programs appealing to older students, the enrollment figures in community colleges are affected most significantly by the number of recent high school graduates. Even though people twenty-four or younger comprise less than half of the student head count,

Table 15.1. Eighteen-Year-Olds in the U.S. Population, 1979–2005.

Year (July 1)	18-Year-Olds	Year (July 1)	18-Year-Olds
1979	4,316	1993	3,349
1980	4,245	1994	3,422
1981	4,186	1995	3,385
1982	4,136	1996	3,540
1983	3,978	1997	3,574
1984	3,774	1998	3,703
1985	3,686	1999	3,883
1986	3,623	2000	3,873
1987	3,703	2001	3,971
1988	3,803	2002	3,964
1989	3,889	2003	3,918
1990	3,601	2004	4,044
1991	3,384	2005	4,060
1992	3,312		

Source: National Center for Education Statistics, 1995a.

that group accounts for 70 percent of the course load. Accordingly, college attendance will be affected notably by the differences in high school graduation rates according to ethnicity. For all seventeen-year-olds, the high school graduation rate remained steady at around 75 percent for the thirty years prior to 1994. However, the graduation rate for African-American students was 63 percent and for Hispanics 50 percent. It seems likely that the high school graduation rates of Anglo students will remain steady over the next several years, while those for minorities will rise; the proportion of minorities in the group comprising all eighteen-year-olds also will rise.

The rate of college going is less predictable. The percentage of students entering college the same year in which they graduated from high school increased from around 50 in the early 1980s to 62 in 1991, but it varied by ethnicity: 64 percent of the Anglo graduates entered college, 47 percent of the African-Americans, and 53 percent of the Hispanics.

Coupled with the discrepant high school graduation rates for the ethnic groups, these figures indicate that 50 percent of the Anglo eighteen- and nineteen-year-olds entered college, compared with 30 percent of the African-Americans and 27 percent of the Hispanics in that age group. But members of the ethnic minority groups are more likely to complete high school after the age of eighteen or nineteen; hence, their rate of college going tends to increase after members of those groups reach their twenties.

The varying rates of high school graduation and college attendance have a notable effect on the community colleges. Around one-third of the Anglos, African-Americans, and Asians entering higher education as full-time freshmen in the mid 1980s began in community colleges, but the rate for the Hispanic full-time entrants so enrolled was 42 percent. Clearly, since the Hispanic students are overrepresented in community colleges, any increase in their rate of high school graduation or college entry will have an accentuated effect on enrollments, especially in states where the Hispanics comprise a large proportion of the population.

In general, the community colleges will sustain their enrollments because the demand for postsecondary education will remain high. They will continue to get their share of eighteen-year-olds because of their traditional appeal: easy access, low cost, and part-time-attendance possibilities. They will continue enrolling job seekers because of the high demand for people in occupations for which some postsecondary training but not a bachelor's degree is expected. According to the U.S. Bureau of Labor Statistics (cited in Palmer, 1988), this demand will be highest for electrical and electronics technicians, computer programmers, real estate salespeople, computer operators, and data processing equipment repair people, along with medical technologists and certain professional specialists, such as commercial artists. The community colleges also prepare people for jobs as retail salesclerks, secretaries, clerical workers, and nursing aides— all in high demand. The only caveat is that competition with the proprietary schools will intensify as long as their students remain eligible for state and federal financial aid.

Assuming that financial aid availability for middle- and upper-income students does not increase so that tuition differentials are offset, the community colleges will get an even greater share of the students as tuition at four-year colleges and universities continues its rapid rise. Assuming that further limitations are not put on Latino and Asian immigration, college enrollments will benefit from those groups. Even without a change in the rates of high school graduation or college going, credit enrollments would surpass six million before the end of the century. The students will continue their intermittent attendance patterns; most will continue to be employed, pursuing work and study as parallel activities.

The National Center for Education Statistics (1995a) predicts that the enrollment of part-time students will decrease slightly, from 65 percent to 63 percent, and expenditures per FTSE will increase slightly, from $3,000 to $3,242 by 2005. The number of associate degrees conferred will rise from 485,000 to 560,000 per year. In brief, we will see a mature set of institutions with some increase in full-time student enrollment and in number of degrees awarded, but very little dramatic change.

There will be increased pressure to sort students at entry. The matriculation plans that have been in effect for several years reveal the persistence of a trend toward regulations demanding that the colleges guide students into programs consonant with their abilities. Texas has an academic skills test, New Jersey a basic skills test, Florida a rising sophomore test, California a matriculation plan. It will be difficult for a student anywhere to find an institution that will allow a random walk through the curriculum. Students will be tested, guided, and matriculated into programs that have measurable entry and exit criteria.

Put in broader terms, the community colleges are experiencing a metamorphosis similar in this regard to that which affected the compulsory sector earlier as state-level testing, curriculum standards, and graduation requirements gained prominence. A laissez-faire approach to student attendance had rather generally permeated community college management, effecting the high ratio of part-timers, the presentation of classes as discrete units, college image, research paradigms, and definitions of college success. Now, the strong moves toward assessment and placement, toward students making steady progress toward completing a program, will change the pattern of attendance toward higher FTSE ratios and more-rapid progress toward program completion. That is the main reason why the number of associate degrees that will be awarded will increase at a rate greater than the number of students served. The concept "Let everyone in and let them take what they want" is being put to rest rapidly.

The Faculty

Because college enrollments will grow slowly, the number of faculty will show similarly small increases. The ratio of full-timers to part-timers has stabilized at just under 40:60 and will likely remain there as administrators' desires to save money by employing part-timers and faculty organizations' ability to protect full-time positions offset one another. A high proportion of full-timers teach additional courses for extra pay, thus making it unnecessary to employ additional staff except in singular areas. Demands that the full-time instructors be awarded rights of first refusal when overload classes are imminent will continue.

Pro rata pay for part-time employment has long been discussed but shows no sign of spreading. As long as full-time faculty are willing to teach extra classes at effectually lower pay rates and as long as administrators need part-time, hourly rate instructors to help balance the budget, pro rata pay will find few champions. Contentions that instructors engage in duplicity when they argue for reduced teaching hours on the grounds that they need more time to prepare for class while simultaneously petitioning to teach overload classes at additional pay will find few ears.

Faculty hiring practices show little sign of change. Affirmative action programs have been in place in all colleges for many years, but progress in employing members of minority groups has been distressingly slow. Nor has there been much progress in preservice preparation for instructors who are inclined to teach across disciplinary lines. The number of career-bound students who take collegiate classes and the number of baccalaureate-bound students in occupational classes seem destined to force some form of faculty crossover to accommodate members of both groups. But the colleges will have to foster their own interdisciplinarians. The greatest need is for faculty who will become leaders in integrating curriculum and assessing outcomes. These will come from within the ranks of the practicing instructors; few people with those skills can be expected to appear as new employees.

The working conditions of the faculty will not change. The faculty will continue to hold solo practice as their primary code. The number of hours that a full-time instructor spends in the classroom has not changed for decades. Few sustained innovative practices that would teach more students with fewer instructor-contact hours are being introduced. Instruction is stubbornly labor intensive. As Bok has pointed out, "College instruction remains among the small cluster of human activities that do not grow demonstrably better over time" (1993, p. 170). If the productivity of college instructors does not increase, and if everyone in the profession is paid and advanced at the same rate, there will be little room for overall pay increases or for individuals to elevate themselves above their colleagues. Teachers cannot anticipate making more money merely because they work harder or are more clever than their fellows.

How might the profession become differentiated? One way would be if instead of—or perhaps in addition to—the image of the instructor in the classroom with a group of students, practicing a profession in solo fashion, the instructor at the apex of a pyramid of paraprofessionals—readers, test scorers, peer advisors, and paraprofessional aides—came to the fore. But there have been few efforts to build teaching assistants into the instructional pattern.

Until recently, moves toward professionalization as evidenced by managerial roles or enhanced productivity have been made by those instructors who have taken command of learning resource centers and various curricular projects designed to maximize student learning by combining instructional and student support services. The next professional enhancements will be led by the instructors who build reproducible learning sequences and interactive media. To the extent they can demonstrate that their efforts have effected greater learning opportunities for less money, they will be recognized as instructional leaders. More than managers of paraprofessionals, they will be involved with new sets of colleagues: media technologists, script writers, editors, and production coordinators. This will happen slowly, and only to the extent that the colleges can make funds available for this expensive effort.

The road to professionalism is a long one, and even though the faculty have made great strides in extricating themselves from the administrator-dominated, paternalistic situation of an earlier time, they have far to go. In some institutions they may settle in to an untoward model: continuing antagonism between themselves and the administrators; isolation and solo performance in the classroom; and periodic battles for smaller classes, augmented salaries, and more far-reaching fringe benefits. The faculty must take care not to act too much like other public agency workers in their negotiating sessions, in the way they seek redress for grievances through legislative action and the courts, and in their inability to police their own ranks as members of a profession must, lest they be viewed as merely another category of civil servants.

A more desirable model is a faculty involved with curriculum planning in the broadest sense: reading and writing in their disciplines and in the field of education; conducting research on students' exit and entrance abilities; and becoming media production specialists, program directors, laboratory managers, or curriculum coordinators. The actuality will be somewhere between the two extremes. In fact, progress toward both civil service status and professionalism can occur simultaneously. In some districts the faculty champion both a union speaking for wages and welfare and a vigorous academic senate concerning itself with curricular and instructional issues.

Organization, Governance, and Administration

Few changes in the pattern of organization and governance in community colleges are evident. The number of institutions will change only slightly as new colleges are formed in those states that do not now have an institution within commuting distance of most of their population. But for the most part, branch campuses, satellite centers, and courses offered off campus in rented quarters will accommodate the need for expanded facilities. Many small autonomous centers or specialized units within larger districts will be built. Some of these centers will emphasize career studies and recertification for paraprofessionals; others, operating much like university extension divisions, will offer courses in numerous locations and over open-circuit television. These types of instructional centers have accounted for nearly all the institutional expansion that has occurred since the early 1970s. Few of them have grown into full-service colleges.

Regardless of calls for expanded functions, the community colleges will still act as schools. The fire department may operate paramedical ambulances, collect food for poor families, and train people in cardiopulmonary resuscitation; but firefighters had best not forget that their main business is to prevent and extinguish fires. If a building burns to the ground while the department is off performing one of its peripheral functions, heads will roll. Community college leaders may take pride in their role in economic development, but their institution loses its credibility if students do not become educated there. The colleges' standing outside the mainstream of graded education that reaches from kindergarten to graduate school has allowed them to adjust to their students' changing desires. But they must avoid moving so far outside that they lose credibility. Accreditation, funding formulas, staff predilections, and community perceptions are the anchors holding them in place.

The trend toward greater state-level coordination will continue at a slow pace. As the states become more involved with college policies, gaps in interinstitutional cooperation will be filled, and criteria for student matriculation and progress will be set. Statewide coordination has also been emphasized as a means of providing proportionate funding, avoiding curriculum duplication, and easing the flow of students from one sector of public postsecondary education to another.

The pressure for state control will result in continued efforts to micromanage the colleges, but it has had minimal effect on instruction and student services. State-level coordination relates more to reporting, compliance with regulations, and accountability for numerous aspects of institutional operations; there is much room for local autonomy within those requirements. Before a major change can be made, the procedure has to be vetted through an incredible array of organizations, especially state-level associations of trustees, deans, presidents, academic senate, humanities faculty, physical education faculty, counselors, librarians, and on and on. Nothing very sudden or dramatic can survive that process. The combination of state and local control is intact.

Administrative patterns will not shift notably. The colleges are public entities. Their support depends on legislative perceptions and available public dollars. Their products are human learning and community uplift. Accordingly, institutional support is sustained in a political arena; it is only tangentially related to outcomes. The administrators work in a milieu of process, not product. They do not give orders to underlings; nor do they sanction subordinates for disobedience. Instead, they attempt to influence behavior by outlining issues and leading by example.

The major changes in local college administration will occur in two areas. The first will be to augment the number of people assigned to collect data and prepare reports showing that the college is in compliance with constantly increasing extramural demands. The second will be in program coordination, with staff members assigned to manage the specially funded programs that the colleges develop both to serve new clients and to enhance budgets. More of this staff differentiation will occur through internal reassignments than through new hires.

Finance

Characteristics of financing community colleges will change little in coming years. Most of the institutions began with substantial funding from their localities, but since then the trend has been toward state-level support. This will not be reversed. The colleges will compete for state funds along with other public agencies, ranging from other sectors of education to state-supported welfare programs, parks, and prisons.

The community colleges have a decided advantage over other higher education sectors in the cost of instruction. Although the precise amounts allocated to lower division instruction in the universities are rarely calculated with any reliability, the overall student cost differential is obvious. Community college instruction costs about one-half as much as the per-student cost in a comprehensive four-year institution and about one-fourth as much as in a public research university.

Enrollment restrictions will continue to be imposed with ever-increasing specificity. As a supplement to, or replacement for, funding on an FTSE basis, state funds may be allocated according to the number of students making steady progress within programs, graduating, or transferring to four-year institutions; the Maryland General Assembly, for example, has considered the latter (Carkci, 1994). It will become increasingly difficult for the colleges to provide instruction at state expense to people who already have college degrees. Lifelong learning will be justified only as it contributes to career upgrading, retraining, or occupational entry skills.

The colleges will be asked incessantly to provide evidence of increased productivity and specific programmatic outcomes. Difficult to achieve in a labor-intensive enterprise, one that has been attuned more to process than to product, these demands for data on expenditures relative to outcomes will lead steadily toward greater efficiencies. Cost savings will be sought in many areas, the most obvious in moves toward year-long calendars and eighteen-hour days. These would relieve capital costs but would also increase costs of campus security, energy use, and building maintenance.

Some commentators have anticipated that the retirement of high-cost senior faculty who entered the institutions during their growth years in the 1960s will lead to lower faculty costs. However, to the extent that the senior instructors are replaced with junior full-timers, the cost savings will be short-lived. Most salary schedules award automatic pay increments for years of service, with no proviso for increased productivity, and the number of years between the beginning and the top salaries is few. The savings in instructional expenditures will come primarily in institutions that convert their staff to a higher preponderance of part-time, hourly rate teachers.

Overall it is quite unlikely that any state will increase its allocations to its community colleges by more than a couple of percentage points a year. Therefore colleges cannot expect to fund wage increases or the costs of new programs, including the widely heralded instructional technology revolution, through traditional budget lines. Similarly, capital funds will be in short supply. Any new construction will have to be supported by special appropriations; the aging buildings will get older.

Because all of the community colleges in a state tend to be funded under the same formulas, college budgets will be augmented to the extent that local leaders are entrepreneurial. Seeking grants from philanthropic foundations, finding public agencies with funds for staff training, and acquiring state funds for unique programs will be rewarded. Leasing the open areas on campus to agencies that want to conduct fairs, shows, swap meets, and the like will become increasingly popular. College foundations will be pursued with increasing vigor. Contract training has expanded rapidly and bodes to continue as a favorite way of mounting new, specialized programs that benefit local businesses while relieving a portion of the overhead that the college-credit programs bear.

Interestingly, the idea that the colleges should be funded programmatically as parks, recreation centers, and libraries are funded has made no headway in state capitols, but it will progress de facto as each college acquires its own funds for special programs. Using the funds generated by higher tuition to support greater aid to low-income students, a favorite concept of the economists who study higher education, will continue getting lip service but little tangible support in state legislatures. Instead, the states will use the higher tuition as an excuse to reject requests for increased allocations.

Instruction and Student Services

Instruction is the process of effecting learning. Learning may occur in any setting, but instruction involves arranging conditions so that it is predictable and directed. Those conditions include access to new information, organization of sequence and content, and, not least, whatever is necessary to keep the learners attendant on the task—a condition that requires traditional instruction. Would that the drive to learn were so powerful that all people engaged themselves individually with learning all they need to know to play valued roles in the society. Absent that, instruction remains essential. Regardless of the spread of multimedia, interactive media, and other distance-learning technologies that are currently available, classroom-centered instruction will not only not disappear, it will not even diminish very much as a percentage of instructional effort.

Some of the more sanguine commentators envision instruction as fully learner-controlled and totally responsive to individual knowledge seekers. Virtual, on-line arrangements would enable the faculty and students to change roles, teaching each other at will. Interestingly, although such a pattern has been given impetus by the availability of the Internet, it actually stems from the philosophy undergirding adult education; Ivan Illich wrote about it in *Deschooling Society* twenty years earlier, and *The Learning Annex*, an informal network of education users and providers, affords a contemporary example.

Before distance learning through any medium can become central to community college instruction, it must be adopted as a desirable concept by the instructors. It is possible for a college to purchase or lease multimedia or interactive instructional programs and present them without involving the instructional staff, but to do so would require a shift in focus from faculty ownership of instruction. Some colleges will do that, leaving the tenured instructors in their classrooms teaching in traditional ways, and building massive instructional programs through ancillary organizations. But most will maintain several instructional forms within the confines of the pre-existing college organization.

It is engaging to reflect on all the media that were supposed to change the conditions of teaching. To the phonograph, telephone, radio, television, and computer have been added the laser-directed disc, satellites and downlinks, and other electronic marvels too numerous to be tabulated. These automated media did indeed change the way that information is transmitted, but not in the way that the educators had hoped. Their primary application has not been in socially valuable directions or even in the schools. It has been in the world of entertainment, where the media have tended to lure audiences away from the imagery occasioned by reading, away from reflectiveness, patience, and perseverance. The dream of students learning on their own while their instructors were freed from information dispensing to engage in creative interaction with them has remained just that—a dream from which visitors to the schools awaken as they walk the corridors and see instructors and students in classrooms acting quite as they did before the microchip, or, for that matter, the vacuum tube.

The concept of instructional productivity will be central to moves toward media production and utilization. Productivity in the university coalesced around ideas of research and scholarship. In the community colleges, productivity has been defined as numbers of students taught per instructional dollar. Incessant demands for accountability and measures of productivity will force continuous review of productivity measures. Even though telecourses have been widespread for decades, questions about the number of students who will use them and the learning they effect are still open. The number of students exposed to an instructional medium, whether in a classroom or on a television screen or computer terminal elsewhere, is only one among many possible measures of productivity. Few auditors will continue to accept instructional productivity as a measure of the number of students within range of the instructor's voice. Changes in instructional form and in measures of instructional productivity will have to proceed in tandem. Eventually, measures of student learning, achievement, and satisfaction will have to be brought forward. One thing is certain: productivity growth is difficult to achieve in the service sector.

Although practitioners of student services have long advocated better integration of their programs with the colleges' instructional efforts, only rarely have strong links been built between the counseling, tutorial, and orientation efforts on the one hand and the instructional programs on the other. More recently, led by managers of instructional resource centers and learning laboratories, student services and instruction have come closer together. Maas, Rao, Taylor, and Associates (1994) have postulated a "Student Success Center," integrating several aspects of student services with instruction. Its components would include computer-based learning for student access to software, tutorial activities, faculty instructional development support, student assessment, and numerous other functions now typically scattered across the campus. The budgetary lines that divide student services from instruction have tended to retard the development of this form of integration. But to the extent its proponents can demonstrate financial savings, it will proceed.

Curriculum

An outline of curriculum classified broadly as career, developmental, community, and collegiate studies can be projected.

Career Education

Career education will remain prominent. There can be no reversing the perception that one of the colleges' prime functions is to train workers, and ample funds are available to support this function. Competition from universities that develop programs in the technologies and from proprietary schools and publicly funded ad hoc job-training programs that teach the more specific skills will not change the central tendency. There is enough demand to keep them all occupied, even as programs within the category rise and fall.

Enrollment and funding caps will limit the introduction of new programs. In 1991, the Texas Higher Education Coordinating Board adopted a policy of linking approval of new associate degrees to the college's job-training record: "An institution must show that 85 percent of the students completing existing technical programs over a three-year period are employed or pursuing additional education" (Aumack and Blake, 1992, p. 2). The specifications for the Job Training Partnership Act put limits on the programs that a community college may offer for adults because educational attainment per se is not considered a successful training outcome. More than in any other area, the specter of institutional accountability looms over the occupational programs. But they are so popular in an era of intense economic competitiveness that modest change in format is about all that will differentiate them from their predecessors.

Developmental Education

Developmental education will also be high on the agenda. It has come to the fore after decades of being treated as an embarrassing secret, as something that the colleges did but that their leaders would rather not publicize. The report of the commission planning for the future of the Alabama college system noted that economic development in the state depends in large measure on the colleges' "establishing innovative solutions to chronic illiteracy" (Alabama State Department of Postsecondary Education, 1987, p. 19). The Commission on the Future of the North Carolina Community College System indicated that the colleges could bring about significant increases in literacy levels by improving the quality of literacy education programs, increasing the number of graduates, and increasing "support among business and government agencies for literacy programs" (1989, p. 20). The Maryland State Board for Community Colleges (1986) and the Board of Trustees of Regional Community Colleges (1989) in Connecticut concluded that community colleges have a primary responsibility to provide remedial education. In California the Joint Committee for Review of the Master Plan for Higher Education (California State Legislature, 1987) elevated remedial education to a priority second only to transfer and occupational studies. Clearly, developmental education has come out of the closet.

Despite all the increases in high school graduation requirements and the apparent increase in the test scores made by prospective college students, remedial education is as big as it ever was. One reason may be that the tests are at variance with the types of learning that the students have attained, a reason implicit in an NCES report on literacy that states that although half the adult students who were tested were reading at the lowest two of the five levels of literacy, most of them thought that they could read and write well (Kirsch, Jugeblut, Jenkins, and Kolstad, 1993). Another clue comes from the pattern of students completing high school: graduation requirements increased during the 1980s, but so did the proportion of students completing high school at twenty-one or older. Although the rate of high school completion for seventeen-year-olds remained static at around 75 percent from the mid 1960s to the mid 1990s, the rate of high school completion for people in their twenties increased from 82 percent in 1972 to 86 percent in 1993. An even more dramatic increase was seen in high school completion rates for twenty-nine- and thirty-year-olds, from 78 percent in 1972 to 87 percent in the early 1980s and succeeding years (National Center for Education Statistics, 1994k, p. x). The students who take longer to complete and receive high school diplomas or equivalency certificates when they are in their twenties either never learned or forgot the dimensions of literacy that the awards purport to certify.

A sizable amount of basic skill development would continue to be necessary for many years merely to accommodate the backlog of functionally illiterate and non-native-English-speaking people in America. The House Subcommittee on Select Education set a goal of "a 90 percent adult literacy rate nationally" (U.S. Congress, 1988, p. 18). The community colleges are the only postsecondary structures likely to provide this essential instruction. They will not only offer it on their own campuses but will also expand their teaching of literacy in universities, lower schools, and business enterprises. Whether developmental education is funded separately, or whether its cost is aggregated along with other curricular functions, it will account for one-third of the instructional budget. This amount will vary widely between colleges; it will be highest where the lower schools pass through numbers of marginally literate students, where college going and immigration rates are high, and where matriculation testing and placement are mandated.

Community Education

Community education expanded dramatically during the 1970s and held its own even in the face of budget reductions in the 1980s. Its proponents have been skilled in effecting cooperative relationships and in securing special funds for it. Nonetheless, its future is not assured because questions of intent, quality control, and institutional credibility have not been answered. Funding will continue to be the most difficult problem to resolve. Although community education advocates certainly will not effect their fanciful dream of serving as the nexus of the region's educational services, their greatest successes will be in rural areas where competing institutions are weakest.

Issues of definition and scope will be no less prominent than they always have been. The notion of community education as "building communities" has no credence. "Communities" typically are defined as including everyone in the district; thus the colleges are supposed to provide something for everyone, an effort that is as mercurial as the vagaries of resources and opportunism dictate. Contract training will do well, personal interest courses poorly unless they are presented on a self-supporting basis.

Collegiate Education

The prognosis for the collegiate curriculum is good. The linkage aspect of the collegiate function, centering on preparing students to enter junior-level programs leading to bachelor's degrees in health fields, business, technologies, and the professions, will thrive because entrance to those programs depends on students' completing courses in the humanities, sciences, social sciences, mathematics, and English usage.

The collegiate function will thrive also as the colleges enroll greater proportions of minority students. Like most students, they want jobs; and, like all students, they need a perspective on the culture, a sense of interpersonal relations, and an ability to analyze situations and to communicate appropriately. Beyond that, students also seek the higher education that they need to progress in the dominant culture: increased literacy, understanding of ethical issues, and realization of past and present time. Someday, readers of today's education literature will react with emotions ranging from curiosity to indignation and shame as they review the allegations that an influx of minority students rationalizes a curriculum centering on the trades that demand only minimal literacy and manual skills. Should we not teach the humanities to Hispanics? The sciences to African-Americans? The social sciences to Asians? Which portions of the liberal arts should we drop so that the minorities can concentrate on their hand tools? Which aspects of general education should we deny to them lest they be encouraged to raise their aspirations? Racism dies hard, and it is distressing to hear commentators suggesting special curricula for those students they euphemistically call "new."

General Education

Integrated general education will make little headway. The heavy hand of the universities will restrict efforts to provide interdisciplinary studies. Fundamental curricular reform occurs very slowly. The clerically dominated classical curriculum was under attack for at least half of the nineteenth century before a secularized curriculum centering on science became the norm. The twentieth century has seen the rise of career education and, most recently, the acceptance of remedial studies as a legitimate collegiate function. A mandated, integrative education through which students gain historical perspective and a sense of the social and environmental trends that affect their future has yet to take center stage. In sum, except in the rare institution, general education will continue being debated in the context of distribution requirements. It cannot become the guiding principle of an institution that is less dedicated to societal benefit than it is to each individual's immediate concerns. It is a centripetal idea that is constantly subverted by the centrifugal forces of staff members and students with their own agenda and by universities that have rarely provided it for their own students.

Research

Research in community colleges should center on assessing institutional outcomes. The classical educational research paradigms apply to the community colleges no less than they do to other forms of schools. Students attend, learn, and move on to other pursuits. Those outcomes can be assessed—as, indeed, they are in many districts and states. More such studies should be done in individual colleges. But too few institutional research officers are available to coordinate them, too few high-level administrators appreciate their importance, and when they are conducted, too many well-meaning but futile attempts are made to relate the findings to particular college practices.

The colleges should be assessed on the basis of their success in promoting individual mobility. How many people used them as a step toward the baccalaureate or higher-status jobs? How many broke out of a cycle of family poverty? How many gained rapid access to society by becoming literate? How many learned to put their own lives together? If the goal of individual mobility is not broad enough for those who seek measures of the colleges' contributions, let them look to measures of what the colleges have done for special populations in the aggregate: the aged, disabled, minorities, at-risk youth, or immigrants.

No institution in American education plays a more difficult role than the community college. Its leaders, criticized for their inability to effect miracles with populations that have proved intractable to the ministrations of other schools and social welfare agencies, sometimes propose goals and functions even more unlikely of attainment. They might better concentrate on the social problems that have the most apparent educational components. Functional literacy affords a prime example. It is familiar to the college staff and public alike. It is amenable to intervention. And it enjoys political support second only to reducing unemployment, with which it in fact overlaps. The colleges could not only build instructional support systems that would enable them to maintain standards of literacy in all their own classes; they also could reach out by enlisting their own students as trainers of tutors for the primary schools and by organizing literacy sessions in the areas of greatest need in their communities. Measures of success would be apparent.

An intriguing but practically difficult question for assessment is: how much do the colleges contribute to the solution of perennial social issues, such as homelessness, a balanced economy, energy conservation, and white-collar and street crime? The most likely answer is: very little. The community colleges—all schools—are limited in their ability to take direct action. Staff predilections, the paucity of leadership, and funding priorities internally, along with the externals of public perceptions, community power bases, and the competing influences of the mass media, ensure that the colleges reflect the times more than they lead them. It would be wonderful if the colleges could reorganize their curriculum and their instructional divisions so that they were providing forms of education that had a direct effect on social problems. But that goal is elusive; all that any school can do is to encourage its students to participate in the polity, to question their own and the community's values, and to consider the consequences of contemporary policies that affect the problems. How much do the colleges contribute to the development of an enlightened citizenry?

An institution whose leaders pride themselves on the number of people attending finds it difficult to provide data in longitudinal format. Furthermore, the college leaders have had ceaseless difficulty in explaining how the students who attend for not more than one or two classes have benefitted. For half the students who enter the community college as their first higher education experience, a course or two before they drop out is the norm. How many of them found what they needed? In an education system designed as a structure to move people from one grade to another, it has been difficult to shift the paradigm and argue that successive enrollments in schooling are not the essential outcome but rather that something else—job skills, a sense of well-being, or some other intangible— has been a positive result.

Who will ask and answer these questions? The coming years will not see augmented institutional research budgets; there is too much competition for discretionary funds, and state legislatures have never been inclined to support research categorically. State agency-based researchers are too busy providing data to justify unique program expenditures to devise overarching research agendas. Some of the answers will be provided by the nationally oriented researchers housed in universities and federally sponsored agencies, but progress will be sporadic. Perhaps research in education must proceed that way: uncoordinated, underfunded, dependent on the interests of people concerned with particular questions and with the time and will to pursue them.

The Social Role

Social changes affect the way the nation views its social structures. For example, health care reform became a prominent issue in the 1990s as health care costs rose and as the percentage of people whose employers included health care among their benefits declined. A shift in the direction of contingent, fungible, and part-time workers reduced the likelihood that people could expect their health care costs to be covered by their employers. Accordingly, the burden somehow had to be shifted to the broader community. The magnitude of this change was similar to that which industrial nations faced earlier in the century when the breakdown of the nuclear family meant that the elderly would have to be supported at least in part by a ubiquitous form of old age insurance—hence, the creation of the Social Security Act.

An analogous situation in education has been developing over several decades. As fewer people are prepared for careers that will sustain them throughout their working life, the need for successive retraining experiences becomes apparent. This retraining is more than merely learning to use the latest developments in technology in one's own field; continuing education offered through professional organizations and companies can accommodate most of that. Retraining is for people who are changing careers altogether, going from production jobs to entrepreneurial situations, or from one trade or profession to another. At best, a person's early education will emphasize flexibility, critical thinking, literacy skills, and social awareness, so that a move between endeavors can be undertaken with facility. At least, an easily accessible, low-cost educational structure should be available for the necessary realignment.

These elements of institutional mission are somewhat different from those that guided the community colleges during the 1960s and 1970s. When the colleges were expanding, one contention was that newly emergent populations of college goers needed access to higher education so that the finest minds among them might be nurtured. A widespread myth was that inequality was caused by unequal access to education. Many analysts opined that talent was distributed more or less at random across gender, ethnic, and social class lines; therefore, as access to higher education became available to everyone, new geniuses would emerge. The more sanguine pundits contended that a readily accessible system of postsecondary institutions would lead to a broad-scale increase in general community intelligence, taste, understanding, political will, and so on. The first contention, that everyone should be given an opportunity, has borne fruit as women have entered careers in business, law, and medicine and as greater numbers of people from ethnic minorities have joined the middle class. The increase in general intelligence and participation in the polity has proved considerably more elusive.

Overall, the community college is a stable institution. Its faculty, curriculum, and number of students change little from year to year. Although innovations in remedial education that were forced on the colleges by ill-prepared students were notable, and although instruction presented through reproducible media found an early home in these institutions, the most successful experiment that the colleges pursued was open access. To a much greater extent than any other postsecondary structure, the colleges opened their doors to all who wished to participate.

The colleges have also contributed to the paradoxes that surround the structure of education. For one, they enhance inequality. Since they are avenues of individual mobility, the more successful they are in attracting students, the greater the resultant societal inequities as the brighter, more motivated, more opportunistic people move out of the social strata into which they were born. At the same time, the colleges often attempt direct social action, organizing food banks, conducting workshops on grant-getting and tax-return filing, seeking enhanced levels of student aid, and in general becoming entrepreneurial in finding opportunities to bring funds into the community.

Although these two functions seem complementary, they are in fact in opposition. The first, the college as an agent of individual mobility, forces it to act like a school. The college must teach reading and writing, basic computation, American culture. It must teach job-related generic skills, from the use of office equipment to enhancing students' propensities for showing up on time. It must maintain an academic posture, one that says that it is a school, a special environment; it is not a rap session or an extension of the street.

The social service or social welfare agenda, taken to the extreme, can lead to an institution that surrenders many of these elements of schooling. Its leaders can say they do not emphasize the teaching of English because many of their students use another primary language. They can justify preparing students for specific jobs through contract training. They can let health services and other ancillary activities become central. They can cultivate an image as a funding channel by continuously seeking dollars to run directly to the community. Some combination should be recognized, because the community colleges should not function as social welfare agencies to the detriment of their teaching and learning core.

One option or bridge between individual mobility and social welfare may be in helping students to develop local businesses and remain in their community. Some colleges have had success in teaching entrepreneurship, business law, small business accounting, and employee relations. This is much more useful for community development than a continuing drum roll of commentary on race relations, capitalistic systems, and disputes over which group is more victimized than another.

Some unstated but obvious lessons in what happens to an institution that drifts away from its instructional core toward a social service role might be drawn from the experience of the American secondary schools. As they reduced curriculum requirements and attended more directly to student welfare and social or community services, several things happened. They began to employ ill-trained teachers; they began passing marginally literate students through; they effectually put a cap on the percentage of students graduating; and they enhanced the separation between teachers and administrators. Not incidentally, they gained a full share of public opprobrium and consequent support for competing institutions.

Within the context of these philosophical anomalies, the peculiarities of individual colleges are obscured. Legislatures see transfer and developmental and occupational education as top priorities, with all else peripheral. If the colleges try to do too much, they may be accused of doing nothing well. The institutional image contributes to its outcomes. If a college has an exceedingly low transfer rate, the academically inclined students shun it and its transfer rate goes down ever further. Similarly, if a college is dedicated more to contract training than to generic occupational education, the students who seek skills that can be related to a multiplicity of jobs may go elsewhere. If student flow is to be a measure of institutional success, then relationships with the secondary schools and the universities will have to be carefully cultivated and monitored. This effects an association between educational structures that might otherwise be competitive for funding, public support, and students; very touchy, but there is no option.

Another paradox is that distance learning, the reconfiguring of instruction that is supposed to save money, may be directed toward the marginal, nondirected, nonserious, casual students. Why a paradox? Because the students from families with a high regard for education will find their way to a campus for a traditional collegiate experience.

One more paradox is that education tends to increase productivity while incarceration decreases productivity; yet the budget for prisons in some states has now reached parity with higher education expenditures. How commentators can call for increased productivity and competition in the global economy while at the same time advocating more money for the corrections system at the expense of support for higher education eludes rationality.

Last, despite massive growth in access to schooling and the vastly greater and diverse numbers who have enrolled, the communities from which they come have been little affected. Do the schools not build a better society? The individual mobility that they effect does not translate into reorganized cities, changed working conditions, modified immigration policies, or much of anything else affecting the quality of life across the community.

A view of social conditions in the United States at the turn of the century provides a view of the context for the colleges:

- High immigration, both in absolute numbers and in percentages of the American population, along with demands for anti-immigration regulations

- Multilingualism, with scores of foreign language newspapers and a population housed in ethnic enclaves

- Overcrowded cities, with unclean pavements and parks and intractable homelessness

- For the work force, practically no fringe benefits; much in the nature of piecework in the workplace and take-home or cottage industries

- Powerful media determining what people think

- A great gap between the rich and the poor

- Producer or assembly jobs, yielding wages insufficient to sustain a family above the poverty line

- Weak trade unions, representing a small proportion of the work force

- For the individual, business entrepreneurship as the path to capital formation

- A seeming paucity of civility when compared with an earlier era

- A tendency of youth to form gangs and engage in various criminal activities

At the turn of which century? The twentieth and twenty-first alike. One thousand community colleges have not changed those conditions. But did anyone but the most passionate, self-deceiving institutional advocates ever think that they could?

The college may have no ostensible reason for existence other than to serve its students and the business community, but it also has a life of its own as an intellectual community. It is easy to reduce the institution's value to the increase in its graduates' social mobility and to ignore its position as a center of acculturation and historical continuity. But the institution's traditions act to ensure that these values are not completely set aside. Learning is infinite. We can always teach more, learn more efficiently, do better. Thus the continual striving for innovation in education, with the innovators occupying prominent places in the system. Too often overlooked is a view of the staff as models of rational discourse.

Educators do not solve problems or cure ills. But neither do they deliberately sell false dreams or spread bad taste. It is only when they imitate the worst characteristics of business corporations and the mass media that they lose the status the public has granted them. They will not betray the virtues that distinguish their calling.

References

♦ ♦

Note: The Educational Resources Information Center (ERIC) documents listed here (including those that are identified as unpublished papers) are available from the ERIC Document Reproduction Service (EDRS), 7420 Fullerton Road, Suite 110, Springfield, VA 22153-2852. Contact EDRS at (800) 443-ERIC for complete ordering information. Abstracts of these and other documents in the ERIC collection are available from ERIC Clearinghouse for Community Colleges, 3051 Moore Hall, 405 Hilgard Avenue, UCLA, Los Angeles, CA 90095-1521.

Abraham, A. A. *A Report on College-Level Remedial/Developmental Programs in SREB States.* Atlanta: Southern Regional Education Board, 1987. 78 pp. (ED 280 369)

Academic Senate for California Community Colleges. "Report of the ASCCC Conference on Academic Standards." Unpublished report, Dec. 2, 1977.

Adams, B., Bodino, A., Bissell, O., and Smith, M. "Writing for Learning: How to Achieve a Total College Commitment." Paper presented at annual national convention of the American Association of Community and Junior Colleges, San Diego, Apr. 14–17, 1985. 38 pp. (ED 258 666)

Adams, J. J., and Roesler, E. D. *A Profile of First-Time Students at Virginia Community Colleges, 1975–76.* Richmond: Virginia State Department of Community Colleges, 1977. 58 pp. (ED 153 694)

Adams, L. *Extended Learning Institute: Policies and Procedures Manual.* Chester, Va.: John Tyler Community College, 1986. 65 pp. (ED 273 313)

Adelman, C. (ed.). *Assessment in American Higher Education: Issues and Contexts.* Washington, D.C.: Office of Educational Research and Improvement, 1986.

Adelman, C. "A Basic Statistical Portrait of American Higher Education, 1987." Paper prepared for the second Anglo-American Dialogue on Higher Education, 1987.

Adelman, C. "Transfer Rates and the Going Mythologies: A Look at Community College Patterns." *Change,* 1988, *20*(1), 38–41.

Adelman, C. *Lessons of a Generation.* San Francisco: Jossey-Bass, 1994.

Alabama State Department of Postsecondary Education. *Dimensions 2000: A Strategic Plan for Building Alabama's Future.* Montgomery: Alabama State Department of Postsecondary Education, 1987. 34 pp. (ED 295 688)

Alfano, K. *A Survey of New Student Satisfaction with Student Services: Matriculation Study 1990–91.* Moorpark, Calif.: Moorpark College, 1990. 39 pp. (ED 325 172)

Alfano, K., Brawer, F. B., Cohen, A. M., and Koltai, L. *The Evaluation of the Effect of AB1725 on State Wide Faculty and Staff Development.* Los Angeles: Center for the Study of Community Colleges, 1990.

Alfred, R. L., and Lum, G. D. "Remedial Program Policies, Student Demographic Characteristics, and Academic Achievement in Community College." *Community Junior College Quarterly of Research and Practice,* 1988, *12*(2), 107–120.

American Association of Community Colleges. *Membership Directory 1993.* Washington, D.C.: American Association of Community Colleges, 1993.

American Association of Community Colleges. *Membership Directory 1995.* Washington, D.C.: American Association of Community Colleges, 1995.

American Association of Community Colleges. *Community Colleges: Core Indicators of Effectiveness.* Report of the Community College Roundtable: Washington, D.C., 1994. (ED 367 411)

American Association of Community and Junior Colleges. *Responding to the Challenge of a Changing American Economy: 1985 Progress Report on the Sears Partnership Development Fund.* Washington, D.C.: American Association of Community and Junior Colleges, 1986. 20 pp. (ED 270 144)

American Association of Community and Junior Colleges. *Community, Junior, and Technical College Directory.* Washington, D.C.: American Association of Community and Junior Colleges, 1955–1992 (published annually).

American Association of Community and Junior Colleges. *Building Communities: A Vision for a New Century. A Report of the Commission on the Future of Community Colleges.* Washington, D.C.: American Association of Community and Junior Colleges, 1988. 58 pp. (ED 293 578)

American Association of Community and Junior Colleges. *A Summary of Selected National Data Pertaining to Community, Technical, and Junior Colleges.* American Association of Community and Junior Colleges, 1988. 24 pp. (ED 307 908)

American Association of Junior Colleges. *A National Resource for Occupational Education.* Washington, D.C.: American Association of Junior Colleges, 1964.

American College Testing Program. *College Student Profiles: Norms for the ACT Assessment.* Iowa City, Iowa: Research and Development Division, American College Testing Program, 1966–present (published annually).

American College Testing Program. *The High School Profile Report: Normative Data. A Description of the Academic Abilities and Nonacademic Characteristics of Your ACT Tested 1990 Graduates. ACT High School Profile Report H.S. Graduating Class 1990. National Report.* Iowa City, Iowa: American College Testing Program, 1990. (ED 325 503)

Anderson, K. L. "Post-High School Experiences and College Attrition." *Sociology of Education,* 1981, *54*(1), 1–15.

Andrews, H. A., and Allen, J. "CIM (Computer Integrated Manufacturing) in Higher Education: A Partnership with IBM." *Community Services Catalyst,* Spring 1992, *22*(2).

Angel, D., and Gares, D. "The Community College Foundation Today." In J. L. Catanzaro and A. D. Arnold (eds.), *Alternative Funding Sources.* New Directions for Community Colleges, no. 68. San Francisco: Jossey-Bass, 1989.

Angelo, T. A., and Cross, K. P. *Classroom Assessment Techniques.* (2nd ed.). San Francisco: Jossey-Bass, 1993.

Anglin, L. W., and others. "The Missing Rung of the Teacher Education Ladder: Community Colleges." Paper presented at the 42nd general meeting of the American Association of Colleges for Teacher Education, Atlanta, 1991. (ED 336 383)

Archer, C., and Archer, A. J. "How Successful Financial Aid Outreach Is Developed and Run." Unpublished report, 1985. 15 pp. (ED 284 613)

Armstrong, C. L. "The Impact of Collective Bargaining at the Rancho Santiago Community College District (Santa Ana College)." Unpublished paper, Pepperdine University (Malibu, Calif.), 1978. 42 pp. (ED 164 043)

Ashworth, P. C., and Vogler, D. E. "Community College Funding Goals: Senate and Presidential Comparison." *Community Services Catalyst,* Winter 1991, *21*,(1).

Association of American Colleges. *Integrity in the College Curriculum: A Report to the Academic Community. The Findings and Recommendations of the Project on Redefining the Meaning and Purpose of Baccalaureate Degrees.* Washington, D.C.: Association of American Colleges, 1985. 62 pp. (ED 251 059)

Association of Independent Colleges and Schools. *Directory of Educational Institutions, 1988.* Washington, D.C.: Association of Independent Colleges and Schools, 1988.

Astin, A. W. *Four Critical Years: Effects of College on Beliefs, Attitudes, and Knowledge.* San Francisco: Jossey-Bass, 1977.

Astin, A. W. *Minorities in American Higher Education: Recent Trends, Current Prospects, and Recommendations.* San Francisco: Jossey-Bass, 1982.

Astin, A. W. "Student Involvement in Learning." Paper presented at annual conference of the California Community College Trustees, San Diego, May 24, 1986.

Astin, A. W., Korn, W. S., and Dey, E. L. *The American College Teacher: National Norms for the 1989–90 HERI Faculty Survey.* Los Angeles: Higher Education Research Institute, 1991.

Astin, A. W., Korn, W. S., and Riggs, E. R. *The American Freshman: National Norms for Fall 1993.* University of California, Los Angeles, 1993.

Astin, A. W., and others. *The American Freshman: National Norms for [1973–Present].* Los Angeles: Cooperative Institutional Research Program, 1973–present (published annually).

Astin, H. S., and Leland, C. *Women of Influence, Women of Vision: A Cross-Generational Study of Leaders and Social Change.* San Francisco: Jossey-Bass, 1991.

Augenblick, J. *Issues in Financing Community Colleges.* Denver: Education Finance Center, Education Commission of the States, 1978. 70 pp. (ED 164 020)

Aumack, B., and Blake, L. J. *Texas State Technical College Review.* Austin: Texas Higher Education Coordinating Board, 1992. 14 pp. (ED 355 993)

Bailey, A. L. "Their Budgets Cut, 2-Year Colleges Turn to Aggressive Fund Raising." *Chronicle of Higher Education,* 1986, *33*(1), 57.

Bailey, L., Buchanan, N. E., and Holleman, M. "The LRC's Role in Helping Faculty Internationalize the Community College Curriculum." In M. Holleman (ed.), *The Role of the Learning Resource Center in Instruction.* New Directions for Community Colleges, no. 71. San Francisco: Jossey-Bass, 1990.

Baker, G. A., III (ed.). *A Handbook on the Community College in America: Its History, Mission, and Management.* Westport, Conn.: Greenwood Press, 1994. (ED 364 283)

Baker, R. G. "A Comparison of College Freshman Achievement in Remedial English Courses and in Freshman Composition Courses at a Two-Year

College." Paper presented at annual meeting of the American Educational Research Association, New York, Mar. 19–23, 1982. 12 pp. (ED 214 615)

Baldridge, J. V. *Power and Conflict in the University*. New York: Wiley, 1971.

Baldwin, A. *Internal Program Review of Associate in Science Programs, 1981–82 Through 1985–86*. Research Report no. 86–83. Miami: Office of Institutional Research, Miami-Dade Community College, 1986. 71 pp. (ED 275 586)

Baldwin, A. *Program Review: Outcomes Measures of Miami-Dade Community College Associate in Science Graduates from 1984–85 Through 1992–93*. Research Report no. 93-14R. Miami: Office of Institutional Research, Miami-Dade Community College, 1993. (ED 366 401)

Barnes, R. A. *Credit Enrollment and the Adult Population: A Comparison of Fall 1991 Credit Enrollment and 1990 Census Data*. Technical report. San Diego Community College District, Apr. 1992.

Bayer, A. E. "Teaching Faculty in Academe: 1972–73." *ACE Research Reports*, 1973, 8(2), 1–68.

Ben-David, J. *Centers of Learning: Britain, France, Germany, United States*. New York: McGraw-Hill, 1977.

Bennett, B. *Diversity in Serving Prison Populations*. Paper presented at the annual national convention of the American Association of Community and Junior Colleges, Kansas City, Mo., Apr. 13–16, 1991. (ED 333 909)

Bennett, W. J. *To Reclaim a Legacy: A Report on the Humanities in Higher Education*. Washington, D.C.: National Endowment for the Humanities, 1984.

Bensimon, E. M. "Understanding Administrative Work." In A. M. Cohen, F. B. Brawer, and Associates, *Managing Community Colleges: A Handbook for Effective Practice*. San Francisco: Jossey-Bass, 1994.

Berger, J. "For Workers, More Paths to Degree." *New York Times*, Mar. 30, 1988, p. B4.

Berman, P., and Weiler, D. *Choosing the Future: An Action Agenda for Community Colleges*. Sacramento: California Community Colleges, Board of Governors, BW Associates, 1993. 134 pp. (ED 362 247)

Bers, T. H. "Articulation and Transfer." In A. M. Cohen, F. B. Brawer, and Associates, *Managing Community Colleges: A Handbook for Effective Practice*. San Francisco: Jossey-Bass, 1994.

Bers, T. H., and Mittler, M. L. *Assessment and Testing: Myths and Realities*. New Directions for Community Colleges, no. 88. San Francisco: Jossey-Bass, 1994.

Bess, R., and others. *A Study of the Economic Impact of Six Community Colleges in Illinois*. Springfield: Illinois Community College Board, 1980. 31 pp. (ED 191 516)

Blocker, C. E. "Are Our Faculties Competent?" *Junior College Journal*, 1965–66, 36, 12–17.

Blocker, C. E., Plummer, W., and Richardson, R. C., Jr. *The Two-Year College: A Social Synthesis.* Englewood Cliffs, N.J.: Prentice-Hall, 1965.

Bloom, A. *The Closing of the American Mind.* New York: Simon & Schuster, 1987.

Bloom, B. S. "Recent Developments in Mastery Learning." *Educational Psychologist*, 1973, 10(2), 53–57.

Bloom, B. S. "The Search for Methods of Group Instruction as Effective as One-to-One Tutoring. *Educational Learning*, May 1984, 41(8), 417. (EJ 299 535)

Board of Trustees of Regional Community Colleges. *Towards 2000: A Long-Range Plan for the Community Colleges of Connecticut.* Hartford: Board of Trustees of Regional Community Colleges, 1989.

Bogart, Q. J., and Galbraith, J. D. "Marketing America's Community Colleges: An Analysis of National Marketing Efforts of Community Colleges. A Final Report on the MECCA Project of the Council of North Central Community and Junior Colleges." Special condensed summary report presented at annual convention of the American Association of Community and Junior Colleges, Las Vegas, Apr. 24–27, 1988. 23 pp. (ED 296 771)

Bogue, J. P. *The Community College.* New York: McGraw-Hill, 1950.

Bohr, D. H., and Bray, D. "HELP: A Pilot Program for Community College High-Risk Students." Unpublished paper, Sacramento, Calif., 1979. 12 pp. (ED 168 635)

Bohr, L., and others. *Cognitive Effects of Two-Year and Four-Year Colleges: A Preliminary Study.* University Park, Pa.: National Center on Postsecondary Teaching, Learning, and Assessment, 1992. (ED 357 707)

Bok, D. *The Cost of Talent.* New York: The Free Press, 1993.

Bonczer, T. P., and Easton, J. Q. *The Effect of Mastery Learning on Student Achievement.* Chicago City Colleges' Center for the Improvement of Teaching and Learning, 1983. (ED 238 505)

Borquist, B. "The Community College Approach to Serving Business and Industry." *Community Services Catalyst*, 1986, 16(4), 19–21.

Bourque, M. P. "On the Fault Line: President Clinton Salutes Community Colleges." *Community College Journal*, 1995, 65(6), pp. 38–42.

Bowen, H. R. "Cost Differences: The Amazing Disparity Among Institutions of Higher Education in Educational Costs per Student." *Change*, 1981, 13(1), 21–27.

Boyer, E. L. *College: The Undergraduate Experience in America.* New York: HarperCollins, 1987.

Boyer, E. L., and Kaplan, M. *Educating for Survival.* New Rochelle, N.Y.: Change Magazine Press, 1977.

Brawer, F. B. *Familiar Functions in New Containers: Classifying Community Education.* Topical Paper no. 71. Los Angeles: ERIC Clearinghouse for Junior Colleges, 1980. 30 pp. (ED 187 412)

Brawer, F. B., and Friedlander, J. *Science and Social Science in the Two-Year College.* Topical Paper no. 69. Los Angeles: ERIC Clearinghouse for Junior Colleges, 1979. 37 pp. (ED 172 854)

Breneman, D. W. "Planning As If People Mattered: The Economy." Presentation to the Society for College and University Planning, Kansas City, Mo., July 1979.

Breneman, D. W. *Guaranteed Student Loans: Great Success or Dismal Failure?* Fishers, Indiana: United Student Aid Funds, May 1991.

Breneman, D. W., and Nelson, S. C. *Financing Community Colleges: An Economic Perspective.* Washington, D.C.: Brookings Institution, 1981.

Brey, R., and Grigsby, C. *Telecourse Student Survey, 1984.* Washington, D.C.: Instruction Telecommunications Consortium, American Association of Community and Junior Colleges, 1984. 61 pp. (ED 255 258)

Brick, M. *Forum and Focus for the Junior College Movement.* New York: Teachers College Press, 1965.

Brick, M. Review of *Student Development Programs in the Community Junior College.* (T. O'Banion and A. Thurston, eds.) *Journal of Higher Education,* 1972, *43*(98), 675–677.

Brightman, R. W. "Entrepreneurship in the Community College: Revenue Diversification." in J. L. Catanzaro and A. D. Arnold (eds.), *Alternative Funding Sources.* New Directions for Community Colleges, no. 68. San Francisco: Jossey-Bass, 1989.

Brinkman, C. *How Will the Implementation of a Differential Tuition Fee Structure at the California Community College System Influence Student Enrollment?* Graduate seminar paper, University of California, Los Angeles, 1993, 44 pp. (ED 359 993)

Brint, S., and Karabel, J. *The Diverted Dream: Community Colleges and the Promise of Educational Opportunity in America, 1900–1985.* New York: Oxford University Press, 1989.

Brown, J. R., and others. *Developmental Studies Department Special Services Project: Rockland Community College, 1988–89.* Suffern, N.Y.: Rockland Community College, 1989. (ED 319 427)

Brum, J. "Effects of Computer-Assisted Instruction on Students; Final Grades: Applied Educational Research and Evaluation." Unpublished doctoral practicum paper, Nova University, 1983. 32 pp. (ED 263 832)

Bullock, T., Madden, T., and Harter, J. "Paired Developmental Reading and Psychology Courses." *Research and Teaching in Developmental Education*, 1987, *3*(2), 22–29. (EJ 413 779)

Burns, J. M. *Leadership*. New York: HarperCollins, 1978.

Burns, J. P., Armistead, L. P., and Keys, R. C. "Developing a Transition Initiative Program for Students with Handicapping Conditions." *Community/Junior College Journal*, 1990, *14*(4), 319–329.

Bureau of the Census. *1990 Census of Population, General Population Characteristics, United States*. Washington, D.C.: U.S. Department of Commerce, Nov. 1992.

Bushnell, D. S. *Organizing for Change: New Priorities for Community Colleges*. New York: McGraw-Hill, 1973.

Butte Community College. *Secondary/Postsecondary Articulation: The Partnership Concept, The Partnership in Action, and Highlights of Partnership in Action*. Oronville, Calif.: Butte Community College, 1990. 26 pp. (ED 322 975)

California Community Colleges. *Student Profile, Fall 1977 to Fall 1986*. Historical Profiles Project. Sacramento: Office of the Chancellor, California Community Colleges, 1987a. 33 pp. (ED 281 589)

California Community Colleges. *Study of Fee Impact*. Final Report, no. 873. Sacramento: Office of the Chancellor, California Community Colleges, 1987b. 89 pp. (ED 284 645)

California Community Colleges. *Report on Staffing and Salaries, Fall 1989*. Sacramento: Office of the Chancellor, California Community Colleges, 1990. (ED 324 055)

California Community Colleges. *Matriculation: A Report on Second Year Implementation, 1988–89*. Sacramento: Office of the Chancellor, California Community Colleges, 1990. 76 pp. (ED 315 131)

California Community Colleges. *Contract Education: A Background Paper*. Sacramento: Academic Senate, California Community Colleges, 1993. (ED 364 281)

California Community Colleges. *Faculty Salaries in California's Community Colleges, 1993–94: A Report to the Legislature and the Governor in Response to Supplemental Report Language for the 1979 Budget Act*. Sacramento: Office of the Chancellor, California State Postsecondary Education Commission, 1994.

California State Department of Education. "Summary of Source and Education Background of New Teachers in California Junior Colleges, 1963–64."

Unpublished report, California State Department of Education, 1963–64.

California State Legislature, Joint Committee for Review of the Master Plan for Higher Education. *California Community College Reform: Final Report.* Sacramento: Joint Committee for Review of the Master Plan for Higher Education, 1987. 50 pp. (ED 282 587)

California State Postsecondary Education Commission. *Comments on the California Community Colleges' Plan for Allocating Board Financial Assistance to Community College Students: A Report to the Fiscal and Educational Policy Committees of the Legislature.* Sacramento: California State Postsecondary Education Commission, 1984. 59 pp. (ED 253 290)

Campbell, D. F. "New Roles for Occupational Instructors." Unpublished paper, Community College of the Air Force (Lackland Air Force Base, Tex.), 1977. 12 pp. (ED 146 967)

Campion, W. J., and Kyle, M. *Components of Quality Community College Child Care Programs.* Ocala, Fla.: Central Florida Community College, 1990. 20 pp. (ED 325 154)

Carey, D., Wark, L., and Wellsfry, N. *Partnerships for Excellence: High Schools and Community Colleges.* ACCCA Management Report, 1986–7/2. Association of California Community College Administrators, 1986. 23 pp. (ED 278 433)

Carkci, M.R. "Legislative Work Group Touches College Financing Issues." *The Bay Times,* Nov. 23, 1994, p. 18.

Carmichael, J. B. "Meeting Small Business Needs Through Small Business Development Centers." In G. Waddell (ed.), *Economic and Work Force Development.* New Directions for Community Colleges, no. 75, 1991. (ED 335 107)

Carnegie Foundation for the Advancement of Teaching. *Missions of the College Curriculum: A Contemporary Review with Suggestions.* San Francisco: Jossey-Bass, 1977.

Carvell, J. B. *On Course: A Report to the Legislature on the Employee-Based Training Program, 1987–88.* Sacramento: Office of the Chancellor, California Community Colleges, 1988. (ED 307 928)

Case, C. H. *General Education at Los Medanos College.* Pittsburg, Calif.: Los Medanos College, 1988.

Center for the Study of Community Colleges. "Science and Humanities Instruction in Two-Year Colleges." Unpublished report. Los Angeles: Center for the Study of Community Colleges, 1978.

Center for the Study of Community Colleges. *Community College Involvement in the Education of Adults: Spring 1986 Student Survey—Frequencies.* Los Angeles: Center for the Study of Community Colleges, 1986.

Center for the Study of Community Colleges. *Community College Involvement in the Education of Adults: Survey of State Directors Regarding Populations Served and Funding Sources.* Los Angeles: Center for the Study of Community Colleges, 1987.

Center for the Study of Community Colleges. *Art Education in American Community Colleges: Final Report.* Los Angeles: Center for the Study of Community Colleges, 1988. 136 pp. (ED 294 640)

Center for the Study of Community Colleges. Unpublished data. Los Angeles: Center for the Study of Community Colleges, 1991.

Center for the Study of Community Colleges. *Entrepreneurship Training in American Community Colleges.* A report to the E. M. Kauffman Foundation, Center for Entrepreneurial Leadership, January 1994. (ED 365 393)

Center for the Study of Community Colleges. "1995 Transfer Assembly Results." Unpublished paper. Los Angeles: Center for the Study of Community Colleges, Mar. 31, 1995.

Chaffee, E. E. *Organization/Administration.* Washington, D.C.: Association for the Study of Higher Education, 1986. 62 pp. (ED 272 129)

Chang, N. *Organizational Structure in Multi-Campus Community Junior Colleges/Districts.* Denver: Community College of Denver, 1978. 137 pp. (ED 158 795)

Chapel, E. V. *Evaluation of College Science and Technology Entry Program (CSTEP), Fall 1987 Through Spring 1991.* Bayside, N.Y.: Office of Enrollment Management, Queensborough Community College, 1992. 64 pp. (ED 354 057)

Chausow, H. M. "Remedial Education: A Position Paper." Unpublished paper, Chicago, 1979. 16 pp. (ED 170 013)

Ciardi, J. "Give Us This Day Our Daily Surrealism." *Saturday Review,* 1971, *54*(24), 48.

Clagett, C. A. *PGCC Transfer Students at Maryland Colleges and Universities.* Research Brief 89-2. Largo, Md.: Office of Institutional Research, Prince George's Community College, 1988a. 14 pp. (ED 300 075)

Clagett, C. A. *Student Retention at Prince George's Community College.* Research Brief RB89–6. Largo, Md.: Office of Institutional Research, Prince George's Community College, 1988b. 11 pp. (ED 300 101)

Clark, B. R. "The 'Cooling-Out' Function in Higher Education." *American Journal of Sociology,* 1960, *65*(6), 569–576.

Clark, B. R. "The 'Cooling-Out' Function Revisited." In G. B. Vaughan (ed.),
    Questioning the Community College Role. New Directions for Community
    Colleges, no. 32. San Francisco: Jossey-Bass, 1980.

Clark, B. R. "The Absorbing Errand." Remarks presented at national conference
    of the American Association of Higher Education, Washington, D.C.,
    Mar. 10, 1988.

Clowes, D. A. "Remediation in American Higher Education." In J. Smart (ed.),
    Higher Education Handbook of Theory and Research, Vol. 8. New York:
    Agathon Press, 1989.

Clowes, D. A., and Levin, B. H. "Community, Technical, and Junior Colleges:
    Are They Leaving Higher Education?" *Journal of Higher Education*,
    May–June 1989, 60(3), 346–355. (EJ 390 779)

Cohen, A. M. *Work Satisfaction Among Junior College Faculty Members*. Los
    Angeles: University of California and ERIC Clearinghouse for Junior Col-
    leges, 1973. 8 pp. (ED 081 426)

Cohen A. M. "Enrollment Trends in the Humanities in the Community Col-
    leges." Presentation to the national conference, Community College
    Humanities Association, San Francisco, Nov. 15, 1991.

Cohen, A. M. "Community Colleges." *International Encyclopedia of Education*.
    (2nd ed.) Elmsford, N.Y.: Pergamon Press, 1994a.

Cohen, A. M. (ed.). *Relating Curriculum and Transfer*. New Directions for Com-
    munity Colleges, no. 86. San Francisco: Jossey-Bass, 1994b.

Cohen, A. M., and Brawer, F. B. *The Two-Year College Instructor Today*. New
    York: Praeger, 1977.

Cohen, A. M., and Brawer, F. B. *The Collegiate Function of Community Colleges:
    Fostering Higher Learning Through Curriculum and Student Transfer*. San
    Francisco: Jossey-Bass, 1987.

Cohen, A. M., Brawer, F. B., and Eaton, J. S. "Policies and Programs That Effect
    Student Transfer." Presentation to the annual convention of the Ameri-
    can Association of Community Colleges, Apr. 24, 1995.

Cohen, A. M., and Ignash, J. M. "Trends in the Liberal Arts Curriculum." *Com-
    munity College Review*, 1992, 20(2), 54–59.

Cohen, A. M., and Ignash, J. M. "An Overview of the Total Credit Curriculum."
    In A. M. Cohen (ed.), *Relating Curriculum and Transfer*. New Directions
    for Community Colleges, no. 86. San Francisco: Jossey-Bass, 1994. (ED
    371 804)

Cohen, M. D., and March, J. G. *Leadership and Ambiguity: The American College
    President*. (2nd ed.). Boston: Harvard Business School Press, 1986.

Cohen, M. J. "Junior College Growth." *Change*, 1972, 4(9), 32a–32d.

The College Board. *College Bound Seniors: The 1994 Profile of SAT and Achievement Test Takers.* Princeton, N.J.: The SAT Program, 1994.

College Entrance Examination Board. *Annual Survey of Colleges, 1986–87: Summary Statistics.* New York: College Entrance Examination Board, 1986. 147 pp. (ED 279 213)

Collins, C. C. *Junior College Student Personnel Programs: What They Are and What They Should Be.* Washington, D.C.: American Association of Junior Colleges, 1967. 57 pp. (ED 001 459)

Collins, C. C., and Drexel, K. O. *General Education: A Community College Model.* Pittsburg, Calif.: Community College Press, 1976.

Collins, E. C. *The Impact of Evaluation on Community College Faculty Effort and Effectiveness.* Gainesville: Institute of Higher Education, University of Florida, 1986. 74 pp. (ED 280 529)

Colorado Commission on Higher Education. *Completion and Persistence Report: Colorado Public Higher Education, Fall 1986 Through Fall 1991.* Denver: Colorado Commission on Higher Education, 1992. p. 189 (ED 354 927)

Commission on the Future of the North Carolina Community College System. *Gaining the Competitive Edge: The Challenge to North Carolina's Community Colleges.* Chapel Hill, N.C.: MDC, 1989.

Committee on the Objectives of a General Education in a Free Society. *General Education in a Free Society: A Report of the Harvard Committee.* Cambridge, Mass.: Harvard University Press, 1945.

Conklin, K. A. *Educational Goal Attainment: A One-Year Follow-Up Study of Nonreturning Johnson County Community College Students.* Overland Park, Kans.: Office of Institutional Research, Johnson County Community College, 1992. (ED 352 074)

Coombs, P. H. *The World Educational Crisis: A System Analysis.* New York: New York University Press, 1968.

Cooper, C. W., and Michael, W. B. *The Relationship of Academic Self-Concept to Persistence or Lack of Persistence of Disabled and Non-Disabled Students in a Small Rural Community College.* Gilroy, Calif.: Gavilan Community College, 1990. (ED 326 288J)

Copperman, P. *The Literacy Hoax: The Decline of Reading, Writing, and Learning in the Public Schools and What We Can Do About It.* New York: Morrow, 1978.

Corson, J. J. *The Governance of Colleges and Universities.* New York: McGraw-Hill, 1960.

Cosand, J. P. *Perspective: Community Colleges in the 1980s.* Horizons Issue Monograph Series. Washington, D.C.: Council of Universities and Colleges,

American Association of Community and Junior Colleges; Los Angeles: ERIC Clearinghouse for Junior Colleges, 1979. (ED 178 146)

Cotnam, J. D., and Ison, S. *A Follow-Up Study of Non-Returning Students.* Rochester, N.Y.: Office of Institutional Advancement, Monroe Community College, 1988. 17 pp. (ED 291 435)

Craig-Claar, D. "Starting SI at Maple Woods Community College." *SI News,* Kansas City: Center for Academic Development, University of Missouri, Summer 1994.

Cross, C. "Community Colleges Lead in Classroom Use of Computers, Survey Shows." *Community College Week,* Nov. 21, 1994.

Cross, K. P. "Access and Accommodation in Higher Education." Paper presented to White House Conference on Youth. *Research Reporter,* Berkeley, Calif.: Center for Research and Development in Higher Education, 1971, 6(2), 6–8.

Cross, K. P. "Toward the Future in Community College Education." Paper presented at the Conference on Education in the Community College for the Non-Traditional Student, Philadelphia, Mar. 31, 1978. 24 pp. (ED 168 626)

Cross, K. P. *Adults as Learners: Increasing Participation and Facilitating Learning.* San Francisco: Jossey-Bass, 1981.

Cullen, C., and Moed, M. G. "Serving High-Risk Adolescents." In J. E. Lieberman (ed.), *Collaborating with High Schools. New Directions for Community Colleges,* no. 63. San Francisco: Jossey-Bass, 1988.

Cvancara, K. J. "In Prison, In College." *Community College Times,* Nov. 1, 1994, 6(21) 1, 4.

Dallas County Community College District. *ITV Close-Up: The First Six Years.* Dallas: Dallas County Community College District, 1979. 60 pp. (ED 171 361)

Dassance, C. R. "Student Services." In A. M. Cohen, F. B. Brawer, and Associates, *Managing Community Colleges: A Handbook for Effective Practice.* San Francisco: Jossey-Bass, 1994.

Deiro, J. *Prior Learning Experiences: Handbook for Portfolio Process. Alternative Learning Experiences.* Bellingham, Wash.: Whatcom Community College, 1983. 93 pp. (ED 227 903)

Deming, E. W. *Out of the Crises.* Cambridge, Mass.: Massachusetts Institute of Technology, 1982.

Devall, W. B. "Community Colleges: A Dissenting View." *Educational Record,* 1968, 49(2), 168–172.

Dickmeyer, M., *Comparative Financial Statistics for Public 2-Year Colleges: FY 1993 National Sample.* Washington, D.C.: National Association of College and University Business Offices, Apr. 1994.

Diener, T. *Growth of an American Invention: A Documentary History of the Junior and Community College Movement. Contributions to the Study of Education, No. 16.* Westport, Conn.: Greenwood Press, 1986. (ED 271 166)

Doty, C. R. "Principles of and Sources for Vertical Articulation of Occupational Education from Secondary Schools to Community Colleges." Unpublished report, 1985. 28 pp. (ED 272 673)

Doucette, D. *Community College Workforce Training Programs for Employees of Business, Industry, Labor, and Government: A Status Report.* Laguna Hills, Calif.: League for Innovation in the Community College, 1993. 43 pp. (ED 356 815)

Doucette, D. S., and Dayton, L. L. "A Framework for Student Development Practices: A Statement of the League for Innovation in the Community College." In W. L. Deegan and T. O'Banion (eds.), *Perspectives on Student Development.* New Directions for Community Colleges, no. 67. San Francisco: Jossey-Bass, 1989.

Doucette, D., and Hughes, B. (eds.). *Assessing Institutional Effectiveness in Community Colleges.* Laguna Hills, Calif.: League for Innovation in the Community College, 1990. 63 pp. (ED 324 072)

Dougherty, K. J. "The Politics of Community College Expansion: Beyond the Functionalist and Class-Reproduction Explanations." *American Journal of Education,* 1988, 96(3), 351–393.

Dougherty, K. J. *The Contradictory College: The Conflicting Origins, Impacts, and Futures of the Community College.* Albany, N.Y.: State University of New York Press, 1994. (ED 369 461)

Dowdy, H. B. *Manual for Trustees of the North Carolina Community College System.* Raleigh: North Carolina State Department of Community Colleges, 1987. 52 pp. (ED 297 823)

Dressel, P. L. *College Teaching as a Profession: The Doctor of Arts Degree.* East Lansing: Michigan State University, 1982. 33 pp. (ED 217 750)

Dubin, R., and Taveggia, T. C. *The Teaching-Learning Paradox.* Eugene, Oreg.: Center for the Advanced Study of Educational Administration, 1968.

Eaton, J. S. *Strengthening Collegiate Education in Community Colleges.* San Francisco: Jossey-Bass, 1994. (ED 367 409)

Educational Goal Attainment: A Three-Year Follow-Up Study of Nonreturning 1986–87 Students. Overland Park, Kans.: Office of Institutional Research, Johnson County Community College, 1990. 30 pp. (ED 327 252)

Eddington, A. *The Nature of Physics.* Ann Arbor: University of Michigan Press, 1958, p. 103.

Educational Testing Service. *The Concern for Writing*. Focus 5. Princeton, N.J.:
    Educational Testing Service, 1978. 18 pp. (ED 187 363; available in
    microfiche only)

Eells, W. C. *The Junior College*. Boston: Houghton Mifflin, 1931.

Eells, W. C. *Present Status of Junior College Terminal Education*. Washington,
    D.C.: American Association of Junior Colleges, 1941a.

Eells, W. C. *Why Junior College Terminal Education?* Washington, D.C.: Ameri-
    can Association of Junior Colleges, 1941b.

Ehrhardt, H. B. "Mountain View College's Cognitive Style Program: A Descrip-
    tion." Unpublished paper, Mountain View College (Dallas), 1980. 18 pp.
    (ED 190 183)

Eissa, D. *GAIN in the Community Colleges: A Report on the 1992–93 Survey on
    GAIN Participation and Funding*. Sacramento: Office of the Chancellor,
    California Community Colleges, 1994. 21 pp. (ED 369 465)

Emmons, J. *Remedial/Developmental Education in Kansas Community Colleges,
    Summer 1987–Spring 1988*. Topeka: Kansas State Department of Educa-
    tion, 1988. 33 pp. (ED 300 078)

Ernst, R. J. "Collective Bargaining: The Conflict Model as Norm." In W. L. Dee-
    gan and J. F. Gollattscheck (eds.), *Ensuring Effective Governance*. New
    Directions for Community Colleges, no. 49. San Francisco: Jossey-Bass,
    1985. 117 pp. (ED 255 276)

Evans, N. D., and Neagley, R. L. *Planning and Developing Innovative Community
    Colleges*. Englewood Cliffs, N.J.: Prentice-Hall, 1973.

Ewell, P. T. *Implementing Assessment: Some Organizational Issues*. Boulder, Colo.:
    National Center for Higher Education Management Systems, 1987.

Ewens, T. *Think Piece on CBE and Liberal Education*. CUE Project Occasional
    Paper no. 1. Bowling Green, Ohio: Bowling Green State University, 1977.

Executive Committee of the Cooperative Study in General Education. *Coopera-
    tion in General Education*. Washington, D.C.: American Council on Edu-
    cation, 1947.

Falcone, A. J. *Project Pathways: A Longitudinal Investigation of Academic Persis-
    tence*. Interim report. Kansas City, Mo.: Metropolitan Community Col-
    leges, 1990. 23 pp. (ED 325 147)

Farb, D. *Word Play*. New York: Vintage Books, 1993.

Feldman, K. A., and Newcomb, T. N. *The Impact of College on Students*. San
    Francisco: Jossey-Bass, 1969.

Field Research Corporation. *Student Socioeconomic Characteristics, Spring 1984:
    First Phase of Fee-Impact Survey*. San Francisco: Field Research Corpora-
    tion, 1984. 298 pp. (ED 283 567)

Field Research Corporation. *A Survey of Community College Enrollment Conducted as Part of Fee-Impact Study: Second Follow-Up Measure, Spring 1986.* San Francisco: Field Research Corporation, 1986. 365 pp. (ED 284 618)

Finley, C. E. "The Relationship Between Unionization and Job Satisfaction Among Two-Year College Faculty." *Community College Review*, 1991, 19(2), 53–60. (EJ 436 343)

Flanigan, P. K. *California Community Colleges Faculty Role in Shared Governance,* 1994. 30 pp. (ED 373 816)

Fletcher, S. M., and others. "Community Education in Community Colleges: Today and Tomorrow." *Community Services Catalyst,* 1977, 7(1), 10–15.

"Flexibility Sought in Award of Educational Credit." *Chronicle of Higher Education,* Feb. 6, 1978, p. 9.

Florida State Board of Community Colleges. *Florida's Community Colleges: An Information Guide for Trustees.* Tallahassee: Florida State Board of Community Colleges, 1990. 78 pp. (ED 315 123)

Florida State Board of Community Colleges. *Report for Florida Community Colleges: The Fact Book, 1991–92.* Tallahassee: Florida State Board of Community Colleges, 1992. 150 pp. (ED 354 025)

Florida State Department of Education. *General Education in Community Junior Colleges.* Proceedings of Florida Annual Junior College Conference. Tallahassee: Florida State Department of Education, 1959.

Florida State Department of Education. *Report for Florida Community Colleges: The Fact Book.* Tallahassee: Division of Community Colleges, Florida State Department of Education, 1987. 134 pp. (ED 282 618)

Florida State Postsecondary Education Planning Commission. *External Funding for Community College Courses and Programs. Report and Recommendation of the Florida Postsecondary Education Planning Commission. Report 3.* Tallahassee: Florida State Postsecondary Education Planning Commission, 1992. 41 pp. (ED 344 646)

Follow-Up of JCCC Career Program Completers, Class of 1992–93. Overland Park, Kans.: Office of Institutional Research, Johnson County Community College, August 1994.

Ford, M. L. "Penn Valley Community College Learning Skills Laboratory: A Resource Center for Developmental Education." In J. R. Clarke and others, *Developmental Education in Higher Education: Advanced Institutional Developmental Program (AIDP), Two-Year College Consortium.* Vol. 2, No. 5. Washington, D.C.: McManis Associates, 1976. 44 pp. (ED 134 272)

Freedman, L. *Quality in Continuing Education: Principles, Practices, and Standards for Colleges and Universities.* San Francisco: Jossey-Bass, 1987. 195 pp. (ED 294 499).

Friedlander, J. "Coordinating Academic Support Programs with Subject Area Courses." In *Literacy in Community Colleges.* Junior College Resource Review. Los Angeles: ERIC Clearinghouse for Junior Colleges, 1982.

Froh, R., and Muraki, E. "Modifications and Discontinuance of Mastery Learning Strategies." Paper presented at conference of the Mid-Western Education Research Association, Toledo, Ohio, Oct. 1980. 50 pp. (ED 194 178; available in microfiche only)

Frye, J. H. *The Vision of the Public Junior College, 1940–1960.* New York: Greenwood Press, 1992.

Fryer, T. W., Jr., and Lovas, J. C. *Leadership in Governance: Creating Conditions for Successful Decision Making in the Community College.* San Francisco: Jossey-Bass, 1991.

Fujita, E. *Community Perceptions of Hudson County Community College.* Special Report 93.02. Jersey City, N.J.: Office of Planning and Institutional Research, Hudson County Community College, Oct. 1993a. (ED 374 869)

Fujita, E. *An Argument for Providing Developmental Education as Part of the Comprehensive Urban Community College Mission of Hudson County Community College.* Special Report 93.04. Jersey City, N.J.: Office of Planning and Institutional Research, Hudson County Community College, Oct. 1993b. (ED 374 870)

Fullerton, F. E., and Hays, I. *Orientation at the Community College: Sometimes, One Size Does Not Fit All.* Paper presented at the meeting of the Missouri Community College Association, Nov. 1993. (ED 364 274)

Gabe, L. C. *College Preparatory Instruction and Student Persistence at Broward Community College.* Institutional Research Report Abstract RR89–14. Fort Lauderdale, Fla.: Broward Community College, 1989. 8 pp. (ED 309 822)

Gaff, J. G. *General Education Today: A Critical Analysis of Controversies, Practices, and Reforms.* San Francisco: Jossey-Bass, 1983.

Gainous, F., and others. *Kansas Community Colleges Business/Industry Relationships Report, 1985–86 School Year.* Topeka: Kansas State Department of Education, 1987. (ED 276 485)

Gallagher, E. A. "Jordan and Lange: The California Junior College as Protector of Teaching." In *Working Papers in Education,* 94–1. Palo Alto, Calif.: The Hoover Institution, Stanford University, Mar. 1994.

Gardner, D. P., and others. *A Nation at Risk: The Imperative for Educational Reform. An Open Letter to the American People.* A Report to the Nation and the Secretary of Education. Washington, D.C.: National Commission on Excellence in Education, 1983.

Garrett, R. L. "Degree of Centralization of Governance of State Community College Systems in the United States, 1990." *Community College Review,* Summer 1992, *20*(1), 7–13. (EJ 454 855)

Garrett, R.L. "A Profile of State Community College System Characteristics and Their Relationship to Degrees of Centralization." *Community College Review,* Spring 1993, *20*(5), 6–15. (EJ 462 968)

Garrison, R. H. *Junior College Faculty: Issues and Problems, a Preliminary National Appraisal.* Washington, D.C.: American Association of Junior Colleges, 1967. 99 pp. (ED 012 177)

Gay, E. J. "Student Affairs—Alternative Roles." In H. F. Robinson and others, *Expanding Student Mobility: A Challenge for Community Colleges.* Workshop Proceedings. Atlanta: Southern Regional Educational Board, 1977. 71 pp. (ED 164 036)

Gell, R. L., and Armstrong, D. F. *The Graduates, 1976.* Rockville, Md.: Office of Institutional Research, Montgomery College, 1977. 54 pp. (ED 142 252)

Gendron, D, and Cavan, J. J. "Managing a Successful Inmate-Education Program: Why and How?" *Community College Review,* Summer 1990, *18*,(1), 31–38.

Geoghegan, W. H. *What Ever Happened to Instructional Technology?* Norwalk, Conn.: International Business Machines Corporation, 1994.

George, E. W. *Employment of Women Holding Tenure-System Teaching Positions at Kentucky's Universities and Community Colleges Hits Record High 1990.* Staff report. Louisville: Kentucky Commission on Human Rights, 1992. (ED 351 961)

Gianini, P. C., Jr. "Meeting the Challenges of the Information Age: Doing More with Less." Paper presented at the ninth annual Computer Conference of the League for Innovation in the Community College, Orlando, Fla., Oct. 21–24, 1992. (ED 352 079)

Gilder, J., and Rocha, J. "10,000 Cooperative Arrangements Serve 1.5 Million." *Community and Junior College Journal,* 1980, *51*(3), 11–17.

Gillespie, D. A., and Carlson, N. *Trends in Student Aid: 1963 to 1983.* Washington, D.C.: College Entrance Examination Board, 1983. 68 pp. (ED 238 379)

Gittell, M. "Reaching the Hard to Reach: The Challenge of Community-Based Colleges." *Change,* 1985, *17*(4), 51–60.

Gleazer, E. J., Jr. *Responding to the New Spirit of Learning.* Washington, D.C.: American Association of Community and Junior Colleges, 1976. 20 pp. (ED 129 381)

Gleazer, E. J., Jr. *The Community College: Values, Vision, and Vitality.* Washington, D.C.: American Association of Community and Junior Colleges, 1980.

Goddard, J. M., and Polk, C. H. "Community College Trustees: Elect or Appoint?" *AGB Reports,* 1976, *18*(3), 37–40.

Golemon, R. B. *A Survey of Non-Traditional Credit in Texas.* Austin: Texas Association of Junior and Community College Instructional Administrators, 1979. 9 pp. (ED 170 008)

Gottschalk, K. "Can Colleges Deal with High-Risk Community Problems?" *Community College Frontiers,* 1978, *6*(4), 4–11.

Green, K. C. *1994 USC National Survey of Desktop Computing.* Teaching, Technology, and Scholarship Project, Los Angeles, Calif.: University of Southern California, 1994.

Green, K. C., and Eastman, S. *Campus Computing 1992. The EDUCOM-USC Survey of Desktop Computing in Higher Education.* Princeton, N.J.: Interuniversity Communications Council; Los Angeles: Center for Scholarly Technology, University of Southern California, 1993.

Green, T. F. *Predicting the Behavior of the Educational System.* Syracuse, N.Y.: Syracuse University Press, 1980.

Gruber, C. P., and Carriuolo, N. "Construction and Preliminary Validation of a Learner Typology for the Canfield Learning Styles Inventory." *Educational and Psychological Measurement,* Winter 1991, *51*(4), 839–855.

Guskey, T. R., and Pigott, T. D. "Research on Group-Based Mastery Learning Programs: A Meta-Analysis." *Journal of Educational Research,* Mar.–Apr. 1988, *80*(4), 197–216. (EJ 378 253)

Hale, E. "Management Perspectives at the State Level." In A. M. Cohen, F. B. Brawer, and Associates, *Managing Community Colleges: A Handbook for Effective Practice.* San Francisco: Jossey-Bass, 1994.

Hamilton, J. M. *Impact of Georgia's College Preparatory Curriculum on Academic Success at Gainesville College.* Gainesville, Georgia: Gainesville College Office of Institutional Research and Planning, August 1992. (ED 349 040)

Hammond, L. N., and Porter, G. N. *Follow-Up Study of 1981–82 Students: North Carolina Community College System.* Raleigh: Division of Planning and Research Services, North Carolina State Department of Community Colleges, 1984. 19 pp. (ED 259 806)

Hammons, J. "The Department/Division Chairperson: Educational Leader?" *Community and Junior College Journal*, 1984, *54*(3), 3–7.

Hankin, J. N. "Who Bargains with Whom: What's Past Is Prologue." Unpublished paper, Westchester Community College (Valhalla, N.Y.), 1975. 37 pp. (ED 100 476)

Hare, J., and others. *Curriculum Guide for Parent Education Programs (Including Special Sections for Rural Parents, Single Parents, Working Parents, and High Risk Parents)*. Pasco, Wash.: Columbia Basin College Parent Education Program, 1987. (ED 296 105)

Harlacher, E. L., and Gollattscheck, J. F. "Editors' Notes." In E. L. Harlacher and J. F. Gollattscheck (eds.), *Implementing Community-Based Education*. New Directions for Community Colleges, no. 21. San Francisco: Jossey-Bass, 1978.

Harlacher, E. L., and Ireland, J. "Community Services and Continuing Education: An Information Age Necessity." *Community Services Catalyst*, 1988, *18*(1), 3–5.

Harman, D. *Illiteracy: A National Dilemma*. New York: Cambridge Book Company, 1987.

Harper, H., and others. *Advisement and Graduation Information System*. Miami: Miami-Dade Community College, 1981. 34 pp. (ED 197 776)

Harris, N. C., and Grede, J. F. *Career Education in Colleges: A Guide for Planning Two- and Four-Year Occupational Programs for Successful Employment*. San Francisco: Jossey-Bass, 1977.

Harrison, D. J. "Changing Tides and Liberal Studies." *Journal of General Education*, 1987, *38*(4), 262–271.

Hawaii State Board for Vocational Education. *Hawaii Annual Performance Report for Vocational Education: 1992–93 for the Vocational Education State-Administered Program under the Carl D. Perkins Vocational and Applied Technology Education Act of 1990*. Honolulu: Office of the Director for Vocational Education, Hawaii State Board for Vocational Education, Hawaii State Department of Education, 1993. 94 pp. (ED 365 800)

Haynes, F. T., and Polk, C. H. "Choosing a Rationale for Continuing Education." *Community Services Catalyst*, 1991, *16*(4).

Heacock, R. C., and Jenkins, J. L. *Howard Community College Enrollment by Census Tract, Fall 1991*. Research Report no. 81. Columbia, MD: Office of Research and Planning, Howard Community College, 1993.

Head, R. B. *The Academic Performance of Piedmont Virginia Community College Students Transferring to Virginia Public Senior Institutions of Higher Education 1991–1993*. Research Report no. 4093 and PVCC Institutional Brief no.

93–6. Charlottesville, Va.: Office of Institutional Research, Piedmont Virginia Community College, 1993. 29 pp. (ED 360 023)

Heard, F. B. "The Development of a Computerized Curriculum Monitoring System to Ensure Student Success." Ed.D. practicum, Nova University, 1987. 44 pp. (ED 296 750)

Heinrich, J. S. *With Eyes of Equality: Older and Younger Students Learn in a Community College Senior Program.* Paper presented at the annual meeting of the Association for Gerontology in Higher Education, Pittsburgh, Pa., Feb. 28–Mar. 3, 1991. (ED 336 151)

Herder, D. M., and Standridge, L. A. "Continuing Education: Blueprint for Excellence." Unpublished paper, Lansing Community College (Lansing, Mich.), 1980. 14 pp. (ED 187 391)

Herzberg, F., Mausner, B., and Snyderman, B. D. *The Motivation to Work.* New York: Wiley, 1959.

Higginbottom, G. H. *Civic Education in the Community College.* Working Paper Series No. 1–86. Binghamton, N. Y.: Institute for Community College Research, Broome Community College, 1986. 15 pp. (ED 272 256)

Higginbottom, G., and Romano, R. M. *Curriculum Models for General Education.* New Directions for Community Colleges, no. 92. San Francisco: Jossey-Bass, 1995.

Hill, M. D. "Some Factors Affecting the Job Satisfaction of Community College Faculty in Pennsylvania." *Community/Junior College Quarterly of Research and Practice,* 1983, 7(4), 303–317.

Hirsch, E. D., Jr. *Cultural Literacy.* Boston: Houghton Mifflin, 1987.

Hobbs, R. L. *Academic and Developmental Services End of Year Status Report, 1987–88: Shelby State Community College.* Memphis, Tenn.: Shelby State Community College, 1988. (ED 305 111)

Hoerner, J. L., and others. "Professional Development Programs, Leadership, and Institutional Culture: Lessons from a Study of Professional Development Program for Community College Occupational-Technical Faculty." Berkeley: National Center for Research in Vocational Education, 1991. (ED 335 530)

Hollinshead, B. S. "The Community College Program." *Junior College Journal,* 1936, 7, 111–116.

Houston Community College System. *A Comparison of Traditional Vocational Training with a Vocational Training Model Infusing Remedial Academic Skills Training.* Final Report. Houston: Houston Community College System, 1986. 44 pp. (ED 281 034)

Howard, A., and others. *Instructional Computing in the Community Colleges of Washington State*. Olympia: Washington State Board for Community College Education, 1978. 148 pp. (ED 172 891)

Hunter, R., and Sheldon, M. S. *Statewide Longitudinal Study: Report on Academic Year 1979–80. Part 3: Fall Results*. Woodland Hills, Calif.: Los Angeles Pierce College, 1980. 95 pp. (ED 188 714)

Huntington, R. B., and Clagett, C. A. *Increasing Institutional Research Effectiveness and Productivity*. Largo, Md.: Prince George's Community College, 1991.

Hurn, C. J. "The Prospects for Liberal Education: A Sociological Perspective." *Phi Delta Kappan*, 1979, 60(9), 630–633.

Husen, T., and Postlethwaite, T. N. (eds.). *The International Encyclopedia of Education*. (2nd ed.). Vol. 12. Elmsford, N.Y.: Pergamon Press, 1994.

Hutchins, R. M. *The Higher Learning in America*. New Haven, Conn.: Yale University Press, 1937.

Iadevaia, D. G. "A Comparison of Full-Time to Part-Time Faculty and Full-Time to Part-Time Science Faculty in Terms of Student Success at Pima Community College" Ed.D. Major Applied Research Project, Nova University, 1991. 133 pp. (ED 339 403)

Ignash, J. M. *The Scope and Status of English as a Second Language in U.S. Community Colleges*. Unpublished doctoral dissertation, Graduate School of Education, University of California, Los Angeles, 1994.

Illich, I. *Deschooling Society*. New York: Harper and Row, 1972.

Illich, I. *Lima Discourse*. Cuernavaca, Mexico: Centro Intercultural de Documentacion, 1971.

Illinois Community College Board. "Curriculum Enrollment Summary in the Public Community Colleges of Illinois: 1975–76." Unpublished paper, Illinois Community College Board, 1976.

Illinois Community College Board. *Illinois Community College Board Transfer Study: A Five-Year Study of Students Transferring from Illinois Two-Year Colleges to Illinois Senior Colleges/Universities in the Fall of 1979*. Springfield: Illinois Community College Board, 1986. 107 pp. (ED 270 148)

Illinois Community College Board. *Follow-Up Study of Students Who Completed Community College Occupational Programs During Fiscal Years 1983–1985*. Springfield: Illinois Community College Board, 1987. 55 pp. (ED 282 614)

Illinois Community College Board. *Student Enrollment Data and Trends in the Public Community Colleges of Illinois: Fall 1987*. Springfield: Illinois Community College Board, 1988. 50 pp. (ED 291 432)

Illinois Community College Board. *Fall 1990 Salary Survey Report for the Illinois Public Community Colleges*. Springfield: Illinois Community College Board, 1991. (ED 327 243)

Illinois Community College Board. *Student Enrollment Data and Trends in the Public Community Colleges of Illinois, Fall 1991*. Springfield: Illinois Community College Board, 1992. 34 pp. (ED 339 449)

Illinois Community College Board. *Student Enrollments and Completions in the Illinois Community College System, Fiscal Year 1993*. Springfield: Illinois Community College Board, 1994. 75 pp. (ED 365 378)

Jencks, C. *Inequality*. New York: Basic Books, 1972.

Jencks, C., and Riesman, D. *The Academic Revolution*. New York: Doubleday, 1968.

Jensen, A. M. *Multicampus Community Colleges: Twenty Years Later*. San Bernardino, Calif.: San Bernardino Community College District, 1984. 43 pp. (ED 256 413)

Johnson, B. E. *Success Rate Comparisons for DeKalb Developmental Studies Students*. Clarkston, Ga.: DeKalb Area Vocational-Technical School, 1985. 14 pp. (ED 254 297)

Johnson, B. L. "The Extent of the Present General Education Program in the Colleges and Universities of America." Paper presented at the University of Florida, July 1937.

Johnson, B. L. *Vitalizing a College Library*. Chicago: American Library Association, 1939.

Johnson, B. L. *General Education in Action*. Washington, D.C.: American Council on Education, 1952.

Johnson, B. L. *Islands of Innovation Expanding: Changes in the Community College*. Beverly Hills, Calif.: Glencoe Press, 1969.

Johnson, D. C. "Managing Non-Profit Marketing." In R. E. Lahti (ed.), *Managing in a New Era*. New Directions for Community Colleges, no. 28. San Francisco: Jossey-Bass, 1979.

Johnson, D. L. "Reinventing the Community College." *Southern Association of Community, Junior, and Technical Colleges*, Occasional Paper, 1990, 8(1). 6 pp. (EJ 427 565)

Johnson County Community College. *Five-Year Report of JCCC Career Programs, Fall 1988 to Spring 1993*. Overland Park, Kans.: Office of Institutional Research, Johnson County Community College, September 1994.

Kajstura, A., and Keim, M. C. "Reverse Transfer Students in Illinois Community Colleges." *Community College Review*, Fall 1992, 20(2), p. 39–44.

Kangas, J. *San Jose City College Withdrawing Students Study, Math 310, LS 340, ENGL 321: Fall 1990–Spring 1991*. Research Report no. 119. San Jose, Calif.: San Jose/Evergreen Community College District, 1991. 35 pp. (ED 348 097)

Kaplin, W. A. *The Law of Higher Education: A Comprehensive Guide to Legal Implications of Administrative Decision Making*. (2nd ed.). San Francisco: Jossey-Bass, 1985.

Kaprelian, N., and Perona, J. "Gateway Technical Institute Competency Based Education: Case Study of College-Wide Instructional Improvement." Paper presented at annual convention of the American Association of Community and Junior Colleges, Washington, D.C., Apr. 20–22, 1981. 11 pp. (ED 203 954)

Karabel, J. "Community Colleges and Social Stratification." *Harvard Educational Review*, 1972, *41*, 521–562.

Karabel, J. "Community Colleges and Social Stratification in the 1980s." In L. S. Zwerling (ed.), *The Community College and Its Critics*. New Directions for Community Colleges, no. 54. San Francisco: Jossey-Bass, 1986.

Keener, B. J., Ryan, G. J., and Smith, N. J. "Paying Attention Pays Off: How to Market Resource Development." *Community, Technical and Junior College Journal*, 1991, *62*(1), 34–37. (ED 364 643)

Kemerer, F. R., and Baldridge, J. V. *Unions on Campus: A National Study of the Consequences of Faculty Bargaining*. San Francisco: Jossey-Bass, 1975.

Kester, D. L. "Is Micro-Computer Assisted Basic Skills Instruction Good for Black, Disadvantaged Community College Students from Watts and Similar Communities? A Preliminary Fall Semester 1981–82 Mini Audit Report Suggests Caution." Paper presented at the International School Psychology Colloquium, Stockholm, Aug. 1–6, 1982. 14 pp. (ED 219 111)

King, T. C. *North Carolina Community College System Annual Data Plan, 1992–93*. Raleigh: North Carolina Department of Community Colleges, 1993.

Kinnick, M. K., and Kempner, K. "Beyond the 'Front Door' Access: Attaining the Bachelor's Degree." *Research in Higher Education*, 1988, *29*(4), 299–318.

Kintzer, F. C. *Organization and Leadership of Two-Year Colleges: Preparing for the Eighties*. Gainesville: Institute of Higher Education, University of Florida, 1980a.

Kintzer, F. C. *Proposition 13: Implications for Community Colleges*. Topical Paper no. 72. Los Angeles: ERIC Clearinghouse for Junior Colleges, 1980b. 39 pp. (ED 188 711)

Kintzer, F. C., Jensen, A., and Hansen, J. *The Multi-Institution Junior College District*. Horizons Issue Monograph Series. Los Angeles: ERIC Clearinghouse for Junior Colleges; Washington, D.C.: American Association of Junior Colleges, 1969. 64 pp. (ED 030 415)

Kintzer, F. C., and Wattenbarger, J. L. *The Articulation/Transfer Phenomenon: Patterns and Directions*. Horizons Issue Monograph Series. Washington, D.C.: Council of Universities and Colleges, American Association of Community and Junior Colleges, 1985. 85 pp. (ED 257 539)

Kirsch, I. S., and Jungeblut, A. *Literacy: Profiles of America's Young Adults*. Princeton, N.J.: National Assessment of Education Progress, 1986. 79 pp. (ED 275 692).

Kirsch, I. S., Jugeblut, A., Jenkins, L., and Kolstad, A. *Adult Literacy in America: A First Look at the Results of the National Adult Literacy Survey*. Washington, D.C.: National Center for Education Statistics, U.S. Department of Education, September 1993.

Knapp, L. G., and others. *Trends in Student Aid: 1983 to 1993. Update*. New York: College Board, 1993. 20 pp. (ED 362 098)

Knapp, M. S. "Factors Contributing to the Development of Institutional Research and Planning Units in Community Colleges: A Review of the Empirical Evidence." Paper presented at annual meeting of the American Educational Research Association, Special Interest Group on Community and Junior College Research, San Francisco, Apr. 1979. 18 pp. (ED 168 663)

Koos, L. V. *The Junior College*. (2 vols.). Minneapolis: University of Minnesota Press, 1924.

Kulik, C.J.C., and others. "Effectiveness of Mastery Learning Programs: A Meta-Analysis." *Review of Educational Research*, 1990, 60(2), 265–299. (EJ 415 887)

Kuttner, B. "The Declining Middle." *Atlantic*, 1983, 252(1), 60–64, 66–67, 69–72.

Lander, V. L. "The Significance of Structure in Arizona Community College Districts: A Limited Study." Unpublished paper, Tucson, Ariz., 1977. 83 pp. (ED 285 043)

Landsburg, D., and Witt, S. "Writing Across the Curriculum: One Small Step." *Innovation Abstracts*, 1984, 6(entire issue 13).

Lange, A. F. *The Lange Book: The Collected Writings of a Great Educational Philosopher*. San Francisco: The Trade Publishing Company, 1927.

Lanham, R. A. *The Electronic World: Democracy, Technology and the Arts*. Chicago: The University of Chicago Press, 1993.

Lawson, J. K. *Instructors as Investors: A Collegial Conspiracy to Improve Classroom Instruction*. Paper presented at the annual International Conference for

Community College Chairs, Deans, and Other Instructional Leaders, Phoenix, Ariz., 1994. (ED 369 464)

Lee, B. S. *Follow-Up of Occupational Education Students: Los Rios Community College District, Spring 1983.* Sacramento, Calif.: Los Rios Community College District, 1984. 77 pp. (ED 241 099)

Lee, B., and others. *Limiting Access by Degrees: Student Profiles Pre and Post the Fees.* Sacramento: Calif.: Los Rios Community College District, 1994.

Lestina, R., and Curry, B. A. "Alternative Education/Alternative Revenue. A. Contract Training: Public and Private Sector Models." In J. L. Catanzaro and A. D. Arnold (eds.), *Alternative Funding Sources.* New Directions for Community Colleges, no. 68. San Francisco: Jossey-Bass, 1989.

Lever, J. C. *Distance Education Resource Guide.* Laguna Hills: California League for Innovation in the Community College, 1992. (ED 356 022)

Levine, D. O. *The American College and the Culture of Aspiration, 1915–1940.* Ithaca, N.Y.: Cornell University Press, 1986.

Lewis, G., and Merisotis, J. P. *Trends in Student Aid: 1980 to 1987: Update.* Washington, D.C.: College Entrance Examination Board, 1987. 15 pp. (ED 288 466)

Lieberman, J. E. (ed.). *Collaborating with High Schools.* New Directions for Community Colleges, no. 63. San Francisco: Jossey-Bass, 1988.

Lieberman, J. E. "The LaGuardia-Vassar Candidates." *Educational Record, 72*(2), 1991, 43–45.

Lindahl, D. G. "Giving Students Credit for What They Already Know." *VocEd,* 1982, *57*(1), 44–45.

Lockett, C. R., Jr. *An Analysis of Current Problems and Procedures Relating to Articulation Between Public Secondary Schools in Duval and Nassau Counties and Florida Junior College.* Final Report. Jacksonville: Florida Junior College, 1981. 76 pp. (ED 230 246)

Lombardi, J. *Managing Finances in Community Colleges.* San Francisco: Jossey-Bass, 1973.

Lombardi, J. *The Duties and Responsibilities of the Department/Division Chairman in Community Colleges.* ERIC Clearinghouse for Junior Colleges, 1974. 21 pp. (ED 089 811)

Lombardi, J. *Riding the Wave of New Enrollments.* Topical Paper no. 50. Los Angeles: ERIC Clearinghouse for Junior Colleges, 1975. 58 pp. (ED 107 326)

Lombardi, J. *No or Low Tuition: A Lost Cause.* Topical Paper no. 58. Los Angeles: ERIC Clearinghouse for Junior Colleges, 1976. 46 pp. (ED 129 353)

Lombardi, J. *Changing Administrative Relations Under Collective Bargaining.* Junior College Resource Review. Los Angeles: ERIC Clearinghouse for Junior Colleges, 1979. 8 pp. (ED 170 015)

London, H. B. *The Culture of a Community College.* New York: Praeger, 1978.

Long T. L., and Pedersen, C. "Critical Thinking About Literature Through Computer Networking." Paper presented at the annual Computer Conference of the League for Innovation in the Community College, Orlando, Fla., Oct. 21–24, 1992. (ED 358 875)

"A Look at Key Federal Programs for Two-Year Colleges." *Community College Week,* Aug. 16, 1993.

Lorenzo, A. L. "Anticipating Our Future Purpose." *Community, Technical, and Junior College Journal,* 1991, 61(4), 42–45.

Lovelace, B. E., and LaBrecque, S. V. *Assessment of Competency-Based Instruction. Final Report. Volumes I–II.* Denton: University of North Texas, 1993a. 542 pp. (ED 366 772)

Lovelace, B. E., and LaBrecque, S. V. *Assessment of Competency-Based Instruction. Summary Report.* Denton: University of North Texas, 1993b. (ED 366 771)

Lucas, J. A. *Follow-Up Study of 1986 Harper Career Alumni.* Research Report Series, Vol. 16, No. 9. Palatine, Ill.: Office of Planning and Research, William Rainey Harper College, 1988. 46 pp. (ED 291 456)

Lucas, J. A., and Meltesen, C. *Longitudinal Study of Harper College Students, 1979–1989.* Palatine, Ill.: Office of Planning and Research, William Rainey Harper College, 1991a, 10(3). 23 pp. (ED 349 044)

Lucas, J. A., and Meltesen, C. *Study of Students Who Withdrew from Courses, Summer 1988–Spring 1990.* Volume 29, No. 5. Palatine, Ill.: Office of Planning and Research, William Rainey Harper College, 1991b. 36 pp. (ED 328 309)

Lucas, J., and Meltesen, C. *Follow-up Study of 1990 Harper College Career Alumni.* Vol. 20, No. 1. Palatine, Ill.: Office of Planning and Research, William Rainey Harper College, 1992. (ED 348 127)

Lucas, J. A., Pankanin, J., and Nejman, M. *Evaluation of Student Activities Through Surveys of Harper Students and Employees.* Vol. 21, No. 6. Palatine, Ill.: Office of Planning and Research, William Rainey Harper College, Feb. 1993. (ED 364 289)

Lukenbill, J. D., and McCabe, R. H. *General Education in a Changing Society: General Education Program, Basic Skills Requirements, Standards of Academic Progress at Miami-Dade Community College.* Miami, Fla.: Office of Institutional Research, Miami-Dade Community College, 1978. 98 pp. (ED 158 812)

Lundgren, C. A. "A Comparison of the Effects of Programmed Instruction and Computer-Assisted Instruction on Computer Achievement in English Grammar." *Delta Pi Epsilon Journal*, 1985, *27*(1), 1–9.

Luskin, B. J., and Small, J. "The Need to Change and the Need to Stay the Same." *Community and Junior College Journal*, 1980–81, *51*(4), 24–28.

Lynch, R., and others. *Community College Involvement in Contract Training and Other Economic Development Activities*. Washington, D.C.: American Association of Community and Junior Colleges, 1991. (ED 339 434)

Lyons, G. "The Higher Illiteracy." *Harper's*, 1976, *253*(1516), 33–40.

Maas, Rao, Taylor, and Associates. "Where Are We Going?" Unpublished paper. Riverside, Calif., 1994.

MacDonald, R. B. "Evaluation of an Alternative Solution for the Assessment and Retention of High-Risk College Students." Paper presented at the annual meeting of the American Educational Research Association, Washington, D.C., Apr. 20–24, 1987. 40 pp. (ED 316 302)

MacDougall, P. R., and Friedlander, J. (eds). *Models for Conducting Institutional Research*. New Directions for Community Colleges, no. 72. San Francisco: Jossey-Bass, 1990.

McGuire, K. B. *State of the Art in Community-Based Education in the American Community College*. Washington, D.C.: American Association of Community and Junior Colleges, 1988. 77 pp (ED 293 583)

McIntyre, J. F. "Individualized Mastery, the Adaptable, Efficient, and Economical Link to the Future." *Education-Canada*, Winter 1991, *31*(4), 36–40, 47. (EJ 438 282)

McKeachie, W. J. "Research on Teaching at the College and University Level." In N. Gage (ed.), *Handbook of Research on Teaching*. Skokie, Ill.: Rand McNally, 1963.

McLean, C. E. *TNCC Student Opinion Survey*. Hampton, Va.: Office of Institutional Research, Thomas Nelson Community College, 1986. 22 pp. (ED 276 479)

Mann, C. M. *Credit for Lifelong Learning*. (4th ed.). Dayton, Ohio: Sinclair Community College, 1993. (ED 361 039)

Marcotte, J. "The Impact of Developmental Education on the Graduation Rate of Students with Low Combined Differential Aptitude Test Scores." Unpublished report, 1986. 10 pp. (ED 271 172)

Marlowe, M., and others. "Adult Basic Skills Instructor Training and Experiential Learning Theory." *Adult Basic Education*, Fall 1991, *1*(3), 155–167. (EJ 466 416)

Marrison, D. L., and Frick, M. J. "The Effect of Agricultural Students' Learning Styles on Academic Achievement and Their Perceptions of Two Methods of Instruction." *Journal of Agricultural Education*, 1994, *35*(1), 26–30. (EJ 480 585)

Martens, K. J. *Project Priority, 1974–1975: An ESEA Funded Project. Final Report.* Albany: Two Year College Student Development Center, State University of New York, 1975. 30 pp. (ED 139 475)

Martinez, A., and Gonis, M. *Continuing Application for Milwaukee Area Technical College High School Equivalency Program, FY 1992–93.* Milwaukee, Wis.: Milwaukee Area Technical College, 1992. (ED 354 959)

Martorana, S. V., and Piland, W. E. "Promises and Pitfalls in Serving Organized Community-Based Group Interests." In S. V. Martorana and W. E. Piland (eds.), *Designing Programs for Community Groups.* New Directions for Community Colleges, no. 45. San Francisco: Jossey-Bass, 1984.

Maryland State Board for Community Colleges. *Statewide Master Plan for Community Colleges in Maryland, Fiscal Years 1978–1987.* Annapolis: Maryland State Board for Community Colleges, 1977. 227 pp. (ED 139 454)

Maryland State Board for Community Colleges. *The Role of Community Colleges in Preparing Students for Transfer to Four-Year Colleges and Universities: The Maryland Experience.* Annapolis: Maryland State Board for Community Colleges, 1983. 27 pp. (ED 230 255)

Maryland State Board for Community Colleges. *Blueprint for Quality: Final Report of the Committee on the Future of Maryland Community Colleges.* Annapolis: Maryland State Board for Community Colleges, 1986. 145 pp. (ED 275 367)

Maryland State Board for Community Colleges. *State Plan for Community Colleges in Maryland: Interim Report.* Annapolis: Maryland State Board for Community Colleges, 1987. 128 pp. (ED 276 486)

Maryland State Board for Community Colleges. *Maryland Community Colleges: 1987 Program Evaluations.* Annapolis: Maryland State Board for Community Colleges, 1988. 178 pp. (ED 285 699)

Mattice, N. J., and Richardson, R. C. *College of the Canyons Survey of Teaching Practices, Spring 1993.* Valencia, Calif.: College of the Canyons, Office of Institutional Development, 1993. 32 pp. (ED 357 776)

Mayhew, L. B. (ed.) *General Education: An Account and Appraisal.* New York: McGraw-Hill, 1960.

Medsker, L. L. *The Junior College: Progress and Prospect.* New York: McGraw-Hill, 1960.

Medsker, L. L., and Tillery, D. *Breaking the Access Barriers: A Profile of Two-Year Colleges*. New York: McGraw-Hill, 1971.

Meier, T. *Washington Community College Factbook. Addendum A: Student Enrollments, Academic Year 1978–79*. Olympia: Washington State Board for Community College Education, 1980. 123 pp. (ED 184 616)

Mellander, G. A., and Hubbard, G. *Drug Abuse: A Community College Response*. Saratoga, Calif.: West Valley-Mission Community College District, 1990. (ED 319 419)

Merren, J. *Curriculum Procedures in Metropolitan Multicampus Community Colleges*, 1992. 22 pp. (ED 350 041)

Miami-Dade Community College. *RSVP: Feedback Program for Individualized Analysis of Writing. Manual for Faculty Users. Part 1: Analyzing Students' Writing*. Miami: Miami-Dade Community College, 1979. 77 pp. (ED 190 167)

Miami-Dade Community College. *Project SYNERGY: Software Support for Underprepared Students. Year Two Report*. Miami, Fla.: Miami-Dade College, Division of Educational Technologies, 1992. 99 pp. (ED 345 804)

Michigan State Department of Education. *Report on the Acceptance of Vocational Education Courses for Admission Purposes at Michigan's Community Colleges and Universities*. Lansing, Mich.: Michigan State Board of Education, 1990. 61 pp. (ED 333 934)

Michigan State Department of Education. *Michigan Community and Junior Colleges: Enrollment Data Profile, 1988–89/1989–90*. Lansing: Community College Services Unit, Michigan State Department of Education, 1991. 263 pp. (ED 333 935)

Middleton, L. "Emphasis on Standards at Miami-Dade Leads to 8,000 Dismissals and Suspensions in Three Years." *Chronicle of Higher Education*, Feb. 3, 1981, pp. A3–A4.

Miller, D. J. "Analysis of Professional Development Activities of Iowa Community College Faculty." Unpublished Master of Science dissertation, Iowa State University, 1985. 121 pp. (ED 260 766)

Miller, R. I. (ed.). *Evaluating Major Components of Two-Year Colleges*. Washington, D.C.: College and University Personnel Association, 1988.

Missimer, C. "Blocking Assures Writing Across the Curriculum." *Inside English*, Oct. 1985, *13*(1), 3. (ED 288 575)

Mississippi State Board for Community and Junior Colleges. *Fall Enrollment Report, 1993. Mississippi Public Community and Junior Colleges*. Jackson: Mississippi State Board for Community and Junior Colleges, 1993. 35 pp. (ED 366 406)

Monroe, C. R. *Profile of the Community College: A Handbook*. San Francisco: Jossey-Bass, 1972.

Mooney, C. J. "Professors Are Upbeat About Profession but Uneasy About Students, Standards." *Chronicle of Higher Education*, Nov. 8, 1989, 36(10), A1, 18–21. (ED 399 291)

Moriarty, D. F. "The President's Office." In A. M. Cohen, F. B. Brawer, and Associates, *Managing Community Colleges: A Handbook for Effective Practice*. San Francisco: Jossey-Bass, 1994.

Moyer, D. F. *A Description of the Senior College Transfer Destinations of Lehigh County Community College Students from August 1986 to July 1991 with Mean Cumulative Grade Point Average Comparison from 26 Transfer Institutions in Pennsylvania*. Schnecksville, Pa.: Lehigh County Community College, 1992. 48 pp. (ED 349 039)

Mullis, I.V.S., and others. *NAEP 1992 Trends in Academic Progress Achievement*. Report no. 23-TR01. Washington, D.C.: National Center for Education Statistics, July 1994. 31 pp.

Mundt, J. C. "State Vs. Local Control: Reality and Myth over Concern for Local Autonomy." In S. F. Charles (ed.), *Balancing State and Local Control*. New Directions for Community Colleges, no. 23. San Francisco: Jossey-Bass, 1978.

Murray, J. P. "The Genesis of the Community College." *Community Review*, 1988–89, 9(1–2), 25–34.

Myran, G. A. "Antecedents: Evolution of the Community-Based College." In E. L. Harlacher and J. F. Gollattscheck (eds.), *Implementing Community-Based Education*. New Directions for Community Colleges, no. 21. San Francisco: Jossey-Bass, 1969. (ED 037 202)

National Center for Education Statistics. *Opening (Fall) Enrollments in Higher Education*. Washington, D.C.: U.S. Department of Education, 1963–1975 (published annually).

National Center for Education Statistics. *Digest of Education Statistics*. Washington, D.C.: U.S. Department of Education, 1970.

National Center for Education Statistics. *Digest of Education Statistics*. Washington, D.C.: U.S. Department of Education, 1980.

National Center for Education Statistics. *Scholarship and Fellowship Expenditures: OERI Historical Report*. Washington, D.C.: U.S. Department of Education, 1986. 6 pp. (ED 282 483)

National Center for Education Statistics. *College and University Libraries*. Washington, D.C.: U.S. Department of Education, 1987.

National Center for Education Statistics. *Directory of Postsecondary Institutions, 1989–90*. Vol. 1. Washington, D.C.: U.S. Department of Education, 1990.

National Center for Education Statistics. *National Survey of Postsecondary Faculty.* Washington, D.C.: U.S. Department of Education, 1991.

National Center for Educational Statistics. *Historical Trends: State Education Facts, 1969–1989.* Washington, D.C.: U.S. Department of Education, 1992a.

National Center for Education Statistics. *IPEDS Opening Fall Enrollment 1992.* Washington, D.C.: U.S. Department of Education, 1992b.

National Center for Education Statistics. *Overview and Inventory for State Requirements for School Coursework and Attendance.* Washington, D.C.: U.S. Department of Education, June 1992c.

National Center for Education Statistics. *Digest of Education Statistics.* Washington, D.C.: U.S. Department of Education, Oct. 1993.

National Center for Education Statistics. *1993 National Study of Postsecondary Faculty.* Washington, D.C.: U.S. Department of Education, 1994a.

National Center for Education Statistics. *Academic Libraries: 1992.* Washington, D.C.: U.S. Department of Education, Nov. 1994b.

National Center for Education Statistics. *Adult Education: Employment-Related Training.* Washington, D.C.: U.S. Department of Education, 1994c.

National Center for Education Statistics. *Basic Student Charges at Postsecondary Institutions: Academic Year 1993–94.* Washington, D.C.: U.S. Department of Education, 1994d.

National Center for Education Statistics. *Characteristics of the Nation's Postsecondary Institutions: Academic Year 1993–94.* Washington, D.C.: U.S. Department of Education, 1994e.

National Center for Education Statistics. *The Condition of Education, 1994.* Washington, D.C.: U.S. Department of Education, 1994f.

National Center for Education Statistics. *Current Funds, Revenues, and Expenditures of Institutions of Higher Education: Fiscal Years 1984 Through 1992.* Washington, D.C.: U.S. Department of Education, 1994g.

National Center for Education Statistics. *Degrees and Other Awards Conferred by Institutions of Higher Education: 1991–92.* Washington, D.C.: Office of Educational Research and Improvement, U.S. Department of Education, 1994h.

National Center for Education Statistics. *Descriptive Summary of 1989–90 Beginning Postsecondary Students: Two Years Later.* U.S. Department of Education, 1994i.

National Center for Education Statistics. *Digest of Education Statistics 1994.* Washington, D.C.: U.S. Department of Education, 1994j.

National Center for Education Statistics. *Dropout Rates in the United States: 1993*. Washington, D.C.: U.S. Department of Education, 1994k.

National Center for Education Statistics. *Faculty and Instructional Staff: Who Are They and What Do They Do?* Washington, D.C.: U.S. Department of Education, 1994l.

National Center for Education Statistics. *Vocational Education in G-7 Countries: Profiles and Data*. Washington, D.C.: U.S. Department of Education, 1994m.

National Center for Education Statistics. *Projections of Education Statistics to 2005*. Washington, D.C.: U.S. Department of Education, 1995a.

National Center for Education Statistics. *Degrees and Other Awards Conferred by Institutions of Higher Education: 1991–93*. Washington, D.C.: U.S. Department of Education, 1995b.

National Center for Education Statistics. *National Postsecondary Student Aid Study: Estimates of Student Financial Aid: 1992–93*. Washington, D.C.: U.S. Department of Education, 1995c.

National Center for the Study of Collective Bargaining in Higher Education and the Professions. *Directory of Faculty Contracts and Bargaining Agents in Institutions of Higher Education*. Vols. 1–20. New York: National Center for the Study of Collective Bargaining in Higher Education and the Professions, 1974–1994.

National Center for the Study of Collective Bargaining in Higher Education and the Professions. *Newsletter*, vol. 23, no. 2. New York: School of Public Affairs, Bernard M. Baruch College, City University of New York, 1995.

National Society for the Study of Education. *General Education in the American College*. Bloomington, Ind.: National Society for the Study of Education, 1939.

Nelson, J. E. "Student Aid at the Two-Year College: Who Gets the Money?" Paper presented at annual convention of the American Association of Community and Junior Colleges, Washington, D.C., Mar. 1976. 12 pp. (ED 124 223)

Nespoli, L. A., and Radcliffe, S. K. *Student Evaluation of College Services*. Research Report no. 29. Columbia, Md.: Office of Research and Planning, Howard Community College, 1982. 75 pp. (ED 229 058)

New Hampshire State Department of Postsecondary Vocational-Technical Education. *Graduate Placement Report, Annual Summary: Class of 1986, New Hampshire Vocational-Technical Colleges and New Hampshire Technical Institute*. Concord: New Hampshire State Department of Postsecondary Vocational-Technical Education, 1988. 14 pp. (ED 292 483)

New Jersey Advisory Committee to the College Outcomes Evaluation Program. *Report to the New Jersey Board of Higher Education from the Advisory Committee to the College Outcomes Evaluation Program.* Trenton: New Jersey Board of Higher Education, 1987. (ED 299 883)

New Jersey Basic Skills Council. *New Jersey College Basic Skills Placement Testing, Fall 1991.* Trenton: Basic Skills Assessment Program, New Jersey Department of Higher Education, 1991. 120 pp. (ED 344 519)

New Jersey Department of Higher Education. *Fall 1993 Basic Skills Test Results: Update and Special Analysis.* Chancellor's Report, April 1994.

Nickens, J. M. "Who Takes Community Service Courses and Why." *Community/Junior College Research Quarterly,* 1977, *2*(1), 11–19.

Noeth, R. J., and Hanson, G. "Research Report: Occupational Programs Do the Job." *Community and Junior College Journal,* 1976, *47*(3), 28–30.

North Carolina State Department of Community Colleges. *A Matter of Facts: The North Carolina Community College System Fact Book.* Raleigh: Division of Planning and Research Services, North Carolina State Department of Community Colleges, 1993a. 148 pp. (ED 361 034)

North Carolina State Department of Community Colleges. *Student Enrollment, Full-Time Equivalents (FTE), Staff/Faculty Information, 1992–93. Annual Statistical Report, Volume 28.* Raleigh: North Carolina State Department of Community Colleges, Division of Planning and Research Services, 1993b. 257 pp. (ED 362 225)

Nussbaum, T. J., and others. *Encouraging Greater Student Participation in Governance.* Sacramento: Office of the Chancellor, California Community Colleges, 1990. 21 pp. (ED 322 955)

O'Banion, T. *New Directions in Community College Student Personnel Programs.* Student Personnel Series, No. 15. Washington, D.C.: American College Personnel Association, 1971.

Oklahoma State Regents for Higher Education. *Student Competencies for College Success.* Oklahoma City: Oklahoma State Regents for Higher Education, 1993a. (ED 365 252)

Oklahoma State Regents for Higher Education. *Student Remediation Study.* Oklahoma City: Oklahoma State Regents for Higher Education, 1993b. 19 pp. (ED 364 297)

Olson, M. A., and others. *Attitudes Toward Videodisc Technology in the Dallas County Community College District.* Dallas: Dallas County Community College District, 1992. (ED 354 953)

Orfield, G., and Paul, F. G. *State Higher Education Systems and College Competition.* Final report to the Ford Foundation, 1992. 121 pp. (ED 354 041)

Osborn, R. "Part-Time Faculty Development: What Do We Know and What Can We Use?" *Community Services Catalyst*, Spring 1990, *20*(2), 17–21. (EJ 417 088)

Ottinger, C. A. (comp.). *Fact Book on Higher Education*. Washington, D.C.: American Council on Education, 1987. 212 pp. (ED 284 472)

Pabst, D. L. "Community Colleges Exhibit New Spirit of Fund-Raising Aggressiveness." *Trustee Quarterly*, Winter 1989, pp. 5–9.

Palmer, J. "The Characteristics and Educational Objectives of Students Serviced by Community College Vocational Curricula." Unpublished doctoral dissertation, Graduate School of Education, University of California, Los Angeles, 1987a.

Palmer, J. *Community, Technical, and Junior Colleges: A Summary of Selected National Data*. Washington, D.C.: American Association of Community and Junior Colleges, 1987b. 20 pp. (ED 292 507)

Palmer, J. "Fall 1987 Enrollment: A Preliminary Analysis." *Community, Technical, and Junior College Journal*, 1988, *58*(5), 62–63.

Parilla, R. E. *Gladly Would They Learn and Gladly Teach*. Southern Association of Community and Junior Colleges, 1986. 6 pp. (ED 263 949)

Park, R. "Proffered Advice: Three Presidential Reports." *UCLA Educator*, 1977, *19*(3), 53–59.

Parkman, F. "The Tale of the Ripe Scholar." *Nation*, 1869, *9*, 559–560.

Parnell, D. *Associate Degree Preferred*. Washington, D.C.: American Association of Community and Junior Colleges, 1985. 90 pp. (ED 255 266)

Pascarella, E. T., and Terenzini, P. T. *How College Affects Students: Findings and Insights from Twenty Years of Research*. San Francisco: Jossey-Bass, 1991.

Pedersen, R. "State Government and the Junior College, 1901–1946." *Community College Review*, 1987, *14*(4), pp. 48–52.

Pedersen, R. "Small Business and the Early Public Junior College." *Community, Technical, and Junior College Journal*, 1988, *59*(1), pp. 44–46.

Pedersen, R. "Workforce Education Too Narrowly Focused." *Community College Week*, March 1994, p. 4.

Penisten, J. "The Effects of Computer Assisted Instruction in a Community College Learning Lab." Paper presented at the annual meeting of the Association for the Study of Higher Education, San Antonio, Tex., Feb. 20–23, 1981. 48 pp. (ED 268 900)

Percy, W. *The Moviegoer*. New York: Avon Books, 1980.

Person, R. J. "Community College Learning Resource Center Cooperative Efforts: A National Study." *Community and Junior College Libraries*, 1984, *3*(20), 53–64.

Peterson, M. W., and Mets, L. A. "An Evolutionary Perspective on Academic Governance, Management, and Leadership." In M. W. Peterson and L. A. Mets (eds.), *Key Resources on Higher Education Governance, Management, and Leadership: A Guide to the Literature*. San Francisco: Jossey-Bass, 1987.

Peterson's Guide to Two-Year Colleges, 1995. Princeton, N.J.: Peterson's, 1994.

Phillippe, K. "Student Financial Aid in Community Colleges." *AACC Research and Data*, November 1994.

Phillippe, K. "More Community College Enrollment Facts." *AACC Research and Data*, 1995a.

Phillippe, K. (ed.). *National Profile of Community Colleges: Trends and Statistics*. Washington, D.C.: American Association of Community Colleges, 1995b.

Piland, W. E. "The Governing Board." In A. M. Cohen, F. B. Brawer, and Associates, *Managing Community Colleges: A Handbook for Effective Practice*. San Francisco: Jossey-Bass, 1994.

Pincus, F. L. "The False Promise of Community Colleges: Class Conflict and Vocational Education." *Harvard Educational Review*, 1980, *50*(3), 332–361.

Pincus, F. L. "How Critics View the Community College's Role in the Twenty-First Century." In G. Baker (ed.), *A Handbook on the Community College in America*. Westport, Conn.: Greenwood Press, 1994.

Platt, G. M. *Necessary but Insufficient: The Learning Center's 1992–93 Annual Report*. Levelland, Tex.: South Plains College Learning Center, 1993. 42 pp. (ED 361 011)

Plucker, F. E. "A Developmental Model for the Community/Junior College." *Community College Review*, 1987, *15*(3), 26–32.

Pokrass, R. J., and others. "Enhancing Student Success Through the Use of Interactive Videodisc Technology." Paper presented at the annual Computer Conference of the League for Innovation in the Community College, Orlando, Fla., Oct. 21–24, 1992. (ED 350 043)

Portolan, J. S. "Developing Statewide Organization and Exploring a Redefined Role for Instructional Administrators in California Community Colleges." Unpublished doctoral dissertation, Graduate School of Education, University of California, Los Angeles, 1992.

Potter, G. E. "The Law and the Board." In V. Dziuba and W. Meardy (eds.), *Enhancing Trustee Effectiveness*. New Directions for Community Colleges, no. 15. San Francisco: Jossey-Bass, 1976.

Prager, C. "Learning Centers for the 1990s." *ERIC Digest*. Los Angeles: ERIC Clearinghouse for Junior Colleges, Aug. 1991. 2 pp.

Preston D. L. "Interfacing Two-Year and Four-Year Transcripts for Transfer Students." Paper presented at the annual Forum of the Association for Institutional Research, Chicago, May 16–19, 1993. 31 pp. (ED 360 017)

Preston, J. *Writing Across the Curriculum. Some Questions and Answers and a Series of Eleven Writing Projects for Instructors of the General Education Core Courses: Energy in the Natural Environment; Humanities; Individual in Transition; [and] Social Environment.* Miami, Fla.: Miami-Dade Community College, South Campus, 1982. 114 pp. (ED 256 414)

Price, E. C. *Learning From the Past as We Aim for the Future Through Identifying Students' Learning Styles to Improve Teaching/Learning Experiences in College Students.* 1991. (ED 364 502)

Purdy, L. M. "A Case Study of Acceptance and Rejection of Innovation by Faculty in a Community College." Unpublished doctoral dissertation, Graduate School of Education, University of California, Los Angeles, 1973.

Quanty, M. *Initial Job Placement for JCCC Career Students, Classes of 1973–1976.* Overland Park, Kans.: Office of Institutional Research, Johnson County Community College, 1977. 61 pp. (ED 144 666)

Ravitch, D. "Curriculum in Crisis: Connections Between Past and Present." In J. H. Burzell (ed.), *Challenge to American Schools: The Case for Standards and Values.* New York: Oxford University Press, 1985.

Renz, F. J. "Study Examining the Issues of Faculty Evaluation." Unpublished report, 1984. 12 pp. (ED 243 559)

Richardson, R. C., Jr. *Reforming College Governance.* New Directions for Community Colleges, no. 10. San Francisco: Jossey-Bass, 1975.

Richardson, R. C., Jr., and Bender, L. W. *Fostering Minority Access and Achievement in Higher Education: The Role of Urban Community Colleges and Universities.* San Francisco: Jossey-Bass, 1987.

Richardson, R. C., Jr., Fisk, E. C., and Okun, M. A. *Literacy in the Open-Access College.* San Francisco: Jossey-Bass, 1983.

Richardson, R. C., Jr., and Leslie, L. L. *The Impossible Dream? Financing Community College's Evolving Mission.* Horizons Issue, Monograph Series. Washington, D.C.: American Association of Community and Junior Colleges, 1980. 58 pp. (ED 197 783)

Richardson, R. C., Jr., and Moore, W. "Faculty Development and Evaluation in Texas Community Colleges." *Community/Junior College Quarterly of Research and Practice,* 1987, *11*(1), 33–37.

Richardson, R. C., Jr., and de los Santos, A. (eds.). *Review of Higher Education,* 1988, *11*(4). (Special issue on minority access and achievement.)

Richardson, R. C., Jr., and Wolverton, M. "Leadership Strategies." In A. M. Cohen, F. B. Brawer, and Associates, *Managing Community Colleges: A Handbook for Effective Practice*. San Francisco: Jossey-Bass, 1994.

Riley, M. *The Community College General Academic Assessment: Combined Districts, 1983–84*. Los Angeles: Center for the Study of Community Colleges, 1984. 59 pp. (ED 246 959)

Roberts, D. Y. "Personalizing Learning Processes." Paper presented at the annual meeting of the American Association of Community and Junior Colleges, Seattle, Apr. 13–16, 1975. 9 pp. (ED 115 322)

Robison, S. "Development of the Two-Year College: Foundation and Techniques of Success." In W. H. Sharron, Jr. (ed.), *The Community College Foundation*. Washington, D.C.: National Council for Resource Development, 1982.

Rothschild, J., and Piland, W. E. "Intercorrelates of Postsecondary Students' Learning Styles and Personality Traits." *Community College Journal of Research and Practice*, Mar.–Apr. 1994, *18*(2), 177–188. (EJ 479 907)

Rotundo, B. *Project Priority: Occupational Emphasis, 1975–1976— AVEA Funded Project*. Final report. Albany: Two-Year College Student Development Center, State University of New York, 1976. 20 pp. (ED 139 476)

Roueche, J. E., and Boggs, J. R. *Junior College Institutional Research: The State of the Art*. Horizons Issue Monograph Series. Los Angeles: ERIC Clearinghouse for Junior Colleges; Washington, D.C.: American Association of Junior Colleges, 1968. 77 pp. (ED 019 077)

Roueche, J. E., Roueche, S. D., and Milliron, M. D. *Strangers in Their Own Land*. Washington, D.C.: American Association of Community Colleges, 1995.

Roueche, J. E., Taber, L. S., and Roueche, S. D. *The Company We Keep*. Washington, D.C.: American Association of Community Colleges, 1995.

Rowh, M. C. "Job Duties of Institutional Researchers in Two-Year Colleges." *Community College Quarterly of Research and Practice*, 1990, *14*(1), 35–44.

Rubinson, R. "Class Formation, Politics, and Institutions: Schooling in the United States." *American Journal of Sociology*, 1986, *92*(3), 519–548.

Rudmann, J. *An Evaluation of a College Orientation Course*. Irvine, Calif.: Irvine Valley College, 1992. 6 pp. (ED 349 056)

Rudolph, F. *Curriculum: A History of the American Undergraduate Course of Study Since 1636*. San Francisco: Jossey-Bass, 1977.

Ryan, J., and Lucas, J. *Report of Interest in an Intramural Program*. Palatine, Ill.: Office of Planning and Research, William Rainey Harper College, June 1992, *20*(7). (ED 348 125)

Ryder, H. D., and Perabo, G. W. *The Complex Challenge of Professional Development: Current Trends and Future Opportunities*. Princeton, N.J.:

Mid-Career Fellowship Program, Princeton University, 1985. 41 pp. (ED 265 911)

St. John, E. *A Study of Selected Developing Colleges and Universities*. Case Study 5: *Valencia Community College, Orlando, Florida*. Cambridge, Mass.: Graduate School of Education, Harvard University, 1977. 52 pp. (ED 153 674)

Salzinski, J. B. "Writing Across the Curriculum: The Crossover Program at Orange Coast College." *Inside English*, May 1987, *14*(4), 4, 6. (ED 281 603)

Santa Rita, E. "The Freshman Experience and the Role of Student Assistants." *Journal of College Admission*, Summer 1992, *136*, 19–22. (EJ 454 152)

Sasscer, M. F. *1976–77 TICCIT Project*. Final report. Annandale: Northern Virginia Community College, 1977. 150 pp. (ED 148 430; available in microfiche only)

Schroeder, C. C. "New Students—New Learning Styles." *Change*, Sep.–Oct. 1993, *25*(4), 21–26.

Schuster, J. H. Quoted in *The Chronicle of Higher Education*, Mar. 29, 1989, p. A17.

Scott-Skillman, T., and Halliday, K. *Matriculation: A Report on Third-Year Implementation, 1989–90*. Sacramento: Board of Governors, California Community Colleges, 1991. 92 pp. (ED 329 315)

Seidman, E. *In the Words of the Faculty: Perspectives on Improving Teaching and Educational Quality in Community Colleges*. San Francisco: Jossey-Bass, 1985.

Selgas, J. W. "1975 Graduates: Spring '77 Follow-Up." Unpublished paper, Harrisburg Area Community College (Harrisburg, Pa.), 1977. 276 pp. (ED 145 869)

Seppanen, L. *Assessment of Meeting Employer Needs and the Labor Market Experience of Job Upgrading and Retraining Students in Washington Community Colleges. A Baseline Report, Operations Report No. 91–3*. Olympia: Washington State Board for Community Colleges, 1991. (ED 345 790)

Servicemembers Opportunity Colleges. *SOC Principles and Criteria, 1995–1997*. Washington, D.C.: Servicemembers Opportunity Colleges, 1995.

Shabat, O. E., and others. *Mastery Learning Conference: Summary*. Chicago: City Colleges of Chicago, 1981. 72 pp. (ED 214 606)

Short, D. D. *Enhancing Instructional Effectiveness: A Strategic Approach*. Norwalk, Conn.: International Business Machines Corporation, 1994.

Silvers, P. J. *Utilization of Associate Faculty at Pima Community College: A Report on Surveys of College Associate Faculty and Department Heads*. Tucson, Ariz.: Office of Research and Planning, Pima Community College, 1990. (ED 329 320)

Sinclair, U. B. *Goose-Step: A Study of American Education*. New York: AMS Press, 1976. (Originally published 1923.)

Singer, E. *Competency-Based Adult Education: Florida Model*. Cocoa, Fla.: Brevard Community College, 1987. (ED 289 532)

Skinner, E. F., and Carter, S. *A Second Chance for Texans: Remedial Education in Two-Year Colleges*. Tempe, Ariz.: National Center for Postsecondary Governance and Finance, Texas Association of Junior and Community College Administrators, 1987. (ED 297 783)

Slavin, R. E. "Mastery Learning Reconsidered." *Review of Educational Research*, 1990, 60(2), 300. (EJ 415 883)

Slutsky, B. "What Is College For?" In M. A. Marty (ed.), *Responding to New Missions*. New Directions for Community Colleges, no. 24. San Francisco: Jossey-Bass, 1978.

Smith, J. D., and others. "PLATO in the Community College: Students, Faculty and Administrators Speak Out." Paper presented at the annual convention of the American Educational Research Association, Los Angeles, Apr. 13–17, 1981. 90 pp. (ED 214 549)

Snow, C. P. *The Two Cultures and the Scientific Revolution*. New York: Cambridge University Press, 1959.

Snow, R., and Bruns, P. A. "A Successful Experiment for Transferring Prior Learning Experience." In F. C. Kintzer (ed.), *Improving Articulation and Transfer Relationships*. New Directions for Community Colleges, no. 39. San Francisco: Jossey-Bass, 1982.

Snowden, B. "The Community College Goes to Prison." *Community Services Catalyst*, 1986, 16(2), 16–17.

Solmon, L. C. "The Problems of Incentives." In H. F. Silberman and M. B. Ginzburg (eds.), *Easing the Transition from Schooling to Work*. New Directions for Community Colleges, no. 16. San Francisco: Jossey-Bass, 1976.

Solmon, L. C. "Rethinking the Relationship Between Education and Work." *UCLA Educator*, 1977, 19 (3), 18–31.

Soltz, D. F. *Johnson County Community College Transfer Students: Their Destinations and Achievements 1992–93*. Overland Park, Kans.: Office of Institutional Research, Johnson County Community College, 1993. p. 43. (ED 360 035)

South Carolina State Board for Technical and Comprehensive Education. *South Carolina State Board for Technical and Comprehensive Education Annual Report, 1989–90*. Columbia, S.C.: South Carolina State Board for Technical and Comprehensive Education, 1990. 110 pp. (ED 335 068)

Spicer, S. L. *Paths to Success. Volume One: Steps Towards Refining Standards and Placement in the English Curriculum.* Glendale, Calif.: Glendale Community College, 1989. 34 pp. (ED 312 021)

Spicer, S. L. *Paths to Success. Volume Two: Student Satisfaction with Support Services (Since the Implementation of "Matriculation").* Glendale, Calif: Glendale Community College, Planning and Research Office, 1990. 35 pp. (ED 325 170)

Stacey, N., Alsalam, N., Gilmore, J., and To, D. *Education and Training of 16- to 19-Year-Olds After Compulsory Schooling in the United States.* Washington, D.C.: Office of Educational Research and Improvement, U.S. Department of Education, 1988. 70 pp. (ED 293 004)

Stanback-Stroud, R. "Contract Education: A Background Paper." Sacramento: Academic Senate, California Community Colleges, 1993. (ED 364 281)

Stanley, L., and Ambron, J. (eds.). *Writing Across the Curriculum in Community Colleges.* New Directions for Community Colleges, no. 73. San Francisco: Jossey-Bass, Spring 1991.

Starrak, J. A., and Hughes, R. M. *The Community College in the United States.* Ames: Iowa State College Press, 1954.

Stern, J. D., and Chandler, M. O. (eds.). *The Condition of Education: A Statistical Report.* Washington, D.C.: National Center for Education Statistics, U.S. Department of Education, 1987. 252 pp. (ED 284 371)

Stolar, S. M. *Non-Traditional Age Students: Attrition, Retention, and Recommendations for Campus Change.* Vineland, N.J.: Cumberland County College, 1991. 49 pp. (ED 335 092)

Stone, I. F. *The Trial of Socrates.* Boston: Little, Brown, 1987.

Study Group on the Conditions of Excellence in American Higher Education. *Involvement in Learning: Realizing the Potential of American Higher Education.* Final report. Washington, D.C.: National Institute of Education, 1984. 127 pp. (ED 246 833)

Suter, M. A. "A Comparison of Grades, GPA, and Retention of Developmental Students at Northwest Technical College." Unpublished graduate seminar paper, University of Toledo, 1983. 24 pp. (ED 254 267)

Swift, K. D. "A Study of the Effects of the Master Contract on the Eighteen Community Colleges in the State of Minnesota." Unpublished doctoral dissertation, Nova University, 1979. 39 pp. (ED 188–651; available in microfiche only)

Talbott, L. H. "Community Problem Solving." In H. M. Holcomb (ed.), *Reaching Out Through Community Service.* New Directions for Community Colleges, no. 14. San Francisco: Jossey-Bass, 1976.

Tang, E. D. "Student Recruitment and Retention." Paper presented at Pacific Region Seminar of the Association of Community College Trustees, Portland, Oreg., June 25–27, 1981. 26 pp. (ED 207 620)

Tatham, E. L. "A Five-Year Perspective on Job Placement for JCCC Career Students (Classes of 1973–1977)." Unpublished paper, Johnson County Community College (Overland Park, Kans.), 1978. 64 pp. (ED 161 508)

Taylor, V. B., and Rosecrans, D. "An Investigation of Vocational Development via Computer-Assisted Instruction (CAI)." Unpublished report, 1986. 20 pp. (ED 281 168)

Terzian, A. L. "A Model in Community College Transfer Programs." In D. Angel and A. Barrera (eds.), *Rekindling Minority Enrollment*. New Directions for Community Colleges, no. 74. San Francisco: Jossey-Bass, 1991. (EJ 430 316)

Thompson, M. O. "Evaluating Adjunct Faculty in an English Program." Paper presented at the College Composition and Communication Conference, Chicago, Mar. 1990. 10 pp. (ED 321 810)

Thornton, J. W., Jr. *The Community Junior College*. (2nd ed.). New York: Wiley, 1966.

Thornton, J. W., Jr. *The Community Junior College*. (3rd ed.). New York: Wiley, 1972.

Tighe, D. J. (ed.). *Poet on the Moon: A Dialogue on Liberal Education in the Community College*. Washington, D.C.: Association of American Colleges, 1977. 21 pp. (ED 145 870)

Tillery, D., and Wattenbarger, J. L. "State Power in a New Era: Threats to Local Authority." In W. L. Deegan and J. F. Gollattscheck (eds.), *Ensuring Effective Governance*. New Directions for Community Colleges, no. 49. San Francisco: Jossey-Bass, 1985. 117 pp. (ED 255 276).

Tinto, V. "College Proximity and Rates of College Attendance." *American Educational Research Journal*, 1973, 10(4), 277–293.

Tinto, V. "Dropout from Higher Education: A Theoretical Synthesis of Recent Research." *Review of Educational Research*, 1975, 45(1), 89–125.

Tollefson, T. A., and Fountain, B. E. *Forty-Nine State Systems, 1992 Edition*. Washington, D.C.: American Association of Community Colleges, 1992. (ED 363 368)

"'Transfer Core' Curriculum, Aimed at Removing Transfer Restrictions, Is Approved by Assembly." *Notice*, 1988, 12(1), 59–64.

Tross, G., and Distefano, M. *Interactive Video at Miami-Dade Community College*, 1983. (ED 230 256)

Tudor, D. E. *Compendium of Selected Data and Characteristics, 1990–91.* Lexington: University of Kentucky Community College System, 1992. 106 pp. (ED 348 085)

U.S. Congress, House of Representatives, Subcommittee on Select Education. *Preliminary Staff Report on Educational Research, Development, and Dissemination: Reclaiming a Vision of the Federal Role for the 1990s and Beyond.* 100th Cong., 2nd sess., 1988.

Upcraft, M. L. (ed.). *Orienting Students to College.* San Francisco: Jossey-Bass, 1984.

Updike, K. M. *A Comparative Study of Contract Training in Select Community Colleges.* Phoenix, Ariz.: Office of Corporate Training and Development, Maricopa County Community College District, 1991. 55 pp. (ED 336 161)

Vaala, L. D. "Attending a Two-Year College After Attending a Four-Year University in Alberta, Canada." *Community College Review,* Spring 1991, *18*(4), 13–20.

Valencia Community College. *Interdisciplinary Studies Program: Introduction to Teacher's Guide.* Orlando, Fla.: Valencia Community College, 1984. 22 pp. (ED 245 768)

Vanis, M. I., and Mills, K. L. *A Countywide Adult Basic Education Program: Final Report, 1986–87.* Rio Salado, Ariz.: Rio Salado Community College, 1987. 9 pp. (ED 286 572)

Vaughan, G. B. (ed.) *Questioning the Community College Role.* New Directions for Community Colleges, no. 32. San Francisco: Jossey-Bass, 1980.

Vaughan, G. B. "Scholarship and Community Colleges: The Path to Respect." *Educational Record,* 1988, *69*(2), 26–31.

Vaughan, G. B. "Effective Presidential Leadership: Twelve Areas of Focus." In A. M. Cohen, F. B. Brawer, and Associates, *Managing Community Colleges: A Handbook for Effective Practice.* San Francisco: Jossey-Bass, 1994.

Veblen, T. *The Higher Learning in America: A Memorandum on the Conduct of Universities by Business Men.* New York: B. W. Huebsch, 1918.

Vocational Education: Status in 2-Year Colleges in 1990–91 and Early Signs of Change. Report to Congressional Requesters. Washington, D.C.: Division of Human Resources, General Accounting Office, 1993.

Von Wald, S. C. *The Student Survey Report.* Grand Rapids, Minn.: Arrowhead Community College Region, Spring 1992. 32 pp. (ED 345 824)

Wagoner, J. L. "The Search for Mission and Integrity: A Retrospective View." In D. E. Puyear and G. B. Vaughan (eds.), *Maintaining Institutional Integrity,* New Directions for Community Colleges, no. 52, 1985, pp. 3–15.

Walker, D. E. *The Effective Administrator: A Practical Approach to Problem Solving, Decision Making, and Campus Leadership.* San Francisco: Jossey-Bass, 1979.

Wallin, D. L. *Faculty Development Activities in the Illinois Community College System.* Springfield, Ill.: Lincoln Land Community College, 1982. 25 pp. (ED 252 269)

Walter, J. A. "Paired Classes: Write to Learn and Learn to Write." Paper presented at the annual meeting of the Community College Humanities Association, Kalamazoo, Mich., Oct. 5–6, 1984. 8 pp. (ED 248 933)

Ward, P. "Development of the Junior College Movement." In J. P. Bogue (ed.), *American Junior Colleges.* (2nd ed.). Washington, D.C.: American Council on Education, 1948.

Warner, W. L., and others. *Who Shall Be Educated? The Challenge of Unequal Opportunities.* New York: HarperCollins, 1944.

Washington State Board for Community and Technical Colleges. *Washington Community and Technical Colleges Fall Enrollment and Staffing Report, 1991.* Olympia: Washington State Board for Community and Technical Colleges, 1992. 51 pp. (ED 356 824)

Washington State Board for Community and Technical Colleges. *Washington Community and Technical Colleges Fall Enrollment and Staffing Report, 1992.* Olympia: Washington State Board for Community and Technical Colleges, 1993. 59 pp. (ED 356 825)

Washington State Board for Community and Technical Colleges. *Transfer Outcomes in Washington Community Colleges: A Baseline Report on Transfer Student Outcomes. Operations Report No. 94-1.* Olympia: Washington State Board for Community and Technical Colleges, 1994, 26 pp.

Washington State Board for Community College Education. *Washington State Student Services Commission: Student Assessment Task Force Report.* Olympia: Washington State Board for Community College Education, 1985. 28 pp. (ED 269 049)

Wattenbarger, J. L., and Starnes, P. M. *Financial Support Patterns for Community Colleges, 1976.* Gainesville: University of Florida, 1976. 127 pp. (ED 132 994)

Wattenbarger, J. L., and Vader, N. J. "Adjusting to Decreased Revenues at Community Colleges in 1985." *Community College Review,* 1986, *13*(4), 20–26.

Weeks, A. A. *CSS One-Hour Content-Correlated Courses.* Poughkeepsie, N.Y.: Dutchess Community College, 1987. 35 pp. (ED 283 543)

Weick, K. E. "Educational Organizations as Loosely Coupled Systems." *Administrative Science Quarterly,* 1976, *21*(1), 1–19.

White, J. F. "Honors in North Central Association Community Colleges." Paper presented at the annual meeting of the American Association of Community and Junior Colleges, Seattle, Apr. 13–16, 1975. 8 pp. (ED 112 995)

White, M. E. *Re-Entry, Recruitment, and Retention: A Community Relations Model for Sacramento City College*. Paper presented at the Annual Speech Communication Association Convention, Nov. 1990. (ED 324 087)

Wilcox, S. A. *Directory of Southern California Community College Researchers*. Los Angeles: Southern California Community College Institutional Research Association, 1987. 30 pp. (ED 287 529)

Wiley, B., and Robinson, J. "An Interdisciplinary Studies Program: An Innovative Alternative." Paper presented at National Conference on Teaching Excellence and Conference of Administrators, Austin, Tex., May 17–20, 1987. (ED 283 553)

Wiley, C. "The Effect of Unionization on Community College Faculty Remuneration: An Overview." *Community College Review*, 1993, *21*(1), 48–57.

Wills, G. "What Makes a Good Leader?" *The Atlantic Monthly*, 1994, *273*(4), 63–64, 67–71, 74–76, 79–80.

Wilms, W. W. "Marching to the Market: A New Tune for Training Organizations." In W. W. Wilms and R. W. Moore (eds.), *Marketing Strategies for Changing Times*. New Directions for Community Colleges, no. 60. San Francisco: Jossey-Bass, 1987. (ED 289 560)

Wilms, W. W., and Hansell, S. "The Unfulfilled Promise of Postsecondary Vocational Education: Graduates and Dropouts in the Labor Market." Unpublished paper, Los Angeles, 1980.

Winner, C. N. *The Role and Function of the Departmental Chairperson at Delaware Technical and Community College*. Three executive position papers submitted as Ed.D. requirements, University of Delaware, 1989. (ED 308 898)

Winter, C. G. *History of the Junior College Movement in California*. Release no. 20. Sacramento: Bureau of Junior College Education, California State Department of Education, 1964.

Winter, G. M., and Fadale, L. M. *A Profile of Instructional Personnel in New York State Postsecondary Occupational Education*. Albany: State University of New York, 1983. 101 pp. (ED 252 261)

Wirth, P. L. *Shared Governance: Promises and Perils*. Marysville, Calif.: Yuba Community College District, 1991. 10 pp. (ED 331 568)

Wisconsin State Board of Vocational, Technical, and Adult Education. *Three-Year Longitudinal Follow-Up Study of Wisconsin VTAE Graduates of 1980–81: Report of Data from Twelve VTAE Districts*. Madison: Wisconsin

State Board of Vocational, Technical, and Adult Education, 1985. 29 pp. (ED 263 326)

Witmer, J. "Development of an Inservice Training Program for Teachers in the Parent Education Child Study Lab Setting." Master's practicum, Nova University, 1990, 59 pp. (ED 325 246)

Witt, A. A. *The Junior College Movement: An Historical Review.* Gainesville: Institute of Higher Education, University of Florida, 1988. 29 pp. (ED 294 627)

Wolfe, R. F. "The Supplemental Instruction Program: Developing Learning and Thinking Skills." *Journal of Reading,* 1987, *31,* 228–232.

Wolford, B. I., and Littlefield, J. F. "Correctional Post-Secondary Education: The Expanding Role of Community Colleges." *Community/Junior College Quarterly of Research and Practice,* 1985, 9(3), 257–272.

Woodroof, R. H. "Doubts About the Future of the Private Liberal Arts Junior College." In R. H. Woodroof (ed.), *The Viability of the Private Junior College.* New Directions for Community Colleges, no. 69. San Francisco: Jossey-Bass, 1990.

Woods, J. E. *Status of Testing Practices at Two-Year Postsecondary Institutions.* Washington, D.C.: American Association of Community and Junior Colleges, 1985. 73 pp. (ED 264 907)

Wozniak, L. C. "A Study of the Relationship of Selected Variables and the Job Satisfaction/Dissatisfaction of Music Faculty in Two-Year Colleges." Unpublished doctoral dissertation, School of Education, Catholic University of America, 1973.

Zwerling, L. S. *Second Best: The Crisis of the Community College.* New York: McGraw-Hill, 1976.

Zwerling, L. S. (ed.). *The Community College and Its Critics.* New Directions for Community Colleges, no. 54. San Francisco: Jossey-Bass, 1986.

Zylinski, D., and Metson, E. *Recruiting and Retaining Underrepresented Groups and Special Populations in Nursing Programs. Napa Valley College, October 1991–June 1992.* Napa, Calif.: Napa Valley College, 1992. 19 pp. (ED 345 768)

Index